*The publisher and the University of California Press
Foundation gratefully acknowledge the generous support of the
Peter Booth Wiley Endowment Fund in History.*

The Road to Resegregation

The Road to Resegregation

NORTHERN CALIFORNIA AND
THE FAILURE OF POLITICS

By Alex Schafran

UNIVERSITY OF CALIFORNIA PRESS

University of California Press, one of the most distinguished university presses in the United States, enriches lives around the world by advancing scholarship in the humanities, social sciences, and natural sciences. Its activities are supported by the UC Press Foundation and by philanthropic contributions from individuals and institutions. For more information, visit www.ucpress.edu.

University of California Press
Oakland, California

Library of Congress Cataloging-in-Publication Data

Names: Schafran, Alex, 1974– author.
Title: The road to resegregation : Northern California and the failure of politics / By Alex Schafran.
Description: Oakland, California : University of California Press, [2019] | Includes bibliographical references and index. |
Identifiers: LCCN 2018019744 (print) | LCCN 2018026250 (ebook) | ISBN 9780520961678 (Ebook) | ISBN 9780520286443 (cloth : alk. paper) | ISBN 9780520286450 (pbk. : alk. paper)
Subjects: LCSH: Regional planning—California, Northern. | Segregation—California, Northern—20th century. | Community development, Urban—Political aspects—California, Northern.
Classification: LCC HT393.C2 (ebook) | LCC HT393.C2 S33 2019 (print) | DDC 307.1/2—dc23
LC record available at https://lccn.loc.gov/2018019744

27   26   25   24   23   22   21   20   19   18
10   9   8   7   6   5   4   3   2   1

For the Bay Area

CONTENTS

ILLUSTRATIONS

FIGURES

MAPS

ACKNOWLEDGMENTS

I owe the deepest thanks to all of the people of East County and the Central Valley who talked to me formally or informally over the years. Thanks to the 79 dedicated professionals who agreed to be interviewed and whose ideas and experiences I came to depend on.

Thanks in particular to Kerry Motts and Casey Gallagher, two friends, colleagues, fellow urbanists, and longtime East County residents, both of whom put me up and put up with me. Thanks to Jessie and Rachel Roseman for making Modesto always feel like home and for helping me understand it better. Thanks to Elias Funez, for teaching me about Patterson and providing a great home for a short time.

This project would have been impossible without constant support and feedback. Academic publishing is an increasingly difficult task, and I am grateful to Niels Hooper, Bradley DePew, and Kim Robinson at UC Press for their support and hard work. Thanks to all the dedicated journal editors and reviewers to whom I have successfully and unsuccessfully submitted work over the years. Those processes, even if at times painful, helped make this project what it is, and I am fortunate to say that some of what you will read has appeared in other forms in the *International Journal of Urban and Regional Research, Regional Studies, Places Magazine, Environment and Planning A, Urban Geography, Critical Planning,* and *CITY.* A similar debt is owed to conference attendees who listened to pieces of this project before it coalesced into a coherent whole.

I am also indebted to the large group of Bay Area scholars upon whose work this project relies. All scholars "use" other scholars work, and I hope I have done right by the long list of people in the References section. Rachel Brahinsky and Louise Nelson Dyble took the time to talk me through San

Francisco and Marin specifically, helping me fill holes in my knowledge late in the game. Dani Carrillo provided incredible comments on an early draft of the full text, and I will always be in her debt. John Stehlin stepped in to find what I could not find, saving me at a critical moment. Erin McElroy became a friend, inspiration, and brilliant sparring partner in the last and most difficult years of this project, and was part of a community of people who read when I needed them to read. Egon Terplan also became a friend, inspiration, and brilliant sparring partner over the years, and he not only agreed to be interviewed and provided great last-minute edits, but gave me the opportunity to share some ideas and research in SPUR's *Urbanist* in June 2012, together with Chris Schildt and Jake Wegmann. This issue, together with a piece authored in *Race, Poverty and the Environment,* provided an invaluable opportunity to write in nonacademic prose, and to speak to the policy and activist community from which I come originally.

The *Urbanist* and *RPE* articles are also some of the many jointly produced pieces of scholarship I have been fortunate to be a part of, and which contribute mightily to this text. I am particularly grateful to co-authors Jake Wegmann, Oscar Sosa Lopez, Lisa Feldstein, and Chris Schidlt, invaluable research and writing partners, not to mention friends, and I look forward to continued collaboration. Jake deserves particular thanks, as portions of chapter 1 would not have been possible without his work, and I am thrilled to be working again with him and Deirdre Pfeiffer on diverse new work on housing in the United States. LeConte Dill and Yvonne Hung were partners on a study that never quite came together as a stand-alone paper, but which was also critical to chapter 1. More recently, I have begun working with new colleagues / friends, Matthew Noah Smith and Stephen Hall, and I am grateful not only for the collaboration but that they allowed me to include some of our collectively developing work in the conclusion.

I am particularly indebted to the people who helped me become something resembling a scholar. Like many books of its kind, this project began as a doctoral dissertation (although I hope it does not read like one). I could not have done anything here without the DCRP staff—Yeri, Malla, Pat, and the late great Kaye Bock. I was one of those students with no secure funding, living semester by semester on teaching assistantships and the odd dollar from the department, and they more than anyone made sure that I had a place in this program. I want to send a heartfelt thanks to Fred Collignon, my original advisor, whose promise of a GSI-ship teaching Intro to City Planning at the University of California led me to turn down fully funded offers from schools in places with no place in my heart. Mike Teitz provided a steady source of encouragement, honest critique, and deep Bay Area planning knowledge, and I will forever remember him as my first interview for the project at hand.

I was also fortunate to teach early and often at Berkeley, and met many incredible students. One, Zac Taylor, is now my PhD student at Leeds, a research partner and the design guru who made my maps and graphics legible, and was a constant source of support throughout. Former students Sean Dasey, Sarah Ehrlich, and Hannah Reed wrote class papers for me that dug deeper on some areas important for this book, and I am proud to cite their work in the text. They were Berkeley at its best.

I could not have asked for a better committee. Malo Hutson showed up just at the right time, providing me with a chance to teach in an incredible environment and constantly making me believe that my work was valuable. Ananya Roy helped me understand that I was an intellectual, helped me understand what that meant, and most importantly what that could possibly be. Richard Walker made me realize that I was at core a historical geographer, provided unparalleled intellectual justification for my view that the Bay Area is the center of the universe, and pointed the way to a literature in which I feel honored to participate. And finally, nobody could ask for more in an advisor than Teresa Caldeira, ever patient, ever steady, a woman of quiet brilliance who was there for me at every turn, even those moments when I was not there for her.

During the five years at Berkeley I spent learning and researching, I met an amazing set of friends and colleagues. Particular thanks are due my brothers Gautam Bhan, Ricardo Cardoso, and Jia-Ching Chen, my sister Lisa Feldstein, and my very old friend Mary Mota, who were there for me every step of the way, especially when I was stuck.

My colleagues at the University of Leeds have built an incredible research environment where I have had the freedom and time to write, and the opportunity to meet and collaborate with numerous brilliant colleagues. I am also indebted to the wonderful network of UK-based urban studies scholars who have welcomed me with open arms, offering me seminars to plead my case and support for my ideas and research. There is no place on earth with a greater density and diversity of smart and critical people thinking about urbanism and urbanization, and I am fortunate to be part of that community.

Frederick Douzet and colleagues at the Institut Français de Géopolitique provided me a critically needed home during my two years in Paris, when this book was first coming together. Frederick provided me with invaluable perspective as one of the greatest non-Californian scholars of California, and along with Yohann LeMoigne and Hugo Lefebvre, I never lacked for people to talk with about California even if I was far far away.

It takes a village to raise a PhD student, but it is even better to have amazing parents. I certainly do, and without Ruth and Warren Schafran, this dream, and many others, would have faded long ago. They both sacrificed quite a lot to provide me a world of opportunity most humans never have, and I could not be more grateful.

Finally, I fell in love just as my field research was coming to a close. A magical nineteenth-century love story in a twenty-first-century setting swept me away to a small apartment on the Place de Clichy, where one Tiffany Fukuma Schafran stood by my side during a year of thousand-word days. That year of thousand-word days then became a complex multinational odyssey which may have delayed the publication of this book, but she stayed with me throughout, no matter how hard it has been. This book may be dedicated to the Bay, but it owes its life to the love and support of my wife.

PREFACE

THE PERSONAL AND THE POLITICAL

This book is an attempt to explain how and why the San Francisco Bay Area, the region where I was born and grew up and lived on and off for more than three decades, became a key epicenter of the foreclosure crisis. It examines how the region ended up as an example of a new form of mobile, regional segregation—a *re*segregation on a megaregional scale. It is an attempt to make sense of the paradox that is my beloved Bay Area: a place of poetic beauty, vast riches, an incredible spirit of innovation, and a proud tradition of progressive politics, yet one that is simultaneously deeply segregated and incredibly unequal. The Bay Area has witnessed and tolerated unacceptable levels of poverty, violence, health inequalities, and environmental injustice. With a still-booming economy and an ongoing housing crisis, inequality is clearly rising rather than falling. While I approach this book as a scholar—I stand by the rigor of my work and the claims and arguments I make unequivocally—my anger and frustration at the present state of my home region have surfaced in my writing despite my best efforts to edit out these feelings, or at least smooth them over. Perhaps by explaining how and why this book came together, what it is and what it is not, I can provide a context for some of this emotion.

Growing up in the Bay Area, I was always confused by what I saw around me. Every November, without fail, my parents and neighbors marched to the polls and voted overwhelmingly for the same party. So did almost everyone in the region: black, white, Latinx, and Asian, environmentalist and union member, middle class and working class, and even many wealthy people. When I started paying attention to politics as a six-year-old, watching the big

TV map turn almost entirely red in 1980 as Ronald Reagan became the vanguard for what was truly a new world order, the Bay Area in large part wanted nothing to do with it. While Reagan's election ushered in a decade and a half of Republican domination, first in the White House, and then in the California statehouse where he once presided as governor, the Bay Area went the other way. By the mid-1990s, Republicans were an extreme rarity in the Bay Area delegation to Sacramento, the state's capital, and to Washington, DC.

Yet what appeared to me at the time as a form of regional solidarity—especially as both Washington and Sacramento increasingly became the epicenters of Reagan's "revolution"—actually masked a lot of deep internal divisions. In 1978, just a few years before Reagan's landmark election, many portions of the Bay Area voted in favor of the equally landmark Proposition 13, the infamous "tax revolt" that among other things froze property taxes for (mostly white, mostly suburban) landowners. As I would soon learn, Prop. 13, as it is known colloquially, helped usher in an era of seemingly constant fiscal crisis. I would discover much later in life that Prop. 13 was only a small part of the story.

In the 1980s, as the Cold War built to a crescendo and then faded, before 9/11 rewrote global geopolitics and the internet rewrote communications and daily life, Californians became used to the language of "pink slips" and budget crises. We always seemed to be talking about teacher layoffs, crumbling infrastructure, and rising university tuition, despite the fact that there seemed to be wealth all around us. Southern California had Hollywood and airplanes, we had banks and a big oil company and Silicon Valley. Sure, it was pre-internet back then, but with Apple and HP and Sun Microsystems, it was still pretty clear even to a teenager who didn't know much about anything that this wasn't the Rust Belt.

The Bay Area also had what appeared to my naive eyes to be a very confusing amount of inequality—poverty, homelessness, racial inequality, environmental injustice, violence and more violence. Gun violence was constantly on the news, but it never occurred where I grew up or spent time. (My biggest problems, as the great Ta-Nehisi Coates [2015] somehow understood, were in fact poison oak and my (absent) love life.) What made it particularly confusing was that not only did the region seem quite rich, but also supposedly super-progressive. As a college student, I took classes on Bay Area and U.S. history, learning how the region was at the center of many incredible political movements, movements that would impact the nation and the world: the gay rights movement, the Black Panthers, Berkeley and the Free Speech movement, San Francisco State and the Third World Liberation Front, John Muir and the environmental movement. Cesar Chavez first trained in San Jose with the Community Service Organization before founding the United Farm Workers.

The story that began to form in my head was one shared by many in the Bay Area, especially the white, liberal, and educated. We, the Bay Area, were smart, progressive, and innovative. We believed that outside forces—a dysfunctional state run by conservatives from Southern California and the Central Valley; a hostile Republican-controlled Washington obsessed with the Cold War and cutting aid to the poor—were to blame for our problems.

As a "progressive" region facing a hostile statehouse / White House combo (both at the time seemingly the fault of Southern Californians), we often forgot to look in the mirror. When I graduated from college and became both politically active and a professional working on some of these problems, I realized that this was the mentality I had adopted, even as the White House changed hands and California began to turn purple and then blue. We were an island of progressivity in a sea of conservatism, or so I thought.

PRIDE AND MIRRORS

My career would eventually take me from a decade of immigrant rights and housing activism back to school, right as the towers came down and the world shifted its political axis. What had long been an amateur fascination with cities and places became a profession. When I arrived in Berkeley, to start a doctorate at the age of thirty-two, I knew that somehow I had to deal with the paradox of the rich, innovative, progressive, yet terribly unequal Bay Area.

How did this region that I loved so much, and to which I had returned with such enthusiasm, end up so wealthy, so progressive, so innovative, yet so unequal? Like many who shared my demographic details—25–45, white, educated, politically "progressive," suburban-raised city-dwellers—what had originally been a form of inequality seen at a distance growing up became part of my day-to-day life, as I and the rest of what I regard as the "gentrification generation" ended up face to face with one of the major forces for change in high-income regions like the Bay Area.

Like many young scholars, I wanted to understand what was happening around me, including in the immediate North Oakland neighborhood where I was clearly part of this paradox in uncomfortable ways. I was lucky that early on in this project, someone asked me the question that many gentrifiers ask: Where are all the people leaving these neighborhoods going? At the time, I didn't know. With a little investigation, I started hearing the same names—Antioch, Pittsburg, Stockton, Vallejo, Fairfield—places that as a geographically minded Bay Area native I knew from a map but of which I had no firsthand experience. These were places that put a premium on high school football, hosted Marine World, places people like me drove through on the way to somewhere else. Hip-hop had migrated north and east and northeast (Chang 2016), but I had not. Nobody I knew lived there, was from there, spent time there. This, perhaps, was part of the story.

Thus began a four-year odyssey to explore my home region in depth. One of the problems facing all regions, but especially massive, sprawling, and incredibly diverse regions like the Bay Area, is that most people know only a very small portion of their region, and this is true regardless of race, class, ethnicity, age, or politics. To this day, most of my friends and colleagues live and work in a small set of spaces, primarily in the region's core. They are aware that I study the outer portions of the region, but most have never been there. While people in the outer region certainly travel more—they have no choice— and many are from the center originally (just as many folks in the center grew up in the suburbs), this doesn't mean that they really know or understand most of the Bay Area. This partly explains why we have never been able to truly develop what the late Mel Scott would have described as a form of regional citizenship, and why the Bay Area has never solved its problems.

But limited vision and knowledge of what is a very large and populated place is only part of the issue. Almost all regions have pride, but few mix that pride with as much ego as the Bay Area. Bay Area progressive politics can be very self-congratulatory, and at times it feels as if people and organizations would prefer to be right rather than to make actual change. I would aver that the region continues to see the source of its problems as the enemy without, not the dysfunction within, when it is clearly *both*.

Many Bay Area readers will find this book too critical. Those who have worked in earnest to make the region more equitable may feel "we did the best we could," and I work hard not to point fingers at individuals. The question I am asking is this: Has the Bay Area really done what it could have done considering its wealth, politics, and privileges? Can we really be proud of our constant affordable housing problem, our role as an epicenter of foreclosure, our health disparities that see a more-than-twenty-year gap in life expectancy within the same county, the racialized violence that claims too many lives, and an ever-widening inequality?

Others may think that I turn this critical eye on the wrong people. Not enough blame is placed at the feet of capital, or the political class, or business, let alone the constant stream of right-wing politics that continues to plague the region, state, and country. Some will argue that this book is too critical of environmentalists. Some will perhaps rightly fear that a self-critical book urging progressives to look in the mirror will be used as a cudgel by those who detest everything the region supposedly stands for. Those who would degrade virtually everything and everyone will use anything to continue their scorched-earth politics, and I am not naive to this fact. But winning this battle means building a true and unassailable majority, and this can only be done by building effective politics of development and urbanization, which I discuss at length in the conclusion.

Others will say that I have not made it clear enough where I am laying blame. This seeming vagueness, this refusal to point fingers exclusively at one set of institutions, is intentional. The only hope of changing the future of the Bay Area is for all institutional actors—nonprofit, for-profit, and governmental, business and community, green and white and brown and black, labor and capital, neighborhood and city and county and regional—to ask more deeply how they could have done things differently to produce a different Bay Area. It is only through building this form of collective responsibility, through leveraging the progressive majority which we have long had, that we can make the Bay Area the shining beacon that it should be. We need to raise collective expectations, to stop being so jaded about what is possible, and to stop incriminating everyone but ourselves. Simply producing yet another screed blaming one group—no matter how much they are to blame—would only contribute further to the political fragmentation that I argue is at the center of the problem.

Still others will say that I focus too much on the Bay Area and California, seemingly giving a pass to the federal government or the country as a whole. I had originally intended to write a final chapter on the federal role, but the book is long as it is, and that would have delayed an already delayed project even further. Moreover, I came to realize that this would require an entire book of its own. Resegregation and the changing nature of segregation are issues in every city and region in the United States. "The Road to

Resegregation, Part 2: The *United States* and the Failure of Politics" is a book that needs to be written, and my only hope is that someone more qualified than I writes it before I do.

The question of responsibility, of holding a mirror up so that we can see ourselves more honestly, is deeply connected to the personal nature of his book. I am a white, middle-class, hyper-educated, progressive environmentalist, son of the hypocritical Obama-voting, affordable-housing-opposing suburbs. I have been part of that "gentrification generation" of (mostly) white children of similar suburbs everywhere participating in the change of places like South Berkeley, North Oakland, and the Mission district of San Francisco, all while working for nonprofits, marching against ill-conceived wars, and trying to make a living and a life. I have never been a techie, but I have too many techie friends to be yet another white progressive who pretends that the tech community in the Bay Area is an other. They are so entwined with everything we are and have been that they are an inextricable part of us. Thus, I focus an added dose of responsibility on the communities I come from, am part of, feel like I have standing to speak to, and at times blunt my critique elsewhere. I hope that other members of other communities write similar books along similar lines. This has become even more important in light of what has happened politically in the United States since I started writing this book.

This issue of who I am and where I am from—both demographically and professionally—structures what gets told in this book and what does not. Although I gathered many personal stories from African American, Filipino, and Latinx families who were part of this suburbanization, stories of homes bought and often homes lost, I don't retell them. I don't tell the stories of those who remained where they were or those who were always there but not counted. I don't tell the stories of the white households who were part of these changing communities in different ways. While I use ethnographic methods and other techniques cribbed from sociology and anthropology, this is not a story of people's lives, of the lived experience of segregation and resegregation.

I have so many of these personal stories because collecting such stories was originally what I thought I was doing. That is, until during the course of my research I was sitting in the kitchen of a friend of a friend, an African American woman in Pittsburg whose friends, family, and professional life were part of many of the changes I was charting. By that point my research had yielded a growing understanding of the political economy of development that had transformed the Bay Area, but I was still struggling with some of the particularities of the actual experience of this change, and how to weave the two elements together. I was well equipped to tell the story of political fragmentation and major planning decisions, less so to tell the complex stories of the individuals and communities caught up in this change.

After the friend of a friend had finished telling me her story, and her husband had told me his, I looked at her and said, "You know, as important as it is, I don't think it's my place to tell your story."

She smiled, and just nodded.

HOW IT ALL CAME TOGETHER

As a research project, this book owes a good deal methodologically to my mother, a collage artist for half a century. It is very much a twenty-first-century hybrid of Levi-Strauss's (1966) bricoleur and engineer, a product of a new world where, unlike in Levi-Strauss's time, the bricoleur's tools and materials are seemingly infinite. Never before have scholars and intellectuals had so much at their fingertips, and I do my best to take advantage of the contemporary moment to tell a contemporary tale. The text weaves together quantitative data, archival research, stories and anecdotes, interviews with politicians, planners, activists, and developers, the results of more than two years of fieldwork in a fifty-mile-long corridor, and the endless reading and rereading of an ever-expanding list of writers who have tried to understand the complexities of urban and regional development and metropolitan segregation since the days of Patrick Geddes and Friedrich Engels. It uses methods borrowed or adapted from social science and history, but the text conforms to neither tradition. It is simply scholarship.

The field research for this book was formally conducted over two years, from May 2009 to April 2011, with significant preliminary work done in 2007 and 2008. The computer, archival, and phone research spanned a longer period, spilling into 2012, with follow-up work from 2014–17. I spent much of 2007–11 traveling between my home in Oakland and eastern Contra Costa County, one of the primary subjects of the book, and the full range of commuter towns in central and western San Joaquin and Stanislaus counties, particularly Modesto and Patterson. I conducted 79 formal interviews with planners, engineers, elected officials, policy wonks, real estate developers, brokers, activists, journalists, academics, longtime residents, and new arrivals. I attended public meetings, festivals, rallies, and high school sporting events. I worked at a farmers market in Brentwood selling ravioli. I was a regular at garage sales, far and away the best and most enjoyable way of chatting with a diverse range of strangers in single-family-home America. Throughout, I had at least as many informal conversations about life, urban change, crisis, politics, crime, and inevitably, traffic, as I did formal interviews, mostly in East County and the San Joaquin Valley.

I read the weekly *Brentwood Press* religiously and the daily *Contra Costa Times* (now *East Bay Times*) almost every day, did archival work in local libraries and historical societies and online, gathering bits and chunks of information, ideas, anecdotes, and conundrums in "discrete patches" for the unwieldy Arcades project that forms the empirical foundation of this book. And of course, in this day and age one can find mountains of quantitative data with a few clicks of the mouse, data that was analyzed and mapped descriptively by myself and to which more complex statistical methods were applied with the help of colleagues far more capable than I. When the text hits a technical bit of data, the endnotes explain what was done.

Considering that my goal from the outset was to write a truly regional book which avoided scapegoating or valorizing any one place in particular, I visited almost every single mapped location in Alameda and Contra Costa counties during that time—sometimes for formal interviews or formal fieldwork, other times just to have a cup of coffee, walk and drive and bike around, and take pictures and chat with people I met. I lived for a summer in Brentwood with a transplant from Pennsylvania (via Walnut Creek) who needed a roommate to avoid foreclosure, in a brand-new half-built subdivision surrounded by empty lots. I spent another winter in Antioch, in a hundred-year-old house downtown with a man in his fifties who had grown up in town and whose great grandfather had built the house we lived in. I spent a wondrous week in Patterson, and crashed on couches and guest rooms in Byron and Modesto over a period of a few years, a Bay Area boy trying to make sense of the vast beyond on the other side of the Altamont Pass. I made friends, drank beer, went to car shows, and spent hours and days wandering around East County and the Central Valley in my trusty Honda Civic or on a beat-up old Trek, talking to people and taking nearly six thousand photographs. From the friendships I made, and from friendships I already had, I built a series of life histories, mostly of people from my generation, stories that helped add a critical backstory to my thinking but that, as I mentioned above, largely remains theirs and do not appear in these pages.

Introduction

GHOSTS IN THE MACHINE

IN 1976, THE BAY AREA RAPID TRANSIT DISTRICT, known as BART, published a report on the possibilities of extending the system eastward. This was advanced planning by definition—the inaugural commuter trains would not start rolling until the following year. But considering how long it took to build a system as complex as BART, initially envisioned in the 1950s, thinking ahead made sense.

The area in question was eastern Contra Costa County, "East County" to locals (see maps 1 and 2). East County at the time was a big place (close to 100 square miles) with a small population. There were just over 50,000 people spread between the two main industrial cities, Antioch and Pittsburg, the old farming town of Brentwood, and a handful of unincorporated communities like Oakley, Discovery Bay, and Byron. Divided as it was from the core of the Bay Area by a series of hills, served only by a small state highway and a few backroads, East County was far from the rest of the Bay, even if it was only about 40 miles from downtown San Francisco at its westernmost point. The east side of East County was geographically part of the great Central Valley, and residents would be as likely to head east to Stockton to do their big shopping as to go over the hills into Oakland and San Francisco.

To planners from BART and Parsons Brinkerhoff Tudor Bechtel, the joint venture that brought together two of the country's most famous planning and engineering firms to build BART, East County represented an opportunity. They produced renderings of modern-looking stations that at first glance could seem fantastical. BART as a system was not yet open, and here they were imagining expensive stations in faraway places miles from the nearest suburb, let alone the major center of employment. But as they wrote in 1976, East County was a unique opportunity for regional planning. It was "an area

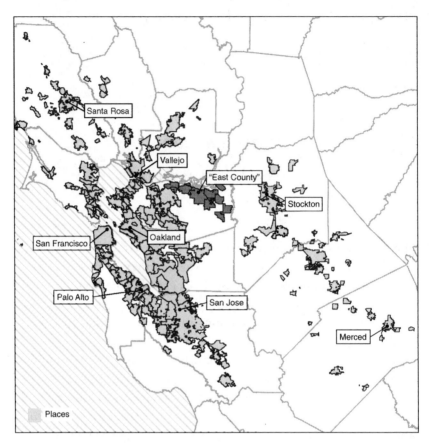

MAP I. Places. Map by author.

where BART can direct growth rather than merely respond to growth" (Bay Area Rapid Transit District n.d.). The plan, although written long before planning dreamed in terms of "sustainability," "walkability," "transit-oriented development," and other contemporary buzzwords, was just that—part of a vision for a different kind of American suburban development.

As far and as empty as East County may have seemed, this wasn't crazy talk. New suburban-style subdivisions had begun popping up in the 1960s in East County. Highway 680, which would connect East County to the Tri-Valley area and Silicon Valley, was opened in 1971. The Bishop Ranch "edge city" was in the planning phase. Things were happening, and they were happening fast.

Yet if BART planners saw East County as an opportunity to finally get out ahead of the growth and to build the region in a new way, they also figured that it was their way or no way. Their words were unequivocal: "without major

MAP 2. The 12-county Bay Area. Map by author.

regional policy changes concerning highway funding and environmental acceptance, the corridor without a BART extension would most likely experience a limited level of growth" (ibid.). We have no way of knowing whether planners were right in believing they could "direct growth rather than merely respond to growth." We do know in hindsight that when it came to growth without BART, BART was wrong. The "major regional policy changes" and "environmental acceptance" never came, but the growth did. In a big way.

WELCOME TO EAST COUNTY

By 1982, without a widened Highway 4 and without a BART system and with no concrete plans for either project, the City of Antioch decided to double its population by adding more than 15,000 units for approximately 45,000 people on 6,500 acres.[1] By the 1990s, the fever had spread east to Oakley, which grew almost 1,000 percent between 1980 and 2000, and neighboring Brentwood, which earned fastest-growing city in California status for the better part of the 1990s (Heredia 1998).

By 2000, East County had more than 230,000 residents, almost four times the 1970 census numbers that had formed part of BART's forecasting baseline. By 2007, as the foreclosure crisis began morphing into a global economic meltdown, more than a quarter of a million people called East County home. Most would consider themselves middle class, whether blue collar and white collar. Many were immigrants or the children of immigrants. More than half were nonwhite.

East County's residents often worked in the building trades, constructing and reconstructing the rapidly growing Bay Area, including the subdivisions they lived in and those like it across a 250-mile-long arc stretching from Santa Rosa to Stockton to Gilroy. They were FedEx and UPS drivers, nurses and teachers, cable guys and repairmen, meter readers and other public employees who had kept the region running for generations. Many worked in white-collar jobs in the booming "edge cities" (Garreau 1991) near San Ramon or Pleasanton, job centers that blossomed during the late 1980s and 1990s along freeway corridors in central Contra Costa County and neighboring Alameda County. Some worked in well-paid executive and technical positions, others as part of the growing and feminized wave of back-office service workers whose work was steadily suburbanized over the past generation (Nelson 1986). Long-distance commuting was a way of life—well-paid local jobs were scarce, and people left home early and came home late, often stuck in terrible bottlenecks on freeways never designed for the traffic load they were now expected to handle.

By 2008, East County had become a national epicenter of the foreclosure crisis. Readers of the *New York Times* were introduced to cities like Antioch, alongside similar communities in neighboring Solano, San Joaquin, and Stanislaus counties. The *San Francisco Chronicle* called Brentwood "the poster child for the housing bust," and reporters from around the world filed stories documenting how the American and Californian dreams were falling apart in subdivision after subdivision along the edge of one of the wealthiest regions in human history (Egan 2010; Moore 2008; Temple 2008). All told, the four major places of East County—Pittsburg, Antioch, Brentwood, and Oakley—and the nearby developer-built project of Discovery Bay saw 6,231 foreclosures in 2008. During the height of the crisis, from 2007–11, these same five communities saw almost 16,000 foreclosures. These communities together had only 90,000 housing units in 2010.[2]

These lost homes were a disaster for the families who lost them, and a fiscal nightmare for the cities in which they were built. Property values cratered, with homes trading at late 1980s prices when adjusted for inflation. This massive decline in real estate values gutted city budgets that were dependent on property tax revenues, pushing cities like Antioch to the brink of insolvency.

East County was not alone in its plight. Thirty miles to the west and across the Carquinez Strait, Solano County's largest city, Vallejo, did go bankrupt. The major cities in southern Solano County and the cities of East County form what I call the "Cities of Carquinez" (Schafran 2012b), and between them there were more than 10,000 foreclosures in 2008 alone. Thirty-six miles to the east of Antioch, Stockton became the largest municipal bankruptcy in American history, as foreclosure swept through the cities in western San Joaquin and Stanislaus counties as well.

By 2016, while prices recovered more in some places than others, virtually all of these communities lost value compared to 2004 (Badger 2016). In Antioch, on Lefebvre Way, an anonymous suburban street where just two blocks lost almost $4.6 million in housing value in the four years following the crash (chapter 3), one could still buy a house actively in foreclosure in 2016 that was worth 40 percent of what it was in 2006.

CHANGING GEOGRAPHIES OF RACE AND CLASS

This was not the case everywhere in the Bay Area. As Americans watched the continued struggle of Rust Belt regions and the now-exposed metropolitan economies of parts of the Sun Belt, the fortunes of the Bay Area as a whole remained golden. Median incomes and property values in San Francisco, Silicon Valley, the North Bay, and the East Bay's Tri-Valley area powered through the crisis.[3] A region made rich on gold and industrialized agriculture stayed at the top of the global economic food chain even after the dot-com crash of 2000 and the disastrous recession of 2008. Between Apple's 2012 announcement that it had $100 billion in cash and the subsequent Facebook IPO, realtors in San Francisco and Palo Alto braced for another uptick in home prices, one which had reached absurd proportions by 2016.

In the more centrally located cities and towns of the region, the crisis was about rising rents and unaffordable homes, not lost equity and destroyed credit. San Francisco's mayor convened an affordable housing task force in 2014, for once again, despite a real estate crash and global economic meltdown, gentrification and affordability were the primary questions of the day, not abandonment and foreclosure (Meronek 2015). Just a few years after Brentwood became the "poster child" for the housing bust, San Francisco emerged as a global icon of gentrification, a force that has more recently brought Oakland to the attention of the national press as well (Wood 2016).

San Francisco's affordability and inequality crisis have become a staple of national and international headlines (Wong 2016), much as East County's foreclosures did during the height of the crisis. National Public Radio ran a special series on income inequality in the region. *Fortune Magazine* and the *Economist* leant their particular perspective to the issue. Newspaper articles and blog posts abounded with well-publicized studies showing just how absurdly the prices had risen. Between 2012 and 2016, San Francisco saw the largest increase in the share of million-dollar homes of any metropolis in the country, followed by San Jose and Oakland (McGlaughlin 2016).[4] This meant that the three largest cities in the region were one, two, and three in the nation in this category, all while homes on the far edge of the region struggled to hold value. By 2016, perhaps only London was on par with the Bay Area as an international symbol of inequality seen through the lens of a growing affordable-housing crisis.

If one digs deeper, the picture of a very unequal region is even more profound. Many of the families that helped East County and the surrounding areas grow were African Americans from Oakland, a city which lost 37 percent of its black population between 1990 and 2014. San Francisco lost 42 percent of its black population during the same time period. The famed university city of Berkeley, just north of Oakland and across the bay from San Francisco, lost more than half of its black community. This meant that more than 100,000 African Americans had left the three cities in the core of the region in 25 years.

The profound changes in the race and class geography of the San Francisco Bay Area are not as simple as a gentrifying core and an impoverished periphery. The full region is a complex, hyper-diverse archipelago that defies easy categorization. Much of East County's growth was driven by Latinx, Asian, and white families whose stories, like those of African Americans, are complicated. San Francisco is very different from Oakland, and Antioch is different from Brentwood. Silicon Valley is an entire ecosystem in its own right.

We should be careful when talking in terms of the Californian *banlieue,* especially since this label is often based on a poor understanding of the actual French *banlieue* (Schafran and LeMoigne 2016). It is not as simple as "two Bay Areas," or what Alan Ehrenhalt (2012) calls "the Great Inversion"— wealthier and whiter folks moving into the city, poorer communities of color moving out.

We must also be wary of focusing too much on the intensely gentrifying centers of the region. As dominating a force as gentrification is in cities like Oakland and San Francisco, we should heed Jeff Chang's (2016: 72) advice: "By itself, gentrification can't explain the new geography of race that has emerged since the turn of the millennium . . . Gentrification is key to understanding what happened to our cities . . . but it is only half of the story."

As Chang notes, it is in gentrifying spaces where the region's growing inequality is most visible, but focusing exclusively on the center means ignoring the larger story at the heart of his work and mine. Even if it is not black and white, in either the literal or figurative sense, the clearly racialized nature of the divide between East County and San Francisco / Silicon Valley provides a clue to the first core argument of this book: what happened in the Bay Area is fundamentally about segregation. I mean this in both in the historical sense of the term, and in the new ways that the transformation of the Bay Area demands we understand it.

SEGREGATION, RESEGREGATION, AND
THE ORIGINS OF AN URBAN CRISIS

While some people of color have prospered as part of the tech and property boom of the past few decades in the Bay Area, the numbers are clear—black, Latinx, Filipino, and Southeast Asian people are overrepresented in communities struggling with foreclosure and bankruptcy, and underrepresented in the more stable, high-property-value communities. Communities of color may no longer be exclusively trapped in underserved and disinvested inner cities, but the racialized map of foreclosure in the Bay Area and its relation to postwar segregation is a clue that one era has not entirely given way to another. This is not your grandparent's segregation—it is as much suburban and exurban as urban; it is multiracial, and not just black and white; it is more about moving too often than not being able to move at all. As I will explain in far greater detail in chapter 1, these changes nevertheless deserve to be called segregation, and this new, more mobile form of segregation is at the heart of the problem.

This new form of segregation, and the crisis it helped produce, is in every way a product of how the postwar segregated metropolis was built, and how we reacted to it a generation later. As I and others have argued previously (Schafran 2012a; Dymski 2009; Harvey 2009), the foreclosure crisis must be understood fundamentally as an "urban" crisis, or better, an "urbanization" crisis. By this I do not mean urban in the sense of cities, for obviously this is a suburban and exurban crisis as much as an inner-city one. By urban I mean rooted in the process of urbanization, in the production of cities and towns and regions, in the building of homes and schools and transport networks.[5]

Every house that was foreclosed upon had to be built somewhere by someone, approved by some council or agency, often as part of a long-term plan. The foreclosure crisis was not the dot-com crash of 2000, where companies with no real value were suddenly valuable, until they were not. Many of the loans that purchased these houses were toxic, both in their terms and in their amount. There was no doubt a radical bubble, with houses trading for two to three times what they should have been worth. But these were still real houses, in real places, mostly owned by real families. While there were plenty of people who overextended themselves into crazy speculation and an investment portfolio built on smoke and mirrors, people also lost homes that had been purchased with prime, fixed-rate mortgages, but at a price point that was unsustainable.

Most critically, this "asset bubble" could only have been built on an asset like the American home, a real thing that is often the source of an outsized dream, and for which there is potent demand. Where this demand came from, and how this demand was stymied in certain geographies and taken advantage of in others, is fundamentally part of the story of the foreclosure crisis. Foreclosure in the Bay Area cannot be reduced to bad banks or ill-informed homeowners.

Instead, we must look at the very foundations of how and for whom the region has been built, and we must do so over a long period of time. One of the many reasons to use segregation to describe what is taking place is that it forces us to see that this is a deeply historical phenomenon, not simply a product of the past decade. So while I and others, such as Chang (2016), refer to what has occurred in the Bay Area as *resegregation,* this book contends that *re*segregation is like *re*financing—it does not imply that one had ended before another began.[6] Resegregation and old-fashioned segregation are happening simultaneously, not only in the Bay Area but throughout the country.

These new forms of segregation are also not the antonym of integration. Antioch is a former "sundown town," a place where African Americans in the postwar era knew they were largely unwelcome after dark (let alone before—see chapter 2). Antioch is thus simultaneously the radical face of integration and a key example of twenty-first-century resegregation. Coming to terms with this paradox is critical to understanding how segregation has changed.

Using the term segregation also reminds us that what is happening in the Bay Area is not about *race* but, as Ta-Nehisi Coates (2015) would explain it, fundamentally about *racism*. The evidence from research shows clearly that the foreclosure crisis hit communities of color the hardest (Hall, Crowder, and Spring 2015), and cannot be separated from the racist production of the twentieth-century American metropolis (Rugh and Massey 2010).

Like all forms of segregation, the racialized and stratified landscapes in which this crisis has played out are not simply products of market forces, demographic change, or economic shifts. They are products of the culmination of innumerable political decisions, some major—like the decision not to extend BART and not to build East County in a different way—and some minor. They are products of specific decisions on land use, housing, transportation, environmental protection, and much more, decisions about how and for whom to build cities and towns and regions and neighborhoods.

Understanding contemporary segregation means grappling with the culmination of multiple generations of decisions. It is a product of many decisions made by many institutions, some of which were outright racist or classist. But many decisions were made by institutions that would contend they opposed segregation, and some of those same institutions have done important work to fight it. Just as importantly, contemporary segregation is the product of many decisions not taken, the product of political inertia as much as the product of bad ideas. When something has been so unequal for so long, it becomes normalized.

ROADS NOT TAKEN

Placing segregation at the center of the explanatory framework does not mean eschewing other well-known explanations for the crisis, but rather incorporating them critically and in pieces so as to avoid common missteps. As the crisis began to unfold and gather media and scholarly attention, prominent voices argued that this disaster proved that those who opposed development on the regional fringe were right all along. America's pattern of rapid, low-density, and resource-intensive suburbanization over the past half-century was not only environmentally destructive but financially unsustainable (Florida 2009). The crisis was an indication—one of many—that suburbs are declining (Kim, Chung, and Blanco 2013). For prominent urbanists like Chris Leinberger (2011), the crisis marked "the death of the fringe suburb," with foreclosure as the well-placed iceberg for America's regional development Titanic.

Especially when compared to earlier crises that involved places being abandoned and immiserated, the foreclosure crisis had a distinctive suburban or exurban quality (Newman and Schafran 2013; Pfeiffer and Molina 2013; Immergluck 2011). The foreclosure crisis can easily be considered the most devastating crisis in the history of American suburbia. Like those critics who pointed the finger at sprawl, suburban decline, metropolitan fragmentation, or other related ills, I also argue that how the Bay Area in particular and the United States in general was built since World War II is at the heart of the problem.

But the fundamental shortsightedness of the sprawl discourse in the United States is that it has a tendency to root the problem geographically: whereas sprawl in theory is a form and pattern of development, it too often becomes a geography of development. Any growth in a place like Antioch, 50 miles from San Francisco, becomes sprawl in the minds of many, especially those in the urban core secure enough to have no need for the affordable American Dream long available only on the urban fringe.

This geographical rooting of the problem makes Antioch and East County the problem in and of themselves. There is a deep tendency in America to assume *problems evident in geography are the result of choices and decisions and events made primarily in that geography*. Local actors are seen to bear primary responsibility, as opposed to the broader system of urban and regional development. Even if one also blames actors at higher scales or in different sectors, actors in other parts of the region like central cities and wealthier suburbs often get a free pass.

The parallels between the blaming of the Antiochs of America for the current crisis and the blaming of the postwar inner city for the urban crisis of the 1950s and 1960s are striking. Robert Beauregard's (1993: 6) statement that talking about the postwar inner-city almost exclusively in terms of decline provided "a spatial fix for more generalized insecurities and complaints, thereby minimizing their evolution into a more radical critique of American society," could just as easily have been written about the flood of post-foreclosure journalism and critique aimed at struggling communities on the metropolitan fringe (Schafran 2013). While we seem to have clearly learned that the struggles of the postwar inner-city were as much about the postwar suburb as they were about the city, places like Antioch have not been given the same benefit of a wider perspective.

When we seek this form of spatial fix, we also trod another all too familiar historical path best left untaken.[7] The "discourse of decline" brewing on the urban fringe has already begun to mark those who live there, a bitter irony considering that many communities who now call places like East County home are survivors of the earlier marking of the inner-city. There is no arguing with some of the facts on the ground, be they questions of rising poverty (Kneebone and Berube 2013) or the lack of social services. American suburbia is struggling in a way it has never struggled before.

Unfortunately, writers and pundits discussing suburbia's struggles use language that is strikingly similar to the language of mid-twentieth-century writers on urban decline—in effect, moving "urban problems" to the "suburban ghetto" (Murphy 2007: 21–37; Lucy and Phillips 2000). This scholarly perspective has been accompanied by a more popular discourse that goes further, again using terms like "slum" and "ghetto" to describe communities facing high rates of foreclosure, increasing poverty, limited fiscal capacity, and newly diverse communities (Schafran 2013).

In regurgitating this deep and dark tradition in American urbanism, in once again looking at problems in communities of color and declaring those places as problems in and of themselves, we again focus on a symptom and not the larger historical system of injustice. Rather than asking pointed questions about segregation, we simply cast aspersions, or discuss the "death" of these places without any regard for those who live there. The fast-growing cities on the fringe of the Bay Area are collectively majority-minority, in some cases more than two-thirds communities of color. Talking of their decline helps nobody.

Fragmentation, Regionalism, and Neoliberalism

Another set of explanations focuses on metropolitan fragmentation—the way in which too many small governments cannot come together to plan regionally. Since the days of Robert Wood's (1961) famous *1400 Governments,* scholars and practitioners alike have pointed to the fact that our regions are chopped up into innumerable overlapping jurisdictions. All of these separate local, county, subregional, and regional governments, authorities, and independent agencies make planning less efficient, limit cooperation, and empower certain jurisdictions to be selfish and exclusionary. The "natural" response to fragmentation, and in turn to the patterns of segregation and sprawl it is thought to cause, is some form of regional governance, itself a century-old dream of planners and political scientists (Weir 2004).

It is a diagnosis that makes sense on so many levels. The idea of defragmenting the region through some form of regional governance would seemingly undo the urban / suburban divide dialectic that has been so harmful. Rusk's (1993) "cities without suburbs" and Orfield's (2002) "metropolitics" appear to be intelligent ways of grappling with both the ongoing divide between cities and suburbs and the increasing division between the suburbs themselves. Place matters as much as it ever has (Dreier, Mollenkopf, and Swanstrom 2001), and these fragmentation / regionalism approaches have immense value.

The limitations of these approaches are much less severe than the sprawl and decline discourses, at least when they are mutually exclusive. Fragmentation and regionalism approaches stumble by making two key geographic errors, one theoretical and one historical. Conceptually, they engage in a common scalar fetishism that sees one particular geographic scale as ideal for the governance of the production of space. If we could only achieve regional governance, or some hybrid between local and regional activity (Katz and Bradley 2013), we would finally be able to achieve some of the long-desired plans, finally be able to counteract sprawl, segregation, etc., or so the argument goes.

To this day, advocates continue to push for more "regionalism," including in the Bay Area. But the production of cities, towns, and region, of homes, roads, jobs, and schools, of space and place, has always been a set of relationships among actors from different sectors operating at different scales (Storper 2014), and one must focus on the broader question of the politics of planning *across* scale rather than the possibility of planning at a particular scale.

This between-scale question is made all the more necessary by the unfortunate tendency to misread history, especially in the Bay Area. The region did not become fragmented, at least in the narrow sense of competing jurisdictions, during the period in question, or even immediately beforehand. The Bay Area was born fragmented and multicentered, spread out and sprawling. The overwhelming majority of growth implicated in the new geography of crisis did not occur in brand-new cities imagined by developers, postmodern versions of Levittown or Lakewood.[8] Virtually all of the major places in this book—East County's Antioch, Brentwood, and Pittsburg; central Contra Costa's San Ramon and Walnut Creek; the core cities of Oakland and Richmond; San Francisco and Silicon Valley and Marin County; the Central Valley cities of Modesto and Stockton—were on the regional map by 1900. In the 25 cities in the greater Bay Area that grew by 50 percent and saw at least 5,000 new residents between 1990 and 2010 (chapter 1), cities which have overwhelmingly borne the brunt of foreclosure, the median founding date was 1873. The Bay Area did not sprawl into an uninhabited desert in the postwar era, but rather grew into a regional skeleton of small industrial cities and old farm towns largely established by the end of the nineteenth century. As discussed in more detail below, the question is less about jurisdictional fragmentation and more about a generalized unwillingness and inability to plan for this region that was basically fragmented from the start.

From Scalar Fetishes to Institutional Ones

The regionalist / fragmentation approach has a strange bedfellow in the discourses of neoliberalism. Neoliberalism became an intellectual catchall during the first decade of the twenty-first century, used to describe a series of actions whereby the "market" was prioritized over the "state," financialization and privatization were rampant (Harvey 2005), and individuals were held to be the primary economic actors in society, heroic entrepreneurs in the mold of Ayn Rand's Howard Roark. Peck and Theodore (2002) divide neoliberalism into "roll-out" and "roll-back" neoliberalism, separating those sets of actions which eroded existing institutions or regulations from those that established new rules and new entities.

There is little argument from critical scholars that one can find direct and indirect relationships between virtually all aspects of neoliberalism and the foreclosure crisis. It was a crisis driven by deregulated capital spreading and taking on new forms while governments at multiple scales largely ignored the ticking time bomb. This bomb was fed by the persistent fetishization and promotion of homeownership, the latter led by an ever-powerful real estate industry and quasi-governmental institutions like Fannie Mae and Freddie

Mac that had been transformed during the past two decades to better serve capital and speculation.

If regionalism stems from a geographic view of fragmentation, scholars of neoliberalism emphasize the fragmentation or "splintering" of the state as a whole (Graham and Marvin 2001; Brenner and Theodore 2002). The question is not simply about the power or number of local jurisdictions, but about the increasing power of private-sector actors in the production of space. For Graham and Marvin (2001) in particular, what has been splintered is the "integrated ideal," in which the state is at the center of infrastructure provision. In its emphasis on the broad political economy of urbanization, the neoliberalism approach more closely resembles my own, and has contributed greatly to my thinking about the crisis in the Bay Area.

Yet there are two aspects of the neoliberalism discourse that are limiting. One is a failing that geographic fragmentation also faces—an at-times incomplete reading of history. To talk of a radically devolved and disempowered state may make sense in Europe or Latin America, but it makes little sense in California and most of the United States, where the brief window of Keynesianism is hardly the historic norm. The idea that intercity competition, private-sector power, or any of the other hallmarks of neoliberalism are somehow new is to misread regional history. These factors, much like geopolitical fragmentation, are virtually inborn in Californian and American urbanism.[9] As Mark Weiss (1987) makes so breathtakingly clear in his under-acknowledged (and underread) classic, *The Rise of the Community Builders*, private-sector actors were at the heart of every stage of the formation of the regulatory and planning apparatus in California. Cities in the western half of the United States were engaged in serious entrepreneurial boosterism (Abbott 1981a, 1981b) before David Harvey was born, let alone before he penned his famous argument about the shift from the managerial to the entrepreneurial city (Harvey 1989) as part of academic urbanism's early engagement with neoliberalism. The line between "state" and "market" actors is so fuzzy in California that the terms lose much of the utility they may have elsewhere.

Scholarship on neoliberalism also has a tendency toward institutional fetishization, a trait it shares with many subgenres of urbanism. This is the viewpoint that favors or blames certain actors—developers, local government, banks, community-based organizations, etc.—an institutional parallel to regionalist pursuit of the proper scale. The power of certain institutions becomes the problem in and of itself, an institutional problem instead of a spatial one. But the production of space in the United States, and especially in California, has always been constituted by an intricate set of relations between a vast number of governmental and nongovernmental institutions at every scale, held together and driven apart at different times by different sets of collective politics and sociocultural / socioeconomic trajectories.[10]

What is needed instead is a deeper sense of political fragmentation, one more akin to historian Robert Fogelson's (1993) depiction of the early days of Los Angeles as a "fragmented metropolis," a sense that went beyond jurisdictions to consider deeper cultural and social issues. This notion of fragmentation goes beyond questions of the state or the number of local governments, beyond the "splintering" of the "integrated ideal" that ushers in an era of privatized infrastructure. As I attempt to show throughout the book, what ultimately drove this crisis was the broad fragmentation of the political economy of virtually every aspect of city- and region-building. Rather than build toward a political economy of development that could have produced a more equitable, environmentally sustainable, and fiscally and economically stable region, the politics became more divided and the economics much more fragile. Rather than recognize what California's long-forgotten 1978 *Urban Strategy* called the "common purpose" that is urban and regional development (California Office of Planning and Research 1978: iii; see also chapter 8), California grew even more divided when it came to building space and places, neighborhoods and regions.[11]

This broader sense of fragmentation enables us to see division where, on paper, there should be solidarity. The Bay Area not only has a reputation for being politically progressive, but over the course of the past 40 years, virtually every major elected official has been a member of the same party.[12] What one could consider the "Obama coalition"—middle- and working-class communities of color and generally middle-class, generally white progressive environmentalists—has been the overwhelming majority in the region for decades. There were no radical ideological differences on abortion, war, gay rights, or civil rights, as there has been in the country as a whole. There was no major reactionary movement that questioned government in every way. Of course there were the typical differences between business groups and environmental organizations, but especially with the ascendancy of the tech industry, many business leaders saw themselves as firmly green. In the hyper-multi-ethnic Bay Area, virtually all institutions avowed that they were progressives on issues of poverty and race. San Francisco became famous for having two types of politics—progressive Democrats and moderate Democrats.

As discussed in chapter 6, one could argue that the high-growth areas on the fringe of the region—areas like East County that built the homes which housed the people who took the loans—are more purple than blue. As you go deeper into San Joaquin County, places become even more Republican, and it was these elected officials who overwhelmingly voted to allow the type of suburban development that became a hotspot for foreclosure. But this type of political stratification on the megaregional scale is still not enough to explain the full story, for again, it would make the error of understanding places like East County only in East County. It does not account for innumerable other decisions made at other scales and in other places, most of which were made by people who voted similarly in November and were not divided by standard American political ideologies. While the relationship between party affiliation and land use politics / urban growth is underexplored, it is only a partial explanation for what occurred.

The stark reality is that faced with the profound challenge of remaking the unequal and unsustainable region built during the postwar era, leaders and institutions at every scale and in every sector in the Bay Area could neither find nor forge this "common purpose" that is urban and regional development, despite voting together in November. It was not simply the formal, jurisdictional political geography of a vast and growing region that had become fragmented, nor the party lines dividing communities on the outskirts of the regions from those in the core. It was the entire politics of planning and development itself. The relative political unity of the region masked the fact that like most of the United States, the Bay Area remained deeply divided over issues of race, space, and place.

To understand this, one has to think historically about how the region of one generation is built in reaction to the region of another. Despite its progressive politics and considerable economic resources, the San Francisco Bay Area was never willing nor able to heal the vast racialized wounds that were so foundational to its history, especially those wounds inscribed in space and place. The region's incredible record of economic and social innovation and environmental preservation was matched by similar innovation in racial exclusion and outright bigotry. Moreover, the radicalism and innovation for which it became famous never materialized into a similar world-class effort to overcome those spatialized inequalities and divisions that the collective racism produced. The Bay Area became more adept at conservation-minded park-building, technology-driven company-building, and preservation-minded neighborhood-building than equity-driven metropolis-building. At times, it also allowed important majorities to believe that these things were mutually exclusive. When the postwar form of ghettoized segregation began to unravel, the region had a chance to do things differently, rather than reinvent segregation on a much larger scale. Instead it fragmented, in this deeper and broader sense of the term, unable to overcome the racial ghosts in the regional machine.

GHOSTS IN THE MACHINE

The second core argument of this book is that this new form and map of segregation, and the foreclosure crisis it helped to enable, was produced by the highly specific way in which the politics of space and place during the more recent era reacted to the ghosts of postwar urbanism. What has occurred is not simply some path-dependent aftermath of the postwar era, the result of a postwar model destined to fail. Nor, as I have stated before, is it simply the result of neoliberalism or bad decisions in the 1980s and beyond. Rather, it is the end result of a "neoliberal era," that period from the mid-1970s until the foreclosure crisis of 2008, built on the ghosts of the postwar era.[13]

When it comes to urbanization and development, the neoliberal era must be conceived as the result of a multiplicity of reactions to the sins and unsolved problems of the urban crisis of the postwar era—the complex math of one era being built in reaction to, on top of, and side by side with another era that never truly went away, etched as it is in the built environment, in political institutions, and in collective memory.[14] This historical residue, from concrete freeways through poor and racialized communities to abandoned plans for regional mobility, from institutional memories of top-down planning to the deep legacy of racial exclusion both residentially and politically, is what I collectively refer to as *ghosts in the machine*. Any understanding that does not hold both eras up to the light simultaneously will fail to understand the contemporary moment.

Postwar sub / urbanization established an unworkable and racialized urban / suburban dichotomy, structuring metropolitan areas into distinct zones of opportunity. It was also wasteful, environmentally destructive, and economically and fiscally unsustainable. What was at times sold during the postwar era as a collective effort was in reality driven by a powerful but narrowly constructed coalition of elites, a top-down "growth machine" (Logan and Molotch 1987) that extended far from downtown, especially in California. Developers, planners, bankers, lawyers, newspaper publishers, unions, real estate brokers, and businesspeople of all types supported, pushed, and boosted this machine that had undergirded the development of California from the outset. The postwar era relied on a blind majoritarian politics to prop up an elite and top-down urbanization that was harmful to minority communities and the natural environment, even as it built needed infrastructure and turned a generation of (mostly white) Americans into a homeowning middle class. State-led urban planning, heavily influenced by modernism, never fully recovered from its involvement with the sins of the postwar period, while never getting the credit it deserved for its profound successes.

The broad implosion of postwar urbanization in the Bay Area and beyond came as a result of an attack on this machine from virtually every side, from left and right, environmentalists and racial justice advocates, local governments and homeowners, suburbanites and urbanites. Opposition to the way cities and towns and the region as a whole were built, planned, and developed began to grow in incredibly diverse circles. Actors in different sectors with different cultures and political beliefs knew that the way the region was growing and building wasn't working and couldn't continue.

But the reaction to this destructive majoritarianism was not a coming-together across various differences and spectrums to build a new, less racist, and more environmentally and economically sustainable urbanism. Instead, the broad opposition led to further fragmentation. Both environmental and racial justice advocates grew more powerful during the neoliberal era, but in different spaces fighting for different things. Local governments, regional agencies, transportation authorities, community-based organizations, unions—virtually everyone involved in the urbanization process found their niche to defend, their issues to promote, and their spaces to build and rebuild, but the collective endeavor needed to meet the truly massive challenge of a post–civil rights metropolis in a booming and gentrifying megaregion was never likely. Developer power did not wane in the least, but they too carved out new spaces and territories and ways of operating, they too retrenched politically. Some focused on building increasingly expensive places for an increasingly rarified elite; others fled over the hills to areas that had not yet rejected their postwar model.

One result of this broad and deep fragmentation was that certain aspects of the modernist planning project which underwrote the postwar era, including the ability to think big and connect far-flung portions of the metropolis, were dramatically undermined even as they remained necessary. The planning and development that emerged from the postwar era was determined to do better at respecting the micro scale, and in this it somewhat succeeded. It could no longer run roughshod over places the way it once did, and the lessons learned from Jane Jacobs and many others about small-scale and bottom-up began to take hold.

But larger-scale challenges—the bigger systems needed to move, house, and educate a growing region that began the day divided and unequal—could not be met by this fragmented body politic. Again, this was not simply a case of local jurisdictions not being able to cooperate or regional agencies not having enough power, but the inability of all of the major institutional actors involved in the production of space to come together to confront the ghosts of planning's past and meet the challenges of a rapidly growing and rapidly changing region still heavily scarred by inequality and beset by the double-edged sword of a beautiful but difficult physical geography.

Not all of the ghosts in the machine involve things done that should not have been done. The notion of ghosts refers equally to what was left on the table—generations of good ideas and worthwhile plans that have gathered dust even as the situation on the ground worsened. Much like the BART plan that opened this introduction, many of the plans and ideas from the 1960s and 1970s show evidence that planners and leaders recognized some of the failings of postwar suburbanization. There was no lack of concrete ideas throughout this entire history on how to make changes.

There were also many who understood the risk of repeating the failures of postwar sub / urbanization once again—only this time farther from the core with hundreds of thousands of new residents. As I mentioned at the outset, even the plans that unleashed growth in East County included ideas which perhaps could have allowed things to unfold differently, ideas which today are taught as contemporary "solutions" to long-standing planning problems, particularly in the suburbs: transit-oriented development, walkable and bikeable communities, improved connections between housing, jobs, and education, local agricultural preservation, and so on. But these ideas, like so many of the time, were left on the table, or left buried in plans on the shelf and never implemented.

The true shame of what happened to East County and to the Bay Area and plenty of other areas like it in the United States is that planners, politicians, activists, and academics long saw the writing on the wall, but were unable or unwilling to build the type of planning politics necessary to alter the direction of history and build a different geography. From the late 1950s up and through the first wave of foreclosures, regional and state agencies, local planning departments, respected consulting firms, powerful advocacy organizations, academic institutes, and developer trade associations knew what was slowly unfolding on the region's fringe. They wrote reports and plans and projections, argued for solutions and fought battle after battle after battle, but little actually changed. Planning failed not because it saw the future incorrectly, but because it saw it all too clearly and failed to adequately intervene. The Bay Area had many good plans, and even more good planners, but at the end of the day the system of planning could not alter the course of history.

What the Bay Area lacked, and still largely lacks, was not good ideas or good policies, but *effective politics*—a politics of development capable of producing the actual existing urban fabric that we all need to survive in an equitable and sustainable way. The true tragedy of the way in which these two eras came together is how both periods combined to undermine any possible faith in the political economy of urbanization. The region had the resources and know-how to avoid its fate, to avoid resegregating itself on a much bigger scale, to avoid becoming such a tempting market for bad mortgage debt, to avoid inhumane and unsustainable commuting patterns, but it could not come together politically to make these difficult decisions. Instead, the region continued to divide itself along false choices—environmentalism or development, gentrification or abandonment. This twentieth-century either / or mentality was ill suited to the twenty-first-century both / and problems the region was facing, and furthered the fragmentation and inertia. This helped reproduce twentieth-century problems and create new twenty-first-century ones at the same time, but in different parts of the region.

Responsibility for this failure of planning, for the continued fragmentation of the politics of urbanization and development, lies in virtually every institution and at every scale; it was driven by developments on the ground and in turn drove those developments. This insistence on a broad geographic and institutional understanding of responsibility for the resegregation of the Bay Area informs the organization of this book. Chapter 1 lays out the case for understanding the transformation of the Bay Area as segregation, and for transforming our understanding of segregation. The second section of the book then examines how this transformation occurred in different parts of the region. It starts in East County (chapter 2), moving west through Contra

Costa County (chapter 3), the cities of Oakland and Richmond and the old military-industrial spaces of the inner Bay Area (chapter 4), and what I call the West Bay Wall—Silicon Valley, San Francisco, and Marin County (chapter 5). This section ends by returning east, over the Altamont Pass and into the Central Valley (chapter 6).

The final section of this book examines why this resegregation was never prevented either at the regional scale (chapter 7) or by the state of California (chapter 8). All throughout these chapters I try to show how "common purpose" was never achieved, and how a series of seemingly paradoxical dilemmas furthered a set of false choices. These dilemmas collectively hamstrung the very possibility of turning the regional ship around, as real solutions became unthinkable. Each chapter bounces back and forth between the historical and the contemporary, a fact that may make orthodox historians nervous but which is a necessary part of grappling with how the past and the present come together in each place to produce the contemporary moment.

As I discuss in the conclusion, building a new, more unified politics of development, this "common purpose," will take time. It will require rethinking who plans and who is a planner. It will require rethinking the very role of urban development in our economy as a whole. It will require that we abandon some of the normative baggage with which we judge places and housing choices, and work to make sure everyone's place and everyone's home is as secure and risk-free as possible. It will require a concerted and honest effort to come to terms with the ghosts of planning past, so that the type of political grand bargain needed to build the homes and transport and communities we all need becomes possible, rather than just another set of good ideas left on the shelf, or good intentions left unfulfilled. And it will require a renewed commitment to combatting exploitation in all aspects of metropolis-building.

One way of reformatting our thinking so that this type of grand bargain becomes possible is to reimagine sustainability. One of the most important planning and development buzzwords over the past two decades, sustainability came to symbolize both the hope and failure to unify environmental, equity, and economic goals. Rather than simply abandoning sustainability as an idea, we need to understand it for what it is and was on the ground—a failed coalition. Only sustainability as a true political coalition among institutions advocating for each of these goals can help us realize the unfounded promise of the Bay Area as the equitable and sustainable region it wants to be but has never been.

ONE

The Suburbanization of Segregation

RATHER THAN WRITE NORTH OR SOUTH OR EAST OR WEST, it has long been a California tradition to indicate directions when getting onto a freeway by giving a major destination farther down the line. On Highway 4 and Interstate 580, the two main east–west roads that connect the Central Valley and the core of the Bay Area, one often sees signs like the one shown in Figure 1—this way to Oakland, that way to Stockton.

These signs unwittingly symbolize the choices given the majority of communities of color over the past 40 years in the Bay Area. Stay in cities like Oakland or Richmond, move to places like Stockton or Antioch. Staying generally meant dealing with issues of poor schools, high crime rates, extreme levels of violence, and deep environmental inequity. It meant staying in communities marked by the type of ghettoized segregation that has made inner-city America an international symbol. The major difference in the Bay Area version compared to some of the truly abandoned places in the country is that these core areas were also gentrifying rapidly.

Leaving often meant grappling with new homes far away from churches, family, and community. It meant congested traffic, very little public transportation access, and cities that grew rapidly and under weaker fiscal conditions than older suburbs. It meant moving to communities challenged by increasing poverty rates and greater numbers of lower-income people, amidst a political culture and social services network less prepared for the challenge than their inner-core colleagues. It meant living in places on the front lines of integration and diversification, massive melting pots with all of the beautiful and difficult aspects of living with difference.

This chapter is not about how and why people made these choices. Nor is it about how it has worked out for individual families.[1] Nor does it seek in

FIGURE 1. Choices. Photo by author.

any way to portray the people involved, nor the communities to which they moved or from which they came, as somehow damaged or pathological. Both Oakland and Stockton are and can be wonderful places. Both decisions to stay and decisions to go can and have been good decisions.

What this chapter focuses on are two interrelated facts. First, this choice—Oakland or Stockton, or the various places in similar situations in both core and periphery—does not represent the full range of choices in the Bay Area at all. There are many other places that are neither Oakland nor Stockton, but such places—fiscally sound communities with good schools and often plentiful jobs and a robust tax base—have remained largely white and largely wealthy throughout a time of major demographic change. Second, all of the cities that became major destinations for communities of color experienced dramatically higher foreclosure rates and major losses of value relative to the region as a whole, even as they continued to represent the hopes and dreams of an entire generation of diverse migrants (Schafran and Wegmann 2012). This finding is consistent with growing evidence from across the nation that communities of color were disproportionately impacted by the foreclosure crisis (Rugh and Massey 2010; Rugh 2014).[2]

Coming to terms with this persistent racialization of regional geographies and its connection to foreclosure means pushing past much of the myopic debate in the United States about whether the country is still segregated, and focusing instead on *how segregation has changed,* both in form and geography. Simply because race and racism is not what it was doesn't mean that either have left the American metropolis, nor are they confined to Ferguson, Missouri, or post-Katrina New Orleans or any other symbolic place.

This chapter, which also serves as an introduction to both the historical and contemporary human geography of the changing Bay Area, argues that the shifts in racial geography in the Bay Area over the past generation, while helping undo old forms of segregation, have helped produce a new geography that one must also call segregation. This is the shift from the *ghettoized segregation* of an earlier era to the *mobile segregation* of today, a process that can be viewed as the suburbanization of segregation. And just to be clear—the development of this newer form of segregation, this *resegregation* if you will, does not imply that the older form of segregation no longer exists. The challenge is to understand them dialectically, as two forms of spatial separation and distinction that operate together.

In what follows, I provide a brief introduction to the history of diversity in the Bay Area, arguably one of the first regions to be born as multiracial, in what was at that time a very two-tone America. I then take a deep dive into the question of segregation, starting with how what became known as the "suburban wall" helped form our ideas of segregation. By examining how this geography has changed, we can begin to see how segregation has changed, moving beyond debates about whether American is still segregated, and instead focusing on what segregation means in the twenty-first century.

As I discuss in the introduction to this book as well as in this chapter, the partial erosion of the "suburban wall" does not mean segregation is dead, but simply that it has changed form and geography. The remainder of the chapter seeks to show and explain this argument, using three different studies, two quantitative and one qualitative, each of which shows in Northern California similar new pattern of more mobile, regional- and megaregional-scale racialized inequality. Taken together, they point to an altered segregation, a set of lines more subtle than postwar segregation but nevertheless real, a twenty-first-century mobile segregation for a massive, wealthy, and globalized regional metropolis.

MULTIRACIAL METROPOLE

From its earliest days, what would become the San Francisco Bay Area had multiracial roots. A mix of Native American tribes, Mexican outposts, and

Californio settlers was turned upside down by an international flood of migrants during the Gold Rush of 1849.[3] Small cities and an interconnected region were born seemingly overnight, in a California where, as the great Carey McWilliams ([1949] 1999: 25) put it, "the lights went on all at once, in a blaze."

It was one of the most diverse migrations in history, and quickly sprouted one of the most eclectic regions in the world. Miners and prospectors came from the Sandwich Islands and Mexico, Peru and Chile, Ireland and Wales. There were Basques, French, Germans, and Britons—refugees from a Europe in upheaval. There were early Oregonians and old-time East Coasters, Australians and New Zealanders, Filipinos and African Americans. By one estimate, half of the 90,000 arrivals who would make San Francisco an instant metropolis were foreign-born (Starr and Orsi 2000).

The Bay Area thus became one of the world's first truly multiracial regions, in a nation constituted largely along black and white lines or Native American and white lines. Chinese immigrants were part of the initial rush, and thousands more would arrive for the building of the transcontinental railroad in the 1860s. Japanese migrants came in earnest toward the end of the nineteenth century. The porous border with Mexico and the fact that California was Mexico meant Chicano farmers and families were part of the California landscape early on.

From the outset, this diversity was regional. Even if San Francisco and Oakland were principal gateways as they became big cities, many of the region's small cities have boasted immigrant communities from their earliest days. This tradition would continue with the next major immigration event after the Gold Rush: World War II. The war and its massive federal investment in shipbuilding and war-related industrialization brought an influx of African American workers to the region, mostly from Louisiana, Arkansas, and Texas. Filipinos also came in numbers during the war, helping to cement what had long been a relatively small but important multiracial minority, alongside significant Chinese, Mexican, and Native American populations. They too settled in the cities of the region, not simply in one center or another—Pittsburg, Vallejo, and Richmond all had war work and hence black and Filipino communities; Latinx communities began growing in historic centers like East San Jose, while Chinese Oakland grew in the shadow of Chinese San Francisco.

The "other" economic miracle undergirding the region's economy, agriculture, also benefitted from immigration and cultural diversity. Japanese, Portuguese, Italian, Swiss-French, and Punjabi farmers were at the heart of an agricultural economy stretching from the vineyards and egg farms of

Napa and Sonoma down through Silicon Valley's orchards and into the industrialized food factory that was California's Central Valley (McWilliams [1949] 1999). Even if San Francisco dominated in terms of the larger population of immigrants and nonwhites, the regionalization of diversity kept pace to a certain degree with the regionalization of the metropolis. Immigrants and nonwhites could be found all along the urban-rural transect.

This regional diversity, which a new generation of revisionist historiography has shown is not entirely unique to the Bay Area (Wiese 2005; Kruse and Sugrue 2006), was by no means inclusionary. The Bay Area was at the forefront of the development of exclusionary practices, many of which underpin American urbanism. In an environment founded upon a "virtual reign of terror" (Castillo n.d.: n.p.) foisted upon Native Americans during the Gold Rush, Northern California aimed its wrath in a more organized fashion at the Chinese. The Chinese became the target of landmark exclusionary laws at the state and federal levels, culminating in the anti-Chinese acts of the 1880s (Walker 2008; Craddock 2000). Even more influential would be the zoning acts enacted in Modesto and San Francisco during this same period that would effectively invent zoning in the United States. The nominal purpose was to prevent laundries from opening in certain neighborhoods, laundries being by that time a primarily Chinese business (Warner 1972; Bernstein 1999).

This attack on the Chinese began a historical wave of reactionary replacement—one group brought in for economic purposes by power and capital, only to then be attacked and replaced by another. The Japanese were explicitly brought in to replace excluded Chinese workers, only to become targets of "yellow peril" race-baiting and warmongering during the first two decades of the twentieth century. This anti-Japanese sentiment reached full tilt when the Japanese neighborhood in the Fillmore district of San Francisco was largely confiscated during World War II. Their homes were often taken over by African Americans brought in for the war effort, a community that was then pushed out in large numbers by postwar urban renewal programs.

The regionalization of diversity does not mean that the Bay Area was not segregated. By the 1970s, the majority of African Americans were confined to a handful of communities—Oakland, Richmond, East Palo Alto, Pittsburg, Vallejo, and parts of San Francisco. Latinx and Asian geography was not quite as confined, but neither was there true integration. As the small railroad towns throughout the Bay Area grew into incorporated industrial cities and suburban commuter towns, racial covenants, FHA loan provisions, steering by real estate agencies, and harassment by law enforcement and hostile neighbors were all brought to bear on nonwhite Bay Area residents, particularly African Americans (Self 2003; Rhomberg 2004). The entire apparatus that sustained pre- and post-war housing discrimination against nonwhites in postwar America (Jackson 1985) was in full force throughout the region. No matter that the twentieth-century Bay Area was at the forefront of many progressive political movements—the full weight of "the great crime of history that brought the ghettoes to be" (Coates 2015: 106) was brought to bear on the shores of the San Francisco Bay.

What is critical to understand is that even in the postwar era, the roots of the region's differentiated segregation are evident. West Oakland, East Oakland, San Francisco's Bayview–Hunters Point, and Richmond's Iron Triangle are classic examples of American racialized ghettoization—inner-city neighborhoods where African Americans were allowed to settle following migration, only to see these communities cut-off, starved of resources, ripped apart by urban renewal, hemmed in by racist housing policies, and often abandoned by the state (Wacquant 1997). But East Palo Alto was different—an unincorporated area on the periphery where suburban factory workers of color were allowed to settle on poor quality land on the edge of the bay. Pittsburg and Vallejo were distant industrial towns. Even by 1970 the writing was on the wall that the segregation of the Bay Area would be both the same as our traditional imagination of ghettoized segregation and something qualitatively different.[4] Even as the Bay Area became home to some of the most famous archetypes of ghettoized segregation, it also was laying the foundation for another form of segregation that was to come.

MENTAL MAPS: THE WALL AND THE GHETTO

In 1971, the City of Los Angeles published a study in which it recreated a more regional version of Kevin Lynch's famed "mental maps." They asked residents of Boyle Heights, a poor, heavily Latinx, East Los Angeles neighborhood with low levels of car ownership, and residents of Northridge, a commuter-heavy middle-class suburb in the San Fernando Valley (north of Central Los Angeles), to draw their version of the metropolis. The composite maps (see Figure 2) have become famous, a perfect crystallization of an older form of segregation, a segregation where one was literally trapped in a very confined neighborhood. Not coincidentally, Boyle Heights is hard up against the factory belt extending east from downtown (but certainly not west), a receiving point for immigrants stretching back to the beginnings of the century.

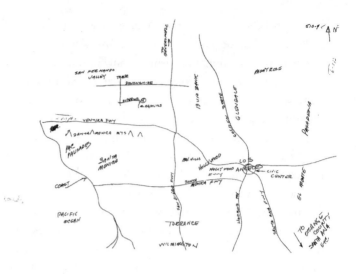

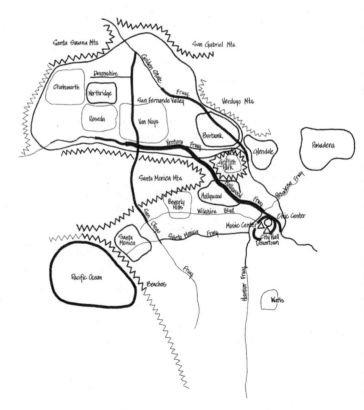

FIGURE 2. Mental maps. This page: San Fernando Valley; facing page: Boyle Heights. Source: Los Angeles Department of Planning, 1971.

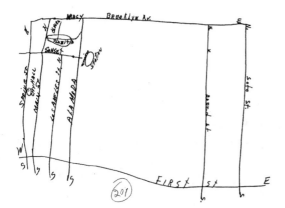

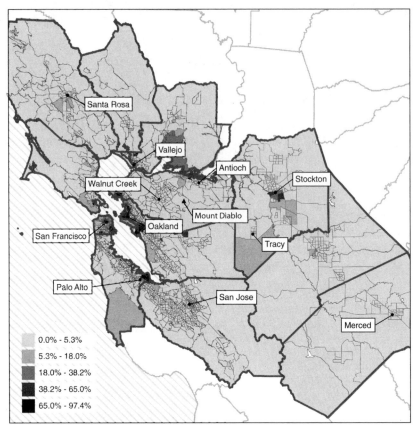

MAP 3. African Americans, 1970 census, by census tract. Source: Neighborhood Change Database (NCDB) at 2000 census tracts.

In the Los Angeles of the early 1970s, as in the Bay Area of the same time period, being a person of color generally meant being trapped in a very limited space—a geography defined in many ways by overt discrimination, a postwar racial map that was born in the violence and genocide of the nineteenth century, hardened through legal and quasi-legal doctrine and enforced through "gentler" forms of steering, "custom," and thinly veiled hostility.

Map 3 shows the above-mentioned regional segregation pattern for the 1970s Bay Area, which was particularly intense for African Americans.[5] One can clearly see the pocket of East Palo Alto, one of the few places a black family could live (and certainly buy) south of the Hayward / San Mateo Bridge. The biggest bright spot on the map is the Oakland-Berkeley-Richmond corridor, historically the center of black life in the Bay Area.

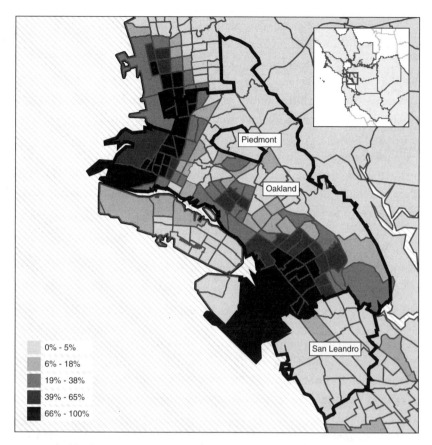

0% - 5%
6% - 18%
19% - 38%
39% - 65%
66% - 100%

MAP 4. Oakland, San Leandro, Piedmont, 1970. The white noose. Source: US Census. Map by author.

Map 4 shows a close-up of one edge of this area, the Oakland–San Leandro border, which would become a national symbol of city / suburban segregation. As Brian Copeland recounts in his memoir, black residents of East Oakland called the line between the two cities the "invisible wall" (Copeland 2006: 12). If you were black it was difficult enough to circulate, what with a police car stationed under the archway of the border on East 14th Street and designated to follow any black motorist who dared enter, let alone buy a home with a real estate industry organized not to sell you one. *Newsweek* featured San Leandro in a 1969 article on Nixon's "forgotten white majority," and by 1971 CBS was back to make a documentary about discrimination and what it called the "Suburban Wall" (Copeland 2006; CBS Films 1971).

Together with other working-class white cities like Alameda, Hayward, and the wealthier Contra Costa County suburbs over the hills to the east, Oakland and Richmond would be surrounded by what historian Robert Self (2003) calls the "white noose"—a classically American form of city / suburb segregation. With the coming of crack cocaine in the 1980s, Reagan-era policies that continued disinvestment, and the beginnings of African American middle-class flight from the neighborhood, East Oakland became even more ghettoized. Immigration from Latin America and Southeast Asia made the neighborhood more ethnically diverse, but violence and the murder rate remained high, schools struggled, and the area ranked as one of the Bay Area's iconic examples of inner-city, ghettoized poverty.

But the San Leandro–Oakland line was not the only suburban wall in the area. When we look at a less well-known wall, and compare it to the current version of San Leandro, we can see one way in which segregation has changed.

Some Walls Stay, Some Remain the Same

Piedmont is an incorporated city entirely surrounded by the city of Oakland. Home to much of Oakland and the East Bay's historic ruling class, it has long been an island of wealth in an otherwise more middle- and working-class area.[6] While San Leandro, a truly blue-collar suburb at the time, was held up to a national TV audience as an example of the cruelty of the white working masses, Piedmont was even whiter, had half the poverty, and a 60 percent higher median income.[7]

San Leandro is now one of the most diverse places in the country, where no major racial group has a majority, and the diversity can be felt in every shopping center and public or quasi-public space. It is a classic inner-ring suburb, full of aging postwar infrastructure, with slightly increased poverty and a host of questions about its future.[8] At least San Leandro, along with most of its kind in the Bay Area, is still growing, more than 20 percent since 1970.

Piedmont, meanwhile, has approximately 250 fewer people than in 1970 (Table 1). It is less white than before, but still not black or brown. There were barely more black people in Piedmont in 2010—approximately 144—than there were in San Leandro when it was famous for not allowing black people to live there (~84 in the 1970 census). And now it has one-quarter the people in poverty and 2.7 times the median income of San Leandro. This is the growing gap between rich and poor, not expressed as a city / suburban phe-

TABLE 1 San Leandro and Piedmont, 1970 and 2010

	San Leandro 1970*	San Leandro 2010**	Piedmont 1970*	Piedmont 2010**
Total Population	68,698	84,950	10,917	10,667
% White	97.0	27.1	96.3	71.5
% Black	0.1	11.8	0.6	1.3
% Asian	1.9	29.3	2.9	18.0
% Latinx	10.5	27.4	0.8	3.9
Median Income	$10,537	$62,609	$16,553	$169,674
Poverty Rate	6.0%	8.6%	3.0%	2.4%

*1970 data from U.S. Census. Race and Hispanicity are not separated, so numbers are more than 100%. California has a very small Afro-Latinx population, so these numbers can generally be subtracted from Whites.

**2010 race data from Decennial Census, income and poverty from 5-year ACS.

nomenon as during an earlier era, but increasingly as inequality between suburbs (Dreier, Mollenkopf, and Swanstrom 2001; Orfield 2002).

The integration of San Leandro from a racial perspective is a clue that the Boyle Heights imagination of segregation has changed, at least on one side of the wall. Racialized poverty still exists on the East Oakland side of the line, but San Leandro—and neighboring Hayward, another part of the "white noose"—have been two of the most important sites of African American, Latinx, and Asian population growth in the region, as the postwar barriers *in some places* were slowly chipped away. San Leandro and Hayward are much more connected to transit, federal freeways, higher education, and other critical infrastructure than East County, but they are not major job centers and have never been wealthy. Their 2008 foreclosure rates (747.5 and 1,113.9 per 100,000 people respectively) were two to three times those of wealthier Fremont to the south (300.6), ten to fifteen times Berkeley (84.1) and Albany (68.9) to the north. The latter two cities have grown steadily less black over the past two decades, while the former is part of the transformed blue-collar zone that is now part of Silicon Valley.

For many, these changes in racial geography suggest questions with regard to segregation that are functionally quantitative, asking whether what is happening means the region is "more" or "less" segregated. But in asking whether places are more or less segregated, scholars have often forgotten to ask whether segregation itself has changed.

Segregation Curtailed in U. S. Cities, Study Finds.

—*New York Times* headline, January 30, 2012 (ROBERTS 2012)

In early 2012, national news outlets eagerly picked up a press release from the conservative Manhattan Institute touting the publication of a report unambiguously titled "The End of the Segregated Century." Written by Harvard economist (and now dedicated urbanist) Edward Glaeser and Harvard-trained Duke economist Jacob Vigdor, the report documented how American neighborhoods had become dramatically less segregated since 1890. All-white neighborhoods were largely a thing of the past, and primarily black communities were the exception rather than the norm.

The report and subsequent media attention elicited responses from some of the most prominent segregation researchers in America. Some pushed back against the broad implications of the report or the report's overall message. The Brookings Institutions' William H. Frey warned that "the report sends a potentially harmful message that black-white residential separation is no longer a priority issue in this country." John Logan told the same reporter that "we are far from the 'end of segregation'" (Roberts 2012). Douglas Massey, whose *American Apartheid* is fundamental to our understanding of segregation in post–civil rights America, was quoted as saying that the erosion of all-white neighborhoods was more due to Asian and Latino in-migration than black integration, an argument echoed by Michigan's Reynolds Farley (2011) when he pointed out that despite gains, blacks remained more segregated from whites than did Asians or Latinxs.

With the steady release of 2010 census data, other reports emerged, arguing with similarly catchy headlines that segregation is ebbing ("The Waning of American Apartheid?") or still resilient ("New Maps Show Segregation Alive and Well") (Farley 2011; Remapping Debate 2011). A mountain of research also parsed every possible permutation of racial and ethnic division, showing new lines dividing and uniting Asians, Latinxs, whites, and African Americans, or debated the role of class in these divisions (cf. Massey, Rothwell, and Domina 2009). We have entered the age of what Rugh and Massey (2014: 205) call "competing claims of persisting segregation and rapid integration."

The study of segregation in the United States and its intertwined variants—ethnic clustering, housing discrimination, integration, geographies of opportunity, public policies designed to deal with said issues, the "underclass" debates, etc.—is a massive constellation of research aimed at understanding the links between geography, membership in a social group, and life outcomes, and it is at the very heart of the American urban social science tradition. From the days of the Chicago School of Sociology, the study of racialized difference across space has influenced not only sociology but the foundations of public policy and public health research. When geographers David Kaplan, Kathleen Woodhouse, and Frederick Douzet attempted to review the literature on segregation (Kaplan and Woodhouse 2004; Kaplan and Woodhouse 2005: 737; Kaplan and Douzet 2011), their review spanned three articles in *Urban Geography,* one dealing with causes, another with outcomes, and a third solely devoted to "measurements, categories and meanings."[9]

This latter category is arguably the most contested, for herein lies the links between segregation and particular outcomes or between specific structural forces and the patterns of spatial separation. When Loic Wacquant (1997) eviscerated "the study of the American Ghetto," one of his primary targets was the vast literature that starts with segregated neighborhoods and attempts to measure outcomes based on life in those places. In Wacquant's mind, this measures the cart instead of the horse, ignoring the historical social and economic forces that created the segregated environment in the first place, the systems of "ethno-racial closure and control" that made San Leandro San Leandro and East Oakland East Oakland.

Since most researchers acknowledge some link between segregation and outcomes, much of the truly foundational debate has occurred around the origins of a segregated environment, manifested in particular in inner-city poverty. Massey and Denton's (1993) now famous argument that racial discrimination is at the root of segregation, which is then the root of racialized poverty and inequality, seeks to draw a more direct link between race relations and segregation than do other arguments that point at economic restructuring and the flight of the black middle class (Wilson 1987), the failures of the state and state policy, or right-wing arguments about individual / communal weakness endemic to "cultures" in poor communities.[10]

What has made this question so complex over the years is that the patterns are constantly changing, driven by innumerable forces, including decades of social policy aimed at either eliminating segregation or mitigating its impacts. Scholars have been tracking the suburbanization or metropolitanization of poverty and segregation for decades (cf. Weiher 1991). Yet one of the reasons why our collective conception of segregation does not seem to have changed is that many of the early and influential authors who have written about the suburbanization of poverty and segregation (Dreier, Mollenkopf, and Swanstrom 2001; Orfield 2002) are also associated with a particular remedy for that problem (either enabling mobility or some form of regionalism or both). The questions "Is the U. S. still segregated?" and "What do we do about segregation?" thus become conflated. There is now an equally fierce struggle between those who believe that the way to combat segregation is to reduce spatial separation between social groups through mobility, and those who believe that the better solution is to solve problems in place, even if it means allowing gross imbalances in what the Europeans would call the "social mix."

These debates reached a crescendo with the publication of a Wacquant-esque attack by political scientist David Imbroscio on what he calls the "mobility paradigm" in American urban policy. For Imbroscio, this paradigm is built on a set of policies that have aimed to deconcentrate poverty through public housing demolition, housing vouchers, attempts to build affordable housing in the suburbs, and other measures. His scathing critique, like Wacquant's, specifically attacks leading academics in the field and offers arguments in favor of community development and other place-based measures. He considers "liberal urban policy" both the "dominant philosophical perspective underlying the development of urban public policy in the United States" and, in no uncertain terms, a failure (Imbroscio 2012a: 1, 2012; Squires 2012; Deluca 2012).

Imbroscio is correct to question the intense policy focus on poverty deconcentration, taking the lead from Ed Goetz's (2003) pioneering work on public housing redevelopment and the mobility issue to challenge a view which argues that agglomerations of poor people are inherently problematic.[11] But this intense focus on whether policy should encourage or discourage poor people from moving neglects that *mobility has long been a fact of life for many communities of color,* especially in places like the Bay Area. This includes those on the lower end of the socioeconomic spectrum for reasons that go beyond policy. These critiques are so centered on countering the idea that mobility is necessary for equality, and with picking apart the limited empirical research on formal mobility programs, that they neglect to examine that in many regions a more mobile set of race and class geographies is a reality.[12] Whether or not it is a good idea to move, or whether policy should encourage or discourage it, the suburbanization of communities of color is a fact, not a question.

In debating the age-old question of who lives next to whom, or whether policy should help people move or help people stay, scholarship can again fail to examine the broad processes under way that are restructuring race and class geographies, processes that go beyond policy or a normative and often paternalistic evaluation of whether the state should or should not encourage poor people or people of color to move. The Glaeser and Vigdor report noted that integration of urban core neighborhoods was "assisted" by gentrification and immigration, while black, Latinx, and Asian suburbanization has helped integrate the suburbs. These changes are nothing new in the San Francisco Bay Area. And simply because the numbers on the ground are not what they were, does not mean the Bay Area is "desegregated."

Bad Maps, Not Bad Measurements

Part of the problem is that a good deal of empirical research—the type of work that attempts to count who lives next to or near whom—is either stuck in an old set of geographies, or has adopted new geographies with little basis in regional reality. As a panel of sociologists noted in 2008, most segregation research has been conducted at the census-tract level, a reflection of the foundational nature of both "invisible wall" and "suburban wall" to segregation research. From early on, this research focused on "the extent to which African Americans and Whites occupied separate urban neighborhoods," a fact which "established a key methodological precedent: measuring segregation with decennial census data for readily available geographic units such as tracts or blocks" (Lee et al. 2008: 2; Reardon et al. 2008). Even research conducted at the regional scale often views the region as an agglomeration of tracts.[13]

Unfortunately, when researchers move up in scale, they often use the metropolitan statistical area (MSA) and its variants.[14] These geographies, like the census tract, are a construct of the Census Bureau, one that does not necessarily reflect regional patterns of economic, social, cultural, or political relationships. In the case of the Bay Area, a much larger scale is needed to capture racialized migration patterns, one that ignores census geography and builds a map based on regional history and on-the-ground research (Storper et al. 2015). Yet virtually every major national study to include the Bay Area and all the interactive platforms—you can now get segregation indices online at the touch of a few buttons—uses census MSA divisions that continue to split the Bay Area into different MSAs, with San Francisco, San Jose, and Solano County being counted as different regions. A nine-county analysis becomes impossible, let alone the type of megaregional analysis needed to understand the questions at hand. Even researchers based in the Bay Area have generally worked only at the nine-county region or smaller, missing many of the important changes in regional race and class geography.[15]

Moreover, the question is not simply one of jumping up in scale, but of asking what truly constitutes a region. Census geography is apolitical—no one votes in a census tract, or in an MSA. Policy and decisions are never made at these scales, unless the MSA also corresponds to a regional agency, which is not the case in the Bay Area. If the literature on fragmentation recognizes the importance of cities and towns, why do many concerned with fragmentation continue to build pictures of the region based on tracts?

This scalar myopia, the vitriol evident in the Imbroscio debates about the proper set of public policies, and the intense reaction to Glaeser and Vigdor by other segregation scholars, stem in part from how the scarring of postwar geographies is visible not only on American cities but on those of us who study them. To argue that segregation has changed is seemingly to state that old-fashioned ghettoization is a thing of the past, even if that mental leap is not necessarily true. To move beyond the policy debates is seemingly to abandon the clear role of policy in both the production and alleviation of segregation, even if policy is only one of many forces, and policy is often contradictory. Postwar racial segregation is the ghost that haunts the machine of American urban studies.[16]

In efforts to remain vigilant in the face of segregation, or to challenge supposed orthodoxy within policy realms, scholars have often failed to be open, creative, and inductive when thinking about what segregation has become. Recent scholarship has worked to be more open to new empirical realities, part of what can be considered the "mobilities turn" in segregation research. This work takes a particularly critical look at the relationship between "physical separation" and "social processes" (Adelman and Mele 2014), and between "places and flows" in Castellsian terms (Van Kempen and Wissink 2014). In particular, it looks at segregation beyond where people live, and incorporates analyses of their daily lives, of patterns of movement and interaction, of where people work and mingle and socialize beyond the traditional measures of segregation based on housing and schooling.

Understanding contemporary segregation in the Bay Area means crafting some sort of hybrid between old and new approaches. We must look beyond traditional geographies and scales of segregation without in any way abandoning the old places. Contemporary segregation in the region is no longer *exclusively* or even primarily about the "invisible wall" and the "white noose," but these geographies and ideas still matter. After all, the market for the subdivisions of East County was often those who were leaving the ghettoized neighborhoods of the postwar era. Moreover, simply because the new geographies of race and class do not look like postwar segregation does not mean they are not still a form of segregation. It is simply a different type of segregation, one designed and built for the neoliberal era. As we dive into the data about how the Bay Area has changed over the past few decades, this hopefully becomes clear.

SEGREGATION ON A MUCH BIGGER MAP

> We must, as a nation, as a state, as a region here in the Bay Area, take seriously the threat of becoming like so many European cities—Paris is the one that often comes to my mind—where you have a precious thriving city core, which is where the tourists come, where the people of wealth live, and then you have the poor people, in Paris it is often the African immigrants—living all in the outskirts, unseen and not having any access to opportunity. It is not a sustainable model.

—ANGELA GLOVER BLACKWELL, KQED's *Forum*, JULY 7, 2011

> San Francisco Moves to Stem African American Exodus: Critics Say Effort to Reverse Longtime Trend May Be Too Late.

—*San Francisco Chronicle* headline, April 9, 2007

One of the few California studies of segregation that truly captures the issue as one of change and process at a large scale is a 2002 study by the Public Policy Institute of California (Sandoval, Johnson, and Tafoya 2002). It examined segregation across California, digging down to the city level and back up to major regions. There are two significant findings that correspond to the broader story of this book:

1. The most diverse and most segregated places in California tend to be suburban cities in large metropolitan areas.
2. Diverse cities with diverse neighborhoods tend to be fast-growing cities with plenty of new and relatively affordable housing (ibid., 11, 15).

It is a haunting study to read, in part because it was written during the years when the real estate market was exploding, before these fast-growing and hyper-diverse cities with "plenty of new and relatively affordable housing" would become epicenters of the foreclosure crisis, impacting the communities that had made these places their home. The links between this growing diversity and foreclosure are what matter here, as they are the linchpin of my argument that this new map also constitutes a form of segregation, even if the places involved may actually be the most diverse.

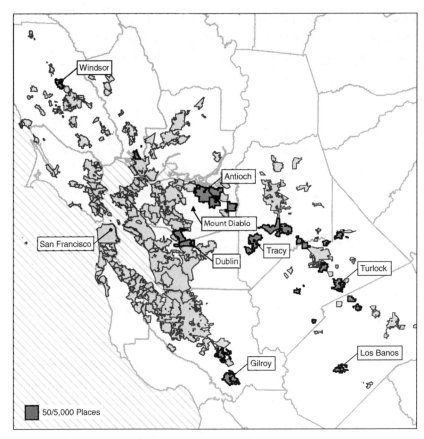

MAP 5. The 50/5000 club. Map by author.

One way of capturing this change is through a crude categorization I call the "50 / 5000 club," a set of places that between 1990 and 2010 grew at least 50 percent and added at least 5,000 people.[17] Map 5 is a simple rendering of places in the San Francisco Bay Area, Sacramento, and the northern San Joaquin Valley that grew rapidly and significantly in the past two decades. The darker places grew by more than 50 percent and gained at least 5,000 new residents between 1990 and 2010. They are mostly incorporated cities and towns, but include a handful of unincorporated areas recognized as "places" by the Census Bureau. The outline is the "Sierra Pacific Megaregion," one of many versions of a Northern California "megaregion" that geographers argue has emerged through the economic (but not political) integration of existing urban regions (Nelson and Lang 2011).

Altogether, these 47 communities are home to more than 1.8 million people. More importantly, they have added a million people since 1990, more than doubling in size during that era. If you take away the suburbs of Sacramento and neighboring counties, the 32 places of the greater Bay Area added almost half a million people, and are now home to 933,179 people according to the U.S. Census, almost 10 percent of the total population of this 15-county region.[18]

If you spend time in many of these places, it feels as if everything is brand new: subdivisions, strip malls, parks, and schools and miles and miles of fresh asphalt. These communities, especially in the banana-shaped arc stretching from eastern Contra Costa County to southwestern Merced County, have been the Bay Area's primary growth frontier over the past two decades. In the 12-county region that is the primary commute-shed for the Bay Area (not including smaller Santa Cruz, Monterey, and San Benito), the twenty-four "50/5000" places added more than 420,000 people, roughly doubling their collective population, compared to an additional million people in the remaining 74 places with a population greater than 10,000 people, places that include major cities such as San Francisco, Oakland, and San Jose, the tenth-largest city in the United States.

Being on the growth frontier means being on the foreclosure frontier. Looking at the full 15-county region, the median foreclosure rate in 2008 was 1,734.5 for the thirty 50/5000 places, versus 300.6 for the 79 others.[19] The numbers are just as extreme at the 12-county level—1,849.8 (n = 25) and 315.7 (n = 73) respectively. On average, the 50/5000 cities were three to four times more likely to have a home go through foreclosure in 2008, the height of the crisis in the Bay Area, an average that stands up to statistical testing at the .001 level.[20]

In the 12-county region, the twenty-five 50/5000 places saw more than 16,400 foreclosures in 2008, 28 percent of the total for places in the region, despite having only 11 percent of the population. What also becomes clear when examined on a map is how much worse the story becomes the farther out from the core of the region one travels. Map 6 shows just how intense the foreclosure rates are for the 12-county region.[21]

The differences are even starker when examined city by city and place by place. The foreclosure rate in Antioch (2,446.6 per 100,000 residents) was almost 13 times that of Redwood City in San Mateo County, and hundreds of times higher than most of Silicon Valley. Lathrop, population 17,063, had more foreclosures than San Francisco, population 808,976.

Yet even if most of the homes and streets and infrastructure in the 50/5000 club are brand new, the places themselves are not. As noted in the introduction,

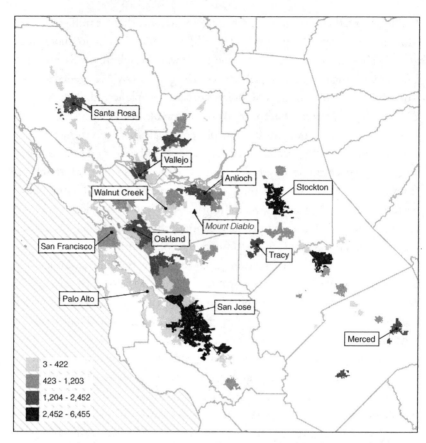

MAP 6. Foreclosure rates per 100,000 people, 2008. Source: California Association of Realtors and DataQuick News, U.S. Census, via RAND California. Calculations by author.

the median founding date for the 25 places in the 12-county region is 1873, the median incorporation date 1914. Only Discovery Bay, built as a real estate venture in the 1970s, can be considered a product of the current era.[22] There is deep history in the 50 / 5000 places, history often ignored in talk about the exurban Bay Area, lumping these places together with postwar Sun Belt urbanization.

The Question of Race

Here the question of racial segregation enters the discussion: of the 456,984 people added to these high-growth, high-foreclosure communities, only 15 percent were white.[23] More than half were Latinx. About eight percent were African American—a seemingly small number, but then the overall region lost African

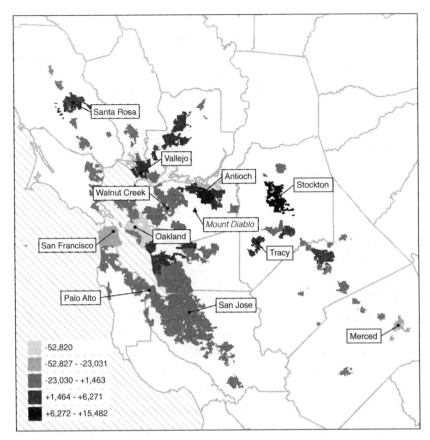

MAP 7. African American growth, 1990–2010. Source: 1990, 2010 U.S. Census Redistricting data. Calculations by author.

American population, and in the 12-county region the 74 places that were *not* part of the 50 / 5000 club lost more than 90,000 African American residents.

Map 7 shows the patterns of African American population change in the 12-county region. Again, like growth and foreclosure, it is a pattern that in general spreads outward from the core, with notable exceptions in the inner-ring suburbs of San Leandro and Hayward in southern Alameda County.

Similar to the link between growth and foreclosure, there are stark and statistically significant differences between racial change in the 50 / 5000 places and everywhere else. The median African American growth rate for 50 / 5000 cities was 429 percent, while for all others it was 11 percent. For Latinxs it was 227 and 90 percent, respectively. Of the roughly 840,000 people who now live in these 24 places, almost half a million of them, or 58 percent, are not white.[24]

In so many ways, this is not your grandparents' suburbanization. The new growth is much, much farther from the region's traditional central cities than was postwar growth and much more diverse. The idea of a majority-minority suburbanization would have been unthinkable a generation or two ago—after all, much of American suburbia was specifically built to exclude people of color, not include them. But traditional suburbanization was not supposed to collapse in a foreclosure crisis and not supposed to leave more than 700,000 Californian homes—in places mostly considered suburbs—at some stage in the foreclosure process by April 2010 (Center for Responsible Lending 2010).

Zones of Value and Loss

The 50/5000 analysis paints the broad picture of migration, growth, and foreclosure, and does it at the critical place-based level, i.e., a "real" geography where people live and vote and with which they identify. It also gets at some of the large, megaregional-scale issues that are inherent to these transformations in the Bay Area, a scale not well accounted for by census geography. Both of these understandings will be critical as a baseline for the following chapters, as I unpack the political, economic restructuring of the region to better understand how this unequal growth was enabled and to see how it interacts with race and class-based migrations.

But the broad picture of inequality is only hinted at. We know that communities of color grew in major numbers in places which experienced particularly high foreclosure rates, but what does this mean beyond foreclosure? Is this a long-term concern?

In a series of papers about the Inland Empire, Southern California's version of East County and the northern San Joaquin Valley, Deirdre Pfeiffer (2011, 2012) examines some of the same questions that drive my research. She is concerned that the African American, Latinx, and Asian communities that have been driving population growth in the outer fringe of Los Angeles may not be getting a fair shake of suburban life, facing questions of high foreclosure rates and a generally more unstable environment in what she calls "post–Civil Rights suburbs." Her work focuses on "neighborhood quality," a complicated metric that evaluates what people who have moved to the Inland Empire think about their new communities, especially in reference to where they came from.

I have taken a slightly different tack by focusing on the simpler question of real estate values. They are a crude measure of value, and are in some ways inherently problematic, given the implicit prioritization of exchange value

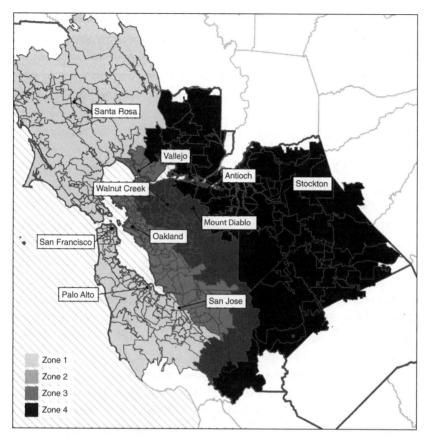

MAP 8. The four zones of the Bay Area. Source: Schafran and Wegmann (2012).

over use value. But in light of the homeowner-driven nature of this growth and the crisis, and the dependency of communities on property value and property taxes, it is an important marker for gauging the impact of the crisis on communities and the people who live there.

Again, using a geography based on the changing megaregion—this time excluding Merced County, which is relatively small and for which we did not have data—my colleague Jake Wegmann and I examined the segregation of the Bay Area using 20 years of real estate sales data gathered at the zip code level (Schafran and Wegmann 2012).[25] One of our analyses was based on a set of four zones that seemed to capture the restructuring of the region. Map 8 shows the four zones of the region, built using zip codes, that take a page from Walker's (1995) use of Banham's (1971) "four ecologies" to show some of the major fault lines of the region.

Zone 1 is the increasingly bourgeois West Bay, stretching from Silicon Valley through San Francisco and into the generally wealthy suburban environs of Marin County and the wine country of Sonoma and Napa. Zone 2 is the industrial garden, the stretch of (in some cases former) working-class industrial communities from East San Jose up the 880 and 80 corridors to Vallejo. Zone 3 is the 680 corridor of edge cities that include the Tri-Valley area of Alameda and Contra Costa counties. Zone 4 is the periphery, the band of fast-growing communities at the heart of this book.

From the following four figures, you can see the broader story of the contemporary Bay Area—all four zones gained population, but none as dramatically as Zone 4, where the majority of the 50 / 5000 cities are located. Whites and especially Asians remained generally stable in terms of their zonal share. The Asian community as a whole grew throughout the region, but grew relatively equally everywhere.[26] Whites continued a long process of leaving Zone 2 (the industrial garden) for Zone 4 (the postindustrial garden), while maintaining strong presence in the wealthier Zones 1 and 3. Unsurprisingly, it was black and Hispanic populations that saw the greatest shift. Zone 4 replaces Zone 1 as the second most important center of African American life, and Zone 4 will soon surpass all other zones as the center of Latinx life.

By virtually every measure, from simple descriptive statistics to a regression model developed by Wegmann, the signs point to a sharp devaluation of Zone 4 relative to the rest of the region following the crash. Consistent with the 50 / 5000 findings, there were also strong correlations with race, particularly African Americans. Zone 2 also suffers to a certain extent, while Zones 1 and 3 continue to hold value. At virtually every scale, the geography of depressed values maps onto the geographies of nonwhite Bay Area, particularly blacks and Latinxs.

Should one be tempted to make the all-too-common racial leap—that all these migrating communities of color brought down property values and caused the bubble to burst—we can demonstrate clearly that this is not the case. The core of the model is a metric we call the Cole Valley Delta (CVD), which measures the median per square foot sales price for each zip code in the 11-county region from 1989 to 2009 and then compares each zip code against the zip code for Cole Valley, a gentrifying area of San Francisco that has seen steadily rising property values over the past few decades (and ultimately few foreclosures). A high CVD means that the zip code gained relative to Cole Valley, a low CVD the opposite.

African Americans were overrepresented in zip codes that *gained* against Cole Valley up until the bubble burst, and subsequently overrepresented in

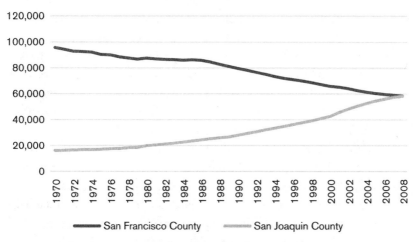

FIGURE 3. African Americans in San Francisco and San Joaquin counties, 1970–2008. Source: RAND California via U.S. Census.

low CVD areas afterward. By 2005, just before the peak of the bubble, the migration had been under way for decades, with no major drag on property values. The opposite was true. Communities of color were making a seemingly rational decision, a collective movement toward places that were gaining in value, even against the expensive core.

The zip codes that gained dramatically until 2005 and then lost it all (and then some) mostly fall into Zone 4. The gap in value between the core and the periphery widened, with the outer-ring counties of Stanislaus, San Joaquin, and Solano all losing far more value against San Francisco than Marin, Sonoma, or the Silicon Valley zones of San Mateo and Santa Clara. The average home in San Joaquin was worth about a third of a home in San Francisco before the crash; by 2009, it was worth about a fifth. It was also around this time that the size of the African American populations in the two counties converged (Figure 3), a generation removed from the heyday of the Fillmore district and a period where San Francisco was a major center of African American culture on the West Coast.

In a 2010 paper about the link between segregation and the foreclosure crisis, Jacob Rugh and Douglas Massey (2010: 629) argue that residential segregation "created a unique niche of minority clients" for subprime lending, now known to be the fundamental economic driver of the crisis. This confirms earlier work by scholars such as Elvin Wyly, Greg Squires, Dan Immergluck, and Kathe Newman, who dig into the racialized nature of subprime lending, some of which sadly predates the crisis by a number of years (Wyly et al. 2009; Squires and Kubrin 2005; Squires 2003; Immergluck and Smith 2004, 2005, 2006; Newman and Wyly 2004). It has since been backed up by further studies by Rugh (2014) and others (Hyra et al. 2013; Hwang, Hankinson, and Brown 2015), work which continues to pile evidence onto the claim that there is a profound link between the crisis and segregation. Badger (2016) reports that this trend continues in much of Zone 4.

What this link between race and subprime often obscures is that this crisis is racialized far beyond people who took bad loans. Diverse migration to these foreclosure zones has been occurring for a generation now, and many people moved before things got too hot, with fixed-rate mortgages on homes that were not initially overpriced. But they too have been impacted, part of the "largest loss of wealth for community of color in US history" (Rivera and United for a Fair Economy 2008: v). The market that had been created was not just for bad loans, but for an entire suburban dream which was profoundly unstable. This is the link between old patterns of segregation and new patterns of foreclosure. Middle- and working-class African Americans, Latinxs, and Asians—business owners and public servants, blue-collar workers and union reps, bus drivers and accountants, nurses and store clerks—had been heading outward for their first collective bite at the suburban apple and pushing away from the older neighborhoods they had been confined to a generation ago. Some, as Angela Glover Blackwell noted in the earlier epigraph, were doing so under pressure from inner core communities that were still failing to provide a safe, healthy, and opportunity-rich environment, especially for families with children. Some were doing so in the face of gentrification and rising real estate prices in the core, pricing out many first-time homeowners.

Some were doing so simply because they wanted to, following a suburban path well trod in the United States. Even if everything had been rosy back in Oakland and Richmond, some families would have made the move regardless. One can debate the "push" and "pull" factors of the most diverse suburbanization process in American history endlessly, but at the end of the day a certain amount of this suburbanization was bound to happen.

The question of inequality and segregation arises when one considers that as communities of color began to pursue the suburban dream, the suburbia they moved to was built on a structurally unsound foundation. This massive, racialized, and unequal new map is a form of segregation for the neoliberal era. It may not be "ethno-racial closure and control," but any time there are strikingly different outcomes linked to a highly racialized map, I argue that we must call it segregation, in part because it forces recognition of the deep historic link to the days of redlining and Jim Crow.

But the segregationist nature of the restructuring of the region goes beyond differentiated real estate values. These places in Zone 2's industrial garden and Zone 4's postindustrial garden are linked to a migratory cycle that sees people of color moving back and forth, while rarely settling down in either Zone 1 or Zone 3. The more mobile nature of twenty-first-century segregation means people move about regularly, often over long distances, but always to a select group of cities, while a large portion of the regional map lies largely untouched.

MENTAL MAPS, REVISITED

Between 2009 and 2011, I was part of a group of researchers studying the impact of violence, policing, and increasing racial and ethnic diversity on young people in Oakland's San Antonio district.[27] Born as a lumber town annexed to Oakland in 1852, development in the 1920s and 1930s turned it into a typical Oakland residential neighborhood—streetcar suburb toward the hills and blue-collar factory town down by the water (Bagwell 1982; Maly 2005). As was customary at the time—Oakland had two members of the Klan serving openly on the city council in the 1920s (Rhomberg 2004)—the neighborhood was kept all-white through racial covenants.

The transition began in the 1960s, as the breakdown of internal segregation in East Oakland saw African Americans arrive in significant numbers. They were soon followed by Latinx and Asian immigrants, part of the post-1965 immigration from which Oakland drew so many new residents. By the first decade of the twentieth century, the neighboring Fruitvale district to the south would be studied as one of the most ethnically diverse neighborhoods in the United States, as refugees from the wars in Bosnia joined Laotians, Vietnamese, Cambodians, and other immigrants who had come to America for more than economic reasons (Maly 2005).

Crack cocaine and violence from the drug trade ravaged much of East Oakland during the 1980s and early 1990s, and San Antonio was not immune, even if it was farther from the epicenters of "Deep" East Oakland and West Oakland (Ginwright 2010). Crime remained a significant issue, as did violence and poverty. The neighborhood is hyper-diverse, primarily Asian and Latinx now that African Americans have moved out, both as part of the migrations charted in this dissertation and ongoing shifts within the city of Oakland. It is poorer than Oakland on average, but not the poorest; unemployment is high, nearby jobs are limited, and educational attainment is low. And although it may not be the poorest neighborhood in Oakland, it is exactly the type of inner-city community often discussed in terms of segregation, with questions about people being confined with limited opportunity. And it is exactly the type of neighborhood from which people go searching for better opportunities—safer streets, better schools, a bigger house, homeownership, or just more affordable housing. It is important to keep in mind that even struggling neighborhoods in Oakland and San Francisco—despite the challenges—are not inexpensive. By 2004, the median per square foot price of a home in the San Antonio district (94606) was 30–40 percent higher than either of Antioch's zip codes (94509 and 94531).[28]

Our study focused on interviews with 38 individuals who were roughly age 13 in the year 2000, meaning that they spent their teenage years in Oakland during the height of the real estate boom, the out-migration, and the bust and foreclosure crisis. The major purpose of the study was to access the role of violence and community change in structuring their lives *within* the San Antonio district. To supplement the interviews with young people (most are now in the early 20s) we interviewed an additional 40 adults, from leaders to social workers to real estate agents. A subsequent parallel study in Elmhurst, deeper into East Oakland, asked similar questions, giving us an amazing data set from which to learn about mobility in inner-city life.

Something fascinating emerged from the study, somewhat by accident. In response to questions about people moving out of the neighborhood, respondents were very specific about where people were moving. We began to notice that in the questions about work, they were specific about their geographies, even talking at times about work patterns of friends and relatives.

Over and over again, we heard the same places—Tracy, Stockton, Antioch, Manteca in the outer part of the region, San Leandro and Hayward next door. Together with my colleague from public health, LeConte Dill, the author of the Elmhurst study, and the youth geographer Yvonne Hung, we started searching for specific mentions of places and mapping them according to why they were mentioned—somebody moved there, somebody lived there, they visited that place for work, fun, or school, or it was a place they aspired to move to. With only 38 respondents, and another 25 from the Elmhurst study, it is a limited sample, but the results were similarly stark. The places referenced as locations people lived or moved to were once again San Leandro, Hayward, or Zone 4, with almost no exceptions. One reference was made to people moving to Dublin, one to Livermore, but otherwise the 680 job belt (chapter 3) is missing entirely. Nor was there any mention of San Mateo and Marin counties, and except for one reference to San Jose, or of massive and wealthy Santa Clara County, home to Silicon Valley.

Expanding the analysis to other references—jobs, school, visits, essentially any mention of place in their lives—the geography grew somewhat, but barely. San Leandro and Hayward became even more prominent, in part because they offer jobs—including low-wage service jobs available to many young people and some of the remaining blue-collar work in the region. San Francisco and Berkeley appeared much more prominently, mostly in reference to schooling, but rarely as a destination to live. Most of the references to living in San Francisco refer to family members who have been there a long time. Walnut Creek and Pleasant Hill now appeared, the former as a job site. Both served as aspirational places—places people would move to if they could. But the high-tech job centers of San Ramon or Pleasanton, Palo Alto or Cupertino? Completely absent.

It is clear that the participants in the two studies are no longer confined to East Oakland, as perhaps their parents and grandparents would have been. Neither are their family members or social networks. The mental map of Boyle Heights is not the map of today's inner-core Oakland, even for the people who remain. But neither do they have full access to the region. Most of the wealthiest, job-rich, low-foreclosure places in the region are not on their maps at all.

When combined with the "50/5000" and "four zones" analysis above, what emerges is a picture of the more mobile form of segregation produced in the neoliberal-era Bay Area. While people appear to be moving freely about the region—for school, for work, for homeownership—in reality certain people from certain communities tend to be occupying only half of it. The half they are occupying is not the wealthy part, not the part with low foreclosure rates, but rather the places far more to the edge. These geographies tend to be marked by similar race and class profiles and, as we have seen, similar experiences of foreclosure.

The questions of race, class, and segregation in the metropolis are far more complex than they were during the postwar era. In the Bay Area, the lines are both east/west and core/periphery, white and Asian and black and Latinx, Chinese/Korean versus Southeast Asian/Filipino, the globalized and educated upper middle class versus the regionalized and less-educated working and slipping middle class, the bourgeois bohemian versus California-style middle America. In previous work (Schafran 2009a) I have talked about it in terms of "endopolis," the city within, versus "exopolis," the city without. One of the troubling aspects of the foreclosure crisis in the region is how those in the increasingly wealthy and generally whiter (and more Asian) center are largely untouched by the crisis on the fringe, in part because they inhabit a different circulatory pattern of metropolitan life, one marked by wealthy suburbs, office parks, and gentrifying urban neighborhoods, connected more to global centers and similar up-market, tech-fueled "creative class" havens than the working- and middle-class communities that increasingly ring the region. There is a mobility to the "segregation" and separation of people all throughout the race, class, and cultural spectrums, part of what makes this contemporary story so difficult to understand yet so important to those with a keen eye for change.[29]

Clearly this is not Engels's Manchester, a class-defined city of a single "good" quadrant surrounded by the working masses, even if this geography still exists, especially in the Central Valley, where cities like Lodi are divided by what side of the railroad tracks one lives on, as if from a novel from a century ago. It is not Self's (2003) Oakland or Sugrue's (1996) Detroit, where people of color were exclusively confined to a handful of places, an extension of earlier eras when the lines of ethnic and racial communities like Chinatown were rigid and enforced through violence, law, and custom.[30]

How precisely to understand this new form and new map of segregation is one of the fundamental questions of twenty-first-century American urbanism. In every region across the country, *some* of the hard old lines are being broken down, while others remain as almost caricatures of inner-city racialized poverty. In every major city across the country, *some* old working-class, black, or ethnic neighborhoods are being integrated at the same time they are being gentrified, while their inner-ring suburban counterparts are becoming more integrated during an age of aging infrastructure and rising suburban poverty. While this newer, more mobile form of segregation is more dominant in the Bay Area, in other places it may be the reverse.[31]

What is critical is that the production of one form of segregation emerged from another, a new map which never completely erased the old map. The two forms of segregation exist dialectically, and this dialectical nature is another reason we must call this newer form of spatialized and racialized inequality segregation or resegregation, rather than changing the language to "exclusion" or another similar term. Contrary to Adelman and Mele (2014), it is separation, isolation, mobility, and other forms of contemporary inequality that need to be seen through the lens of segregation, not the other way around. The fallacy of a postracial America, exposed on international TV and social media throughout the world as people took to the streets of Ferguson, forces us to reengage with the meaning of segregation in twenty-first-century America,

TABLE 2 Reframing Segregation

	Ghettoized Segregation	Mobile Segregation
Era of Dominance	Pre-war, Keynesian	Neoliberal, contemporary
Market Mechanisms	Racial covenants, housing discrimination	Subprime lending
Policy Mechanisms	Redlining, two-tiered housing program, urban renewal	Housing choice voucher, banking deregulation
Policy Responses	Vouchers, anti-housing discrimination laws	Shifting anti-poverty resources to the suburbs, anti-foreclosure legislation
Iconic Space	Inner-city neighborhood	Inner-ring suburb, exurb
Dominant Scale	Neighborhood/City	Regional/Megaregional
Metaphor	Trapped in a lack of opportunity	Opportunity is offered but never secure

rather than allow it to be imagined as only part of our historical mental map. While helpful, the question of whether the era of segregation is ebbing misses the ways in which this spatial process has morphed over the past generation. Rather, segregation needs to be reframed, as a conversation between two types, each with an era of dominance that varies regionally (Table 2).

As mentioned at the outset of this chapter, this book focuses on the historical, political economy of how this new form of segregation was produced in actual places while simultaneously reproducing older forms of segregation in others. In the next five chapters, I build a zone by zone analysis of how each part of the region contributed to this resegregation, starting and ending out on the fringe. This is what I call the road from Babylon to Brentwood, how the Bay Area in general and the East Bay in particular, which Robert Self chronicled in *American Babylon*, became the foreclosure crisis in places like Brentwood. If the starting point for this book is a new way of seeing segregation on a bigger scale, the heart of this book is understanding how this segregation was in part produced and reproduced by a fragmentation of the political economy of place and the political economy of development. In many ways, these two foundational processes—segregation and fragmentation—also function as dialectic, and this book, like the process itself, is a constant conversation between the fragmented political economy of development and the constant mutation of segregation. Understanding how this all came together over the past 35 years in the San Francisco Bay Area starts in East County.

TWO

The Postindustrial Garden

ON THE OLD PITTSBURG-ANTIOCH HIGHWAY, just west of Hazel's hamburgers and Antioch's downtown, is a small and lightly used wetlands preserve. The light is stunning, especially at sunset, and the delta breeze provides a respite from the often brutal heat which reminds visitors that, geographically, they are in the Central Valley. Despite Contra Costa County's roughly 30-mile-long shoreline on the San Joaquin River, access can be hard to find, cut off by heavy industry, the military, and a coastal marshland best suited for birds, making this respite even more precious.

To the west are the remnants of East County's industrial life: a Calpine energy plant steaming ominously and just the faintest glimpse of USS Posco's massive steel facility. To the south, over the light industrial park and self-storage units, the signs for Antioch's Auto Center and the various shopping centers of Somersville Road seem to blend perfectly with the din of Highway 4, the area's overworked highway. In the not-too-distant hills, bright green in winter and burnt beige in summer, East County's suburban subdivisions crawl unevenly up the hillsides. To the east are baseball fields and the historical society cum sports museum, testimonies to Antioch's love for sports and nostalgia. Just beyond sits the struggling historic downtown. Across BNSF's railroad tracks and the San Joaquin River to the north is a sea of windmills jutting out of southern Solano County's vast delta wetlands, churning out green energy for the region as a whole.

Each aspect of the view from the wetlands holds a clue to the larger story of how East County was transformed from a set of relatively isolated small towns to a national center of the foreclosure crisis and a point of concern on the map of one of the wealthiest and supposedly most progressive regions in human history. The single-family homes on the hillsides are a direct result of the decision in the early 1980s by Antioch's leaders to bow to massive pressure from developers and dreams of local glory to approve a doubling of Antioch's population in one fell swoop. The decision paved the way for growth in other East County towns like Oakley and Brentwood. It bolstered an already strong Pittsburg growth machine to the west, where a local developer was poised to become one of the largest single-family home builders in the United States.

All this was done with the idea that jobs and transportation infrastructure would arrive in tow, helping to support a rapidly growing region also facing the decline of its industrial base. While the growth came, the transport and jobs largely did not. Moreover, the competition between local cities, which had always been fierce, would take on new meaning following the passage of Proposition 13 in 1978, a ballot measure that dramatically limited how cities raised revenue.[1] Sales tax revenue and shopping malls became even more critical, at the same time as intralocal cooperation would be required for things never before demanded of cities, like building regional highways.

What is remarkable about East County's suburbanization is how different the rules of the game were from its postwar counterpart. For Robert Self (2003: 28), postwar suburbanization can be thought of as the "industrial garden." The industrial garden was "a coordinated middle landscape that joined economic progress and social stability." It was a model underscored (and ultimately undermined) by deep racism, a paternalist political structure, economic inefficiency, and environmental destruction. But, at least at that time, it provided for white families the stable home ownership, fiscally sound infrastructure, schools and recreation, and freeway access that became central to the production of America's first mass middle class.

The model hit rough times in the 1970s, both in reaction to its racism and its economic, social, and environmental limits. What replaced it was a new regime of suburbanization with the same basic physical structure, and the same dreams of homeownership and social stability through urban development, but in a more racially diverse environment with less economic progress and less coordination. There was less support from higher levels of government and much more unstable forms of capital, while at the same time old rivalries and old lines of power remained entrenched. And in the Bay Area, like in many regions throughout the country, this new version of suburbia was much farther from central cities than the industrial garden.

East County, and the many far-flung, hyper-diverse, post-1980 suburban and exurban places like it, are what I call the postindustrial garden. They reflect the same basic idea as the industrial garden, but with different people in different places and a very different underlying political economy. However, when it came time for people of color to suburbanize en masse, something they did alongside many working- and middle-class whites, the red carpet laid out by the postwar U. S. government had been worn out and not replaced. Instead of fixing suburbanization so that communities of color could enjoy what they had been excluded from, newly suburbanized communities were increasingly abandoned to their own devices.

This chapter examines key moments and symbolic struggles in the production of the postindustrial garden in East County, from decisions to build to racial struggles in the face of integration, from foreclosure to highway-building to downtown planning. Unlike Self's industrial garden, nobody set out to build the postindustrial garden. Planners, politicians, developers, and homeowners in East County largely thought they could keep reproducing a model that seemed to have worked in the past, or were actually putting in changes to make it better, not worse.

As I discuss in more detail in chapter 5, the sins of both modernist planning and mass suburbanization in the postwar era had soured the collective view of planning, but not of suburbanization. America in general and California in particular continued to let towns make decisions to grow, but stripped them of the needed institutional and physical infrastructure to make that growth liveable, sustainable, and equitable. These newly suburbanized places were forced to band together to produce their own splintered simulacra of the Eisenhower era, backfilling services in a hopeless race with legs tied together at the ankles. The fact that they struggled with internecine rivalries, often with deep race and class undertones, is their fault. The fact that they had to cooperate because the game had changed is not. And the fact that the suburbs impacted by this shift tended to be those that demographically were the opposite of postwar white suburbia was no coincidence.

THE DOUBLING

[Editorial] Prop. 13 Caused Fiscal Crisis
The Lender Is Foreclosing—Debt Is on Everyone's Mind
Layoffs Slated for Two Area Plants
Reagan Forecasts Hard Times
— *Antioch Daily Ledger* headlines, November 10, 1981

House Loans Risky

—Antioch Daily Ledger headline, November 15, 1981

The die is cast for a community with too many homes and too few jobs.

—Antioch Daily Ledger, February 5, 1982

Area's BART Plans Derailed

—Antioch Daily Ledger headline, February 7, 1982

There is an eeriness to the pages of the *Antioch Daily Ledger* from the early 1980s.[2] Read today, they are a constant reminder that virtually every major issue haunting post-foreclosure East County existed in some form in 1981. The headlines and editorials about fiscal crisis, industrial layoffs, foreclosures, and nationwide recession were the shot across the bow, announcing that the neoliberal era in the United States was well under way.

The headlines came just after the first formal piece of a two-part decision by the city to leap out of its industrial past and into the suburban era. This is the first line of the fateful article from early November, 1981: "With little discussion among themselves and no comment from the public, the Antioch Planning Commission members Wednesday endorsed a final plan for development that would nearly double the city's population" (Ginsberg 1981). The first part of the plan, 3,433 homes on 854 acres in the Hillcrest corridor, had gone through the planning commission earlier in the year. When the city council finally ratified the 11,567 homes on roughly 3,000 acres in the Lone Tree portion of the plan, more than 40,000 residents were officially scheduled for Antioch's next three decades.

Unlike the largely silent planning commission meeting, the final city council meeting in February 1982 was positively boisterous. More than 100 people attended the council meeting, and after a session where 10 of the 13 speakers spoke in favor of the larger of the two specific plans, the council voted 4–1 to approve. Rejecting calls for another study, councilmember Walter Pierce avowed, "That's what's wrong with this city. There's too much studying and not enough action." Following the objections of the one councilmember, Wilhemina Andrade, who opposed the plans, a resident speaker retorted, "Any organism has to change, or it dies" (Ginsberg 1982b).

Andrade's objections were rooted in the lack of jobs in the plan—the quote "too many homes and too few jobs" is hers. But if her objection proved prescient, it technically was addressed. The plan very clearly stated that new employment centers would "provide employment opportunities for up to sixty percent of the residents of the community." Even better, they would be developed concurrently with housing so that workers would be able to bike and walk to work.

If only it were so easy. In the context of Antioch's history, the idea of local jobs serving local residents made sense. Founded as Smith's Landing in 1850, Antioch is one of the oldest towns in California, and was the first incorporated place in Contra Costa County. From the discovery of coal a decade later, the city's economy revolved around industrial production in one form or another for more than a century. Coal fields in the Diablo foothills south of the town fed the brickworks and distilleries, which were gradually linked by railroad entrepreneurs to the larger statewide and regional networks that dominated California's early political economy. In 1889, paper came to Antioch, and industry grew to dominate Antioch's politics, economy, and odor until the 1970s. In the 1950s, at a time when the town had less than 13,000 residents, 6,500 people worked at Fibreboard's plants and local subsidiaries in town (Bohakel et al. 2005).

The postwar boom stoked the development of power plants and building materials industries, including some of the biggest names in San Francisco and Oakland industry—Pacific Gas & Electric, Crown-Zellerbach, Kaiser. The presence of San Francisco's industrial capital on the shores of the San Joaquin River was part of a historical wave of the suburbanization and exurbanization of heavy industry from San Francisco that began in the 1880s (Walker 2004b). As the population of San Francisco grew in numbers and in wealth, the dirtiest and heaviest industries were no longer desirable. Cut off from any southward movement along the peninsula by the estates of the wealthy, the sparsely populated Contra Costa coast became the favored site of glue factories, dynamite plants, power generating facilities, and oil refineries.[3] To this day, all four of the region's oil refineries are along the San Joaquin River, part of a massive geography of energy production that accounts for two-thirds of the electricity produced in the region.[4]

Both the presence of major San Francisco capital and the development of building industry supply factories presaged the coming of the suburban wave. Kaiser's cement and gypsum factory, opened in 1956, fed the growing demand for sheetrock in the booming postwar suburbs just over the hill in Concord, Pleasant Hill, and Walnut Creek. At the time, Antioch was largely content with its historic role as part of the massive economic hinterland of the San Francisco Bay Area, feeding the latter's demand for energy and material while remaining physically and culturally apart. Farming and ranching still dominated the lands south and east of town, including then-unincorporated Oakley and neighboring Brentwood, which in 1960 had fewer than 4,000 residents between them.[5] They were part of the truck farming and canning economy that was integral to the region's economy for its first century.[6]

As early as the 1960s, the writing was on the wall that Antioch would eventually be sucked into the regional sphere as more than a node of industrial production. It had been included in the original 1956 BART master plan for the second phase, and was no doubt part of newspaper mogul Dean Lesher's famous airborne proclamation that this was where the growth would go (Leykam and Concord Chamber of Commerce [Calif.] 1989). Albert Seeno, Sr., a developer from neighboring Pittsburg, had already begun buying land in East County, in anticipation of suburban growth for what would soon be one of the region's most important and controversial development empires.

Future plans aside, things in Antioch were still relatively small scale and small town in the postwar era, with houses built by a quartet of locally owned and operated developers whose names evoke the influence of Italian immigrants in the area: Seeno, Garro and Vetrano, Vonccio and Sobrante, Catalini. Antioch did not get its first professional city manager until 1958, and in the immediate aftermath of World War II the consulting engineer for the developer signed off on projects. The city council often met over dinner in the back of a restaurant to decide city business and approve development. In the words of one longtime city employee, the original developers "didn't pay for anything—we had few inspectors, they did what they wanted, and we even found water lines that were missing."[7] Things began to improve following the passage of subdivision regulation in 1962 (not to mention the 1953 Brown Act, which required that council meetings be truly public), part of the steady stream of regularization and professionalization of the planning and development process in the postwar era.[8] While the politics of development and the fiscal challenges of today are very different, the basic struggle between municipalities and developers over quality of work and financial responsibility for infrastructure is as old as suburbanization itself.

At the dawning of the 1970s, critical changes occurred in the political economy of development that set the stage for the 1982 Specific Plans. Congress passed the National Environmental Protection Act (NEPA) in 1969, followed almost immediately by California's "little NEPA" in 1970, the California Environmental Quality Act (CEQA). CEQA would play a fundamental role in altering the rules of the development game, giving opponents of both specific developments and large-scale suburban development in general—a movement just beginning to coalesce in California—a potent legal means of delaying or stopping development. At virtually the same time, a new developer arrived in town, not the son of an immigrant fisherman from Pittsburg but a prominent and wealthy developer who had already built hundreds of homes just over the hill in Pleasant Hill and Concord and down the San Ramon Valley into Dublin. Perhaps as an indication that there was a cinematic quality to his role in the story, legend has it that Tom Gentry arrived in a helicopter.[9]

Gentry had actually purchased 500 acres just south of Highway 4 in 1966.[10] It was to be his first master-planned community, and the first significant development by a major Bay Area developer in Antioch. "Gentrytown" was a critical opening round in what would ultimately be a new wave of development both geographically and economically. It was one of the first major residential subdivisions south of Highway 4, setting the stage for the Southeast Area expansion a decade later, not to mention numerous other subdivisions that followed soon after.[11] Gentry "brought a flood in with him"—the flood being major regional developers, land speculators, brokers, and real estate investors. East County was set to be the new zone of growth, as real estate development capital sought out new greenfields in the booming Bay Area. By the time the bubble burst a half century later, to find out who was building in Antioch one simply had to, as one local planner put it, "look at the NAHB (National Association of Home Builders) roster—we had everyone who was on it."[12]

The "flood" that followed Gentry was part of California's long tradition of merchant builders who helped pioneer land development and large-scale suburbanization, i.e., developers who were particularly adept at maximizing land yields (Landis 2000).[13] They had developed a model of house-building that they had no interest in changing, even as the original postwar suburban belt in the Bay Area—central Contra Costa County; the Tri-Valley area of Alameda County; key parts of Marin, Sonoma, San Mateo, and Santa Clara counties—turned against the pro-growth model that had dominated California up until the 1970s (Walker 2007).

When cities started turning against growth, emboldened by Petaluma's famed 1974 limit on growth and Livermore's attempt to cap population in

1975, the residential development industry simply looked over the hill to where Gentry had gone, and to where land speculators like Seeno had quietly been buying up land in anticipation of the next wave of suburbanization.

Large-scale residential builders do not simply switch models from stick-built detached housing to skyscrapers. Their network of lenders, subcontractors, investors, and sales staff is set up to manufacture a specific type of product, and they will move their operations more readily than change them to suit new constraints, especially if it means only going over a few hills.[14] They opted for the market risk of exurban suburbia rather than the political and economic risk of either learning to do inner-core redevelopment or trying to wedge in more suburbia in anti-growth suburbs.

The two Specific Plans of 1981 and 1982 thus were originally rival plans for two separate corridors, but their developer sponsors eventually agreed they could coexist in the remaking of an entire subregion.[15] The city they proposed to double was still a "gritty blue-collar 'old mill town'," with a strong union base and a deep concern about the obvious decline in industrial jobs. Moreover, Proposition 13 had raised a whole new level of issues in terms of the fiscal future of the area, which had a small, local-serving commercial sector but certainly nothing able to compete with the sales tax–generating machines in other parts of the region. Undoubtedly, many in Antioch stood to profit from land sales, legal and accounting fees, the new construction jobs, and other aspects of the suburban growth machine. But when combined with a promise of jobs and tax base from developers and with the expansion of the BART system on the books (being paid for by local property taxes), it is no wonder these massive plans sailed through with little objection and almost no fanfare. It was "action" in the face of uncertainty, predicated on a handful of ideas central to planning at the time—the belief in the jobs-housing balance as a goal and state and federal infrastructure as a matter of course.

As I will show in chapter 3, Antioch's jobs-housing balance fell victim to the push for the same balance in the wealthier former-bedroom communities of central Contra Costa County, while its infrastructure needs would be ignored in the era of Ronald Reagan. The end result—tens of thousands of new homes with few local jobs and terrible traffic on overworked arterials with no real regional transit—was the ultimate in neoliberal-era infrastructure planning. The cities of East County had to build their own freeway.

The Bypass

Because the state wasn't stepping up, the locals had to be creative.

— Former County Transportation Planner, Contra Costa, 2011

Antioch is a cul-de-sac.

— Former Antioch Government Planner, East County, 2010

Brentwood is a cul-de-sac.

— East County Journalist and Resident, 2011

When you drove east on Highway 4 from Martinez in 2010, it was generally smooth sailing over Willow Pass and down into Bay Point and Pittsburg. In tragically symbolic fashion, the freeway bottlenecked a few miles past BART's last station in Bay Point, as the highway dropped from four lanes each way to two. This was the most brutal stretch, through Pittsburg and into Antioch.[16]

An odd thing would have happened as you passed the Hillcrest exit in Antioch, one of the focal points of the 1980's Specific Plans. The road widened to six lanes, and was clearly newer than what you just drove through. A flyover offers passage to Highway 160 and the Antioch Bridge and the towns of the delta. A large green highway sign beckoned you the other way, down the smooth new road with the simple phrase—"Bypass."

This is the Highway 4 Bypass, known locally as simply "the bypass." What it is bypassing are the historic downtowns of Oakley and Brentwood, for the original state highway goes right down Main Street. The original passage of Highway 4 was codified as such in 1934 when the state of California named and numbered its highways, and it used to connect to downtown Pittsburg and Antioch, as well.[17] Slowly but surely, as East County grew, Highway 4 was pulled off the main street and turned into a freeway. The section from Railroad Avenue in Pittsburg to A Street in Antioch was completed in 1953, and the section from A Street to the Antioch Bridge in 1971. And then it stopped.

By the mid-1980s, local leaders in East County realized that the houses were coming but the freeway was not. Highway 4 had never been made part of the vaunted Eisenhower system, never benefitting from the 90 percent federal funding that had paid for the rapid and sustained growth of the now-wealthy 580 and 680 corridors and the destruction of low-income and

African American neighborhoods throughout Oakland. The cities were dependent on the state of California alone.

CalTrans, the state highway and transportation agency that owns and operates all highways in the state (including ones paid for by the federal government), had been part of the late 1980s East County Corridor Study in which the idea for the bypass emerged. The original goal of the study was, in part, to link the growing communities of East County to the jobs centers sprouting up on the 580 corridor to the south in Alameda County. This would also have solved the cul-de-sac problem, as it would have given East County residents better access around Mount Diablo, connecting the Highway 4 and Interstate 580 corridors. It would also have marked a continuation of highway-building into less developed areas, which was increasingly politically infeasible given the increasing power of the environmental movement at every scale.

When local officials went to CalTrans to ask them to pay for the bypass, CalTrans refused. With federal monies drying up, state monies impacted by Prop. 13, and an increasing backlash against highway-building, especially on the urban fringe, Caltrans had an easy time saying no. The locals were on their own.[18]

Nevertheless, the cities of East County felt that they had to do something in the face of rapid population expansion and mounting traffic problems. By 1989, they had hammered together a Joint Powers Agreement involving the county and the cities of Antioch, Pittsburg, and Brentwood.[19] By 1994, an Environmental Impact Report (EIR) had been approved that would allow the authority—now known as the State Route 4 Bypass Authority—to design and build a four-lane limited-access highway to connect Highway 4 from the 160 interchange to Vasco Road, the two-lane connection between Brentwood and Livermore. While the idea all along was for the highway to be built to CalTrans standards and for the state to take over the road once it has been completed, it was the locals who banded together to design, build, and pay for the bypass.

It is in the financing of the bypass where the true changes from the earlier era are apparent. Rather than being paid for by federal dollars via gas taxes or other tax-related financing mechanisms common in large-scale transportation projects, the bypass was paid for by one-time development fees charged on each new home and office built in East County.[20] The fees were collected by a separate authority, the East Contra Costa Regional Fee and Finance Authority (ECCRFFA). ECCRFFA was charged with doling out this fee money to various projects, including both the bypass and the local matching funds for the long-delayed widening of Highway 4 and the extension of BART. The fees were structured differently based on geography. For Antioch, Oakley, and Brentwood, fees began at $4,500 per single-family residential unit, growing quickly to $7,500 per single-family unit in 2002 and ultimately to $18,048 by 2009. Pittsburg, in deference to the power of local developer Albert Seeno, set its fees significantly lower: the 2002 fee was $1,364 per single-family residential unit, less than a fifth of the other cities.[21] Between 1994 and 2002, with relatively low fees and solid development growth, ECCRFFA raised $73 million, an average of more than $9 million annually. With the housing boom at the beginning of the decade and rapidly increasing fees, money poured into the fund and construction began in earnest on the bypass.

In theory, the logic of development fees is brilliantly simple and politically enticing—make development pay for itself. Why should longtime residents bear the tax burden to pay for infrastructure demanded by growth? Shouldn't developers pay for more of the infrastructure they need? Given the experiences in Antioch in the 1950s and 1960s, where developers often left the city to foot the bill for basic things like sidewalks, it seemingly made sense as a planning evolution.

Fees became a major budgetary item for cities, at times even paying for the planning and development staff that oversaw project approvals, as was the case with the county and the local cities in East County.[22] This skewed the political calculus of development, as cities grew more and more dependent on new development to pay for basic services. Fees were also almost always restricted to capital costs, not to maintenance, creating an even greater long-term burden and necessitating tax assessment districts for maintenance on top of already high fees.[23]

The development fee / regional transportation infrastructure linkage effectively tied the development of already needed infrastructure to continued high rates of growth. This was infrastructure designed to serve an already existing population and an already *planned* population, yet it required the continued approval of new development above and beyond what had come before. Fees were collected once, and only once, and with such severe restrictions under Prop. 13 in terms of future assessments and property tax rate increases, cities were locked into a veritable Ponzi scheme—suck as much out of a development as possible, and then move on to approve the next one. East County became like a shark—it had to keep swimming or its sources of basic capital funds for infrastructure died.[24]

The end result was not only that the ECCRFFA fees dried up when East County growth hit a wall in 2007, but the sad fact that the bypass remained incomplete, 25 years after it was conceived and 15 years after the first fees were collected. This was not merely the result of poor engineering or bad project management, but of a financial and regulatory regime that in its fragmentation produced literal fragmentation. Each section of the bypass had to be funded separately, from this highly insecure source of monies and limited outside support. Each piece had its own EIR, and was bid and built separately. For the theoretically minded, the bypass is the epitome of what one Contra Costa County transportation planner called "institutional structures being formed in absence of the state."[25] Peck, Brenner, Theodore, and other theorists of neoliberalism could not have said it better (Brenner and Theodore 2002; Peck and Tickell 2002).

By 2012, after sailing through the beautiful three lanes after the bridge, you quickly merged down to two lanes by Laurel Avenue in Oakley. Next, a rough stretch tight against a soundwall, with oncoming traffic just inches away, past the popular Streets of Brentwood mall and onto Balfour Way. Accidents were notorious in this part, with semi-regular news reports of bloody crashes and local fear and indignation over a road that was too necessary to avoid and too dangerous or traffic-clogged to depend on. It is now officially Highway 4, officially state property, but it in no way resembles other state freeways and the Eisenhower system undergirding so much of suburbia.

SMALL TOWNS, BIG PLACES

The rivalry between Pittsburg and Antioch is legendary in East County, and it would be an appealing tale of small-town America if the enmity were restricted to the football field. But it runs much deeper than the "Little Big Game," embroiling city leaders and government officials in a century's worth of petty bickering, foot-dragging, and municipal petulance with ugly race and class undertones.

Antioch vs. Pittsburg

East County's oldest rivalry dates back to the first days of post–Gold Rush fever, when Pittsburg's founders named it "New York on the Pacific" and

Antioch's leaders declared it "the metropolis of East County." This was during an era when regional superiority was not a given—nearby Benicia and Vallejo were state capitals during the Gold Rush, and San Francisco was not yet the city it would become.

One highly symbolic moment in this rivalry is easy to document, as it is etched on a plaque in front of what is now the Antioch Historical Society. As San Francisco grew into the actual "New York on the Pacific" and the local towns settled into a relatively quiet life centered around railroads, ports, coal, industry, and agriculture, Pittsburg and Antioch came together to build the first high school in the county in 1911. The charming, red brick neo-Italianate school was erected on donated unincorporated land located on a crest between the two towns overlooking the San Joaquin River. The money for it came from the first bond passed jointly by Pittsburg, Antioch, and three smaller towns that no longer exist—Nortonville, Somersville, and Live Oak. The goodwill didn't last. By 1925, Pittsburg and Antioch dissolved the union, and the last class graduated in 1931, just 20 years after the building was constructed.[26]

World War II brought significant changes to East County, including Camp Stoneman, an army training and staging area set on more than 2,800 acres south of what is now Highway 4. It was land whose transformation in the 1950s and 1960s into suburban tract homes would be one of the first acts in the suburbanization of East County, but the transformation wrought by Camp Stoneman, Port Chicago, and Vallejo's Mare Island across the river was a human one—racial diversity returned to East County. As with other waterfront locations throughout the region, the wartime industry brought African American and Filipino laborers over the hill, and they settled in unincorporated West Pittsburg and in Pittsburg itself. By 1950, Pittsburg's African American population numbered above 1,800, more than 14 percent of the total population. The community remained throughout the 1950s, and by 1960 more than one in six Pittsburg residents was nonwhite.[27]

Antioch, meanwhile, counted 11 black residents in 1950 and 53 "others" out of a community of more than 10,000. By 1960, the census found two—yes, two—black residents in a community of almost 18,000. The color line between Antioch and Pittsburg was not as famous as the line between Oakland and San Leandro, but it was just as real.

Discrimination in Antioch went beyond who could live where, for that type of segregation was prevalent in Pittsburg as well—certain parts of the city, in particular the new sections sprouting up south of the highway off

Buchanan Road, were off-limits to blacks. But if you were black in East County in the 1950s, you simply were not welcome in Antioch. As one African American Pittsburg native put it, "You wouldn't try to go to downtown Antioch. The Sears was down on 2nd Street—the building is still there—that was the only place you could go. This was in the 1950s, but no theatre, nothing like that."[28] Even up through the 1970s, before she moved to Berkeley and Oakland, she would not go to Antioch unless she had to. "They would call me n———, like it was the South." One prominent local politician put it this way, "If you had a Pittsburg name, you wouldn't dare go to Antioch."[29]

The race line between the cities did not hold, but the racialized animosity between the cities remained. As Antioch began to diversify in earnest in the 1990s, and Pittsburg steadily transformed into a majority-minority community, some longtime white residents moved eastward into the more recently suburbanized cities of Oakley and Brentwood.[30] As both cities grew rapidly in the 1990s and 2000s, development and diversity became issues. Especially for Brentwood, which shares a long and contested border with Antioch in the heart of the growth zones tight against the Diablo foothills, Antioch was transformed into the racialized other that Pittsburg had been a generation ago.[31]

Brentwood vs. Antioch

Tensions between the cities go back to the days of Antioch's Specific Plans, when both cities jostled for control of Deer Valley, a picturesque swath of the Diablo foothills running south from Antioch and west of Brentwood (Lovejoy 1981).[32] In language that typifies the annexation quarrels of the time, the *Antioch Daily Ledger* wrote that "Antioch's ultimate sphere overlaps the Brentwood sphere, and goes to the border of Brentwood's 10-year sphere."[33] In the heady days of the early 1980s, the arguments were about the control of annexable land with potential for growth.

By 2006, political tensions and underlying social distinctions came together in the controversial Brentwood City Council candidacy of Brandon Richey. Richey, a Concord police officer and former Antioch resident, ran on a very unambiguous platform. "If there is one reason I am running for Brentwood City Council," his campaign literature stated, "I would say that I am worried that without careful planning, Brentwood will turn into another suburban Antioch with massive housing, mega-traffic, overcrowded schools and big-time drug dealers and gang-related crime" (Norris 2006). Richey won relatively easily in a wide-open race between ten candidates for two open seats, and reiterated his pledge to keep Brentwood from turning into "another Antioch" in statements after the election (Sherbert 2006: F4).

Richey's election could perhaps be dismissed as the sole doing of one ambitious politician had the "Antioch issue" not returned front and center four years later in a brutal internecine fight in Brentwood over an expansion of the urban growth boundary. Brentwood's political class—with the notable exception of Richey—was supporting a local ballot measure (Measure F) that would have established a new urban limit line for the city, changing the boundaries set at the county level as part of a series of negotiations following the passage of the Measure J transportation tax in 2004.[34]

Not coincidentally, the parcels in question in Measure F were on the edge of the aforementioned Deer Valley, just east of Antioch's city limits and sphere of influence. Early on, Antioch emerged as a critical point of reference—for both sides. In campaign literature, newspaper articles, one-on-one conversations, and particularly in the vibrant discourse in the letters to the editor section of the *Brentwood Press*, Antioch got dragged into the fight as both a political entity and a symbol.[35] Pro–Measure F forces argued that if Brentwood did not expand its growth boundary and annex and develop this land, then Antioch would do so, and it would literally become Antioch. This despite the fact that Antioch was at the time reeling from the foreclosure crisis, had a massive fiscal deficit, and neither the intention nor ability to expand. Anti–Measure F forces, of whom Richey was a key part, used a variation of his campaign argument—if Brentwood kept expanding and developing, it would become "another Antioch."

It was a battle filled with endless conjecture about what Antioch would or would not do, what the developers would or would not do, and whether the Local Area Formation Commission (LAFCO) would ever approve an Antioch annexation.[36] In an extremely controversial move that garnered a series of public reproaches, two LAFCO members joined the fray by suggesting that the board would be amenable to an Antioch petition should the measure fail (Lemyre 2010). The measure did fail, and spectacularly, despite its opponents being outspent more than 30 to 1.[37] Depending on one's perspective, the defeat of Measure F was either a critical sign of resident backlash against rampant development or part of a process where middle-class suburbanites lash out at the process that brought them there in order to protect what they have. Yet regardless of one's perspective on development, both sides of the fight marked a low point in the ongoing place wars in East County, where as one longtime planner and resident put it, "Brentwood is the 'good place,' and Antioch is the 'bad place.'"[38] As one local journalist said in the aftermath of Measure F, "There was a lot of anti-Antioch feeling before Richey, but he put it on a sign, and it got him elected."[39] Measure F was also a continuation of a long tradition in East County of casting places in racial terms, a tradition dating back long before Richey made the move one town to the east. The line in this case had simply moved, and Antioch found itself being treated as it had treated Pittsburg.

Pittsburg vs. Everyone Else

In the aftermath of the Measure F fight, one local elected official offered that they "really wished the Antioch issue hadn't happened." The cynic would argue that they was simply upset that their side had lost. The politically astute would observe that the Antioch vs. Brentwood conflict deferred attention from what had, ironically, become their common problem—Pittsburg.

If Pittsburg was the victim of outright racism on the part of Antioch for two generations, it has certainly worked diligently to make up for it by being the least cooperative member of the East County four over the past decade. Some of the anger from Antioch and others is mere jealousy—Pittsburg was incredibly aggressive in their use of redevelopment as a tool, remaking huge swaths of their downtown, including a condo complex, new streetscapes, and a new home for the legendary New Mecca restaurant.[40]

But Pittsburg's actions on regional transportation issues, the lifeblood of the Bay Area's largest cul-de-sac, should not be seen as mere intra–East County sniping or a further edition of "who's whiter and who's classier," unless one wants to argue that this is Pittsburg's revenge, served very cold. There have been long-running skirmishes over valuable fiscal territory on the border between Pittsburg and Antioch for years, driven by the prime location of border territory for tax-generating retail—land between the cities can capture commerce easily from both communities.

There are also questions of both physical and financial obstacles to improved transportation. For years, Pittsburg approved development, much of it by Albert Seeno, right against the existing two-lane Highway 4, even though plans had long existed to widen the freeway. This freeway edge development, some of it on disputed land, drove up both acquisition costs and overall costs, requiring an expensive sound wall and contributing to what has been a decades-long lag in the widening of Highway 4.

There were many who hoped that ECCRFFA, which included Pittsburg and was a historic moment of cooperation in East County, would mark the end of the era of constant bickering. Between ECCRFFA and TRANSPLAN, the subregional committee of the Contra Costa Transportation Authority that worked to make collective East County decisions about transportation priorities under Measure J (chapter 3), the cities were more and more tied together institutionally in a way that at least somewhat mimicked their social, geographic, economic, and historical relationships. And although much progress had been made and there was a good deal on the ground to suggest improved cooperation, 2010 saw even those hard-fought alliances begin to fracture. After a year of "saber-rattling," Pittsburg formally withdrew from ECCRFFA in July 2010, citing a disagreement over funding priorities and the failure of the Authority to build an extension to James Donlon Boulevard, which runs east–west between Antioch and Pittsburg and was seen by Pittsburg as key to alleviating traffic on arterial roads at peak hours, especially when Highway 4 was backed up for miles (Radin 2010).[41]

Pittsburg's withdrawal was simply the latest and most onerous instance in decades of internecine fighting.[42] Pittsburg had a significant geographic advantage in East County, as it was closest to the core of the Bay Area, the first to get BART, and the first to get a widened freeway. Rather than use its advantage to press for a complete East County, it pushed an isolationist agenda that alienated its neighbors and delayed much needed improvements, in part by giving regional agencies an excuse to ignore them.

The pettiness one saw in East County and the lack of subregional solidarity is not a trait unique to the cities east of Willow Pass. Much of the literature on "home rule," local autonomy, and segregation is filled with stories of municipalities behaving badly, erecting every barrier possible, cooperating only reluctantly, and often biting off their nose to spite their face. The tragedy in the case of East County is that because of where it stood historically and geographically in the Bay Area, it needed to cooperate far more than did suburbs during an earlier era that could count on infrastructure from above and a fiscally sustainable and flexible tax structure. Few municipalities in the Bay Area seem to have truly pushed past the high school football mentality, but it is only in East County where the tragedy of small-town thinking is evident every day on the streets and roads and in the ghosts of transportation systems not yet built.

THOSE PEOPLE

I don't envy you. In order to talk about Antioch you have to talk
about uncomfortable things.

—Antioch Activist and Resident, East County, 2009

Spend a Saturday afternoon touring garage sales in the subdivisions of
East County and you will rarely meet two families of the same racial or
ethnic group in a row. Spend five minutes at a high school football or
basketball game, or at any of the local swimming pools when it hits 105 in
the shade in August, and you will see the diversity that places like East
County have become home to. Brentwood's Orchard Park might not be
San Francisco's Golden Gate Park, but it is unlikely the latter has hosted
a Tea Party rally and a large African American family reunion side by side
on the same day.

If East County suburbia at times seems to lack in social diversity—at least
for those over 18—its role as the primary purveyor of middle-class, family-
oriented, child-friendly, (mostly) single-family homeownership American
life means that it is the space where diversity and integration are everyday
lived questions, not simply subjects of academic debate. As the wealthier
suburbs have managed to avoid the full spectrum of Californians via exclusionary methods and the market-based exclusion fostered by an increasingly
unequal society (chapters 3 and 5), it is the working- and middle-class places
like East County where integration, with all of its challenges, happens on a
daily basis.

This reality is critical for anyone from outside East County who seeks to
point out that among what makes East County infighting "uncomfortable"
are the underlying race and class tensions between and within the towns,
neighborhoods, and communities. Observers from the bourgeois core of the
Bay Area who deride the area's infighting or struggles with the results of their
rampant growth must recognize that to live in East County today means to
grapple with profound challenges under conditions of racial, ethnic, cultural,
and political integration unheard of during an earlier era of suburbanization.
One planner who has worked for the City of Antioch for decades put it most
clearly:

Communities like Antioch should get plaudits for what [they have] done over
the past twenty years. Instead we are portrayed as tools of greedy developers. We have done our best to make a quality community with demographics

that would challenge the UN, while places like Orinda (a wealthy, heavily restrictive suburb just over the hills from Berkeley) argue about what color the movie theatre should be.[43]

The "Melting Pot Happening"

While the UN General Assembly or famed polyglot neighborhoods like Queen's Jackson Heights are in no danger of being surpassed by East County in terms of global diversity, the 2000 census counted 39 languages spoken in East County homes by almost 58,000 people, more than a quarter of East County residents.[44] The sounds of Spanish, Italian, Portuguese, and Tagalog long common along the San Joaquin River were joined by Vietnamese, Chinese, and the languages of South Asia and the South Pacific. The Asian community in East County grew significantly since 1980, and by 2000 numbered more than 28,000, roughly 10 percent of the total population. Pittsburg in 2000 was more than 15 percent Asian. The ethnic amalgamation of East County eventually included more than 1,500 people of sub-Saharan African descent.[45]

By 2000, more than one-third of East County residents identified as Hispanic or Latinx, with no major racial group being less than 13 percent. The majority of unincorporated Bay Point's (formerly West Pittsburg) roughly 20,000 residents are Latinx, making it one of the few majority Latinx communities in the Bay Area. Pittsburg is more than 40 percent Latinx, and the Mi Pueblo market is one of the top sales tax generators in the city.

Yet, like so many times in American history, it is the growing presence of the African American community in East County that gets noticed, written about, and talked about. The numbers are certainly noteworthy—a population in Antioch that numbered 42 people in 1970 and 615 in 1980 numbered more than 17,000 by 2010. Brentwood had nine African American residents in 1980 and more than 3,000 by 2010. All told, more than 36,000 African Americans called East County home in the 2010 census, virtually the same number as live in longtime African American communities like Richmond and the cities and towns of West County. Regardless of whether one takes a regional or local perspective, this is a dramatic shift.

This shift did not come without tensions, particularly, and perhaps unsurprisingly, in Antioch. "Antioch," to quote one local minister active with social justice issues, "is the melting pot happening."[46] Its newness to integration and diversity means that, in the eyes of one local leader, Antioch has not built the "social infrastructure" necessary to cope with diversity. "Their leaders grew a community without engaging the citizens to help them understand that it isn't the small quaint town that it used to be."[47]

Part of this lack of "social infrastructure" comes from the "one foot in, one foot out" nature of many migrants and their formal communities. Even though the African American community has been building its presence in East County for some time, old churches from the core and new ministries took a long time to develop in numbers sizable enough to have an organized community and cultural presence. A common story heard when chatting with African American residents was how they still went back to San Francisco and Oakland for church.[48]

The political and cultural infrastructure also took time to catch up. For many years, Mary Rocha was the only nonwhite elected official from Antioch. Reggie Moore became the first elected African American councilmember in 2006, six years after former Pittsburg councilmember Federal Glover became the first African American member of the county board of supervisors. Even with a fairly active NAACP branch in East County, Antioch's first city-sponsored Martin Luther King Jr. Day celebration came in 2009.

Yet if there was been progress in terms of political and institutional integration in East County, the challenge of integration remained, especially when problems arose under conditions of uncertainty. Things get "uncomfortable" in East County when the problems and the perceived problems of the region—foreclosures, graffiti, crime, blight, loss of cultural identity, essentially everything but traffic—are conflated.

"Crime, Blight, Behavior, and Nothing Else"

In 2010, with Antioch teetering on the brink of insolvency and the real estate market still in shambles, a new citizens group came together to combat what it saw as a rise in graffiti and crime in Antioch. Take Back Antioch (TBA) quickly drew a lot of attention on Facebook and in the local media. Despite not having incorporated as an organization, it managed to push the city council into accepting it as a voice in the city, allowing them to "adopt" a local park and partner with the local police on a graffiti abatement program.

TBA was at the time only the most recent iteration of citizen's groups focusing on law and order and vandalism in Antioch. One version from the

1990s, Not in Our Neighborhood, conducted letter-writing campaigns focused on removing "problem" neighbors, either through campaigns with landlords, the housing authority, or homeowner's associations using alleged Covenants, Conditions and Restrictions (CC&R) violations. A far more prominent effort began in early 2006, when United Citizens for Better Neighborhoods (UCBN) was formed around the same issues, but with a much more specific target: Section 8 residents.[49]

UCBN's birth coincided with the formation of a special unit of the Antioch Police, known as the Community Action Team (CAT), to respond to resident complaints about neighborhood crime and "persistent nuisance, health and safety issues" (Costa 2009). Within a few months, Antioch was embroiled in a dispute about race, class, behavior, crime, and policing that would make the city the focus of lengthy articles in the *New York Times,* Associated Press, and *Wall Street Journal.* UCBN began holding rallies and flyering homes of suspected Section 8 residents with threatening messages: "No More Renters. No More Section 8. Save Antioch NOW. We THE RESIDENTS are watching YOU" (Public Advocates, Inc., and Bay Area Legal Aid 2007). The CAT team was accused of racial discrimination and sued by a coalition of legal advocacy groups on behalf of Section 8 residents. The local newspapers covered the issue closely, the local NAACP and the Black Political Association held counter-rallies, and hours upon hours of angry testimony from residents and leaders was heard by the city council at formal meetings and at the new "quality of life" forums that began around the same time. Even though Section 8 had been around for years and the geographies of race and class had been in transition for decades, it was the conflict in places like Antioch that people stood up and noticed (Kirkpatrick and Gallagher 2013).

Fear and Crime and Race

This is not about racial profiling, it's about statistics.

—White Woman, Antioch Resident, Testifying in Front of the
Antioch City Council, September 25, 2007

People who say that it has nothing to do with race need to take off the blinders and get an education.

—African American Woman, Antioch Resident and Legal Plaintiff,
Same Meeting, 20 Minutes Later

In statement after statement at council meetings, in newspapers, or quality of life forums, residents argued fervently that this was or was not about race. People concerned about racial profiling and the actions of the CAT team cited statistics from an ACLU study showing that referrals of African Americans by CAT team members to the county's Housing Authority were disproportionate to their representation in the city's Section 8 program. Supporters of the CAT team and UCBN members argued that this was about crime rates, not race. Darnell Turner, a local leader in the African American community, argued: "This is about race, and this is about class, but honestly it is more about class than about race."

What often goes missing from these discussions is precisely what we mean when we say "about race." "About race" to those arguing against race is an attempt to diffuse the charge of racism, an attempt to say, "I am against these activities because of what is being done, not who is doing it." Arguments that this is "about race" from communities of color, in particular African Americans, point either to specific acts of discrimination by the CAT team or to the broader experience of being black in Antioch. In testimony after testimony at the September 2007 meeting quoted above, African American residents spoke not about the CAT team but about other forms of discrimination they had experienced. Two black homeowners came to testify in support of Section 8 renters, one because of repeated stops by the police, the other because someone sprayed the n-word on his car and burned his lawn. While UCBN members regularly attempted to contain the issue to specific acts of "behavior," many black residents wanted to talk about the bigger picture, including the historical one.

This is an issue that came up again at a 2010 quality of life meeting, a meeting generally marked by calmer rhetoric, which one resident claimed was "the best one I've been to." After the testimony of a few TBA members, a prominent African American leader publicly asked TBA to change their name. She praised their energy and enthusiasm, but asked them to change the name "because what it means to people who look like me."[50] This same women three years earlier had defended the chief of police and the CAT team against the lawsuit. In that instance, she could separate the broader experience of being black in Antioch from the specific question of policing, but she remained diligent in terms of the broader question of race. In an interview, she was clear that she was optimistic about TBA, hoping that they would not resort to the "vigilante" tactics she felt characterized UCBN.

TBA would subsequently make some efforts to watch its language, even if it refused to change its name "until we take Antioch back."[51] Yet what is evident is that they, like many in Antioch, including some like Gary Gilbert who are black, refuse to acknowledge what Omi and Winant would deem the "racial project" of East County suburbanization. Omi and Winant (1994: 56) define a "racial project" as "Simultaneously an interpretation, representation, or explanation of racial dynamics, and an effort to reorganize and redistribute resources along particular racial lines."

For many African Americans in Antioch, or for a largely racialized group of Section 8 recipients, the broader issue of crime, police, and community response cannot be separated from the larger question of racial dynamics or the question of the distribution of resources, be it housing, security, or peace of mind. The same thing goes for many white and / or middle-class residents of East County. In conversation after conversation, and throughout the in-depth coverage in the local media of the original Section 8 / CAT team uproar, local residents blame more powerful actors at higher scales—the cities of San Francisco and Oakland, the counties of Alameda and Contra Costa, and the federal government—for making them and their neighborhoods guinea pigs in a different strategy of reorganization and redistribution along race and class lines. One group is looking at local history, another at regional responsibility. Even if they are coming from opposite sides of the racial and political spectrum, both are aware that at least they are having the debate. So many of the wealthier and more "progressive" parts of the region can avoid Antioch's overt racial tension by avoiding racial diversity altogether.

Just like the internecine rivalries between towns, these race and class divides within communities made it all the more difficult to come together for a common purpose, and because of its circumstances this fragmentation mattered in East County in a way it did not in wealthier or older parts of the region. After years of talking past each other and failing to focus on the broader questions of shared residence in an incomplete and structurally unsound subregion, residents and leaders were ill prepared for the most unifying question of all—foreclosure.

FORECLOSURES ON LEFEBVRE WAY

There is a street in southeast Antioch with a name totally at odds with the Winterglen Ways and Country Hills Drives that it intersects: Lefebvre

TABLE 3 The Houses of Lefebvre Way in 2015

Status	Number
Original owner (1990–92)	15
Foreclosure 2006–11	11
Owned since 2000	6
Owned post-2001	9
Received notice, nothing further	2
Likely short sale	2
Pending foreclosure notice (2015)	1
No data	3
Total	49

SOURCES: foreclosures.com, zillow.com, Contra Costa County Assessor

Way.[52] It is a quiet, unassuming street in Antioch's postindustrial garden, with relatively mature trees and the beige color scheme that is omnipresent throughout much of California exurbia. It is short, only two blocks long, and home to precisely 49 houses.[53] The houses north of Country Hills were built in 1990; those to the south in 1992.

Lefebvre Way illustrates in one brutal data snapshot the absurdity of the housing bubble, the diffuse nature of its geographic actors, and how severe the foreclosure crisis is for a place like Antioch. Of the 49 houses on Lefebvre Way, 11 were foreclosed upon between 2006 and 2011 (Table 3). Another had a notice of default pending, while two others received a notice and either refinanced or survived another way, and a fourth went through a short sale. This means that more than one in four houses went through some aspect of foreclosure during 2006–11, a slightly higher rate than the roughly one in five in the city of Antioch during roughly the same time period.[54]

One look at the loan numbers for the 15 homes that experienced some part of the foreclosure process shows the obscenity of the real estate bubble and unsustainable mortgages. The median loan amount for the 15 was $412,000, more than twice the current estimated value of each home and 1.5 times the average sales price of the entire 94531 zip code in 2000.[55] One house that sold for $252,000 in 2000 sold for $550,000 in 2005. Another down the street went for $143,000 in 2000 and $530,000 in 2005, an increase of *370 percent.*

The latter sale was made possible by a $424,000 loan from Home Loan Services Corporation in Fort Worth, Texas, a company which shared a PO

Box with Fremont Investment and Loan, the owner of a defaulted loan down the street for $416,000 on a house that was "valued" at more than three times its 1994 price just ten years later. Small and unknown financial players, from Fort Worth and Addisson, Texas, San Diego, San Francisco, and Burbank, were joined by virtually all of the major banks—Wells Fargo, Chase, Washington Mutual, and Bank of America. One was owned by Fannie Mae.

Lefebvre Way is a good place to think about how it all came undone, parsing the arguments that pointed fingers at Wall Street (the big banks), the small-time sharks operating under multiple names like Home Loan Services, the Republican's favorite target, Fannie Mae, and the Right's other favorite target, the individual homeowners who took these bad loans. As I made clear at the outset, my argument for adding another piece to this story—looking back on how and where, with what infrastructure and for what people these homes were built in the first place—should not deflect from an equally critical argument about shared, multiple responsibility. This is even more critical in the racially charged class politics of Antioch, for you can see both on Lefebvre Way and in the city as a whole that this crisis took everyone down with it, regardless of responsibility.

The Crash

Academic research has shown convincingly that foreclosures impact the value of neighboring houses (Immergluck and Smith 2005), but as discussed in the previous chapter, it is the larger question of the housing market crash that is relevant in the case of Antioch. Nestled in among the foreclosures on Lefebvre Way in 2011 were 15 houses owned by the original owners, and another six who had owned their homes more than 10 years, before the prices went sky high. Nine were owned by people unfortunate to have purchased after 2001, when the prices began to climb rapidly.

The critical thing to keep in mind in Antioch is that everyone was impacted, regardless of when you bought or who you were. Without adjusting for inflation, 21 of the 46 homes with available data showed negative equity, an average loss of almost $45,000. But if you adjust for inflation for the year of purchase, the numbers are staggering. Forty of 46 houses showed negative equity in 2011, an average of over $100,000 per house and a median of more than $85,000. Even if you bought in 1990 or 1992, when the houses were new and affordable, even if you bought with a fixed-rate loan that you could afford and have paid the house off, you lost an average of $90,000 in

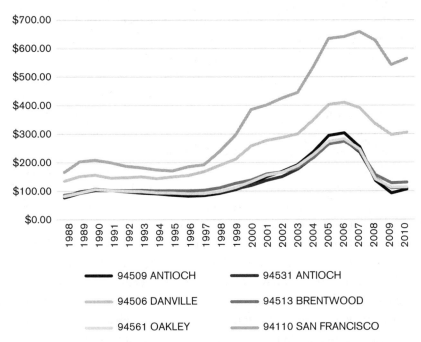

FIGURE 4. Real estate sales price per square foot, 1988–2009, inflation adjusted. Source: DataQuick.

adjusted dollars on what is for most families their largest source of equity. Houses purchased afterward fared even worse, losing an average of almost $160,000 more than the earlier homes. But the real brutality can be seen when added together—the two little blocks of Lefebvre Way lost a combined $4.6 million in equity. Two blocks.

The name of the street is as important as it is unusual, and my choice to use it as a symbol was as deliberate as finding the street was accidental. Henri Lefebvre's (2003; see also Lefebvre and Goodewardena 2008) conception of the "Right to the City" is one of the most influential ideas in contemporary urban activism, and is rooted in the right of urban denizens to "use value" over "exchange value," i.e., the value one gets from using a place as opposed to buying and selling it. What makes the crash on his eponymous street the most bitter of pills is that it represents the abject destruction of both.[56]

The broader story of lost equity is just as striking at the city level. Compare Antioch's two zip codes, 94509 and 94531, or Brentwood and Oakley's zip codes, with their wealthy Contra Costa neighbor of Danville, just over Mount Diablo from East County (see Figure 4). The East County towns blur together, making it almost impossible to separate them, even if Brentwood and Oakley would insist that they are different and the 94531 would resist comparison to the 94509. Everyone gained during the boom, but East County gained a much higher percentage, almost quintupling its value between 1988 and the peak in 2004–05. Following the crash, East County has lost everything, trading at roughly 2001 prices, while Danville has lost only the peak of the boom. If you compare it to a gentrifying neighborhood in San Francisco, the differences are off the chart.

When I first set foot on Lefebvre Way in 2007, the first wave of foreclosures had begun to hit, and lawns were littered with yellow Bank-Owned signs and other homeowners desperate to get out.[57] Homeowners watered lawns and dug out dead trees in neighboring yards to keep up appearances. One house around the corner was boarded up. Abandonment was a real fear, stoked by the discourses of decline and the seeming "end of suburbia."

Nevertheless, the first wave of foreclosures did not give way to widespread abandonment. Lefebvre Way saw only one foreclosure notice for what appears to be a "second wave" foreclosure, i.e., one caused by the post-crash economy and job loss as opposed to bad debt, even as the block slowly transitioned from majority homeowners to a mix of renters and homeowners.[58] But the larger structural problem of stagnant real estate prices continued to be troubling for East County, even as other parts of the region had the opposite problem. The fiscal challenges for Antioch remained significant, a brutal interaction between state-level policy and house-by-house losses in tax base. Sadly, the shared economic reality of East County did little to create major new bonds or overcome old barriers during the immediate aftermath of the crisis; instead it merely ratcheted up the level of tension as integration and infrastructure were managed under conditions of extreme anxiety and uncertainty. Part of the problem is that Antioch became large without ever becoming a center.

POSTCARDS FROM DOWNTOWN

If you walk into the back entrance of the Antioch Historical Society, located in the former high school, you are greeted by a series of photocollages done by students at the local community college. One of the collages contains a worn photocopy of a nineteenth-century photograph showing a handful of men in downtown Antioch crowded around a massive sign. The sign proclaims "Antioch, Metropolis of Eastern Contra Costa County," part of the boosterism common at the time and a reminder that the entrepreneurial city was not a neoliberal invention.[59]

One can also read this bold proclamation as a statement of fact: Antioch was the oldest city in the county, and when the photo was taken its downtown and its industry the most developed. In 1880, its population of 626 was the largest in the county. By 1910 it had been surpassed only by the fellow waterfront industrial cities of Richmond, Martinez, and Pittsburg, remaining larger and more economically vital than Concord, Walnut Creek, and the now wealthy suburbs of Central County (chapter 3).[60] The shift in population and wealth was not cemented until postwar suburbanization, a story that will be told in more detail in the next chapter.

This history is evident in the bones of downtown Antioch, a stretch of classic American grid running from the old high school eastward, up the slopes of Prosserville and through the remaining historic commercial buildings of 2nd and 3rd Streets and the Victorian mansions a few blocks south. At first glance, the downtown seems almost completely empty, possessing an almost surreal quietness on the blocks near City Hall or on 2nd Street down by the waterfront, broken only by the occasional train traffic and passing young men driving sound systems on wheels. If you look more closely, you come to realize that there is more life to the downtown than is initially apparent, more businesses open, even if they are spread out and mostly silent. But that only makes it more embittering—one should not have to seek out signs of life downtown.

Like so many issues in this book and the history it covers, the moribund state of downtown Antioch is not for want of "planning" or, perhaps more accurately, plans. A 1955 county plan examined downtown Antioch in its context as part of a generally inaccessible shoreline, a problem that remains today. The 1963 Antioch Waterfront and Vicinity Plan acknowledged the prominent role of the train and private industrial uses in blocking access, and proposed to remediate the problem. A decade later, in a 1973 supplement to the general plan, the city acknowledged that "none of these proposed improvements had materialized," and that some form of decline in the downtown had already begun in earnest (City of Antioch 1976). The bicentennial year (1976) saw an inspired plan by two interns from UC Berkeley's planning program under the supervision of city planning staff, a plan that examined the possibilities of utilizing air rights downtown to overcome the train problem and revitalize downtown through its waterfront. The plan specifically references and reprints Antioch's ghost in the machine, the renderings of the downtown Antioch BART station that never was.

By 1978, a new plan by a local consultant emphasized transit and environmentalism, albeit with an explicitly anti–downtown BART stance. "Revitalization plans of this study will severely reduce the desirability and practicality of a BART station and related parking facilities," the plan states, referring to a set of renderings and ideas rooted in a new "theming" of downtown. The plan was also rooted in a series of assumptions: that Antioch would be the beneficiary of significant spillover in the 1980s in terms of commercial development from Central County, that 500 units of housing would be built downtown, and that the new city hall would be a catalyst for development.

Just six years later (and a year after the Specific Plans), the city paid for another downtown plan, a simple urban design plan that pushed even further away from the real economic and infrastructural challenges toward the hope that new facades and sidewalks would make a change. The general plan of 1987 and an economic development plan of 1995 both mention the state of downtown, leading to a final downtown plan in 2006, just before the crash. This plan, a 178-page behemoth, was written by the same major national consultants responsible for Baltimore's famous Inner Harbor redevelopment (ARCADIS and City of Antioch 2006).[61] The ARCADIS plan, which is now a ghost in and of itself, is the ultimate in high-end planning fantasy, a $585 million dream based almost exclusively on private investment where the plan itself admits "the financial feasibility of private development in downtown Antioch could be characterized as indefinite at best given prevailing market conditions" (ibid., VI-14). Although this plan, like all previous downtown plans, recognized the problem with the train, the lack of public transportation access, and the challenge of competing growth absolutely everywhere in Antioch *except downtown,* it offered nothing but renderings, pro formas, SWOT analysis, and platitudes.[62] When the plan was delivered in August 2006, Antioch had suffered only three foreclosures the month before. By August 2007, Antioch had three foreclosures per day.

This accumulation of plans is a deeply Western variation on the multiplicity or absence of spatial plans and property documents that Ananya Roy (2002) found in Calcutta. Rather than use the "ambiguity" of the unmapped as a strategy for the production of space, local governments often buy plans (with their now mandatory if thin public processes) to put on the shelf to create the appearance of planning and action (in the case of downtown), or to satisfy mandates from higher levels of government (in the case of general plans). At least the plans of the 1970s have the courage to mention politics, to recognize the interconnectedness of Antioch to the region's decision-makers, and to set forth arguments acknowledging that to build a downtown is not simply a question of market share, financing, and urban design—creating a center during an era of peripheralization is an inherently political act, one that Antioch's leadership and populace never truly embraced.

Urbanists like myself are often accused of fetishizing the quaint downtowns of yesteryear, a continuation of Jane Jacobs's (1961) Hudson Street imagination.[63] The failure of downtown planning efforts should not be examined because they failed to create a neo–Greenwich Village on the San Joaquin, but because they failed to recreate a center at the precise moment when they were being sucked into the periphery of a hungry metropole. Lefebvre's Right to the City is also partly a right to the centrality that cities represent, and in this too Antioch and East County were unable to escape their growing peripheralization.

This lack of a central point—one rich in jobs, tax base, public space, transit, local history—worsened the fiscal and economic impact of foreclosure, and made recovery all the more difficult. Residents of East County could never come together around a common purpose, riven as they were by so many seemingly insurmountable lines. The county's physical spaces epitomize that fragmentation, and depending on the degree to which one adheres to various forms of environmental determinism, helped reinforce and coproduce its fragmented nature.

It is not a coincidence that the last Antioch plan with a strong emphasis on regional transportation infrastructure, and the last with any reasonable chance of forming a central node in the city, was written in 1976 as the last plan made by the city for the city and not bought from consultants. Nothing epitomizes the change in eras like the gap between that plan and the ARCADIS plan, the former a grounded infrastructure-focused effort versus the latter's market-driven fiction.

In the stories of East County—the great doubling of Antioch, the building of the bypass, the small-town mentalities and race / class tensions, the foreclosures, and the unbuilding of downtown—one can see deeper structural issues inherent to the production of East County. These are questions about planning itself, about centrality and peripherality in the contemporary moment, and about what critical legal scholars like Gerald Frug and David Barron discuss as the inherent fallacies in our conceptions of "home rule"—

the very American idea that towns are powerful (Frug 1980, 1984, 1993, 1996, 2001a; Barron 1999, 2003).

The cities of East County were never truly powerful, not powerful enough to control their own destiny. Unfortunately, they were powerful enough to be affected by their constant reiteration of the fragmented politics of development in California, riven by lines between neighbors, between forces internal to the cities, and between the cities themselves. Again, this did not make them different from most other places; however, their inability to overcome these barriers affected them more than it did other places.

But as much as East County must acknowledge its profound role in determining its fate, what one must not do is consider the structural instability of the postindustrial garden on its own, and particularly not only in its own geography. The "postindustrial garden" in East County was no more the sole production of its physical home than the industrial garden was a production in and on San Leandro. To understand how it all came together in East County, the next step involves a geography often ignored by urbanists toggling between cities and regions—the county. For East County is nothing if not a product of Contra Costa County, and it is in the development politics of Contra Costa County that one can truly see fragmentation. It was a geographically divided county, but is also became the site of the classic impasse of neoliberal-era development politics, an impasse I call the Dougherty Valley dilemma.

THREE

The Dougherty Valley Dilemma

And in fact, over that ridge—the Contra Costa County Line—
and through that tunnel, one does enter into the economy and
mindset of a different world.

—JOEL GARREAU, *Edge City* (1991: 312)

CONTRA COSTA COUNTY LIVED UP to its name for approximately three years. One of California's original 27 counties, its naming was a critical symbolic defeat for the "New York on the Pacific" boosters and other early denizens who hoped that the metropolis of the Bay would border the San Joaquin River rather than the Golden Gate. On February 18, 1850, Contra Costa County was formed as arguably the only county in the nation to be exclusively named in relation to another place—it was the "other coast" to San Francisco's ascendant metropolis. Barely three years later, it undoubtedly became the only county in the nation named after a relational geography it no longer possessed. Alameda County was formed from pieces of Santa Clara County and the entirety of Contra Costa's San Francisco–facing waterfront, leaving Contra Costa as the gateway to the delta rather than the center of the East Bay.

A more accurate and suitable name would have been Diablo County, after the sprawling peak that anchors the center of the county like a medieval citadel. Mount Diablo is known for its intense wildflower blooms, its close-in camping and occasionally snow-capped peaks, and for the once in a blue moon chance at the Shangri-La of views, a glimpse of both the Farallon Islands off the coast of San Francisco and Yosemite's Half Dome from the same point, one of the longest views on earth.

If you look down on your visit to the viewpoint, you will notice another factoid with greater historical and metaphoric importance—Mount Diablo was one of three survey points for the establishment of property boundaries in California and Nevada. This "initial point" was designated by the United States Public Land Survey System in 1851 to carve up the spoils from the Treaty of Guadalupe Hidalgo, the nine million acres of ranchos that would arguably be the most profitable war bounty in the history of the United States.[1] It is fitting that Contra Costa would be the central point for the creation of Northern California's real estate grid, for real estate has long been at the center of Contra Costa County.

Diablo's summit is also an unparalleled vantage point for a panoramic view of the living paradox that is the Bay Area. On clear days after a rain, the green hillsides and rolling hills seem to blend effortlessly with the waters of the bay and the vast yet seemingly content metropolis lining valleys and waterfronts for miles around. The Great Central Valley agro-economic miracle stretches from the eastern base of the mountain to the Gush Rush peaks of the Sierras, California's true primitive accumulation. Kerouac's "fabulous white city of San Francisco on her eleven mystic hills" looks magical in the distance (Michaels, Reid, and Scheer 1989: 145), and you can feel for just a minute the hyperbolic love people have for the place, the sense as Julián Marías would have it of "entering into the land of Paradise" (ibid., 13).

Come on an infernally hot summer day and the smog from the 150 million miles of daily driving and the four massive oil refineries that make this sprawling life possible dims the color of the water and makes the hills look even more burnt than usual.[2] The Central Valley is a blur of tract homes stretching out into a sky more brown than blue, and both the Sierras and San Francisco are visible only in the mind's eye. You have to look down rather than out, and the questions about the mansions and subdivisions and gated communities and office parks ringing the mountain start multiplying.

If the Bay Area were as honest as it was innovative, it would rename itself the Mount Diablo metropolitan region. It is far more accurate geographically, uniting the Central Valley and the Bay region in name as they have been united economically, woven together by traffic patterns, long-distance commuters, and out-migrants, the true center of a "megaregion." Yet one does not even need to think megaregionally to see the centrality of Diablo, for it is also the focal point of Contra Costa County, a massive, fragmented, and diverse set of political, cultural, and physical lines that is a microcosm of regional fragmentation.

The past 35 years of county history included important decisions and developments that helped produce East County and its colleagues in the Central Valley. The house-rich and job-poor spaces of the postindustrial garden were only made possible by the development of job-rich and housing-poor "edge cities" in the heart of the county.[3] This furthered the evolution of the county into distinctly different zones of privilege, politics, and poverty, and exacerbated tensions over traffic, growth, and rapid change throughout the county.

Amid rising tensions over this development in the 1980s, leaders of the development and increasingly powerful environmental communities worked with local and county officials to establish an historic "grand bargain." This compromise paved the way for new investment in transportation and seemingly united the different geographies of the physical county and the different geographies of its planning and development politics. Although this bargain developed new planning institutions, helped implement new planning policies, and stirred much-belated infrastructure investment in what had become a much bigger county seemingly overnight, it failed to weave together the increasingly contentious development politics of the county.

Just a few years after this bargain, this political goodwill fell apart, and Contra Costa County became one of the great battlegrounds in the planning fights of late twentieth-century California. Environmentalists and developers, both powerful and wealthy, battled to an expensive and politically costly draw over a development in the heart of the county called Dougherty Valley. In the end, little progress would be made in the deeper struggle against the unsustainable, unequal, and rapidly resegregating region, in part because no matter which side had "won" the battle over Dougherty Valley, the region and those impacted by its fragmentation and segregation would have lost. This is what I call the "Dougherty Valley dilemma"—a political stalemate in which real solutions are never possible, and the majority lose regardless of who wins a costly fight between two powerful and privileged sets of institutions.

EL CONDADO

> City governments cannot always assume the sole responsibility for the solution of these pressing urban problems. I repeat, they cannot—our state governments will not—the federal government should not—and therefore you on the county level must.
>
> —JOHN F. KENNEDY, Address to First National Association of Counties (NACo) Urban County Congress, 1959

The county as a political entity in America is notable for both its ubiquity and its status as the "forgotten government" in our complex and variegated set of federalist hierarchies (Benton 2005: 462).[4] Descended from the shire system of pre-Norman England—from which county-level offices like sheriff, coroner, and justice of the peace emerged—counties were readily adopted in the colonial United States, although with a key geographic variation. The more rural south generally adopted a relatively strong county system (mimicking the English), while the more urban north vested little power in counties. Pennsylvania was a hybrid, vesting power at the county level while maintaining at-large elections. As the country expanded westward, southern states tended to maintain the strong county system pioneered by Virginia, while western states generally followed Pennsylvania's lead.

Counties were targets for professionalization and political reform during the Progressive Era alongside cities and states, and there exists a robust if wonkish literature among public administration scholars in regard to virtually every aspect of county government.[5] The historic and generally fixed nature of county boundaries has reified political lines in a way that the more fluid lines of cities and town are less likely to have done, especially in the newer cities of the West. California, which in 1911 became the first state in the nation to grant counties extensive home rule, has not had any major changes to county geographies in more than a century.[6]

Urbanism and identity are often also constituted at the county level, both in rural and nonrural contexts. In much of rural America, people live in unincorporated space, receive services from county agencies, and go to school with people from their county, not just the named place where they live. While suburban scholars may talk of Levittown, New Yorkers of Nassau and Suffolk and Westchester, and Southern Californians of the famous OC (Orange County), all are shorthand for broad swaths of suburbia and recognition that identity is constructed as much at this larger scale than in the innumerable small towns, many of which are actually unincorporated. If you ask anyone from my hometown of San Anselmo, or any of the nearby towns and cities, where they are from, they will likely tell you the same thing—Marin County. The construction and defense of suburban life may festishize the small town, but it is often constructed politically, culturally, socially, and economically on the historically rooted geography of the county.

In urban studies and planning, we are so often in a hurry to rush from the local to the regional or the global that we forget these in-between geographies. Both legal jurisdictions like counties and sub-county areas like East County are places in their own right, with particular histories, identities, and sets of relations that create a unique sociopolitical economy. The production of East County is not only impossible to understand without an analysis of the role of Contra Costa County's board of supervisors and county government in the production of growth, it is impossible to understand without some conception of Contra Costa County as a place: its socioeconomic divisions, its stark multipolar geography defined by a pronounced physiography and a fragmented transportation infrastructure, its spider web of ever-changing agencies, authorities, districts, and municipalities, its powerful and outsized real estate industry, or its cultural and environmental politics where "green" has racial undertones.

In a period of 35 years, Contra Costa County transformed itself into the 37th largest county and the 10th largest suburban county in the nation. It is home to more than a million people, yet its largest city, Concord, has less than 125,000 people (hence the definition as suburban). It built "edge cities"—massive complexes of office and commercial development in existing towns and on old ranches in unincorporated territory—transforming the Bay Area's human and economic geography far beyond the county lines. How it did this and why it did it is just as important to understanding the story of East County as are the actions of East County itself, or the changes wrought at higher scales or in different places. Contra Costa County was a pro-growth space in a more reluctant region, a place with an attachment to the rural ideal largely lost in the rest of the urbanized metropolis, one of the few places in the most famously liberal region in the nation where Republicans live in numbers and where right-wing politics is not exclusively a pejorative. Contra Costa County is Northern California's "postsuburbia"—a place of suburban employment and not just bedrooms—its slice of Orange County wedged into the Bay Area (Kling, Olin, and Poster 1995). The problems of East County can partially be traced not to the creation of postsuburbia, but to the inability to fully embrace it. The new job centers of central Contra Costa would be just as incomplete as the bedroom communities like East County on its periphery.

THE COUNTIES OF CONTRA COSTA COUNTY

There is not really a sense of being part of a whole in any of the places—because the distances are so significant, the physiographic dividers are pronounced, and the socioeconomics so different.

—Longtime County Planner, Contra Costa, 2010

A common aside in Contra Costa political circles is that the county is actually three counties, or four, or five, depending on who is doing the counting or what gets counted. The physical county is the most starkly defined: sprawling west to east from the San Francisco Bay to the Central Valley, Contra Costa spans two sets of hills and more than 60 miles of shoreline. The county's almost 720 square miles are inhabited in three broadly defined zones— the western coastal zone along the bay, the San Ramon and Diablo valleys at the center of the county, and East County's arm of the Central Valley. The hills in between are noted not for how many people live there but for how wealthy they are.

These physical boundaries help define the overlapping layers of the county's economic history. As I have noted, the northern shoreline of the county from Richmond in the west to Antioch in the east has been home to the Bay Area's heaviest and dirtiest industry since the late 1880s. Agriculture is still prominent in far East County, while ranching holds on in isolated spots throughout the central portion of the county, often integrated with an increasingly important network of preserved open space and a complex public / private regime of open space preservation. The 1980s office boom went not to the postindustrial landscape along the waterfront but to the tony suburbs of the Diablo and San Ramon valleys.

The physical and the economic intersect at distinct historical moments with the county's transportation networks. Water and rail serviced the burgeoning industries on the coast for the first century of Contra Costa's economic history, only to take a backseat to the auto-oriented dominance of the twentieth century. Had you told a county resident in 1900 that Walnut Creek and San Ramon would one day dominate the county's wealth generation, and anchor one of the wealthiest suburban clusters in the country, they would likely have looked at you with disbelief. But starting with the 1937 opening of the Caldecott Tunnel (running through the Berkeley Hills between Oakland and Orinda)—little more than six months after the Golden Gate Bridge and barely a year after the San Francisco–Oakland Bay Bridge—the central part of the county was linked by well-funded freeways to the burgeoning metropolis of the Bay Area.

Growth came slowly. When Catherine Bauer Wurster studied the largest 13 cities in the Bay Area in 1960, not a single one was in Contra Costa County (Bauer Wurster 1963). The 1960s and early 1970s saw the construction of Interstate 680 from San Jose up the spine of the San Ramon and Diablo valleys, linking the center of the county with Silicon Valley, and providing an express connection to Alameda County's Livermore and Amador valleys. This paved the way for the San Ramon Valley to redefine itself as part of the wealthy, cross-county "Tri-Valley" area, a subregion that would become ground zero for edge-city office growth. When BART came at the end of the 1970s, it did not follow the old waterfront rail corridors through Richmond and Martinez, but rather the new suburban pathway through the Caldecott Tunnel and down the center of interstate system—a system that never went over Willow Pass into East County.

To add to the complexity, Contra Costa County boasts one of the more unfathomably complex political geographies in the state, a maze of incorporated and unincorporated space, epitomized by Richmond's boundaries that owe more to a Rorschach test than good governance. One of the poorest parts of the Bay Area—North Richmond—is actually an unincorporated spot on the map surrounded by Richmond. On the flip side are Alamo and Diablo, two of the wealthiest zones around, which along with the business center of "Contra Costa Center," the working-class community of Pacheco, and the East County farm towns of Byron and Knightsen, remain unincorporated spaces under control of the county.

The historical layers of political, economic, transportation, and physical geographies map onto a socioeconomic map that leaves people in each part of the county separated by far more than mountains and freeways. The flats of West County—much of the cities of Richmond and San Pablo, the unincorporated pockets of North Richmond, and parts of Rodeo and Crockett— feature struggling communities still grappling with the environmental impacts of energy production and heavy industry, but without the employment base these industries once assured. As I discuss in the next chapter, unemployment, poverty, environmental health impacts, and high levels of violence coexist on a human map that is highly racialized, with African Americans, Latinxs, and Southeast Asians bearing the brunt of some of the unhealthiest living conditions in California.

The flats of West County lead up to the Berkeley / Oakland Hills, a space that oscillates between middle-class tranquility and upper-class gilt, and which extends through the wealthy enclaves of Lamorinda and into the Diablo Valley.[7] Walnut Creek, the geographic and commercial heart of the county, is a demographic crossroads (Garreau 1991: 315). To the south, the San Ramon Valley is one of the wealthiest portions of the *country,* boasting four of the top 101 zip codes in Forbes' List of the most expensive in the nation,

TABLE 4 The Five Counties of Contra Costa

Place	Total Population	% NH White	% NH Black	% NH Asian	% NH 2+ Races	% Hispanic
Contra Costa County*	1,049,025	47.8	8.9	14.2	3.8	24.4
East County	292,232	38.1	12.5	9.8	4.0	34.4
West County	248,270	25.0	18.5	18.8	3.6	33.0
North County	207,827	57.3	3.1	10.7	4.0	23.9
South County	224,959	67.0	1.7	19.4	3.6	7.8
Lamorinda	65,855	77.7	1.0	10.9	3.8	6.0

SOURCE: California Department of Finance Public Law 94–171 Redistricting Data, via U.S. Census Bureau. Generated March 8, 2011.

*THE totals in the DOF's data for the county exceed the combined totals of each Census Designated Place by approximately 10,000 total.

including the aforementioned unincorporated spaces of Diablo and Alamo.[8] To the north, the Diablo Valley is decidedly more mixed and middle class, as the old Air Force town cum "boomburb" (Lang and LeFurgy 2006) of Concord more closely resembles East County than either West County or the San Ramon Valley.

The divisions in terms of class parallel stark divides in terms of race. Table 4 shows the result of the 2010 Census in five areas—West County, East County, North Central, South Central, and Lamorinda. Only when it comes to the Asian American community (and mixed-race individuals) are the communities somewhat evenly divided. East and West Counties are majority-minority, while Lamorinda and South County—which are grouped together for transportation planning purposes—are more than two-thirds white, less than 2 percent African American, and collectively have roughly half of the number of Hispanic residents as the city of Richmond, with almost three times the population.

The divisions in terms of income and poverty are even starker. Map 9 shows the divided nature of the county, with clear difference between south and west, and some variation in North and East County. This is in part what makes East County a true frontier, enmeshed in a complex grid of interactions and migrations across race and class lines, but nevertheless it is united to some degree more with Richmond in the west than with San Ramon in the south.

This racialized socioeconomic geography, when viewed alongside a coproduced historical geography of political lines, economic functions, physical

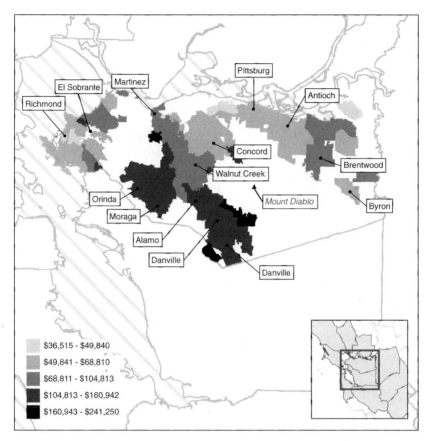

MAP 9. Contra Costa Median Household Income, 2010. Source: 2010 U.S. Census.

barriers, and transportation networks, evokes a second imagery beyond the archipelagos of the four or five counties. Viewed from above, the panorama of Contra Costa shows two distinct axes. The east / west axis is the Highway 4 corridor, the industrial and maritime corridor on which the county was built. The north / south axis is the newer, federally produced 680 / 24 corridor, a viaduct for capital and wealth at the forefront of suburban office development and exclusionary suburbanism. It is a geography that brings to mind an inverted variation of Lucio Costa's early renditions of Brasilia's famed Plano Piloto, its arms weighed down not by modernist expectations, but by the reality of working-class suburban life in a postindustrial, post-Keynesian, and postmodern world.

From Edge Cities to an Axis of Exclusion

> Perhaps the quickest way to learn about the hottest issue in Contra Costa County is to drive its length north to south on Highway 680. From Martinez to San Ramon, it's easy to see why this area's reputation as a suburban oasis has now changed to office construction mecca.
>
> —THOMAS SWEENEY, *San Francisco Business,*
> September 1986

> If you look at the underlying land use plans for those (the Highway 4 corridor) communities, they desire to see that (office development)—the market has never manifested itself.
>
> —Longtime County Planner, Contra Costa, 2010

During the postwar era, much of the San Ramon and southern Diablo valleys remained sleepy bedroom communities and small towns, with just smatterings of the growth seen in San Leandro and Alameda's "industrial garden" corridor from Oakland to Milpitas. Walnut Creek had fewer than 10,000 people in 1960, and most of the area to the south in the San Ramon Valley was unincorporated. But the writing was on the wall—small areas of suburban growth in Concord and Pleasant Hill would soon be connected to Alameda County and San Jose via Interstate 680, which was completed in 1971. Although BART would eventually bypass the San Ramon Valley and take an extra generation to reach Pleasanton and Dublin to the south, the 1977 opening of BART in Walnut Creek and Concord was presaged by a more than two-decades-long planning process that saw the rendering of the San Ramon Valley as part of the BART system in 1956. There was nothing foreordained about urbanization, wealth, or economic growth following what would become the 680 corridor. That would require intervention.

At the heart of the San Ramon Valley lies Bishop Ranch, an extensive office complex that became the region's leading example of "edge cities" (Garreau 1991)—major office developments in suburban areas. Planning for Bishop Ranch began in the 1950s, as county planners designated the ranch at the heart of the San Ramon Valley for economic uses. The language of the 1958 San Ramon Area General Plan proposes a light manufacturing center. They see the transformation of the area into a variation on the "industrial garden" communities—mostly middle-class industrial workers in a "well-balanced" community (San Ramon Planning Area General Plan quoted in McGovern 1998: 251). It was government planners and not real estate developers who carried the torch for economic / industrial uses on Bishop Ranch for more than two decades, as the development community angled instead for suburban housing. After a deal fell through for Western Electric Company to build a telephone factory on the site, planners rejected an initial proposal for a huge residential subdivision from new owners and eventual Bishop Ranch developers Masud and Alex Mehran.

The county's concern with tax base—an issue in pre-Prop. 13 California as well—was joined by the same planning principle that guided development in East County: the jobs-housing balance. With concerns about traffic, sprawl, and congestion joining issues of economic and fiscal sustainability, the magical balance was seen as a means of mitigating the effects of growth and creating a "well-balanced community," overcoming the one-dimensionality of the postwar suburb—although without integrating land uses. As Patrick McGovern (1998: 250) points out in his study of "edge cities" in Contra Costa County, this planning-driven belief was enabled by state legislation that mandated general plans for all jurisdictions—cities and counties—but no regional planning or regional coordination: "The general plan legitimized the idea that each local community was on its own in seeking development and tax revenue. General plans became documents of boosterism and visions of urban centers for even the smallest communities, exacerbating the fragmentation of land use regulation, which had already led to metropolitan sprawl." Merely hinted at by McGovern and by other studies of edge cities is that white-collar office development helped solve a class problem as well. The limited suburbanization of the San Ramon Valley to that point had been fairly genteel, "big homes in bosky glens" as Garreau would have it, and the San Leandro in the San Ramon Valley vision of the 1958 plan did not fit with the residents' view of the area. There was a "mismatch with an upscale housing stock," as McGovern describes it.

The people who did work in the area largely fit the dual profiles of the labor force that would constitute a big portion of the initial wave of white-collar employees—overwhelmingly male corporate executives, who had already begun transforming the ravines of largely unincorporated Lamorinda, Danville, and Alamo into an upscale suburban escape, and their underemployed but college-educated wives.[9] This availability of labor and proximity to the new homes of the executive class, combined with clear support from the planning staff at the county and the City of Walnut Creek, newly minted transportation infrastructure, and a handful of eager property developers, helped convince skeptical capital to invest in what was essentially a suburban downtown.

And invest they did. Bishop Ranch grew from two initial buildings in 1981 to more than 10 million square feet of office space housing 33,000 workers and 550 companies in 14 complexes.[10] The initial commitment of Toyota to house a small operation in 1981 quickly led to the massive corporate office relocations of Chevron and Pacific Bell. The "city" now boasts restaurants and a hotel, and is one of the most important economic agglomerations outside of San Francisco and Silicon Valley.

But Bishop Ranch, originally planned by the county—San Ramon would not incorporate as a city until 1983—was only the largest of what would be a series of smaller office building clusters along the 680 corridor. While Bishop Ranch was a greenfield development, the City of Walnut Creek redevelopment plan centered around the new downtown BART station. The "Golden Triangle" became six million square feet of commercial space between the late 1970s and the mid-1980s (Walnut Creek General Plan 2025 [1979] in McGovern 1998).[11] The Contra Costa Center, an unincorporated zone in the political fabric between Walnut Creek and Pleasant Hill, would be another 2.4 million square feet of office and commercial space.

When combined with the Hacienda Business Park node at the 580 / 680 interchange to the south, and the smaller cluster of office development around Concord's BART station, the area was transformed from a series of isolated edge cities to a new corridor of work and consumption that radically altered not only the county's geography but that of an entire region. Overall jobs-housing balance was achieved in Central County—it has hovered at roughly nine jobs for every ten units over the past two decades, with Walnut Creek and San Ramon exceeding 2:1—but in a manner that impacted everywhere else.[12]

By the time the foreclosure crisis hit, more than 28,000 East County residents commuted to the 680 corridor (including Pleasanton), along with roughly 10,000 residents of Solano County—Contra Costa's neighbor to the north. More people commuted to Central County from San Joaquin County (~3,000)—over Altamont Pass in the Central Valley and outside the formal Bay Area—than from BART-connected San Francisco (~2,500).[13] When Bishop Ranch opened, transit use for workers relocated from San Francisco fell from 58 percent to less than 3 percent (Cervero and Landis 1992). The edge cities blew apart a regional economic geography that was never particularly dense to begin with. By the mid-2000s, the Bay Area was the ninth most-sprawling metropolitan region in terms of job sprawl (Kneebone 2009).

Like virtually every other "problem" in the region, the more powerful and more geographically blessed locales were able to "solve" their issues by merely pushing them elsewhere.

Not Just Any Jobs

The location of the new workers and the transit-unfriendly commutes of this new regional economic geography is only part of the story of the edge-city influence on geographies of race, class, and real estate. Many of the jobs were high-income, white-collar jobs in finance, insurance, and real estate (FIRE). Between 1969 and 2000, San Francisco saw sporadic, up-and-down growth in the FIRE sector, while Contra Costa more than tripled the number of jobs, roughly equaling that of Alameda County.[14] By the height of the boom, Contra Costa had outstripped Alameda County by more than 4,000 jobs in this most lucrative of sectors.

The good-paying jobs were a boon to real estate prices in the southern portion of the county, as values throughout Lamorinda and the San Ramon Valley skyrocketed. This was fine if you were an executive at an insurance company, but not if you were the secretary, the janitor, the mid-level account executive, or the many other back-office workers who made up the numerical bulk of the new workforce. It was a double-edged sword for a new suburban working majority, for the job growth in Central County was not matched in any way by housing to meet the needs of these workers.

Between 1980 and 1985, Walnut Creek added $250 million in nonresidential construction but less than 5,000 residents, and saw its median housing value jump almost 17 percent against the rest of Alameda and Contra Costa counties (Kroll 1986). San Ramon's massive gains in office development would come in the second half of the decade, and although it made a better effort to build housing than its neighbors, the larger story for the subregion remained the same—especially considering that the now exceptionally wealthy cities of Lamorinda and Danville had incorporated and were fiscally secure enough to build very little. Figure 5 tells the story more starkly: for most of the past two decades, East County built more homes than the larger, more job- and transit / transport-rich 680 corridor. It is this simultaneous development of tax revenue and jobs producing commercial development in one place and workforce housing in another that is so critical to understanding the physical sprawl which engulfed East County and beyond.

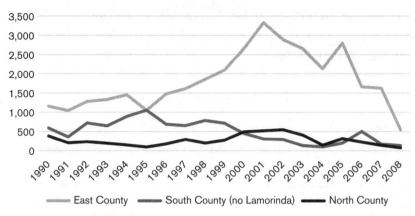

FIGURE 5. Residential units by Contra Costa subregion, 1990–2008. Source: RAND California via Construction Industry Research Board.

With the evolution of central and southern Contra Costa into both job-rich edge city and exclusive suburb, one can see some of the roots of East County's plight. One can also see the futility of the one-dimensional arguments for explaining urban change. Bishop Ranch would never have been built without the efforts of planners to hold back suburban housing developers keen on cashing in on a booming postwar market. Had those cities been more amenable to density, more housing in the corridor would have been built, but many of the cities incorporated precisely to prevent such an occurrence. Had capital and developers not become so myopically focused on certain types of development, pitting housing against jobs rather than encouraging them together, better planning could have resulted. This new geography was reacting to a shifting means of production and the growing inequality that has marked the postindustrial economy. The brand-new, externally funded freeway and BART system played a role, as did fiscal stress under a new regime of federal / state / local relations.

The transformation of the 680 corridor, like all complex urban spaces, can never be reduced to a single explanation, regardless of one's politics. State and market are internally linked and equally guilty, and one would do better to understand the linked nuances of history and geography than rehashing tired ideological and methodological battles. Central Contra Costa had the perfect geography at the perfect (and perfectly deadly) moment in history for edge cities—while the paint was still drying on the postwar infrastructure, and before a concerted anti-growth effort could arise to rein in growth. The transition to a more austere regime spurred an already willing planning apparatus to continue its push for jobs-housing balance, even if it meant negative externalities beyond the narrow confines of the 680 corridor. Initial resistance from a real estate development community accustomed to subdivisions and a capitalist class used to downtowns quickly gave way to a suburban office boom repeated all over the nation—in certain suburbs, but not others.

Which raises the question: How did the creation of edge cities in one part of the county interact with the broader political economy of Contra Costa County? Part of the limitations of authors such as Garreau is that they willfully ignored most of the real political economy of edge cities (Kling, Olin, and Poster 1995; Lewis 1996). As Paul Lewis (1996: 45) wisely points out about Garreau, the latter's inability to see governance as anything other than a "swirling of gnats" means he does not understand how "in a politically fragmented region, the social, geographic, and power inequalities that mark a region inhere in governing institutions and serve to perpetuate disparities in development."

Partly in reaction to the edge-city boom and to a pro-growth county political machine, Contra Costa's development politics shifted while the edge cities were being constructed. Contra Costa's fights over incorporation, housing growth, and the growing environmental movement may have largely been born in the foothills of Mount Diablo, but they quickly spread—all while state and federal investment in infrastructure was significantly reduced. The growth wars had come to Contra Costa County, and they played a key role in making sure that the new geographies of Contra Costa County—four or five counties on two axes—hardened in place.

A PLAYER IN THE DEVELOPMENT GAME

There was a feeling about the 1970s and 1980s board of supervisors that they would approve development in the next valley over on any given Tuesday.

— County Planner, Contra Costa, 2010

When Bishop Ranch landed Chevron and Pacific Bell in one fell swoop in 1982, the popular conception of Contra Costa's economy began to shift. The focus on the FIRE sector, and the growth of management and back-office positions for virtually every type of corporation in the region, gave parts of the county a generic corporate feel. With such a physically divided county,

TABLE 5 Real Estate Industry Location Quotients, 2005

Industry	California	Alameda County	Contra Costa County	SF County	Santa Clara County
Construction	1.06	1.16	**1.53**	0.57	0.85
Building Material and Garden Supply Stores	0.9	0.93	**1.26**	0.29	0.75
Real Estate Credit	1.53	0.73	**2.34**	0.21	0.54
Mortgage and Nonmortgage Loan Brokers	1.9	1.81	**2.55**	0.63	1.03
Real Estate Investment Trusts	2.02	3.07	**1.68**	11.72	0.43
Real Estate and Rental and Leasing	1.15	1.01	**1.35**	1.37	1.04

NOTE: Location Quotient is ratio of analysis-industry employment in the analysis area to base-industry employment in the analysis area divided by the ratio of analysis-industry employment in the base area to base-industry employment in the base area.

SOURCE: Bureau of Labor Statistics.

one has to dig into the data to get a proper sense of what was happening. Often lost in the fervor over new office parks was the industry that built them in the first place.

From the early days of the post-Caldecott boom, real estate and real estate development were the county's economic backbone. In virtually every aspect of the real estate industry, from construction to finance to sales to leasing, Contra Costa slowly built itself on the building of Contra Costa. These were generally small firms—around ten people on average for construction and real estate finance firms, smaller for REITs and mortgage brokers. But they were numerous—the county averaged around 3,500 firms involved in all aspects of real estate and real estate development from 1990–2010, an economy that generated 40,000 jobs by the height of the boom in 2005 and $3.3 billion in wages.[15]

Table 5 shows the location quotient, a measure of relative over- and under-representation of certain industries relative to a base geography and industry (in this case all jobs in the United States). What is most striking are not the construction jobs nor the day-to-day work of renting and leasing real estate—as a growing suburban region, one would expect slightly higher than average levels for those sectors—but the mortgages and real estate credit, two sectors that we now know lie at the root of the foreclosure cum financial crisis. In both areas, Contra Costa County had more than twice its share of the national average, far more than neighboring counties, including wealthy San Francisco and booming Santa Clara.

As a former developer turned real estate and planning consultant noted, "You saw a massive increase in 1990s and 2000s in new financial institutions, just here in Contra Costa County. There was a flood of capital into various real estate markets."[16] This "flood" can be seen in dividend, income, and rent (DIR) data collected by the U.S. Bureau of Economic Analysis—income derived from ownership. From a point of relative parity with surrounding counties, the state, and the nation in 1970, Contra Costa County's per capita DIR grew steadily; by the height of the boom it was almost 50 percent higher than the national average and 33 percent higher than neighboring Alameda County. Only Santa Clara County, with its Silicon Valley tech boom, and San Francisco, with its long-tenured asset-owning gentry, fared better on a relative scale.

East County was not solely a victim of Wall Street brokers, some form of anonymous "accumulation by dispossession" (Harvey 2005) from afar; it was also a victim of a real estate credit industry nestled between its hilltops and anchored in the new glass-and-steel office complexes of its new economy. This was not just wealth created in Contra Costa but *on* Contra Costa *by* Contra Costa. It was part of a larger political economy of real estate that vested particular power in some of those very edge-city office parks that tilted the employment geography of the entire region. And it was located in the "forgotten government" in Martinez, the quaint historic county seat and former home of legendary conservationist John Muir.[17]

The Forgotten Government

Contra Costa County was unique in the Bay Area in that the county regime was not only pro-growth but an active player in the development game of the vast areas of unincorporated space where it has the final word on land use. The planning of Bishop Ranch was, after all, done by the county.[18] County activity was not limited to the 680 corridor—West County is riven with populous unincorporated areas from North Richmond to El Sobrante, while East County's Oakley had almost 25,000 residents by the time it incorporated in 1999.

Over the course of the past two decades, a time period that included some political shifts at the county level which actually made it less pro-growth than in the 1970s and early 1980s, Contra Costa County still permitted 25,000 residential units in unincorporated space. Within the context of the nine-county Bay Area, this set Contra Costa dramatically apart from the rest of the region. Whether you examine total valuation or the total tally of units, the numbers tell the same story. Not only did Contra Costa County permit from two to ten times more housing in unincorporated space than neighboring Alameda County, but for almost the entire 1990–2008 period it allowed more unincorporated units than Alameda, San Mateo, and Santa Clara counties combined.[19]

The county's active role in suburbanization was a result of an intense politics of development at the county level. The county's growth machine had been powerful since the postwar era, when local newspaper magnate Dean Lesher made his famous airborne proclamation mentioned in the previous chapter that Contra Costa County was going to be a primary site of the region's growth. He did everything he could to make it possible—his *Contra Costa Times* empire grew to be the only daily newspaper in the county, slowly buying up the local dailies, including the *Antioch Daily Ledger*. Lesher may never have achieved the power of an earlier generation of California media moguls like the Chandlers and the De Youngs, but he steadfastly used his influence to push and prod growth, even if it brought controversy (Steidtmann 1985).[20]

As Dan Walters (1989: 75) put it, "ContraCostopolis . . . occurred because the local power structure has been dominated by pro-development forces—developers, bankers, newspaper publishers and politicians—hoping to cash in on the surge." In 1984, Lesher was elected head of the Contra Costa Development Association (CCDA), an organization which to this point had been a publicly financed organization promoting economic development in the county since before World War II. Supported by Bishop Ranch developer Alex Mehran, Lesher quickly took the organization private, selling not-inexpensive memberships to local business leaders and establishing what would eventually become the primary business voice in the county, the Contra Costa Council (Steidtmann 1985; Goldman 2003).

Lesher's transformation of the CCDA was partially in response to the first appearance of an organized anti-growth backlash in Contra Costa County, part of a wave of anti- and slow-growth movements that had transformed local planning politics since Petaluma's landmark growth control ordinance was passed in 1975 (Dowall 1984; Levine 1999). If the county political apparatus was firmly in support of and actively producing growth, tied as they were to Lesher's growth machine, the populace had been "decidedly ambivalent" for some time (Goldman and Wachs 2003: 97). A cross-county freeway system that would have linked Moraga and Antioch through Walnut Creek had been rejected decades earlier, and the preservation of the area's rural character was important for many residents (ibid.). Starting in early 1985, local initiatives in Walnut Creek and Pleasant Hill began to restrict the very same edge-city development that had transformed the corridor and provided Walnut Creek with a tax base which remains significant today. Building heights were restricted, growth-management activists began winning seats on city councils, and a movement began to make developers pay a larger share of the costs of development, including roads and other infrastructure (Haeseler 1985; Diringer 1985a). The combined era of development fees and growth management had begun.

Linked to the growth issue was the emergence of powerful environmental organizations, both locally and with connections to major regional actors. Save Mount Diablo was begun in 1971, originally to focus on expanding the eponymous state park. By the 1980s it had begun to focus on the broader issue of development as a whole, in part due to their broader geographic focus on the East Bay Regional Park system and on open space in general. Opposition in the 1970s to the high-end Blackhawk development led to support for downzoning the Tassajara Valley in 1980.[21] Save Mount Diablo steadily grew to be the most powerful local environmental organization in the county. Regional groups like People for Open Space, which in 1987 became the Greenbelt Alliance, and local chapters of national organizations such as the Sierra Club grew in membership and stature, and began weighing in on growth issues, not just on open space preservation or conservation.

Unlike more urban areas, where pro-growth politics are often contested by powerful community organizations focused on affordable housing, the rights of the homeless or low-income groups, or racial or ethnic-based politics, growth politics at the county level in Contra Costa began primarily as a matter of green versus growth, with critical consequences. A primarily white, middle-class movement, the environmental and anti- / slow-growth activists focused mainly on questions of preservation—preserving quality of life, preserving the environment. The Walnut Creek and Pleasant Hill fights, which were paralleled in jurisdictions throughout the region, were, in the oft-quoted words of then Concord mayor Steve Weir, "an absolute signal to every middle-class suburban community in the Bay Area that if these issues are not resolved by the elected officials, the public will step in and do it" (Diringer 1985b).[22]

From the very beginning of the "growth wars," as they were called locally and throughout the state, Bruegmann's (2005: 163) argument for the strange ideological bedfellows produced by the anti-growth or anti-sprawl movements becomes clear: "One of the oddest aspects of the anti-sprawl campaign is the way it has altered the relationship between progressive and conservative ideas ... The anti-sprawl movement is a powerful compound of this new progressivism and a traditional conservatism."[23] Too late to stop the 680 corridor growth, activists instead fought to contain it, tamp it down, and prevent it from spreading. But the regional die had been cast, and there were major unsolved issues of equity and inclusion caused by the same office growth that had spurred the backlash.

But in the 1980s, equity and inclusion were for the most part missing from environmental organizations' list of priorities. Growth in East County was seen as a repeat of the errors of 680, rather than as a reaction to these new jobs centers, let alone the deeper issues of racial exclusion and racial segregation in which the whole county was a full participant. Despite the fact that concerns about housing affordability had been percolating in the Bay Area for some time now, and regardless of connections between environmental preservation and higher-density development around transit, the initial wave of slow-growth populism was aimed at restricting density around BART stations in Central County, instead of increasing it to house more workers. Fearing the continued rise of anti-growth sentiment would threaten growth at a more fundamental level—Walnut Creek had already gorged itself on office development, and the Contra Costa Center was in unincorporated Pleasant Hill—the growth machine took to the ballot box to propose an innovative measure aimed at the one problem everyone could agree had come from growth—traffic.

THE GRAND BARGAIN

State and Federal funding for local roads and transit has been permanently reduced. This loss must be replaced locally.

—Yes On Measure C Ballot Argument, 1986 (Contra Costa County Elections Department [1986] In Goldman 2003: 103)

In 1984, as the Reagan-era program of devolution and retrenchment marched forward and California began 16 years of Republican governorship under the then six-year-old regime of Proposition 13, local demands for infrastructure improvement continued to pile up. Reagan's federal government, meanwhile, continued a process of cutting into California's system for paying for infrastructure that his state government had started almost two decades earlier. Which did not mean that California stopped growing or that it changed its collective expectations to accept worse conditions. The state of California needed to step in, but its legislators lacked the political fortitude to pass a gas tax in the face of an anti-tax lobby that was stronger than ever after 1978. Instead, it passed the buck, crafting enabling legislation that would allow counties to pass voter-approved sales tax increases with the additional monies earmarked for transportation projects.[24] Santa Clara County acted almost immediately, passing a measure that year to expand three highways to serve the county's booming tech industry.[25] Alameda County followed in 1986, as counties around the state began to look into following the Santa Clara model, even if the politics were growing more complex.

Growth interests and growth managers in Contra Costa County were similarly interested in a sales tax measure, not simply because of the dollars it would provide to alleviate clogged freeways, but because of the growing backlash against growth. Mehran and Lesher had begun rallying the business and development community around the idea even before Santa Clara passed its measure. The anti-growth backlash threatened the interests of the developers, and of the business leaders in the developers' camp. The Walnut Creek–style backlash and mounting incorporation fights meant that local residents could clamp down on all growth, including the burgeoning edge cities. Of course this impacted those already heavily invested in the edge-city properties. But for developers less tied to specific lands and happy to build in the politically and geographically wide open spaces of East County, the fear was of a new financing method being cooked up to meet the post–Proposition 13, neoliberal-era infrastructure problem: development fees, just like those that would eventually be used to build the bypass discussed in chapter 2.

The first step was the formation of a Transportation Advisory Committee (TAC), chaired by a county supervisor who was also a member of the Metropolitan Transportation Commission (MTC), and including five city representatives, two developers, a major East County employer (Dow Chemical), a second supervisor, and the League of Women's Voters. The TAC first took on the task of reorganizing planning efforts at the county level in order to create a more streamlined process for transportation planning and construction. This new and more powerful agency, which would eventually become the Contra Costa Transportation Authority, required an act of the state legislature. As forces gathered around a bill sponsored by a Concord-based assemblyman, the first real divisions began to appear. MTC feared ceding its limited authority to this new agency "below" it, and cities feared a new powerful agency "above" it. After lengthy negotiations and a slight reorganization of the TAC, MTC and county officials worked out a deal that would functionally mimic the Santa Clara system: counties could authorize a tax provided it had an expenditure plan approved ahead of time by local governments, the board of supervisors, and a majority of voters, and just as importantly, they could administer these new funds themselves if they chose to do so.

Hoping that technical expertise would seem more appealing than increasingly unpopular developers, the TAC and its political and corporate backers asked public works engineers to draft a plan for the ballot. Ranking 158 candidate projects on congestion, traffic accidents, and traffic volumes, the engineering experts were politically savvy—they consulted public opinion polls to determine what types of projects would be popular, and chose high-profile projects they felt would generate county support. In the end, 18 projects would be financed by a half-percent sales tax over 15 years, for a total of $590 million. It included almost all of the major projects in the county, among them a BART extension to Pittsburg and the widening of Highway 4.

Only one major project failed to make the list, scuttled by objections from nearby homeowners: a light rail line in the San Ramon Valley along the now burgeoning job centers of the 680 corridor. This line would have connected Pleasanton and Walnut Creek through the increasingly wealthy and now incorporated valley. Central County now had its own ghost in an increasingly exclusive machine.

From Failure to Unholy Alliance

The remainder of the story is well known in county planning and development circles, always popping up in interviews with political actors of the time, for it signaled a new era of development politics and a new set of political relations and a new group of institutional structures. Backed by virtually the entire growth machine—most major elected officials, business groups, major employers like Chevron and Pacific Bell, civic associations, labor unions, and the newspapers—and confident in the polling data, supporters of what had become known as Measure C were confident going into the campaign. They raised more than their $600,000 goal, had four full-time campaign workers, and a campaign they felt acknowledged some of the criticisms of the plan as a developer bailout. It was touted as part of an "integrated program" including development fees that would ensure that "future growth pays its own way" (Contra Costa County Elections Department [1986] in Goldman 2003: 103).

The opposition was smaller, less known, and much less flush, raising only $1,400 for their campaign. Led by Concord Citizens for Responsible Growth director Byron Campbell, the volunteer-driven effort, which included the still-separate People for Open Space and Greenbelt Congress and local chapters of the Sierra Club, launched an attack against the measure as "developer relief, not traffic relief" (ibid.). It simultaneously raised concerns about the inherent regressiveness of a sales tax with its unfair impact on seniors, the poor, and the noncommuters.

But there was a geographic component to their objections. Too much money, too many projects, and too much power in the new CCTA, which would be funded as part of this measure, went to East County, as opposed to "most needed" projects in Central County. East County projects should be financed with development fees, argued the measure's opponents, rather than the tax dollars of the county as a whole.

Despite polling numbers that showed support for the projects themselves, the measure lost. As one longtime transportation planner explained it, the only true sense of urgency came from developers and opponents—there was no real popular base for support. It was never clear if voters understood what was on the ballot, part of California's tradition of voting on complicated infrastructure financing bills that would confuse even an expert.[26] Yet there is an easier explanation for why the 1986 bill failed: East County (54 percent) and West County (55 percent) both supported it, but it got crushed in Central County, getting less than 43 percent of the vote in Pleasant Hill, Walnut Creek, Lafayette, Clayton, and Moraga.

Supporters quickly regrouped, and this time they reached out to the environmentalist coalition that had helped to defeat them. In what the *San Francisco Chronicle* called an "unusual coalition," what many locals referred to as the "grand bargain," and what one prominent player in the new coalition called an "unholy alliance," Campbell and many key opponents agreed to come on board in exchange for two things: a seat at the bargaining table (which they retain to this day) and an innovative growth management plan, which would establish the first urban growth boundary in the county and require that each municipality have an approved growth management plan in order to receive funds under the measure.

Despite continued objections from some environmental, slow-growth advocates and the region's most legendary active conservative politician, Assemblyman Bill Baker, the second Measure C passed easily with 57.5 percent of the vote, 10 percent higher than 1986. One look at the vote totals by county shows that the environmental coalition brought on board was not county-wide, but represented a very specific group of people—Central County supporters. The percentage of Yes votes in Danville, Lafayette, Moraga, and Walnut Creek jumped more than 15 percentage points, and a majority of voters in every municipality were now on board, despite the fact that the list of projects, supposedly a developer sellout that too heavily benefitted East County, barely changed at all.[27] With power to draw up growth management plans in the hands of local jurisdictions, East County municipalities largely remained free to do what they pleased. Essentially, Central County growth opponents secured their own power to further clamp down on growth in their backyards. At the same time, they made themselves a force to be reckoned with in county development politics for years to come.

Ghosts in the Unholy Machine

The innovativeness of the growth management program, which established mechanisms for CCTA to require municipalities to submit growth management plans to receive Measure C funds, garnered national attention, and much has been made of the unholy alliance and the grand bargain. Lost in the story are the "equity" concerns and the geopolitics of East County versus Central County. East County was constantly portrayed as a tool of developers, its residents as newcomers who should pay their own way. But the residents of Central County had never paid their own way—East County residents had paid for BART as long as they had with no service to show for it. The nation and the state built Central County a freeway, all during a time when developers ran their politics just as much as they did in East County in the 1980s.

The logic of development and developers paying their "fair share" or their "own way" makes inherent ahistorical sense, but it becomes problematic when seen against a historic geography of wealth created under different conditions. The demands for reform from relatively wealthy Central County residents on the newly developing east are reminiscent of the debate between the developing world and the developed world over greenhouse gas emissions. The developed world wants the developing world to limit its impact because the impact on climate change by two centuries of Northern industrialization has taught us that this is bad, while the global South says no—you got yours, now we need ours.

Ultimately, Measure C provided millions of dollars in transportation financing that made a BART extension to Pittsburg and an initial Highway 4 widening for East County possible. Both Measure C and its renewal, Measure J, cannot be seen as anything less than "fair" in terms of their geographic distribution.[28] But for East County, it was still too little, too late. The self-help efforts of local jurisdictions, the locals being "creative" to replace funds locally, was not enough to offset the absence of major top-down funding and the geohistoric advantage of Central County.

Moreover, the ghost of the missing light rail line, sacrificed in an effort to appease Central County voters, furthered the division of the county. Just like countries of the global North, the wealthy residents of Central County were not willing to make "sacrifices" to their quality of life—in this case a mass transit line to potentially connect thousands of workers to the new job centers in their backyards, even if it would have reduced emissions and preserved the environment they supposedly cared for. Those sacrifices needed to be made over the hill in East County, for, after all, that was where the sprawl was, and thus they were the problem.

The rail line, which was designed to run along the old San Ramon Branch Line of Southern Pacific, is still owned by the public, which purchased it for a transit right of way following the end of train service in the 1970s. Today it is the Iron Horse Regional Trail, an incredibly pleasant biking and walking trail that bisects the wealth of the 680 corridor, primarily carrying residents fortunate enough to live there on their evening strolls and weekend bike rides. With great access to multiple BART stations, it is central to the hopes of local bike planners for more "sustainable" forms of mobility. Yet as John Stehlin (2015) shows in San Francisco, this new sustainable form of mobility is increasingly reserved for the wealthy. Moreover, wealthy residents' livability and "sustainability" came at the expense of the region's version of the same.

In a piece for the *San Ramon Patch,* local resident and writer Camille Thompson unwittingly summed up the attitude perfectly. Chronicling the "brief history" of the Iron Horse trail, Thompson recounts how "concerned citizens" spoke out against using the corridor for mass transit in the early 1980s, "citing the potential hazard for area children, given the fact that seven schools bordered the strip of land." This was the first step in obtaining votes by the San Ramon, Danville, and Pleasanton city councils to oppose transit and favor a biking/walking trail, decisions soon imitated at the county levels in both Contra Costa and Alameda counties. With classic nostalgia and absolutely no sense of irony, she concludes by inviting readers to stop and "listen closely" the next time they are on the trail, for "with a little imagination, you might be able to hear a train whistle off in the distance."[29]

DOUGHERTY VALLEY

Dougherty Valley offers an alternative way of life. Instead of contributing to the distant sprawl of suburbia, Dougherty Valley is a proposal for an infill development—a residential community planned as a cluster of neighborhoods.

—1992 Dougherty Valley Specific Plan, P. 1–1

One should not mistake the "grand bargain" for peace accords—it was more like a cease-fire. Less than four years later, the county was embroiled in a development controversy whose impacts would be felt all the way to Sacramento. The fight is famous in California planning and development circles for spurring both questions and legislation regarding the link between water, water agencies, and urban development. What gets less attention is how the Dougherty Valley debate fundamentally raised, and never came close to answering, a second geopolitical question: what is infill development? It is in this question where one sees just how dysfunctional the politics of development can be, and how any true "solution" to workforce housing and sprawl issues was never really on the table.

Dougherty Valley was a fairly desolate stretch of unincorporated grazing land when Measure C passed in 1988, literally the next valley over from the San Ramon Valley and Bishop Ranch. Rob Haeseler's (1995: A1) imagery of "burned-out and bullet-riddled cars [as] the only sign of human passage" is an excellent reminder of just how far out Contra Costa's undeveloped valleys can feel. Recognizing that the valley was the next big battleground for development, slow-growth advocates attempted to restrict growth in the valley in the 1988 general plan, only to be rebuffed.

Emboldened by their new political position and growing base, the slow-growth community came back with a proposed ballot measure in 1990, which would have effectively pushed the county out of the development business by severely restricting unincorporated development. The county countered with its own proposal that was much more pro-development, one that maintained the possibility of unincorporated development but created an urban limit line to map and define the county's urban future. The proposal called for a 65 / 35 split, with 65 percent of the county's land mass reserved for open space, agriculture, and other nonintensive, nonurban uses (although permitting exclusionary five-acre ranchettes). In a very strategic move, the county, backed by development interests, named their measure Measure C, after the landmark transportation bill of the great compromise. It won, and the environmentalist bill, Measure F, lost.

At the same time, two major developers, Shapell Industries and Windemere Ranch Partners, working together with the county's planning department, unveiled plans for an 11,000-unit, 30,000-resident development on almost 6,000 acres. The Dougherty Valley plan, as it became known, would generate multiple lawsuits and a steady stream of controversy long after the lawsuits were settled in 1995. All told, eleven groups—four cities, five environmental groups (including Greenbelt Alliance and the Sierra Club), an Alamo community group, and the East Bay Municipal Utility District (EBMUD)—sued the county on two occasions different following the 1992 approval. The developers sued EBMUD for failing to provide water. The developers also raised money to defeat environmentalist directors at EBMUD. Meanwhile, an anti–Dougherty Valley candidate won election in November 1992 to the county board of supervisors on virtually this item alone—but the development still passed.

When one reads the earnest language of the 1992 Dougherty Valley Specific Plan, it is written in the language of infill and sprawl-busting, specifically aiming at providing workforce housing for the new edge-city workers. It states: "Dougherty Valley represents one of the few remaining large sites close to existing and expanding job centers and major transportation corridors" (2–3), arguing as well that the constant grazing over the years means it is not a particularly environmentally sensitive site, capable of development with limited impacts. It is two miles from Bishop Ranch, approximately five miles from the new West Dublin BART station. The plans called for 25 percent affordable housing, some townhome and apartment buildings in addition to single-family homes, and biking and walking trails linked to nearby shopping.

In many ways, it reads a lot like Antioch's Southeast Specific Plans, full of ambitious language about transit, jobs-housing balance, pedestrian and bike paths, anything but typical suburbia. There would be mixed use in higher density nodes around a new light rail line running up from 680 and a future BART station. It repeatedly emphasized its contribution to providing homes for local workers priced out of the increasingly unaffordable housing in the Tri-Valley area. The authors argued that the plan was consistent with Measure C, falling inside the voter-approved urban limit line and "consistent and supportive" of the ideas at the heart of the measure. Moreover, they clearly recognized the power of the environmental organizations, stating, "this plan appears to be in keeping with the policy recommendations of various organizations, such as the Greenbelt Alliance, Bay Vision 2020, Sierra Club and Bay Area Council, in creating a jobs / housing balance in the region" (3–8).

The rhetoric of supporters mixed classic disdain for the new geographies of sprawl that Dougherty Valley was meant to contain with righteous concern. Here is Tom Koch, who made his name in the county as the spokesman for this development before moving on to the Measure F fight in Brentwood: "People might be able to find a job in San Ramon but they have to live in Manteca or some other Godforsaken place. Rather than throwing our hands up, we're trying to address it foursquare and proactively . . . We'll probably provide housing to people who make as little as $30,000 a year" (quoted in Haeseler 1995). In approving the project, board of supervisor chair Sunne McPeak, whose tenure on the board was part and parcel of the pro-growth 1980s, argued that the project was necessary to provide housing for the estimated 100,000 people forecast to work in Tri-Valley office buildings in coming years. "If the housing is not in the Dougherty Valley for those jobs, it will be in Modesto or Tracy," McPeak said. "We need to have housing for jobs" (quoted in Hallissy 1992: A19).

Nevertheless, environmental groups protested virulently, including groups like Greenbelt Alliance that were specifically founded with an urbanist bent, recognizing that density in the core was critical to open space preservation on the fringe. Their argument was not against affordable housing, but that this was not really "infill."[30] As they made clear in a 2003 policy memo, infill in their eyes would be on the 680 corridor itself, not a valley away (Greenbelt Alliance 2003). Their argument about another ballot measure—that it used "environmental rhetoric to gloss over a business-as-usual approach"—could easily be applied to key objections to Dougherty Valley. The gist of their argument was that the development claimed to be affordable infill development for the masses, but it was just sprawl with better bike paths.

Pro-business groups like the Bay Area Council countered with accusations of NIMBYism, and Dougherty Valley slowly chewed up headlines and hearing time as it became a lightning rod for the growth and development wars of the early 1990s. When the last of the lawsuits was settled in 1995, the development was allowed to proceed largely as it was designed, with some additional open space and money for an environmental fund, not to mention promises of affordable housing and the tantalizing potential of mixed use and transit.

Now, almost two decades later, Dougherty Valley is a place, part of the city of San Ramon, somewhat finished and seemingly incomplete. One can sense why the residents of the newer part of Brentwood look to San Ramon for inspiration, for the two places feel similar—everything new, lots of golf courses, cul-de-sacs, schools and streets named after wildlife, the bright green lawns made brighter by fairly barren hillsides generally burnt beige by the arid California climate.

The main drag of Bollinger Canyon Road has a landscaped median, a three-dimensional space of drainage and foliage that at times feels like part of one of the golf courses it bisects. This is the space for the light rail that was never built, which was never going to be built, and which, in the words of the developer who sold the project to citizens in part based on the promise of something different, is never going to be built "in your or my lifetime" (quoted in Farooq 2005). The idea keeps percolating, and along with plans for various formulations of BART and light rail for the 680 corridor, is occasion-ally studied, including a detailed analysis in preparation for the renewal of the transportation sales tax in 2004. (Like the other light rail plan in 1988, this never made it into the measure.) Not only would it cost billions now, but many anticipate that the new residents of Dougherty Valley, who moved into a development offering "an alternative way of life," would oppose it (ibid.; Dougherty Valley Specific Plan, p. 1–1). The only thing that can be argued that is truly "alternative" about Dougherty Valley from previous iterations of suburbia is that it is roughly half Asian.[31]

The Dougherty Valley Dilemma

Twenty years in the making, few would argue that Dougherty Valley did much of anything to stop the overflow into the Central Valley or East County or set an example for the rest of suburbia. The developer-driven Specific Plan was never a true plan, not one backed by the full force of both state and capi-tal like the earlier plan to build Bishop Ranch. Bishop Ranch is at least an example of a plan that did what it was intended to do: it provided an ongoing economic and employment pole in what had previously been a bedroom county. It transformed Contra Costa County, which was its purpose. Dougherty Valley may have transformed local development politics and helped spur legislation at the state level regarding water and planning, but as a development it is just another upper-middle-class, relatively low-density, entirely suburban node in an ever more exclusive and expensive suburban valley.

The true tragedy of Dougherty Valley is not the lost hilltops, or that the developers failed to live up to their rhetoric, or that politicians bought into it or were bought by it.[32] The tragedy is that Dougherty Valley defined the planning of that time, a "debate" that was a colossal waste of time and resources on both sides. Rather than emerge from the "grand bargain" of Measure C with a new sense of the possible in the face of mounting evidence that both the postwar and neoliberal forms of suburbanization were not working, Contra Costa settled into a vicious and petty set of expensive, internecine, and completely unproductive wars.

Developers were emboldened by Dougherty Valley and kept up the pressure—next came the Tassajara Valley one ridge over, followed by New Farm in 2010, while East County went from Cowell Ranch to Measure F. Surely, significant gains were made to parks and open space, but the basic issues of core affordability, reducing the massive outpouring of people outside the transportation grid and the traditional Bay Area, shoring up the growing communities of East County that were increasingly relying on unsustainable development fees and more and more predatory debt—these did not get serious attention.

The "possible" in Contra Costa County was reduced to minor extractions from developers, a bit of parkland here and a better water and sewage plan there, nothing that was going to alter the increasingly unequal status quo. It was a status quo that benefitted both developers and the wealthy Central County suburbs whose residents made up the base of the environmental activism. And neither group deigned to alter their own land use and housing plans in a way that would make a difference for the region or those excluded from its wealthiest places.

Jim Blickenstaff, a leader with Sierra Club and Save Our Hills during the fights over Dougherty Valley, argued in the face of the final settlement of the lawsuits that the very limited gains from years of fighting, thousands of hours of work, and untold economic and political resources represented "a pragmatic solution to an imperfect world" (quoted in Ambruster 1995). With apologies to John Dewey and Charles Peirce, developers won the battle for the heart of Contra Costa County in part because they dictated precisely what was possible and therefore "pragmatic." The only power base in the county strong enough to oppose them—the environmental community—went along with the mediocre, as they were not impelled by questions of want or need but rather of preservation and conservation of a lifestyle granted them by a previous generation's racialized creation.

The end result is a politics of planning, and therefore a planning itself, which is sclerotic, fragmented, and ineffective.[33] This is what I call the Dougherty Valley dilemma: two well-armed sides, each with seemingly noble ambitions—building housing for the masses versus preserving the environment and way of life—and a bevy of lawyers, studies, and ideological frameworks, battling it out from ridgeline to ridgeline as the larger problems of society mount *regardless of who wins*. "Victory" for either side would not have solved the major problems of either housing or the environment, and certainly would have made little difference in the lives of those impacted by segregation. Dougherty Valley became the rock and the hard place of Bay Area planning, and a sad synecdoche for the region as a whole.

At its root, the Dougherty Valley dilemma is about two things. One is the comfort and wealth of both the developers and the Central County residents who fought them. They could afford to waste time and money on a battle where no matter who won, the majority of the region lost. Second, it is about the profound limits regarding what had become possible by the 1990s.

Neither the Dougherty Valley that was proposed nor the one that was built would have truly helped prevent the sprawling exurbanization of the working class and communities of color, despite the claims of its developers. Yet the site is within two miles of the most important job center built in the region in half a century, two miles from a major federally funded freeway that was part of a half-century-old mass transit plan, and only five miles from one of the few new BART stations built in the past two decades. If viewed from the regional scale, the Dougherty Valley is actually central to a major economic node, even if it was undeveloped at the time. It was not *urban infill* as commonly thought of, but it was certainly *regional infill*.

Unfortunately, our conception of what is sprawl and what is infill are determined too often by questions of form. As built and designed, Dougherty Valley is just what the environmental groups said it was, a version of upscale single-family housing, with a sprinkling of alternate forms mixed in. But once the decision was made to transform the 680 corridor and the Tri-Valley area into a massive economic cluster, the Bay Area had created a new centrality in a place that was previously peripheral. Yet the region did not shift its politics, policies, and collective imagination to embrace this new centrality. It did not act to fully connect this new center to the new peripheries that had sprung up as a result—places like East County—or transform this new center into a true and complete center. If East County's problem is that it remains incomplete, East County's problem is also that Central County remains incomplete. The problem with Dougherty Valley is not that it was developed, but that it was not developed enough. Central County had a chance to use its new centrality in a way to truly benefit all the counties of Contra Costa County, and it refused.

This failure to change conceptions of what was central and what was peripheral, of what is infill and what is not, and to act boldly and accordingly, is not only the fault of Contra Costa's divided, entitled, and sclerotic politics of development. Dougherty Valley's centrality, its "infillness," is something that can only be seen at the regional scale, not the county or the local scale. Seen only from Walnut Creek or Lafayette, it is the undeveloped fringe. But from the regional perspective, the Bay Area as a whole failed to adjust to the new centrality of the edge cities, to understand the postsuburban possibilities and build this job- and freeway-rich intersection of Contra Costa and Alameda counties into a true new center. Part of the problem is that some saw anything built in Dougherty Valley as sprawl and as suburbia, a view which reinforced the ample and powerful local inertia for limited and unequal development, leaving the region trapped in a planning and political paradigm that foreclosed the possibility of meaningful change.

Adding to this problem was that regional agencies and leaders of the core cities were trapped in their own forms of fragmented inertia, an inertia which both continued to freeze communities of color from having a meaningful role in regional-scale politics and reproduced many of the problems in the inner-city communities whose former residents sought opportunity in East County. This is what I refer to as the reproduction of Babylon, and it came with its own dilemma—the gentrification dilemma.

FOUR

The Reproduction of Babylon and the Gentrification Dilemma

Load up the U-Haul and go back to Richmond or Oakland.
— Hate Letter Sent To Antioch Resident, Read Aloud By Recipient
At Antioch Quality Of Life Meeting, July 14, 2007

Black people have been the canary in the mine.
—ANGELA GLOVER BLACKWELL, KQED's *Forum*, July 7, 2011

Oakland's Housing Crisis: "I'm the Last One Here. I Don't
Know If I Can Stay or Go."
— *Guardian* headline, April 21, 2016 (Berg 2016)

AT THE END OF THE FORD PENINSULA IN RICHMOND, just past the old Ford factory, is a small park named after Lucretia Edwards, a longtime environmental activist credited with helping to add a string of parks along Richmond's shoreline to the East Bay Regional Park District. On clear days it has one of the most stunning views you can find, from the edge of Angel Island past San Francisco and down the peninsula, over to Oakland's skyline and sea of container cranes. The Bay Trail, a planned 500-mile odyssey around the San Francisco Bay that is the result of decades of effort (with more than 350 miles completed), passes through the park.

Richmond was a cornerstone of the region's original industrial geography, at the center of the previously discussed nineteenth-century suburbanization of heavy industry. This northward tilt of the heaviest and dirtiest of industries matched the general orientation of the region's military-industrial base, both before and during its wartime expansion. With a handful of important exceptions—lead smelting in San Jose, Moffett Field in Mountain View—both heavy industry and the military bases of the region primarily stretched in an arc from southeast San

Francisco over the bay to Oakland and Alameda and northeast along San Pablo Bay and the San Joaquin River. This is also where the major manufacturing plants were located before postwar transformation—the Ford plant was in Richmond on its eponymous peninsula, Chevrolet (later General Motors) was in the heart of East Oakland.

It is to these types of places that many communities of color, especially African Americans, migrated during the war. The history of diversity in the Bay Area is specifically tied to military-related industry. The presence of African Americans and Filipinos in Pittsburg and Vallejo is not the generalized result of industrialization or the Great Migration, but specifically related to jobs that grew out of World War II and the military complex which evolved from it. The early history of African Americans in Richmond cannot be told without the history of Kaiser's shipyards, in San Francisco without Hunters Point Naval Shipyard.

Standing at Edwards Park, one is tempted to focus on what has changed, on the sailboats occupying the cove that Henry Kaiser used to build the most productive World War II shipyard in the country, or the partial transformation of the old Ford plant right next door into a mix of event space, a hip restaurant, and a solar power corporation. But to only see what has changed on Richmond's waterfront masks two other transformations that are more difficult to see from Edwards Park, transformations which would lay the foundation for the building of East County and Contra Costa County, and for the development of this new, more mobile form of segregation.

The first is hard to see because it largely occurred at the other end of the bay. If Richmond and the "Cities of Carquinez" were at the heart of the nineteenth-century Bay Area economy, the postwar and neoliberal-era economy would re-center itself in the South Bay. Over the course of the second half of the twentieth century, Silicon Valley and Santa Clara County became the major economic and employment engine of the region. Santa Clara County would become a jobs machine, pushing San Jose past San Francisco in population. San Francisco, which had largely avoided the abandonment that befell so many central cities in the United States during the postwar era, toggled between its longtime role as an economic and cultural center and its new life as an expensive, urbane suburb of Silicon Valley, ultimately becoming both. All of this economic growth meant that between 1970 and 2012, the Bay Area generally ranked first or second in terms of per capita income for large regions in the United States (Storper et al. 2015).

What had once been a relatively wealthy region known for its culture, politics, and landscape became a global economic icon.

The second is hard to see from Edwards Park because it is behind you, blocked by yet another highway built through a historically black community. This is the center of Richmond, the Iron Triangle, a neighborhood that is symbolic of the fate of the racialized cities and neighborhoods of the old, heavy industrial part of the bay. At the same time during which Silicon Valley was transforming into an economic supernova, large parts of military-industrial cities like Oakland and Richmond, and especially its trapped communities of color, faced a daunting problem of growing and endemic poverty, violence, and environmental illness.

One part of the region was able to embrace full-tilt economic transformation while largely preserving its housing stock and natural environment. The investments in suburban residential developments in East County and "edge city" office developments in Contra Costa County and east Alameda County paled in comparison to the massive infusion of capital into both the companies and built environment of Santa Clara County specifically and Silicon Valley more generally.[1] Silicon Valley grew primarily in the light industrial zones of postwar suburbia (which it would pollute and then somewhat clean up [Pellow and Park 2002; Szasz and Meuser 2000]), not the heavy industrial zones that had been marked much earlier and then became the sight of heavy wartime industry.

Meanwhile, another part of the region largely stagnated economically, unable to redevelop economically or in land use terms in a way that would have overcome the immense challenge of a racist and environmentally destructive past. Deindustrialization and containerization transformed the waterfront; the closure of Hunters Point Naval Shipyard in 1974 presaged post–Cold War demilitarization in the late 1980s and early 1990s. Freeway-building during the era of urban renewal hemmed in many of these communities against an increasingly polluted and decreasingly economically vibrant heavy industrial grid. What was left behind were often either semi-derelict brownfields or high-polluting, low-employing refineries that the region needed to survive but which were dangerous to live next to.

While some cities that were home to heavy industry saw some redevelopment, what did get redeveloped was fragmented—cut off physically or fiscally from the cities and neighborhoods and people it needed to help. The major brownfield sites along the waterfront, the places that tended to be connected physically to communities of color, largely remained underdeveloped. This was particularly true of the old military sites that ring the shore, with the exception of the two bases *not* attached to communities of color.

Thus while one part of the Bay Area cemented itself as the center of global venture capital, another part saw conditions worsen and urban inequality deepen, in part because it could not equitably transform (or transform at all) the military-industrial legacy upon which these ghettoized communities were built in the first place. This was the Bay Area's original Faustian bargain—this deep link between military-led, waterfront industrialization and racialized communities—coming back to haunt it. The end result was that despite the immense wealth created over this period, redevelopment and reinvestment in the spaces and places that helped lay the foundations for both the region's economy and its diversity did not occur at a scale which would have potentially made a difference in regional restructuring.

This highly uneven redevelopment helped further the historic socioeconomic and racial gulf between the West Bay and the East Bay, between Zone 1 and Zone 2 in the analysis shown in the first chapter, between the nexus of Silicon Valley and San Francisco and that of Oakland and Richmond. The transformation of the former is the subject of the next chapter, one that also examines the steady closing off of the two suburban counties—Marin and San Mateo—which were best positioned geographically to house workers from the job machines of San Francisco and Santa Clara, or those displaced by crime and violence in Oakland and Richmond. They instead became larger versions of Contra Costa's Lamorinda—wealthy, white, environmentally aware but increasingly exclusive.

This chapter focuses primarily on Richmond and Oakland and the military-industrial spaces of the Bay Area, on important African American places that struggled with the long legacy of ghettoized segregation and its geographic relationship to highways and heavy industry. While the production of East County and the new map of segregation is about far more than the African American experience, as Angela Glover Blackwell's quote at the beginning of this chapter makes clear, there is much to be learned by studying what happened to black cities and places during this period. The hate mail that also opens this chapter may be ignorant of the long and diverse history of people of color in places like Pittsburg and Vallejo, but there is a basic truth to this racist allegation. Many of the people of color, and people in general, who comprised the Cities of Carquinez and the fast-growing communities of the northern San Joaquin Valley home did come from Richmond and West County, from West and East Oakland, from the Bayview–Hunters Point neighborhood in San Francisco or the other racialized pockets of the region impacted by crime, struggling schools, environmental illness, and other classic "inner-city" problems. For despite vast economic growth, an increase in elected power for communities of color, ample development possibilities, and much more, parts of Self's Babylon got reproduced or, in some cases, got worse.

In continuing this book's focus less on the sociology of why people move in favor of the political economy of why they had to, most of the chapter looks at the changes that did or did not happen in these spaces. It examines the struggles of downtown development, brownfield redevelopment, and the lost opportunity that has been the redevelopment of the old military bases. It examines the interlinked violence of air pollution and homicide that plagued these communities during this era, part of a set of issues which the fiscally challenged cities were unable to meet.

In doing so, it highlights the same mix of local responsibility and collective failure that marked the previous chapters. But it also discusses a profound dilemma particular to these communities. During this entire period of fiscal stress, development woes, rising air pollution, and horrifying homicide statistics, housing prices kept rising, even in the most impacted communities. Oakland, Richmond, San Francisco's Bayview, and most of the communities at the heart of the earlier maps of segregation became less healthy and more expensive simultaneously.

This paradox is one part of what I call the gentrification dilemma. On the one hand, conditions for longtime residents do not necessarily improve, but housing prices still rise, making the decision to leave all the more logical. On top of this, the only pathway to much-needed transformation on offer is one whereby the communities who need the change are pushed aside in favor of wealthier newcomers. Local actors are then forced to choose between gentrification and abandonment, between investment that does not help them and disinvestment that makes things worse but never more affordable. As in the case of Dougherty Valley, it is a dilemma whereby no matter which option is chosen, the change that is needed does not happen. When combined with expensive standoffs like Dougherty Valley, it is a formula for a regional political economy of development utterly unable to deliver the type of region its residents need.

One of the challenges of writing about the struggles of places like Oakland and Richmond is that even balanced work can reinforce problems. We have a terrible habit in America of denying places their complexity, of finding perverse comfort in one-dimensional views of communities, be they tony suburbs or impoverished urban neighborhoods or entire cities like Detroit. Richmond is as complex as they come—hyper-diverse with a cutthroat politics of race, class, oil, economics, and environmentalism; a middle-class suburb and postindustrial city all in one; a massive, sprawling, and fragmented place where the collective urban future will be made and where the past hangs as heavily as anywhere in the Bay Area. Oakland is the eighth-largest city in California, with a political, cultural, and economic diversity that is impossible to boil down, in part because it is constantly changing. Both are heavily embedded in a fast-moving and free-flowing region, where the political lines that in theory define them as cities mean less and less.

Understanding complexity is not the true challenge—representing it is. Representation often reinforces problems, even those it is attempting to combat. To write this section accurately, I must talk about pollution and violence, but to do so risks reinforcing the idea that Richmond and Oakland are dirty and violent ontologically, i.e., at the core of their being, almost by definition. But the truth is that they are places with violence and air pollution, not inherently violent or dirty places. This violence—for as environmental justice scholars Lindsey Dillon and Julie Sze (2016) have made clear, "toxic ecologies" are a form of violence, especially when distributed in unequal and racialized ways—is not evenly distributed within these cities or among its residents, workers, and visitors.[2] But by quoting homicide statistics—numbers that capture a tragic reality which was all too real—one runs the risk of furthering the reputation of these places as places to avoid. This furthers the cycle of abandonment, and as I will discuss at the end of the chapter, deepens the grip of the gentrification dilemma that forecloses even more the possibility of real transformation.

Focusing on problems also risks misrepresenting the complexity of people's lives, and limits their agency in making decisions, a problem that again tends to plague studies of African American lives, especially by white researchers. Since the earliest days of mass suburbanization, there has been a debate about why people move. Are they being lured out to the suburbs by what is on offer, or pushed out by problems in the inner city? This debate has had a particular salience in research on African American suburbanization (cf. Marshall and Stahura 1979). While the "pull factors"—larger, more affordable homes, yards, better schools, etc.—may be equally tempting across racial lines (even if what is on offer is far from equal), push factors are imagined to be a greater factor for communities of color who are stuck in ghettoized forms of segregation.

The limited studies that have been done on motivations for African American suburbanization in the Bay Area show a complicated story full of both push and pull factors (Ginwright and Akom 2007; San Francisco Mayor's Task Force on African-American Out-Migration 2009). This was corroborated by fieldwork done for this project. While many African Americans I spoke to formally and informally referred to wanting to get away from certain aspects of where they had come from, many others moved for classic suburban reasons—bigger houses, a lawn, an investment opportunity. While we should be concerned about the push factors which are stark and troubling, we must be vigilant in remembering that there is nothing unusual about black suburbanization. In a nation that built an economy and a middle class and a way of living around a particular urban form, why would it be a head-scratcher when people move? As I discussed in chapter 1, Jake Wegmann and I also found definitive proof that this was an economically rational decision when it was made at the time. There is nothing abnormal about people of color suburbanizing. It is not a "problem" in and of itself.[3]

Moreover, some of this migration was driven by an even older migratory push, one that far predates suburbanization: family. In situation after situation, people I spoke to in the exurban Bay Area had moved there from the inner Bay Area because someone—a parent, a sibling, a child—had moved there before them. Push factors may give these processes their start, but there is a certain degree of path dependency that is then created. This is true for migration all over the world, as family is known to be a critical reason for movement, especially outside the conflict zones and refugee crisis (cf. Santacreu, Baldoni, and Albert 2009).

Yet with all these caveats in mind—the need to be conscious of representation, or the concern about treating African American suburbanization as somehow bizarre or other—there are some overwhelming push factors that coalesced during the 1980s and 1990s in particular to make "exit," in the language of Hirschman (1970), seem necessary. Push factors for certain communities in key parts of the Bay Area were so numerous and so powerful over the past 40 years that the only debate can be over how they interact.

Another challenge of representing places like Oakland and Richmond is the tendency to focus only on problems—which reinforces the negativity—or the inverse focus on rays of light and accomplishments in the face of daunting challenges. Filed under the latter category are the many ways in which Bay Area activists have helped make the notion of environmental justice (EJ) mainstream. This is particularly true in Richmond, where the work of groups like the West County Toxics Coalition and the Laotian Organizing Project have helped the city counteract the purely negative image it often has, instead becoming known as a "cradle of the environmental justice movement, here and across the world" (Karras quoted in Bernard 2012: n.p.).

EJ activists in West Oakland have worked diligently to document levels of toxicity many times the norm for the county as a whole (Pastor, Sadd, and Morello-Frosch 2007). Diesel pollution in 2003 in West Oakland was six times the per capita average and 90 times the per square mile average than the state as a whole (Palaniappan, Wu, and Kohleriter 2003). In Richmond and along the Carquinez corridor, West County Toxics Coalition spent 20 years fighting issues of "flaring" from local refineries, part of a long history of airborne pollution that left areas of Richmond heavily impacted. A sulfuric acid release by General Chemical Co. in 1993 sent 20,000 people to local hospitals; a 1989 refinery fire in Richmond killed eight and left a cloud over the city for almost a week (Bernard 2012).

Pollution is of course not confined to these two communities, but that does not mean it is not racialized at the regional level. A 2007 study by Pastor, Sadd, and Morello-Frosch showed distinct patterns of racialization in the region as a whole when it came to living in proximity to toxic emissions. According to their study, African Americans are three times more likely, and Latinxs twice as likely, to live within a mile of a toxic emission site than whites. They found similarly racialized patterns when it comes to non–point source pollution—i.e., pollution from cars and diesel trucks instead of factories and refineries, a fact consistent with the West Oakland study.

This combination of pollution from refineries and freeways is also symbolic of the way in which spatial inequality is often a result of multiple eras coming together, not simply the sins of one generation. In Richmond, the refining and chemical industry established long before the war mixed with postwar freeway-building to produce a particular toxic stew. Deindustrializing Oakland saw many of its factories replaced with warehouses and highways, as it embraced its expanding port in a bid to stave off economic decline. This meant exchanging one form of pollution for another.

It is these types of connections between seemingly different issues or different historical periods that have been the hallmarks of environmental justice thinking. In the words of Robert Bullard (1996), EJ is about far more than where waste facilities are cited, or about toxicity or pollution, even if that is its foundation. Over the course of more than two decades of activism and research, EJ has been used by activists and scholars to connect structural racism, patterns of segregation, environmental health, public policy, and community organizing in cities around the world. While the record of success in forcing corporations and governments to improve environmental conditions is mixed in places like Richmond, activism has helped push both Contra Costa and neighboring Alameda County health departments to be among the most progressive and aggressive in the nation when it comes to documenting and publicizing environmental health disparities.

A clear target of EJ work has been the poor environmental health in parts of the East Bay, issues that result in alarming health disparities. A prominent 2008 report from the Alameda County Public Health Department, entitled "Life and Death from Unnatural Causes," showed a stark and growing gap in life expectancy in the county between African Americans and whites. A follow-up report (Alameda County Public Health Department 2013) revealed that an African American child born in the flats of East Oakland had a life expectancy 15 years less than a white child born in the nearby Oakland hills.

In 2010, reporters Sandy Kleffman and Suzanne Bohan collaborated with Alameda and Contra Costa health departments to map these disparities at a zip code level.[4] They found similarly massive gaps in life expectancy between relatively nearby places. A resident of zip code 94597 in Walnut Creek would live an average of 15 years longer than one born in the 94603 zip code in East Oakland, where childhood asthma rates were more than six times higher. The life expectancy gap between Berkeley's 94708 and Richmond's 94801—a zip code that includes the Iron Triangle—was 10 years. The distance between the two is less than 10 miles.

It should come as no surprise by this point that the racial disparities between the Walnut Creek / Berkeley and Richmond / Oakland zip codes are stark. The former were 68 and 77 percent white in 2010, with Walnut Creek's 94597 being barely 2 percent black, roughly the same percentage that Oakland's 94603 was white. Richmond's 94801 was almost 60 percent

Latinx, and its counterpart in East Oakland 52 percent Latinx and 37 percent black.

One finds these gaps in so many basic facets of life. The Academic Performance Index, a measure used to grade California public schools, shows significant differences in school performance across these same boundaries. The simple availability of fresh food, and the excess availability of cheap liquor, vary significantly along these same postwar lines that have so long been entrenched in the Bay Area (Alameda County Public Health Department 2013). While a new map of segregation has been created, one based on mobility and not ghettoization, this does not mean that the "suburban wall" and the "white noose" have been entirely erased. The old dividing lines still matter, and their reproduction continues to be part of the process of forcing families and households to make decisions about whether to stay or go. No dividing line is starker, or more brutal, or more publicized, than homicide.

Unsafe Spaces and Breathing Room

Virtually every article written about African American out-migration from the region's core (cf. Hendrix 2001), backed up by the African-American Out-Migration Task Force and by almost every conversation I had with people who either had made the move themselves or had family who did, mentioned violence and crime as an factor. In some cases, it was more the allure of what East County and similar places offered in the positive sense. It meant the return of seemingly older forms of life no longer possible in the places where they came from—leaving your garage open, the lack of sirens, the general "quiet" that came up in many conversations.

The numbers are just as clear. Figure 6 shows the violent crime rates for the heart of the period in question.[5] While crime declined in both Oakland and Richmond during the 2000s, the 1980s and 1990s were brutally violent, and even the 2000s saw the two cities maintain violent crime rates far above state averages. Even though places like Antioch and Pittsburg were closer to the state average than uber-safe areas like Walnut Creek, it still represents a significant improvement for those who headed east.

The numbers are even more staggering when one considers homicide. Richmond and Oakland regularly made local and national headlines for high homicide rates during this era, and while the portrayal and hysteria left something to be desired, the reality of the numbers is stark. The two cities combined generally had a homicide rate 4–5 times the state average from

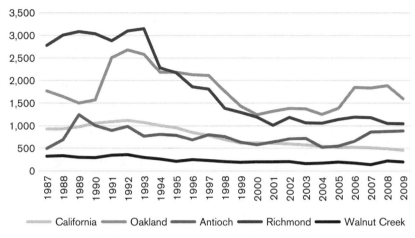

FIGURE 6. Rates of violent crime by city, 1987–2009. Source: RAND California via FBI.

1980–2014. In the horrible year of 1997, when Richmond alone saw 206 murders, the two cities combined for more than 12 percent of the total murders in the entire state, with roughly 1.5 percent of its population.

There was a deeply racial tinge to this homicide. Of the 4,279 homicide victims in Oakland between 1980 and 2014, 73.5 percent were black. Of the 4,626 homicide victims in Richmond during that time, 77.8 percent were black. During this period, 6,743 African Americans were victims of homicide in Richmond and Oakland combined, the overwhelming majority men, the overwhelming majority young. The median age of murder victims during this period never exceeded 33, and was generally in the mid-20s. In 2003, the median age of the 135 people murdered in Richmond was 23. That means half of the people murdered were 23 or younger.

As has become clear of late, but has long been an issue, violence and insecurity were not just factors for policing, but factors of policing. As part of research done on African American migration from San Francisco in general and the Bayview–Hunters Point neighborhood in particular, the San Francisco Mayor's Task Force on African-American Out-Migration (2009) found that not only were black youth disproportionate victims of homicide like in Oakland and Richmond, they were disproportionate victims of criminalization. Between the Riders scandal and the killing of Oscar Grant, Oakland made headlines because of police abuse and fatal killings of young black men, years before it became regular national news. Between 2005 and 2014, roughly half of the arrest- and custody-related deaths in Alameda and

San Francisco counties were black, far disproportionate to population.[6] When added to the homicide rates cited above, it fed what one African American leader called "the perception that this is not a safe space for young men."[7]

Dillon and Sze (2016) have recognized the linkages between unbreathable air in racialized places like San Francisco's Bayview and the struggle of African Americans with police-related violence. In an essay entitled "Police Power and Particulate Matters," they show how in many ways both of these factors are part of the "toxic ecologies" to which many African Americans specifically and people of color more generally have been subjected in the American metropolis. They quote Supreme Court Justice Sonia Sotomayor, who also uses the canary in the coal mine metaphor, but this time in reference to police violence, not new geographies of suburbanization. "No one can breathe in this atmosphere," she states unequivocally (quoted in Dillon and Sze 2016: 8).

For Dillon and Sze (2016: 7), it is the combination of violences "which have denied breath and healthy breathing spaces to low-income communities of color." Places like Antioch and Pittsburg, although not at the level of Walnut Creek or the Berkeley Hills in terms of any of the measurables discussed above, were a far better cry than the Iron Triangle or West and East Oakland. Asthma rates, violent crime rates, school performance rates—all were universally somewhere in the middle. East County was not paradise, but as I discussed in chapter 3 and will revisit in the next chapter, most of the places where the chances of dying are lowest were closed off to all but the wealthiest of newcomers. The new subdivisions out on the fringes of the region may not have been paradise as far as the numbers are concerned, but they were spaces where people could breathe. They were also a better deal.

Prices and Paradoxes

Of all the paradoxes that underlie the recent history of the region—politically progressive yet increasingly unequal, increasingly wealthy yet unable to channel that wealth into equitable city- and region-building—none seems more perplexing on the surface than the fact that the problems laid out above never made these communities noticeably cheaper to live in.

Frequently lost in the research on ghettoization, abandonment, and gentrification—three of the most fundamental processes of postwar American urbanism—is how they often go together in strange ways. Urbanism is not a

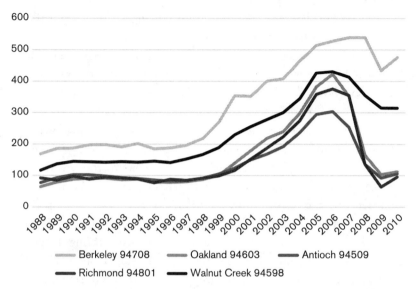

FIGURE 7. Real estate prices for 5 zip codes, 1988–2010. Per square foot, adjusted for inflation. Source: DataQuick.

zero-sum game, and housing prices are not an indicator that things are "better" or "worse" for the place as a whole.

Nowhere is this truer than in the communities discussed in this section. Using the same dataset relied on by Jake Wegmann and myself and used in chapter 1, Figure 7 shows the per square foot price of homes for sale in the four zip codes from Berkeley, Walnut Creek, Oakland, and Richmond, as well as that of Antioch. The pattern is clear. During the economically more stagnant years and hyper-violent years of the late 1980s and early 1990s, prices in 94603 Oakland and 94801 Richmond never dropped noticeably.[8] They were also in lock-step with prices in Antioch—you could essentially trade houses, which many people did. The Berkeley Hills and Walnut Creek remained one and two price levels above these communities at all times.

With the onset of the first dot-com boom in the late 1990s, prices start to rise all around. But notice the beginning of separation in Oakland and Richmond in the 2000s. They become appreciably more expensive than Antioch, even if the indicators in terms of health and life expectancy do not change greatly. By the time the crisis hits in 2007, and despite the fact that Antioch prices were buoyed by an absurd bubble, there is an undeniable gap.

As I showed in chapter 1, all of this was occurring within a regional context whereby places like Antioch were still gaining value relative to the core. If you were a homeowner in Oakland or Richmond, it seemed to make financial sense to sell out and leave. Your house in 94603 Oakland could buy the same or more house in 94509 Antioch, where it was safer, the schools were better, and the air more breathable. If you were a renter looking to become a homebuyer, the same situation was logical. You wouldn't have known that the foundation upon which Antioch was being built was so shaky. It was the logical move—according to the classic political economy framework, both your use value and your transfer seemed to gain by moving to East County.

For renters, the situation was similar.[9] If one examines the U.S. Department of Housing and Urban Development's (HUD) calculation of Fair Market Rents (FMR) for two-bedroom apartments during the period 1983–2012, two things jump out.[10] FMR for Alameda and Contra Costa area rose 27% higher than inflation, never dropping significantly during this time. But the San Francisco, San Mateo, and Marin FMR rose 53% during this same time period. Santa Clara County rose 44%. Meanwhile, FMR rose only 13% and 14% in Solano and San Joaquin counties, and Stanislaus rents in 2012 were actually cheaper when adjusted by inflation in 2012 than in 1983.

Every subregion in the Bay Area became more affordable vis-à-vis San Francisco between 1983 and 2012.[11] When examined as a percentage of San Francisco FMR, Alameda / Contra Costa went from roughly 91% of San Francisco in the late 1980s to roughly 70% by the early 2000s. Solano dropped from 86% in the early 1980 to a low of 55% in the early 2000s, never reaching above 70% during the remainder of the decade.

This multitiered rent picture created two simultaneous effects for Oakland and Richmond residents. Their rents were going up, but not as high as those in San Francisco, Santa Clara, and the West Bay. This meant that lower-income people from those areas, or increasingly middle-income renters, got pushed into the East Bay. Meanwhile, the relatively stable rent prices farther out made those areas more attractive.

As research by Jane Rongerude and Monica Haddad (2016) showed, renters with housing vouchers increasingly used them to move out from the core, in search of more affordable rental housing and more bang for their buck. They overwhelmingly located in places like East County, the Cities of Carquinez, and the Central Valley areas explored in chapter 6.

Like homeowners, it was a situation where often both price and amenities were in their favor farther away. It was affordable breathing space. As this book has tried to make clear, part of what makes this search for breathing space so problematic is that it was done under much less equitable conditions, and remained much less secure, than it had been in earlier generations for white families searching for the same space. The more affordable prices on the fringe and seemingly better life conditions masked an underlying instability when it came to transport, fiscal issues, and long-term community stability.

The brutal mix of poor life quality and high prices is a central part of the gentrification dilemma in the Bay Area, and raises the question as to why these combined push factors could not have been addressed. Why was breathing room rarely possible or affordable in Oakland and Richmond, and why did it have to be sought much farther away? It is a problem that returns us to the familiar topics of resources and responsibility and leadership, of development and redevelopment, both that which happened and that which did not. The answers are related—the inability to develop and redevelop helped drive unaffordability, and helped undermine the fiscal capacity of the cities to deal with problems.

It is a topic that brings its own racialized component, for during most of the 1980s and 1990s, both cities were led by black mayors and a black political establishment. But just like with suburbanization in East County, the achievement of political power for African Americans in certain cities came under very different structural conditions than it had for others a generation earlier.

RACIAL POLITICS AND DOWNTOWN
REDEVELOPMENT

The political clout they (African Americans) have had has not translated into real advantage.

—ANGELA GLOVER BLACKWELL, KQED's *Forum*, July 7, 2011

As in East County, many of the challenges facing leaders in Oakland and Richmond were not of their making. They had more resources than their small-town counterparts, but then they had more challenges. By the time Lionel Wilson was elected as the first African American mayor of Oakland in 1977, capital was already headed toward Bishop Ranch and Silicon Valley. The federal government was already cutting back, poverty was already entrenched and racialized, and many of the above problems had begun to emerge in force. The industrial base was struggling but still polluting, and the 1980 deregulation of trucking would open the door to the massive growth of a goods movement industry in the area. This would help add the diesel exhaust and nonpoint pollution from Oakland and Richmond's port-trafficked freeways to the top of the already long list of environmental injustices. Add in the 1978 property tax revolt that would undermine city finances for a generation, and you have a recipe for difficult times.

One must keep in mind just how daunting a challenge African American leaders faced when they were finally able to achieve formal electoral power. They took over struggling industrial cities with entrenched urban poverty long after the bloom on the industrial rose was gone and the checks were coming due. The military occupied huge portions of the industrial waterfront, making conversion difficult, expensive, and time consuming, and the land would be held decades past its local utility as global geopolitics plodded along. In both cases, capital was able to hold them hostage. Oakland was an in-between place with neither the investment and history of San Francisco nor the wide-open possibilities of 1970s-era Contra Costa County. It also had an entrepreneurial and parasitic municipality, Emeryville, tucked between its downtown and its more bourgeois north side.

Richmond was held hostage by a different source of capital and power, Chevron, which had run the city from behind the scenes long before Kaiser built ships. Unfortunately, like their counterparts in East County and Contra Costa and Santa Clara counties, the political and economic establishment in Oakland and Richmond made critical errors, and like in these other places, the type of city and region that needed to get built or rebuilt was not.

Oakland's Loss

In 1977, following a half-century of African American struggle for power and respect in a city they had long participated in building, Lionel Wilson was elected mayor. He held the office for 12 years, becoming one of Oakland's longest-serving mayors and beginning two decades of African American presence in the mayor's office. In many ways, the Wilson administration understood the fundamental importance of urban land and development, and sought to tackle the profound need for racialized wealth redistribution by targeting black developers. But rather than recognize that decades of discrimination had left Oakland without a large enough and capable enough black development community to handle the full development needs of a mid-size deindustrializing city, they hunkered down, preferring to let projects stagnate rather than push forward.[12]

Capital was already skittish and fickle about Oakland, and in its profit-driven way cared little about their historic responsibility for Oakland's woes. They saw only crime and "bad demographics," developer code for low incomes and people of color. With powerful unions digging in their heels amidst a declining industrial base, rampant problems of cronyism and corruption, and seemingly arbitrary permit denials, Oakland quickly developed a reputation in the 1980s as a bad place to build.

This was not solely about alienating the existing growth machine but about the attempt to replace it with a black-run growth machine at a time when Oakland was becoming increasingly multiracial. By the early 1980s, Latinxs and Asians had begun to clamor for a political voice and a more multiracial form of coalition government, a push that the African American leadership, frozen out of power for so long by a white conservative establishment, resisted (Douzet 2007, 2008, 2009). Racialized controversy even raged over plans to redevelop the old University High / Merritt College site into a shopping mall, a project already dogged by allegations of corruption. When the sole viable bid on the second attempt at development was from Asian investors, some activists balked.[13]

This stagnation was critical in Oakland, but not because development is a panacea or that new offices and shopping centers would necessarily have put its struggling communities back to work, although it might have helped. It mattered because under the new fiscal rules of post–Prop. 13 California, the development was critical to staying fiscally viable to pay for the social agenda needed in Oakland—better schools, workforce development programs, crime prevention, and after-school programs. There was also a question of whether they dragged their feet. As one longtime participant in Oakland's development wars during the 1980s attested, "It was a tremendous squandering of resources in a crucial time," for two vital threats were brewing, threats that would set the city back for years.[14]

One was a threat over which they had no control: the 1989 Loma Prieta earthquake. The earthquake, made instantaneously famous nationwide as it hit on national television just before a World Series game between the Oakland A's and San Francisco Giants, punished downtown Oakland much worse than San Francisco. It fractured many of the older buildings, including numerous historic structures. This kicked an already down city, just months before the 1990 recession would make it worse. Add in existing problems like an already undercapitalized downtown core, suburban flight that was now decades in the making, a massive 1991 fire in the Oakland hills, the aforementioned environmental issues, and a violence epidemic peaking in the aftermath of crack cocaine, and things went from bad to worse. The City of Oakland ended up giving three entire blocks of valuable city-owned downtown land to the federal government for a major office complex, in the futile hope that the public sector jobs would counter the lack of tax revenue in a post-earthquake downtown.

The second fiscal threat was not an act of nature, but one very much produced by state and regional politics, a product and symbol of the region's fragmented political and economic geography. One of the many reasons capital did not have to reinvest in troubled Oakland, whether its brownfield sites or struggling downtowns, is that it could exploit a spatial loophole just next door. This loophole had a name: the City of Emeryville.

Emeryville's Gain

Emeryville was incorporated at the end of the nineteenth century as an industrial and gambling haven barely two miles from downtown Oakland. The city's claim to fame was as "the rottenest city on the Pacific Coast" during the first half of the century.[15] Deindustrialization left ample brownfields in a city that by 1970 had less than 3,000 residents. But the city had something Oakland and Richmond lacked as they faced the prospect of redevelopment— actual politics. There were few citizens in Emeryville, let alone citizens groups. They were not hamstrung by a legacy of urban renewal, racialized struggles for power, unusable military bases, or cutthroat neighborhood politics.

The leaders of Emeryville had two things in their favor as they began a redevelopment process that would see them universally lauded by redevelopment professionals and hailed as a success story for brownfield redevelopment (Dayrit, Arulanantham, and Feldman 2002; East Bay Alliance for a Sustainable Economy 2007). They had a prime location wedged between Berkeley and Oakland at the base of the Bay Bridge linking the East Bay to San Francisco, with multiple freeway off-ramps on two different interstates. And unlike Oakland, where projects could get held up for decades, they could approve a $50 million project in an hour. To quote one former practitioner who worked for the city during the 1990s, "It was like working for a corporate board of directors. You had three or four people at a city council meeting, not like 300 in Oakland."[16]

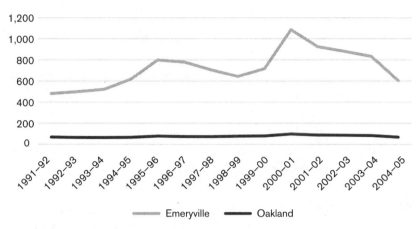

FIGURE 8. Sales and use tax revenue per capita, Oakland vs. Emeryville, 1991–2005. Source: www.californiacityfinance.com from State DOF and Controller Data.

Meetings with development staff were "like Sim City," as anything seemed possible. When Steve Jobs wanted to relocate Pixar from Richmond, Emeryville's city manager went down immediately and cut a deal. Chiron was able to locate two million square feet of a biotech plant in a project that was controversial by Emeryville standards—it took six months to approve because of a union labor question.

But the coup de grace for Oakland was the emergence of Emeryville as a retail monster. What began with the Public Market, a cinema, and a few shopping plazas in the 1980s grew into a redeveloped behemoth featuring the area's sole Ikea, Best Buy, Home Depot, and high-end "lifestyle center." With a perfect location close to increasingly upscale Berkeley and the some of the wealthiest portions of Oakland (Rockridge, the gentrifying Temescal), Emeryville massively outstripped Oakland in terms of both nonresidential investment and sales tax revenue. By the year 2000, Emeryville had almost ten times the per capita sales and use tax revenue as Oakland (Figure 8), generating roughly a third of its municipal budget from sales taxes compared to less than a sixth in Oakland during the same time period. From 1990–2008, Emeryville built 18 times the per capita value of nonresidential real estate as Oakland during an era where Oakland was more than twice as dependent than Emeryville on property tax income as a source of general revenue.[17]

There is a labor side to Emeryville's free-trade-zone-esque presence. The addition of high-tech companies like Chiron and Pixar was outpaced from a labor market perspective by the more than 7,500 service sector jobs added between 1984 and 2001. Many of these jobs are low wage, often with limited or no health insurance, and many did not pay enough to cover the basic household expenses of living in the expensive Bay Area. More critically, only 9 percent of low-wage workers surveyed in a 2003 studied lived in Emeryville—more than half lived in Oakland. In a municipal version of a 2011 campaign speech by Elizabeth Warren, Emeryville earned the profit (taxes) off of the labor that other cities like Oakland housed, educated, and kept safe (or tried to), a municipal Walmart dependent on outside public entities to bear the burden of reproducing its low-wage workforce (East Bay Alliance for a Sustainable Economy 2007).[18]

Emeryville's utter lack of organized politics would seem to some to be the antidote for Oakland's excess of politics. Oakland's leadership and community actors bear responsibility for not being able to craft an urban development politics capable of putting the city in a better place, a challenge that would continue throughout this entire period, regardless of who was in the mayor's office or the city council. There was undoubtedly some creative work done in Emeryville, and converting brownfields at the heart of the region should be lauded on principle.

Yet we must be wary of the tendency to celebrate the structural inequality reconstituted at the subregional level by a corporation-controlled municipal fiefdom. Emeryville took advantage of its lack of real politics, unearned geography, and historical moment to effectively steal from a much bigger neighbor. A fickle and mobile capital regime was all too happy to look elsewhere, content to choose the market and financial risk of Emeryville's toxic physical landscape over what they saw as the toxic political landscape of Oakland, much like they made the same choice between East County and Central County. Meanwhile, Oakland (and to a lesser extent Berkeley) bore the burden of educating and housing Emeryville's workforce *and* customers amidst growing inequality.

The fact that Emeryville stands as the region's most "successful" case of large-scale brownfield redevelopment should not be seen as a victory over fragmented politics, but a victory of fragmented politics. Capital exploited a spatial loophole—the existence of an incorporated city with limited population and politics surrounded by a city with a large workforce and consumer base and dysfunctional politics.[19] But while Oakland bears some responsibility for allowing Emeryville to happen, at least Oakland's leadership did not remain as closely tied to the corporate bosses who helped build the landscape of inequality in the first place, unlike their neighbors to the north.

Unlike Oakland, where African American leadership was forced to wait until the end of the 1970s to assume power, Richmond was a pioneer in black electoral representation.[20] Housing segregation, poor living conditions, and "urban renewal" evictions in the immediate aftermath of World War II led to significant community organizing. This resulted in two African American city council candidates in 1947, and the construction of Parkchester Village in 1949, one of the region's first suburban-style single-family-home developments open to African Americans. In 1959, George Carroll became the first African American candidate to run for council with both black and white support, and when he won on his second try in 1961, he became only the second African American elected city councilmember in the Bay Area. In 1964, he was chosen as mayor by his colleagues on the council, three years before Richard Hatcher in Gary, Indiana, or Carl Stokes in Cleveland, making him one of the first African American mayors of a city in America.[21] He was joined on the council in 1965 by George Livingston, and by 1969 African Americans held three council seats, the mayorship, and the vice mayorship.

Although it ebbed and flowed over the intervening years, African American political power remained consistently strong—only once between 1965 and 2006 did representation on the city council dip below two members, and that window lasted only for a year. An African American was mayor for 26 out of those 42 years. But again unlike Oakland, the larger relationship with the power structure that had existed before black ascendancy was a close one. African Americans became an integral part of the growth machine's pro-business coalition anchored by the Chamber of Commerce, the Council of Industries (COI, representing industrial companies like Chevron), and local unions, including the powerful firefighters union. Strong African American political action committees like Black Men and Women (BMW) grew to be a West County force, part of a larger, and generally conservative, African American political establishment.[22]

Nowhere is the relationship between African American political power and corporate Richmond more prevalent and more controversial than with Chevron. Chevron, the Bay Area's member of the "seven sisters" that dominated global oil production in the twentieth century, has been in Richmond since before the city incorporated in 1905. Its role in the city's politics is legendary; its century-old refinery "towers over the city both literally and figuratively" (McCarthy 2008: n.p.). Chevron largesse supported political candidates, civic functions, and for generations it has been the city's largest single taxpayer.[23] This also meant support for the African American political establishment, including longtime mayor Irma Anderson, in exchange for two things—keep the taxes on Chevron low, and allow them to keep refining as they saw fit, even if it meant increased pollution (Geluardi 2006).

It was a calculation that helped the conservative African American establishment remain in power long after the demographics had begun to shift. Like Oakland, Richmond became an almost evenly divided multiracial community. Environmental justice advocates—including many progressive African Americans long silenced by the conservative majority—began to point to the harm that the heavy industry–friendly policies of the city were having on its residents, particularly its poorest.[24] It would take until 2006 before a multiracial coalition on the Left would unseat Anderson and Chevron, but that was far too late to make a difference for the many Richmonders who had already moved (Schafran and Feldstein 2013). The leadership had made too many decisions that kept places like the Iron Triangle even more isolated than in the postwar days, none more important than Hilltop and Marina Bay.

Development Mistakes

If its political incorporation was the antithesis of Oakland, the situation on the ground bore striking similarities. Local private industrial employment was never strong for African Americans following the war, as discrimination made good-paying industrial jobs hard to come by. What remained were military-based jobs, especially at Vallejo's Mare Island, and public-sector jobs.[25] Industry was critical to the city's tax base, and the city struggled to attract capital investment and new employment amidst restructuring and rising social struggles. The environmental legacy of Richmond's almost century-long relationship to the heaviest of industry—oil refining and petro-chemicals—and the new menace of a diesel-fueled trucking boom was beginning to take its toll, even if the environmental movement had not yet begun to focus on environmental injustice and community health.

Richmond's development errors were less about stagnation and more about bad decisions—decisions that were simply following development trends at the time. The first was a decision to develop a large mall outside of town to generate tax revenue in the face of a struggling downtown. Hilltop Mall, opened in 1976 on Chevron-owned land four miles up the interstate from downtown, was a controversial attempt to increase city revenue when the downtown was struggling. The city's quasi-suburban status and 1961 annexation of even more suburban land up the freeway helped the land deal make sense. The developer, Alfred Taubman, had already built many successful suburban malls in the East Bay, including ones in Concord and Pleasanton. Richmond could cash in on the suburban wave by annexing land and building its own suburbs.

The problem was that the mall devastated what remained of the downtown, and the downtown was part of and adjacent to the Iron Triangle, the poorest and most African American of Richmond's neighborhoods, while the mall was closer to the more middle-class hills. The impacts of the shift on the fragile economy and urban fabric of one of the Bay Area's most vulnerable communities was enormous. Almost immediately after opening, what businesses remained in the downtown began a quick migration to Hilltop. By the 1980s, downtown Richmond, physically central to many low-income residential communities, was a virtual ghost town, despite the presence of both BART and an Amtrak stop.[26]

The combined fiscal impacts of poor downtown redevelopment in Richmond and Oakland, and the emergence of fiscal parasites like Emeryville, could not have come at a worse time. Repairing the communities impacted by the historical legacy of ghettoized segregation and the toxic mix of deindustrialization, environmental injustice, violence, and suburbanization that so many black-run cities had had foisted on them during this period required resources that better decisions could have somewhat helped provide. Like the cities of East County, the leaders of Oakland and Richmond missed the limited and narrow window of opportunity to make structural changes early enough to change the map unfolding in front of them, for different reasons and under different but equally troubling structural conditions.

The failure of downtown development and its related fiscal issues were just one of many fiscal, economic, and redevelopment problems facing these communities at this time. Even more symbolic of the reproduction of Babylon is the stagnation that occurred in the very spaces which were most foundational to the region's original geography of diversity—its military bases.

During this same era, as Silicon Valley soared, Emeryville was redeveloped into a municipal tax shelter, and Oakland and Richmond struggled with their downtowns and their tax bases, some of the region's most important historic spaces stagnated. For a region so identified with its waterfront, efforts to transform the major waterfront industrial locations that built the region dramatically lagged behind other flows of investment. Brownfields and underutilized factory spaces still line the waterfronts of Richmond, West Oakland, southeastern San Francisco, and the San Joaquin River.

Nowhere is this lost capital more evident than in the massive gray spaces of the region's numerous former military bases (Map 10). Urban development throughout the state was incredibly intertwined with defense-related industries from the very beginning (Lotchin 2002). If Southern California is more known for its twentieth-century military economy, it is Northern California where the armed forces made their most spectacular physical imprint, in more than a dozen bases and supply depots strung like a necklace along the shores of the bay.

These bases did more than define a shoreline—as discussed earlier, they helped usher in the largest wave of diversity in the region's history. African Americans moved en masse during the war years, populating not only San Francisco's wartime waterfront but the shores of Contra Costa and Solano counties—Richmond, Vallejo, and Pittsburg (Archibald 1977; Moore 1989). By the end of the war, more African Americans worked at Hunters Point Naval Shipyard than had lived in the city prior to the war (Broussard 1981, 1993). Richmond's African American population went from 270 in 1940 to 13,780 in 1947 (Wenkert et al. 1967). Filipino migration, which had begun in the aftermath of the Spanish American War, shared a similar military geography with African Americans, especially after the war, when restrictions on Filipino immigration were eased and communities developed around naval bases, including Vallejo's Mare Island, which had a small Filipino community even before the war (Bonus 2000).

The impact of these bases on the surrounding landscape was physical as well as human. Mare Island employed 50,000 workers at its peak, Hunters Point close to 20,000. This meant massive needs both during and after the war for housing, schools, roads, and community facilities, let alone the significant physical impact of the bases themselves. Huge parts of southern Richmond in particular were physically reconfigured to make room for

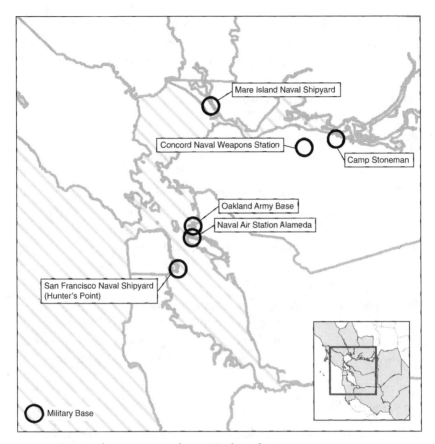

MAP 10. Bay Area bases, current and past. Map by author.

Kaiser's shipyards and the new workers, who quadrupled the city's population seemingly overnight.[27]

The economic boom was short-lived. Although one tends to think of base closure and base reuse as a contemporary phenomenon in the post–Cold War era, Kaiser's Richmond shipyard, which produced more ships during the war than any other facility in the country, closed at the end of the war. Hunters Point, the heart of the city's wartime jobs machine, shut down in 1974. Mare Island, the navy's first base on the Pacific Ocean, also built the first nuclear submarine in 1954—only to build its last less than two decades later in 1970. Even though Mare Island remained an important source of jobs through its closure in 1996, and is now home to an interesting experiment in modular housing manufacturing, it has never came close to approaching earlier levels of economic activity.[28]

It would take Richmond decades to fully redevelop Kaiser's shipyards. It was the major redevelopment effort of the 1980s, transforming the old shipyards just east of the Ford Peninsula into the Marina Bay Community. Like Emeryville, it is an impressive case of brownfield redevelopment, as the shipyards left a toxic legacy that lasted long after the last Liberty ship rolled down the gangway. With approximately 2,500 housing units, a 750-boat marina, and numerous small businesses, it certainly helped keep and attract some middle-class residents at a time when Richmond was facing the type of postindustrial struggle more common to Gary and Detroit than much of the Bay Area.

Unfortunately, Marina Bay exacerbated the physical and social fragmentation of Richmond begun by the 1961 annexations and the building of Hilltop. Marina Bay is a mix of gated and semi-gated communities completely cut off from the rest of the city, a development that chops up Richmond's industrial waterfront and further isolates the Iron Triangle neighborhood north of the newly constructed Interstate 580. If you lived in the Iron Triangle, struggling with the poverty seen earlier, you were trapped between a downtown undone by Hilltop Mall and poor decision-making, a pollution-rich and job-poor Chevron complex, and a southern waterfront whose redevelopment is more keen to keep you out than help you up.

BRAC and the Glacial Pace of Redevelopment

By the time the Cold War ended and base reuse was formally part of the agenda, the communities surrounding the bases were already struggling to one degree or another. The physical proximity of racialized poverty to wartime industry meant the end of the Cold War was a golden opportunity, not just for the local impoverished community but for the rapidly sprawling Bay Area. It was no guaranteed panacea, as the remaining industry on Richmond's waterfront had produced almost 20,000 jobs by 2000, yet only 3,500 were held by Richmond residents (Schafran 2008). Only 5 percent of Chevron's employees lived in the city (East Bay Alliance for a Sustainable Economy 2007). Local industry did not mean living-wage jobs for local residents, but it was certainly better than a mostly empty military base cum brownfield.

The federal government began the process of unloading excess military land, Base Realignment and Closure (BRAC), in 1988, before the Cold War was officially over. Hunters Point and Hamilton Field both functionally closed in 1974. Hunters Point was closed formally in 1991 and turned over to San Francisco in 1993; the Presidio in 1994. The Oakland Army Base was closed in 1995, Mare Island in 1996, the Alameda Naval Air Station and Treasure Island in 1997, and Richmond's Point Molate in 1998. The biggest piece would come last—Concord's 12,800-acre Naval Weapons Station, half of which was conveyed in 2005.

But progress was achingly slow, despite more than two decades of planning time and more than a decade of local ownership. The number of jobs, housing units, new schools or parks or community facilities remained negligible during this entire period. Vallejo followed an unsuccessful downtown redevelopment—its attempt to attract white-collar business—with a head-first dive into suburbanization. It cashed in on its land reserves north of the waterfront core, eventually joining Antioch and Pittsburg in experiencing both deindustrialization and suburban foreclosure (Freire-Gibb 2012).

Hunters Point faced a similar story. Poverty and joblessness were already issues in the surrounding Bayview neighborhood in the 1960s before the shipyard's closure. Although long part of San Francisco's material and political culture, city leaders reacted to the growing problems in the vicinity of Hunters Point by casting it aside, distancing itself from this deeply historic industrial corner of San Francisco and painting it as "a container of social and cultural difference" (Dillon 2011: 21).[29]

A 2007 report commissioned by the City of San Francisco estimated that the inability to redevelop Hunters Point and the Alameda Naval Air Station meant more than 1,000 units of affordable housing and close to 16,000 jobs—more than were employed when the bases close—existed in plans but not in reality (Economic and Planning Systems 2007).[30]

When added together, the nine bases conveyed to local governments in the Bay Area, bases that employed more than 17,000 civilians when they closed, remained largely in the planning stages while East County was being built, while edge cities were suburbanizing jobs, and while Silicon Valley was exploding. Hunters Point, closed in 1974, did not break ground on its redevelopment until 2013. What is finally being built will be far too late and with far too little affordability to make a difference to a community already cut in half. Oakland's Oak Knoll Naval Hospital redevelopment crashed during the downturn due to shaky debt from Lehman Brothers, debt which brought down the SunCal Corporation that was the developer for the Alameda Naval Air Station as well. The Oakland Army Base saw multiple plans come and go, including a Wayans' brothers movie studio. Treasure Island largely remains a multi-billion-dollar vision that houses and employs few, with new development only recently beginning.

This generalized stagnation helped reproduce the racialized poverty in close proximity to the military and industrial complexes that helped produce the region's diversity in the first place. In the four well-populated census tracts wedged between Richmond's Point Molate Naval Fuel Depot and the former Kaiser Shipyards, the overall poverty rate toggled between 25% and 31% from 1970–2000, for a community which grew from 20,000 to 25,000 residents during that time. [31] This was a community that in 1980 was 76% black, with a black poverty rate of 31%. By the year 2000, the black population was only 46%, but the poverty rates for the more than 8,500 Hispanic residents and almost 2,000 Asian (primarily Lao and Southeast Asian) residents were still high—24% and 15% respectively. As Richmond's post-military neighborhoods grew more diverse, its poverty remained entrenched.

The same numbers are evident in the areas surrounding the Oakland Army Base / Alameda Naval Air Station and the Hunters Point Naval Shipyard in San Francisco. The 18 tracts in West Oakland and Alameda closest to the military agglomeration lost people from 1970, as its poverty rate jumped from 23% to 31%. By 1980, more than half the residents were black, more than a third of them were poor, and more than 70% of the people living in poverty were black. By 2000, the poverty rate had only gotten worse: black poverty was now at 41% in a community still roughly half black, but the Asian and Hispanic communities had roughly doubled, and they too had poverty rates above 20%.

Around Hunters Point, the overall poverty rate fluctuated between 24% in 1970 and 21% in 2000 amidst black poverty, which reached a high of 29% in 1990 and was 27% in 2000. By that time, the community had already lost 20% of its black residents, part of a citywide trend that would see San Francisco's overall black population cut in half by the arrival of the foreclosure crisis. In the meantime, the shipyard remained a shell, both of its former self as a jobs generator and its supposed future self as home to thousands.

COMMUNITY BENEFITS AND
THE GENTRIFICATION DILEMMA

It is tempting to view the trials and tribulations of development and redevelopment in the region's historic industrial cities through some of the simplistic lenses that urban observers like to use. The "success" of Emeryville seemed to many an example of what can and will happen when development is largely unfettered, when it occurs in the absence of politics. Redevelopment will move faster, brownfields can get cleaned up, decaying spaces can be made more economically active. The logic of the deregulationists is that if more cities were like Emeryville, the development that was needed to reduce the affordability problem and the subsequent fiscal strength needed to address community ills would have been there.

Yet this absence of politics occurred only because of a geographic loophole in the fiscal fabric of the region. The retail-heavy nature of the project meant mostly low-wage jobs. The tax revenue generated did not help regional residents, especially those who needed it. The benefits accrued almost entirely to capital, in part because the "city" of Emeryville was able to reinvest its part of the windfall to attract more capital and keep the cycle growing.

But it is not just Emeryville that is the problem. The Marina Bay redevelopment project left an entire community once dependent on that waterfront in no better shape than it had been earlier. It provided housing that largely did not help the affordability problem and contributed little fiscally during a period of great need. Marina Bay is a beautiful space, but it is not a particularly productive or inclusive space. And unfortunately, it is hard to find evidence in the Bay Area where major benefits did accrue to impacted neighborhoods, especially without being extracted from developers.

There is undoubtedly a heavy dose of political dysfunctionality in the previous sections, failure by local officials, greed by local developers, and short-sightedness by many other actors. As I will discuss in more detail in subsequent chapters, there were also many failings at higher scales, with ineffective and elitist regional governance and a state politics that could not make critical changes. There is no doubt that reform to California's CEQA law, which governs environmental review, could have made a difference. And it is clear that effective development of old military spaces was never a top priority of the military, nor did it get the attention and resources from Washington needed to make a difference.

But there is a deeper issue that must be raised about the challenges of transformation in the spaces which had been demarcated by earlier eras of ghettoized segregation. Part of the challenge of redevelopment is that both the failures and "successes" of the period sapped the political belief that positive redevelopment was even possible. Projects increasingly either did not happen after years of debate, or when they did, did not seem to benefit the people who needed them the most.

The loss of political faith is the second part of the gentrification dilemma, and works together with the seeming paradox of rising real estate prices amidst urban suffering—the simultaneous abandonment and gentrification of certain spaces. If you are a community dealing with the ravages of abandonment, poverty, disinvestment, and economic restructuring, dealing with the aftermath of redlining and postwar segregation, it seems that the only offer is change which does not help or change which does not come. Damned if you do, damned if you don't. Meanwhile, young men of color keep dying on street corners near poor performing schools and corner stores with booze and little else, all while housing prices keep ticking upward.

As I will discuss in more detail in the next chapter, some of the sclerotic politics of development that have become the hallmark of the larger cities in the region—not just Oakland but San Francisco as well—have everything to do with the loss of faith in the very possibility that building something new will make a place better. This is not just NIMBYism, for it isn't just coming from communities of wealth or from communities trying to preserve the status quo.

This is an aspect of gentrification that gets lost amidst the obviously critical focus on displacement and other factors of this now-global process (cf. Brown-Saracino 2010; Lees, Slater, and Wyly 2007)—the way in which it contributes to the general dysfunctionality of urban politics. Why would you support a development when the jobs would not go to locals, when the houses would be unaffordable, when the spaces would be inaccessible? Why would you support development when it begins to seem that all development and redevelopment was designed to benefit someone wealthier?

Part of the reason why Hunters Point took so long is that local activists had to fight tooth and nail for every single local benefit. Like with the environmental justice movement, this was an active period for community activism, but so much energy had to be put into eking out the most basic benefits from development and redevelopment that larger, more systematic and structural changes did not become possible.

The Search for Community Benefits

Evidence for the above comes in part from the emergence of "community benefits" movements and the agreements they developed during the 1990s and 2000s, in which the Bay Area was once again an important hub (Parks and Warren 2009; Wolf-Powers 2010). One of the most iconic and well known was the 2006 Oak-to-Ninth agreement. A major local developer wanted to transform the waterfront in East Oakland near Jack London

Square, and their original proposal was typically heavy on luxury housing and light on most everything else that would have benefitted the lower-income communities around them.

Yet rather than simply state their opposition, pushing the gentrification dilemma even more prominently to the surface, numerous community organizations, environmental justice organizations, and labor unions banded together into what became the Oak-to-Ninth coalition (de Leon and Greenwich 2006). They attempted to take a positive stance toward the development, to overcome the loss of faith that the gentrification dilemma had ingrained in progressive urban politics. They would support growth only if the developer agreed to concrete benefits—affordable housing, local jobs, open spaces, schools and public facilities—and put the agreement in writing. After a three-year campaign, they won benefits ranging from an increase in the number of affordable units to local hire and job training problems.

Again, people wanted development; they knew it was critical both for the actual homes and jobs and spaces it could produce and for the fiscal benefits its localities so desperately needed in post–Prop. 13 California. Solving the affordability problem, the gentrification problem, the violence problem, and the environmental justice problem increasingly were recognized as part of the same problem. Many recognized that oppositional politics were not effective. Houses were not getting built. Communities and cities did not have the resources to make improvements.

Some scholars have raised questions from a legal perspective as to the viability and legality of community benefits agreements (CBAs) (Gross 2007). Others have raised the important question of whether these private contracts between community groups and private developers are an abdication of public responsibility (Sheikh 2008). There is also a question of whether they work (Wolf-Powers 2010). But why they matter in this case is that they show the depth of the gentrification dilemma, and the way in which almost any development of size and scale required—and still requires—a major organized campaign in order to get basic affordability and local benefits. The development community may complain about how hard it is to get anything built, but they have regularly resisted attempts to legislate the types of benefits that need to be a given if the politics are going to change. After all, the handful of high-profile CBAs are few and far between, and in the greater historical sense too little too late.[32] What is often rightfully hailed in the community organizing community as a great success in the midst of strident opposition is also a sign of the unproductivity of our political economy of development. Each development had to become a campaign and a new coalition just to eke out benefits that could have and should have been commonplace. But as I will discuss in the conclusion, they also represent a kernel of hope for overcoming the gentrification dilemma and finding "common purpose."

Seen from a regional perspective, the gentrification dilemma represents an urban counterpart to the Dougherty Valley dilemma, an equally disheartening political bind where fights are long and intense and nobody wins no matter the result. The failure to find "common purpose," the failure to build a functional and productive urban politics capable of making the spaces and places necessary for basic life, is in part a result of both of these dilemmas occurring simultaneously. They epitomize what California and Bay Area planning and development politics became during this period, and help to explain why the reproduction of Babylon was allowed to continue almost unabated.

The problem of the gentrification dilemma is partly evident by the fact that two major bases were significantly redeveloped during the period of question. They were the two bases that not coincidentally fall outside of the racialized Hunters Point–Mare Island military-industrial arc. Hamilton Field in mostly white and very wealthy Marin County, which like Hunters Point closed in 1974, went to bid for reuse 25 years later. This base, in the northern stretches of suburban Marin County, is now a community of 1,000 homes, with some affordability and diversity. Unfortunately, as I discuss in the next chapter, whatever diversity and affordability was built into Hamilton would be the exception in Marin County during this period, not the norm.

But the truest symbol is San Francisco's Presidio. A historic landmark at the center of the region's history, this half-park, half-base was redeveloped under a unique public-private partnership. Redevelopment and reuse was pushed through by a power elite in the early days of the Clinton administration, so that it went from the BRAC list in 1989 to a park in 1994 and the unique public-private trust in 1996. It has attracted more than a billion dollars in private capital, rebuilding its airfield into a world-class park, constructing a digital arts campus anchored by Lucasfilm that employs more than 2,000 people, all on the edges of some of the wealthiest zip codes in the world. There was little gentrification dilemma here, for this was already predominantly the space of the gentry.

Make no mistake, the Presidio is a wonderful place, by virtually every measure. It is and should be praised, both for its natural beauty and the incredible work that went into its transformation. But one cannot escape the symbolism. The cleanest, nicest, whitest base at the foot of the Golden Gate Bridge, a perfect outpost for a "Silicon Valley by the Bay," became a gem for an increasingly white and wealthy city, while the bases that could have made a difference in the lives of so many communities of color were left to stagnate. It is also a perfect metaphor for the transformation of San Francisco, Silicon Valley, and the entire western side of the bay as a whole.

FIVE

————

Silicon San Francisco and the West Bay Wall

PERCHED ATOP A SMALL PLATFORM in the middle of a fountain in the Presidio's Letterman Digital Arts Center sits a small statue of one of the Bay Area's most famous natives. Between its historic embrace of the City Beautiful Movement and long progressive and countercultural history, San Francisco has no shortage of statues and monuments and public art projects. They honor and depict all manner of historical figures, mythical deities, and native fauna. But few embody the success and ultimate duplicity of the region quite like the statue of Yoda.

For all of the economic success that emerged from the semiconductor industry and its hardware and internet successors, *Star Wars* and the local digital animation industry it helped spawn are as much a source of regional pride as Google or Apple.[1] The latter companies may be a sign of the region's intelligence, entrepreneurial spirit, or inventiveness, but the former is a true fusion of culture and technology. As Fred Turner (2006) makes clear, what we know of as the contemporary Silicon Valley is not simply a by-product of the semiconductor industry, for other regions had made advancements in that area during the height of Cold War–era defense spending and scientific and engineering progress. Silicon Valley as we know it emerged in part from encounters between the technology of the valley and the Bohemian culture of San Francisco.

This San Francisco–Silicon Valley nexus would produce one of the most dynamic economic growth stories any region has ever seen (Saxenian 1996; Storper et al. 2015). Over the course of the latter part of the twentieth century, this encounter eventually turned both San Francisco and Silicon Valley into massive jobs engines. Venture capital poured into the region's companies.

Even amidst the cycles of boom and bust, amidst leading companies rising and falling, the engine kept churning.

This chapter examines the spaces where this engine was most powerful, the places that drove the economic cart which attracted so many new residents and so much investment. These are also the places that largely did either very little or not enough to house the people who held these jobs. They did even less for those who had suffered under the segregated conditions of the earlier era. The West Bay and the South Bay were whiter and richer than the East Bay and the Cities of Carquinez when the Silicon boom happened, and the developments over the course of the neoliberal era did nothing to change that.

In Santa Clara and San Mateo counties, it meant lots of jobs, not enough housing, few African Americans, and a Latinx community struggling to hang on even as they provided key labor that kept the place going. For San Francisco, it meant deep divides and internecine and seemingly eternal development battles, a struggle for its soul driven by two interwoven forces. One was its decreasing centrality economically, as one of the world's most famous cities became a suburb of its own suburbs. The second was a complex fusion of the gentrification and Dougherty Valley dilemmas, a process made more challenging by the city's refusal to accept its secondary status to Silicon Valley and its subsequent reassertion of its economic place.

In wealthy Marin County, it meant building a political wall, preserving an incredible natural environment while epitomizing the exclusivity of white, wealthy suburbia. A western side of the Bay originally walled off to people of color through pure racism kept the walls up through economic growth, land-use regulation, transportation policy, and class privilege. Throughout this time the wealthiest people in the region proved either unwilling or unable to contribute *effectively* to common purpose and a new development politics. They were happy to finance new stadiums, art museums, or major parks in their communities, or to otherwise work to undo some of the environmental contradictions that underlay the region's economic foundation. They worked diligently to make their communities nicer and more livable. But they did little to address the deep race and class lines upon which their region and their wealth was built, instead allowing these lines to expand over the hills and far away, into East County and beyond.

THE DUELING CONTRADICTIONS
OF SILICON VALLEY

> The growth of Santa Clara County during the years since the
> Second World War has been explosive. It has also been highly
> contradictory (Saxenien 1983: 237).

In a 1983 article, Anna Lee Saxenien, who would emerge as one of the most important scholars of Silicon Valley's transformation, provides a haunting account that feels like it could have been written today.[2] She portrays a valley that grew in every sense during the postwar era—adding 350,000 jobs between 1940 and 1970, increasing median incomes to above state and national averages, but also adding a million people.

But by the late 1970s, the contradictions had emerged. Santa Clara County supervisors made the fateful decision in 1957 not to participate in BART (*Mercury News* 2005). They wanted to build freeways instead. By 1975, Saxenian (1983: 238–39) writes, "Silicon Valley was distinguished by unbearably congested freeways, dangerous levels of air and water pollution, and a no-growth movement calling for a halt to further industrial growth. Today the county also boasts among the highest average housing prices in the nation."

As the 1970s morphed into the 1980s and 1990s and beyond, some things changed and some things did not. The freeways would remain congested, but the air pollution would slowly improve. In the late 1970s and early 1980s, Santa Clara County exceeded the state one-hour ozone standard almost once per week on average.[3] By 2000, the rate would fall to less than once per month.

The industrial growth would also continue. The torrent of venture capital had only just begun. In 1999, at the top of the dot-com boom, the Bay Area received twice as much venture capital (5.5 percent) as the next largest metro area, and almost 10 times the U.S. Metro average (Atkinson and Gottlieb 2001). The postwar job growth that saw Santa Clara equal both San Francisco and Alameda counties in terms of number of jobs would see it rocket past both during the neoliberal era (Figure 9). By 2010, even with the decline caused by the dot-com crash of 2000 and the 2007–08 downturn, Santa Clara County still had 50 percent more jobs than San Francisco. Its contradictions would also remain ever present, both ones that Saxenian identified and one that she did not.

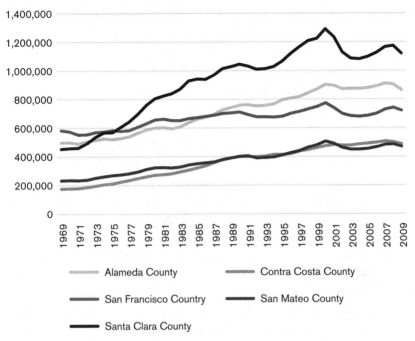

1,400,000

1,200,000

1,000,000

800,000

600,000

400,000

200,000

0

1969 1971 1973 1975 1977 1979 1981 1983 1985 1987 1989 1991 1993 1995 1997 1999 2001 2003 2005 2007 2009

- Alameda County
- Contra Costa County
- San Francisco Country
- San Mateo County
- Santa Clara County

FIGURE 9. Full-time employment by county, 1969–2009. Source: RAND California via BEA.

The Birth of the Valley

During the height of the postwar era, Santa Clara County epitomized the suburban growth machine (Walker 2007; Cavin 2012). Leaders in San Jose specifically looked to Los Angeles as an example, annexing territory left and right in the 1950s and 1960s, growing the city seemingly overnight. The city approved almost 1,400 annexations in that 20-year period (Trounstine and Christensen 1982), adding an incredible 132 square miles (more than three Parises) to its domain. It used its monopoly of the area's sewage system to force residents and small towns to agree to annexation (Trounstine and Christensen 1982). Such actions, led by City Manager "Dutch" Hamann, saw San Jose grow into the "poster child of postwar sprawl" (Walker 2007: 144). Hamann's aides became known as the "Panzer Division" for their relentless efforts to convince farmers and landowners to acquiesce to urbanization (Trounstine and Christensen 1982).

The transformation of the Santa Clara Valley from a land of fruit and nut orchards into the sprawling urbanization of Silicon Valley was Contra Costa

County at an even bigger scale. San Jose went from less than 300,000 residents to more than a million between 1950 and 1970. The city in particular was "a paradise for developers" (ibid.), a growth machine even more powerful and more aggressive than in Contra Costa County. Joe Ridder of the *San Jose Mercury News* played Dean Lesher's role as a leading booster. "Prune trees don't buy newspapers" would become his most famous comment, summing up the demise of what had once been one of the valley's most important industries and the growth machine's logic in the same sentence (Rogers 2002).

The radical transformation of San Jose in particular and Silicon Valley in general spawned a backlash. Hamann retired in 1969, and the political regime he represented was replaced almost immediately by a more growth-skeptical regime. San Jose and neighboring cities began reining in growth, limiting development, and trying to change the rules of the game that had required so little of developers and left the city on troubled fiscal and environmental ground (Rogers 2002; Walker 2007; Trounstine and Christensen 1982). The nascent environmental movement grew in strength, preserving open space, cleaning up watersheds, and doing much to clean up the damage that had been caused both by sprawling urban development and by the highly toxic semiconductor industry that drove it.

A rash of incorporations had partially halted San Jose's physical growth in the 1950s, and Silicon Valley was now a series of smaller cities stretching the length of northern Santa Clara County from the Alameda County line in the east around the bay to the San Mateo line on the other side. Stanford University's Palo Alto, long at the center of the technological side of the valley, would be joined by Mountain View, Sunnyvale, Cupertino, and Santa Clara. With Milpitas to the east and other cities to the southwest, the valley's smaller cities would eventually surpass San Jose in international fame, despite the latter's claim to being the "Capital of Silicon Valley." Apple and Google took root in Cupertino and Mountain View respectively, and these cities found themselves at the heart of the jobs machine. Although the backlash against growth did rein in the worst of local industries' environmental practices, and some cities took important steps to make companies better environmental citizens (Walker 2007), the first source of Silicon Valley's contradictions became the jobs-housing balance. Rather than put a halt to industrial development, local growth politics ended up restricting housing production instead. Housing prices at the top of the national charts only got worse, as housing production failed to keep up with job growth. One part of the postwar growth machine kept going, the other did not.

TABLE 6 Jobs-Housing Imbalance in Two Ratios

County	Average Ratio of Residential to Nonresidential Construction 1990–2010	Jobs:Housing Ratio				
		1970	1980	1990	2000	2009
Alameda	1.36	1.32	1.35	1.51	1.67	1.48
Contra Costa	2.9	1	1.07	1.26	1.34	1.22
Marin	2.73	1.02	1.19	1.5	1.69	1.61
San Francisco	0.87	1.85	2.07	2.17	2.23	1.91
San Mateo	1.26	1.23	1.38	1.59	1.94	1.73
Santa Clara	0.86	1.36	1.7	1.93	2.23	1.77
Solano	2.23	1.45	1.17	1.15	1.19	1.1
Sonoma	2.29	0.95	1.08	1.28	1.48	1.29

SOURCE: (Construction) RAND California; calculations by author.
SOURCE: (Ratio) U.S. Census; calculations by author.

Jobs-Housing Balance?

At first glance, the cities of northern Santa Clara County did build a lot of housing. Even if anti-growth measures began to come online in the 1970s, the smaller cities of the northern part of the county still added more than 50,000 units during this decade. San Jose added 80,000 by itself. Despite mounting anti-growth measures, the cities still added housing between 1980 and 2010.[4] Santa Clara and Sunnyvale each added more than 10,000 housing units during that period, Cupertino and Milpitas more than 8,000. San Jose was no longer the growth monster it once was, but it still added almost 100,000 housing units in those 30 years.

It simply was not enough to keep pace with the economic monster. During the period 1990–2010, only two counties in the region averaged more investment in nonresidential property (as a factor of value) than residential (Table 6): San Francisco, which one would expect given its historic role as the business and economic center of the region, and Santa Clara County. Contra Costa County, despite Bishop Ranch, still saw almost three dollars invested in housing for every dollar in nonresidential construction.

The end result was a steady and slow worsening of the jobs-housing imbalance. The almost 350,000 jobs added between 1970 and 1980 came with only 137,374 housing units. Job growth fell to just under 240,000 in the 1980s, but housing growth fell to half the previous decade. At is nadir in the 1990s, the county added 245,707 jobs and saw housing units grow by only 39,089, a ratio of more than six jobs for every housing unit.

While San Jose was part of the problem, its neighboring smaller cities, many of whom benefitted directly from the tax dollars generated by the tech companies in their city, were even worse. From 1980–2000, when the county saw its jobs numbers rise 60%, San Jose grew by 30% and the 12 other cities of northern Santa Clara County only grew by 20%. Cupertino and Milpitas were the only cities to come close to matching the county's job growth rate in terms of units added (49% each). Mountain View, home to Google and Facebook, grew by only 13.5%. Palo Alto, which helped launch the valley in so many ways, grew less than 10%. Only the cities of Morgan Hill and Gilroy, at the southern end of the county, 30 and 40 miles from Cupertino respectively, matched the county's job growth rates. Not coincidentally, these are the only cities in the county that are part of the 50 / 5000 club.

Neighboring San Mateo County was almost worse. It used its position in between Silicon Valley and San Francisco, with its international airport, two major federally funded north–south freeways, and a commuter rail line, to get in on the job growth, adding almost 100,000 jobs per year between 1970 and 2000. But in that same time, it added only 70,000 housing units. It added 4.2 jobs for every housing unit in the 1980s and a whopping 12 jobs for every unit in the 1990s. If it wasn't for Marin County, San Mateo would have been the worst regional citizen of the inner bay counties when it came to houseless job growth.

In a different region at a different time, these growth rates would have been fine. On the surface, they are probably ideal in terms of infrastructure, planning, and environmental impact. Growing housing units by more than 50 percent per decade is very difficult to do well and sustainably, especially if those units are built at low densities. It made sense to put an end to Hamann's "Panzer Division" and an unsustainable and wasteful era.

But the cities and counties tried to have their cake and eat it too, gorging on industrial development while not making the changes needed to house the workers demanded by such growth. They constrained only one type of growth, not another. The relationship between Santa Clara County and the region as a whole became simply a larger version of what occurred between Bishop Ranch and the rest of Contra Costa County. One place mostly adds jobs, another place builds houses. Except in this case, the two counties in the nine-county region that built housing in significant numbers vis-a-vis jobs were quite far away from Santa Clara—Contra Costa and Solano.[5] Because

Santa Clara's leaders decided in 1957 not to be part of BART, the only way to get from the house-rich places to the job-rich places was via long, polluting commutes on freeways that remain congested and overcrowded.

Throughout this time, Silicon Valley activists, leaders, and tech companies saw that the problem was growing. The valley had largely shifted from manufacturing to a mix of R&D, corporate headquarters, internet, software, and venture capital. These industrial transformations essentially offshored the class tensions that Saxenian (1983) revealed—between blue-collar manufacturing workers and white-collar engineers and executives. It also sent the pollution generated by chip manufacturing overseas. But these class and environmental problems were simply replaced by new ones. The economic divide became more about tech workers versus nontech workers (teachers, firefighters, retail workers, janitors, etc.), the latter providing the basic social reproduction needed by the former but unable to afford to live in the communities they served. And the environmental problem came from the pollution produced by all those workers commuting in from long distances to a valley that was happy to employ them but not house them.

Efforts were made. The Silicon Valley Manufacturing Group, which would become the Silicon Valley Leadership Group, partnered with Santa Clara County, local activists, businesses, and foundations to create a housing trust fund in 1998. The fund has raised more than $100 million, helping provide 12,000 affordable homes. Activists brought attention to the constant specter of rising rents and evictions, not just the problem of rising home prices. The tech industry has even begun to propose housing on its sprawling and expanding campuses. After initially rejecting it in a 2012 General Plan update, the City of Mountain View has now embraced significant housing in the area immediately surrounding the "Googleplex" (DeBolt 2012; Donato-Weinstein 2015).

But all of this is far too little, far too late, especially to offset the dark days of the 1980s and 1990s when so little housing was built. Part of the problem is that the valley's tech leaders focused more during this period on undoing the environmental contradictions of its rapid and toxic growth than it did on the human contradictions. The $100 million raised for affordable housing in two decades is half of what the Peninsula Open Space Trust was able to raise between 2001 and 2006 alone. The personal foundations of Intel and Hewlett-Packard co-founders each gave $50 million during this campaign to preserve open space, more than 25 times the donation of their companies to the affordable housing trust fund (Walker 2007; Silicon Valley Housing Trust 2016).

While the tone shifted as the problem became a full-blown crisis, the fact remains that over the past four decades, Silicon Valley leaders were more intent on undoing the terrible environmental legacy of the postwar growth machine than on correcting the inequality produced during the same era. Like leaders in central Contra Costa, Marin County, and most of the wealthy parts of the region, they chose to combat one set of contradictions rather than another. This decision was made easier by local voters and elected officials, who were in no hurry to change the status quo, especially since the growth machine had already provided the homes and communities that they needed.[6]

All this occurred in a Santa Clara County that remained largely closed off to African Americans. While Silicon Valley became increasingly Asian and international, and San Jose maintained a large and long-standing Latinx population, the pattern of exclusion that began during the war continued through the boom years. This is the other foundational contradiction of Silicon Valley, the one on which Saxenian did not focus. The valley was built from the beginning to be unequal and exclusionary, the former if you were Latinx, the latter if you were black.

Transformation and Exclusion

Most of the cities that became part of Silicon Valley—with the exception of Stanford University's Palo Alto—were not too dissimilar from the postwar "industrial garden" cities of the East Bay like San Leandro and Hayward. Like their fellow "industrial garden" cities, they reaped the benefits of significant postwar infrastructure building and reinvestment, particularly in the form of freeways.[7] They had similar median incomes and were a mix of working-class and middle-class whites, the former being turned into the latter by well-paying industrial jobs and secure FHA loans.

They even had median incomes that were similar to Richmond, Vallejo, Oakland, and Pittsburg. The significant gap that would open between the East Bay and the South Bay with the growth of Silicon Valley was yet to occur. As late as 1959, there was little difference in the median family incomes in cities like Fremont or Milpitas and their Carquinez cousins farther north. The East Bay and most of the South Bay, although still divided by race, was one large blue-collar zone. But by 1999, Milpitas and Sunnyvale had almost twice the median family income as Richmond or Vallejo. Cupertino, home to Apple, has almost three times the median income. This is the epitome of the Silicon divide.

Part of the story is that the South Bay cities never had to deal with significant poverty, having wholeheartedly embraced the Babylon-era restrictions on who could live where. Poverty rates in the South Bay almost never exceeded 5%, while rates in the northern industrial cities often exceed 15%. Fremont, Sunnyvale, and Cupertino were never more than 5% African American, and Milpitas has declined from roughly 7% black at its peak in 1980 to less than 3% in 2010.

This exclusion was a fundamental part of the growth machine in Santa Clara County. Racial covenants were the first barrier. *Shelley v. Kramer* in 1948 outlawed these covenants, but even that decision and local activism by Mexican American and Japanese American residents could not defeat the FHA. No county received more FHA funding than Santa Clara County (Cavin 2012). This meant that the FHA's explicitly racist redlining had a profound effect. African Americans, who were not a major part of the older, agricultural county, would not be allowed into most of the new county being built. Japanese Americans and Mexican Americans, who had been integral to the county's canning and nut industry, would be ghettoized. As Aaron Cavin (2012: 191) makes clear, "the FHA remade the Santa Clara Valley's racial landscape, segregating the area on a scale never before seen."

What was left for people of color, outside of older parts of San Jose and some parts of the smaller cities, were often "pocket ghettos" (Proposal for a Metropolitan Bay Area Housing Development Corporation n.d., quoted in Cavin 2012: 195). These were small, underinvested, and often physically disconnected communities, generally in unincorporated areas. Some, like East San Jose, were heavily Mexican American, and represented a continuation of earlier patterns of racial and economic discrimination that were part of the valley's agricultural heritage (Pitti 2003).

Others were created during the postwar era to house communities of color barred from the all-white developments of the "white noose." Perhaps the most infamous was East Palo Alto, a small former farming community at the foot of the Dumbarton Bridge. As postwar industry began migrating south—including the GM plant moving from Oakland to Fremont, on the other side of the bridge—African American workers came for jobs but struggled to find housing. Mimicking what happened in San Francisco, East Palo Alto's earlier residents had been Japanese American farmers, interned during the war. East Palo Alto would become one of the only places African Americans could live on either side of the bridge, as Fremont was just as racially restricted. As close as it is to Stanford University's Palo Alto, most of it is separated by a major highway. It is also separated politically—it is across the border in San Mateo County.

More integrated diversity only began to come to the Santa Clara County following the 1965 immigration reform. Civil rights activism forced changes to federal law, and educated immigrants, primarily from Asia, began to slowly become a major part of the county's workforce. South Asians, Chinese, and Koreans in particular helped make Milpitas and Cupertino almost two-thirds Asian by 2010.[8]

Yet despite these important gains, the racial inequality and exclusion continued, and began to be noticed not just by advocates and academics but by the tech industry itself (Silicon Valley Institute for Regional Studies 2015). Some of the inequalities have emerged within the Asian community. As Willow Lung-Amam (2015: 23) argues, the valley has been witness to "deepening fissures" between East Asian and Southeast Asian communities who find themselves on different sides of the growing economic divide in the area.

The Latinx community remains a vital portion of the population and the workforce, but they continue to be much poorer and largely excluded from the property wealth created by high home values. By 2014, the Latinx poverty rate was almost three times the white poverty rate in Santa Clara County.[9] As can be seen from Figure 10, the Latinx community is overwhelmingly less wealthy than the white population, with far fewer high earners. More than 60 percent of Latinx households rent (compared to 35 percent of white households) in a county built on and largely for homeownership.

The African American community continues to be excluded, both from the Silicon Valley workforce and its houses. Report after report has highlighted continued struggles for blacks (and Latinxs) in the tech industry. One recent estimate is that blacks are only 4 percent of the tech industry.[10] Yet residential exclusion is even worse. By 2010, Vallejo, population 115,942, had twice as many African Americans (~25,000) as the combined totals for Fremont, Milpitas, Sunnyvale, and Cupertino, population ~480,000 people. Santa Clara County—population 1.78 million—had barely 40,000 African American residents in 2010 (2.2 percent).[11] This number, as small as it is in a region with such a significant black population, was still a 20 percent loss from 1990.

The only county in the region to lose a higher percentage of its black population during this same time period was San Francisco, a time when both Silicon Valley's contradictions and the city's own helped turn it simultaneously into an international symbol of gentrification and a suburb. San

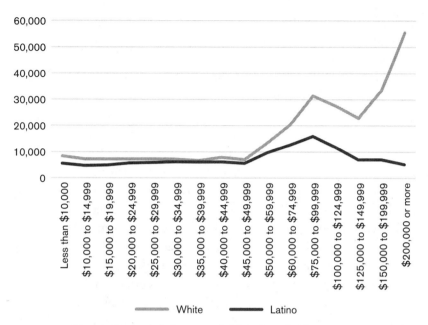

FIGURE 10. Households divided: Latinx and White household income in Santa Clara County, 2010–14 ACS.

Francisco, as the center of the region geographically and culturally, would eventually embody virtually all of the contradictions and dilemmas found in this book, fusing the Dougherty Valley–type fights and the gentrification dilemma. As the forces changing and pulling apart San Francisco grew, the city managed to regain its lost economic centrality while become a smaller and smaller piece of a larger and larger region.[12]

THE SUBURBANIZATION AND
GENTRIFICATION OF SAN FRANCISCO

Gentrification in San Francisco has now been a critical force for enough time that one can think about it in historical terms (Castells 1983; Godfrey 1988). Concerns about rising rents, the displacement of people of color, artists, and low-income residents, and the eviction of rent-controlled tenants go back decades in San Francisco. As noted in chapter 1, displacement is almost inbuilt in the city, and has had a racial tinge since the earliest days of anti-Chinese zoning ordinances and outright racial animosity (Craddock 2000) and invocations of "yellow peril" against the Japanese migrants who replaced them, all against the backdrop of a complicated city that seemingly appeared overnight.

Although "the City," as it is known locally, largely escaped the abandonment that plagued central cities throughout the United States, it did not escape urban renewal. Led by San Francisco Redevelopment Agency director Justin Herman, San Francisco's answer to the modernist planner as demagogue that so tarnished the profession, San Francisco embraced neighborhood clearances and freeway-building with abandon. During the 1950s and 1960s, redevelopment particularly targeted African American neighborhoods, including the Fillmore district, where Japanese American residents had been evicted a generation earlier during internment. Herman was famously called the "the arch villain in the black depopulation of the city" by local African American journalist Thomas Fleming in 1965 (Hartman [1984] 2002: 18). The timing of that statement is an important reminder that the processes which have driven the resegregation of the region have early roots. The black population of San Francisco, which had grown exponentially since the war, would peak soon after Fleming made this statement. The 1970 census showed 96,078 African Americans in a city of just over 715,000, roughly 13.4 percent. It has declined dramatically ever since. The 2010 census showed San Francisco with just 46,781 African Americans, less than half of 1970, in a city that had added almost 80,000 people.

Herman's freeway plans, which succeeded in building a waterfront freeway and a series of spurs into neighborhoods, never managed to crisscross the city as shown in the famous 1948 picture that has come to epitomize the folly of that era. They did succeed in helping launch the freeway revolts of the 1950s and 1960s, in which San Francisco would play a leading role, as it did in so many social movements of the time. Herman's redevelopment machine also famously targeted the South of Market area (SoMa), home to a diverse mix that included numerous former sailors and Filipinos, part of the legacy of the city's maritime past. This would be one of many flashpoints of downtown redevelopment over the years, as concerns and social movements grew not only to combat displacement but to confront the question of the "Manhattanization of San Francisco" (Hartmann [1984] 2002).

By the 1980s, San Francisco had begun to show clear signs of virtually all of the contradictions and fragmentations found in the region as a whole. The southeastern portion of the city, the primarily African American neighborhood of Bayview–Hunters Point, had more in common with West Oakland

and Richmond than most of the rest of the city. Its residents struggled with bad air and high levels of violence. It had suffered from capital flight and disinvestment by both public and private sectors (Brahinsky 2014). The trauma of urban renewal and the ghosts of the more explicitly racist postwar era weighed heavily on the community. Freeway-building had surrounded the neighborhood and cut them off even more from the rest of the city, and clearances had torn apart the city's other major black community, the Fillmore. Hunters Point, far and away the most polluted of the former bases (Dillon 2011), sat largely dormant as the neighboring community struggled with the toxic public health aftermath of its continued presence and the toxic economic aftermath of its shutdown.

As southeast San Francisco struggled with one side of the gentrification dilemma—essentially continued abandonment for most of this period—the lower-income neighborhoods in the rest of the city felt the full force of gentrification. Population in the city, which had stagnated and even dipped during the 1960s and 1970s—even if there was little true abandonment—rebounded. Housing prices rose steadily. Per capita income went from roughly the same as the region as a whole in 1979 to 37 percent higher by 1989, with steadily rising rates of high-earning residents with bachelor's degrees and virtually any other marker of wealth and privilege. The mid-1990s brought the first dot-com boom and tech wealth, and the slow demographic change of the city began to be officially noticed, such as the African American out-migration, already long discussed in the black community. Rebecca Solnit's 2002 *Hollow City* captured a creeping set of changes in which artists, activists, nonprofits, and many others felt that the welcome mat of the city had been rolled up. The "hollowing" that Solnit chronicled during this first boom reached absurd heights a decade later—rents soared beyond belief; evictions skyrocketed, almost doubling between 2010 and 2015.[13] This became the San Francisco discussed in the introduction, the one that makes international headlines as an icon of gentrification.

While the role of Silicon Valley in the production of this new map of regional segregation is somewhat straightforward, San Francisco's story is much more complicated. As Silicon Valley grew, San Francisco became a suburb of its own suburban economic wunderkind, while also fighting to maintain and regain its economic standing. Both of these phenomena—its transformation into a suburb and its economic rebirth—exacerbated gentrification pressures. Meanwhile, its internal politics was better equipped to defend and conserve than to radically expand its housing stock, in part because the housing on offer was never going to solve the problem for those who needed it. In this it somewhat succeeded, in ways that do not get enough credit. In the face of enormous pressure and through a variety of strategies, San Francisco activists and leaders succeeded in keeping many of its low-income residents in the city.

But the constant battles over housing in San Francisco eventually evolved into an internecine version of the Dougherty Valley dilemma, with "demand-side" and "supply-side" factions sowing division rather than building common purpose. The increasingly harsh rhetoric, which often neglected the fact that most people agreed on most things, helped fuel an inward-looking myopia. San Francisco had become a smaller and smaller portion of the region that bore its name, and its solution and the region's solution were always going to be one and the same.

San Francisco's Changing Role

The data in the first part of this chapter showed how Santa Clara County became the jobs center of the region, followed by San Mateo a few decades later. Figure 11 shows the impact of this transformation on commuting. It charts the ratio of people commuting into and out of San Francisco by county of origin / destination. In 1970, San Francisco was a prototypical central city, receiving far more people from Alameda, San Mateo, and Contra Costa counties. But by 1990, San Francisco had become functionally a suburb of Santa Clara, sending more people south in the morning than it received. Highway 280, which runs along the foothills of the Pacific range in San Mateo County, became famous for its "reverse commute," as San Mateo as well almost achieved equity with San Francisco in terms of inflow and outflow.

This almost unheard-of reverse commute was part of the general transformation of San Francisco into a dormitory for Silicon Valley. With tech salaries already high and equity in increasingly valuable stock a common way of paying employees, the slow but steady "suburbanization" of San Francisco helped offset the negative impacts that suburban job centers had on other central cities in the United States. Silicon Valley–driven regional growth helped prop up San Francisco, even during the 1970s and 1980s when so many American cities continued to decline.

There are two other critical things about this process. First, virtually the opposite happened in Solano and Contra Costa counties. Prior to 1970, few

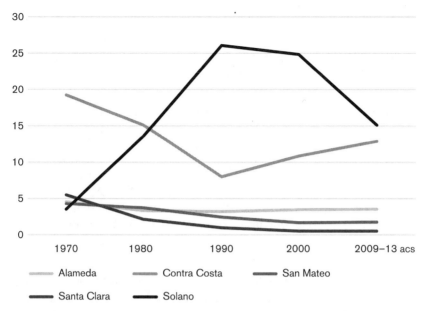

FIGURE 11. Ratio of San Francisco in-commuters to out-commuters, by county. Source: U. S. Census, American Community Survey.

people commuted to San Francisco from Solano County, or vice versa. By 2000, more than 10,000 Solano residents commuted on a daily basis to San Francisco, a sevenfold increase from 1970. The same reverse commute did not occur. Contra Costa did not see the same exponential growth, but the overall numbers were far greater. By 2000, almost 50,000 daily commuters came into San Francisco from Contra Costa County, and less than 5,000 went the other way.

These numbers epitomize the dual role that San Francisco came to play in the region. It became an unaffordable central city whose lower-paid workers and former residents lived in the Cities of Carquinez and beyond. More than a third of its workforce commutes *in* from other counties, far above the national average (U. S. Census Bureau 2013). At the same time, it became the suburban home to the wealthier tech workers of Silicon Valley, with more than 60,000 workers heading south every morning. This is the phenomenon that helped produce, at the same time, "tech buses," foreclosure, gentrification, and the suburbanization of segregation.

One also notices the stabilization of both job numbers and commuting ratios beginning in the 1990s. If the postwar era, and even the 1970s and

1980s, were about Silicon Valley outstripping San Francisco, the city fought back. Its jobs numbers stabilized. It started to build a little more housing, ending its exponential postwar decline vis-a-vis San Jose. More importantly, the city began to reestablish itself as a center for technology and investment. The transformation of the valley from hardware and microchips to software and search engines helped. The first dot-com boom in the 1990s saw start-ups moving into San Francisco, even as the center of the industry remained in the valley. But the post-dot-com crash was very different. Tech began spending the day in San Francisco, not just the night. Whereas less than 1 percent of the city's jobs were tech related in 1990, by 2000 it had tripled to 3 percent and by 2012 to 6 percent. Tech was responsible for the overwhelming majority of job growth in San Francisco post-foreclosure crisis—one of the many reasons why it emerged so unscathed (Lamb 2013).

With this growth came high-profile tech companies headquartered in the city—Twitter, Instagram, Uber, Lyft, Airbnb. Some venture capital firms, long a key engine of Silicon Valley and often associated with one road in Palo Alto, moved as well (Florida 2013), or like the companies they fund, started in San Francisco. By 2013, as the Bay Area maintained its dominant role in U.S. venture investment, it was not Silicon Valley but San Francisco that had the two zip codes with the greatest volume of investment in the United States.[14] These two neighboring zip codes in the South of Market and Inner Mission areas of San Francisco generated over $2 billion in high-tech investment. Palo Alto was third, and another neighborhood in southeast San Francisco was fourth. All told, the five leading zip codes in San Francisco proper outstripped the eight leading zip codes in Silicon Valley by roughly $100 million in investment.[15]

This torrent of venture capital was something that few places have ever witnessed. Added to the earlier eras of growth in the valley, the gentrification pressures on San Francisco grew from intense to insane. San Francisco housing politics had always been sclerotic and intense, and this phenomenon simply made things worse. In the face of a gentrification dilemma whereby preservation did not mean abandonment, stasis became a more appealing and infinitely more feasible route than change, as what was generally on offer would not have saved people from displacement. San Francisco got dragged into a Dougherty Valley–style debate for all the world to see, at a time when the real political capital needed to be spent on the rest of the region, which has long been San Francisco's only hope.

Success and Failure

Although famous internationally for its progressive politics, San Francisco has long served as a prime example of growth machine politics at their most intense. It is no accident that John Mollenkopf's classic *Contested City* is in part a case study of San Francisco—since its earliest days, it is a city remarkable for just how contested it has become. As Grey Brechin (2006) chronicles in his magisterial *Imperial San Francisco,* these growth politics were part of the foundation of the city from the earliest days of the Gold Rush. They involved both the constant exploitation of the city itself, and of its hinterland. But as San Francisco's progressive side worked to stem the abuses of the former, it was less successful in combatting the latter. This inward-looking gaze only grew more trenchant with the increasing pressures of absurd wealth.

Although never truly abandoned, the San Francisco of the late 1970s and early 1980s did not entirely escape the malaise of postwar American cities. Herman and the growth machine so overreached in the 1950s and 1960s that the scars ran deep and the ghosts were omnipresent. Progressive communities and communities of color had grown deeply skeptical of growth and change, as they did in so many places. Then, in a nine-day period in late November 1978, the city was rocked by two tragedies. In Jonestown, Guyana, cult leader Jim Jones, who had been head of the city's Housing Authority, orchestrated the mass suicide of more than 900 people, including more than 300 children, and the killing of local congressman Leo Ryan. A little more than a week later, Supervisor Harvey Milk, the first openly gay elected official in Californian history, and Mayor George Moscone were assassinated in City Hall.

The killings cast a pall over the city, but did little to halt its growth politics. By that time, San Francisco had already begun to be divided between "progressives" and "moderates," a distinction largely based on land use and economic development politics (McDaniel 2015). Opposition to freeways developments in the 1960s gave way to the fight against high-rises in the 1970s. San Francisco Forward was formed to represent the growth machine, San Franciscans for Responsible Growth to represent growth control and neighborhood activists. The former used the slogan "Don't Los Angelize San Francisco"; the latter, "Don't Manhattanize San Francisco." The high-rise question would dominate much of the early 1980s, culminating in one of the most restrictive growth measures in any American downtown—1986's Proposition M, which capped office growth at roughly a half million square feet a year (Paul 1999).

Proposition M symbolized the growth fights at their most cantankerous, and set the table for a long and contentious series of decades. Social movements also rose up to defend communities impacted both by redevelopment and by the gentrification that would start soon afterward. Many were preservationist and increasingly middle class and wealthy in nature, helping defend the Victorian neighborhoods that gave the city its architectural identity. Others grew up in the racialized neighborhoods of Bayview–Hunters Point, the Mission, SoMa, and many more. The Chinese community grew massively, and it too developed moderate and progressive wings. A powerful set of housing and homeless advocates emerged, alongside an even more powerful set of homeowner, neighborhood, corporate, landlord, and business interests. Each worked to build power, to defend their corner of the city or their personal or institutional interests in what was becoming some of the most valuable real estate on earth.

The undulating and fractional coalitional politics created an opaque and byzantine planning process designed to slow growth, not encourage it. There were constant fights over the rules of politics, district elections, and planning policy, and a seemingly endless series of ballot box measures that often targeted development. If the postwar era in San Francisco was, as Chester Hartman (2002: 392) writes, "overwhelmingly dominated by business interests," the resulting years ended in a stalemate. As Richard DeLeon (1992) argued decades ago in a study that still rings true, a broad coalition of "progressives"—made up primarily of civil rights and social justice advocates, environmentalism and left-wing populists—grew strong enough to defeat the growth machine, but not enough to replace it with a progressive version of growth. What remains is an "anti-regime," a "defensive system of governance designed to block and filter big business power and to protect [the city] from unregulated market forces and grandiose progrowth schemes" (1992: 11, quoted in Judge, Stoker, and Wolman 1995).

When viewed in hindsight, it is clear that the result of this anti-regime development politics meant that not enough housing was built for a city with the economic and population demands of the 1990s and onward. As in Silicon Valley, the era of the 1970s and 1980s, when the rebellion against growth was at its height and when the economy was not quite the engine it would become, was the most stagnant. The city added roughly 6,000 units in the 1970s and barely twice that in the 1980s, growth rates of just 2 and 4 percent respectively. Things would pick up in the 1990s and 2000s, with the city managing to add 30,000 units between 2000 and 2010. But even so, some of the delays were absurd. As discussed previously, Hunters Point languished while the community nearby suffered. Land made available by the demolition of the Central Freeway in the aftermath of the 1989 Loma Prieta earthquake would not become occupied housing for more than 25 years.

But there are critical differences with Silicon Valley. As DeLeon makes clear, this was not simply the exclusionary politics of a wealthy and overwhelmingly white set of suburbs focused on repairing and maintaining its natural environment while ignoring the human costs of its segregationist past and job-machine present. San Franciscans often fought to maintain local diversity, with the ghost of Herman ever present. During the neoliberal era, the city enacted and maintained rent control, one of the most misunderstood and misrepresented yet important policy tools in the fight against displacement.[16] It built a supportive housing apparatus that is the envy of advocates around the country, preserving thousands of units of housing for the most vulnerable members of society right in the heart of the city's downtown. It maintained one incredible indicator: San Francisco had almost to a person the same number of people living in poverty in 2010 as it did in 1970. Many of the poorest residents of the city remained, despite its steady transformation.

In testament to some of the true successes of its progressive housing movement, neighborhood planning efforts, and long history of activism (Castells 1983; Brahinsky, Chion, and Feldstein 2012), some communities of color in particular were miraculously successful in warding off what could have been even worse displacement. There were almost the exact same number of Latinx residents in the greater Mission in 2000 (31,370) as there were in 1970 (31,067).[17] Bayview–Hunters Point remained a strongly African American neighborhood into the new millennium, despite losses and years of hardship.[18] It is understandable and fully warranted that most of what we read and write about gentrification in San Francisco focuses on displacement, but we need to recognize that San Francisco's deep history of social movements has enabled some communities to survive and persevere against a tidal wave of wealthy in-migration and massive capital flows into local real estate and local companies. Even if it never found what one nonprofit housing director and growth control advocate called "a vision of our city's future that is any better than 'national trends'—and the guts to make it happen" (Elberling quoted in Hartman 2002: 394), at least the city did not bury its head in the sand as so many other parts of the increasingly elite West Bay did during this time.

As gentrification pressures intensified, so did political tensions. Two important tropes emerged, both with kernels of truth but both problematic in their one-sidedness. The tech industry had come under greater scrutiny, as its leaders asserted greater political power and its workers became a greater percentage of the city's residents. Both leaders and workers made major missteps, playing power politics rather than forging common purpose, exposing themselves as elitist with little sympathy for or understanding of the diversity around them, wrapping themselves in privatized privilege even as the public infrastructure around them crumbled (McNeill 2016). A particularly symbolic and now infamous event involved employees of Dropbox attempting to kick local Latinx kids off a Mission district soccer field because they had reserved the field using an app (Wong 2014).

Excoriations of the sins of the tech elite were matched by similar diatribes against the sins of the progressive anti-growth coalition. In a piece about the global urbanism internet, Gabriel Metcalf (2015), longtime head of the San Francisco–based planning organization SPUR, blamed the city's housing woes on progressives who had either allied themselves with NIMBYs or become NIMBYs themselves. This sparked a vicious back and forth, with activists who agreed on many things repeatedly "talking past each other" (McDaniel 2015).

Yet there are as many fingers to point as one has fingers. Developers used the 1990s boom to go on a loft-building frenzy that brought back memories of Herman's tenure and furthered the argument that new housing supply was only designed for the wealthy and would drive up prices (Brahinsky, Chion, and Feldstein, 2012). Their switch to elite housing towers with very limited affordability in the 2000s did nothing to dispel this notion.

The old elite, often with old money made new again by tech profits, continued to channel its money into projects like the Presidio, new arts museums, and new stadiums. There was no lack of money to be spent on infrastructure and urbanism, but only certain infrastructure and certain urbanism. The Presidio saw more that $1.6 billion in investment between 1998 and 2012, most of it private. Money from the heirs to the Levi's fortune paid for the reconstruction of Chrissy Field. The aforementioned Letterman Digital Arts Center was an investment by Lucasfilm, part of the controversial demand that the Presidio become a self-sustaining public-private partnership following decommissioning. The board of this partnership, the Presidio

Trust, included a who's who of Bay Area real estate, tech, and industrial elite—among them, Bishop Ranch developer Alex Mehran (Presidio Trust 2012). It was not a coincidence that the Presidio is essentially the backyard of some of the most exclusive neighborhoods in San Francisco.[19]

Private wealth also drove the building of a new San Francisco Museum of Modern Art (SFMOMA) in the mid-1990s, a new starchitect-designed De Young Museum in 2005, and then shut SFMOMA for three years for a $610 million expansion.[20] Two-thirds of the money for a completely rebuilt California Academy of Sciences—like the De Young, a major Golden Gate Park institution damaged in the 1989 earthquake—was privately raised. San Francisco saw the first privately financed Major League Baseball stadium in a quarter century built in the late 1990s, a project which cost almost a half billion dollars in 2016 money (Associated Press 2002). This was followed by the controversial move of the San Francisco 49ers football team into a $1.3 billion privately financed stadium—with public guarantees of almost $1 billion—in Santa Clara (*San Francisco Chronicle* 2016). The Golden State Warriors basketball team is currently building its own half-billion-dollar arena in San Francisco, leaving its longtime home in Oakland for wealthier pastures.

Just as with Silicon Valley and open space money, these public space, sports, and arts projects are vital, and many of them should have been privately funded. It is to the region's credit that its sports stadiums have largely not been a tool for the fleecing of public coffers by wealthy owners, as they are in so many other cities.[21] But they are yet another example of the vast wealth of the region being used for certain projects that the wealthy like and enjoy, without addressing the deeper human contradictions which the production of wealth has entailed. The longtime power nexus of the region—tech, old money, and environmentalism (Storper et al. 2015)—was just as inward looking with its public-facing investment as San Francisco was with its housing politics in Silicon Valley.

As I will discuss in the conclusion, responsibility is a factor of power. But even if one maintains that those with more power bear more responsibility, what Rebecca Solnit (2002: 120) wrote in the aftermath of the first dot-com–induced housing crisis remained true in the post-2008 boom: "In the debate over the fate of San Francisco and whose fault it is, there is a lot of hatred of a usually faceless 'them' distinguished from us."

Some have tried to adopt an "it's pretty much everyone's fault" line, including a brilliant 2014 diatribe by local tech journalist Kim-Mai Cutler,

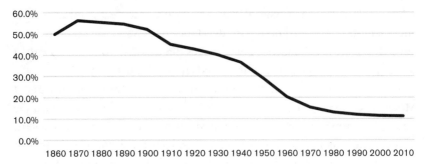

FIGURE 12. San Francisco as a percentage of the nine-county region (population). Source: Bay Area Census via U.S. Census; calculations by author.

who draws equal attention to the sins of Silicon Valley as to those of various sides of San Francisco's battles. But what is often missing from discussions of San Francisco is perspective on the city in relation to the region. During this same era, while the city gentrified and fought over its own gentrification, it steadily became less important as a population center. Its cultural, economic, and political might and international reputation helped promote a form of provincial myopia where the region upon which it has always depended (Brechin 2006) became blurred in its limited vision. San Francisco not only became a suburb of Silicon Valley, but an increasingly small part of an increasingly large region.

One of the most important factoids one can produce on San Francisco's role in the resegregation of the Bay Area and the production of crisis can be seen in Figure 12. Its economic and cultural dominance was once a factor of its relative size. For the first half century of its existence as a city, it was more than half the population of the Bay Area. That began to change with the earthquake and fire of 1906, a catastrophe that accelerated the development of the East Bay in particular. Yet it remained not only the economic, political, and cultural capital of the region through the first part of the postwar era, but its largest city and home to at least a third of the population of the region.

All that changed with the postwar boom, but again, not because San Francisco lost significant population, but because the region grew without it. Even with some progress in building housing units after a stagnant 1970s, the city is now home to barely one in ten residents of the region as a whole.[22] Even hyper-abandoned Detroit has a greater percentage of its metro area (14 percent in the 2006–10 ACS) than San Francisco. Almost a third of the population of greater New York lives in New York City; Chicago is closer to half. Los Angeles may be part of the famously postmodern and multicentric Southern California metropolis, but it is closer to 20 percent of the regional population, twice that of San Francisco. One would be hard-pressed to find a major city in the world that is so small a part population-wise of the region at which it is nominally the center.

This decreasing centrality in terms of population could have been partially combatted by a different housing regime, but only a Singapore-style overhaul that was unthinkable even to the most ardent modernists would have changed the numbers dramatically. Even without the freeway revolts, high-rise ordinances, and the rest of the growth restrictions, the Bay Area was founded as a regional metropolis and was always going to become a more regional one over time. San Francisco was never going to be able to solve the problems it helped create in the region that bears its name entirely within the confines of a 49-square-mile city that had been built out long ago. But part of the problem with its intense politics was that it exacerbated a myopic vision which prevented the type of radical, regional vision that would have been necessary to prevent the city from being a linchpin in the resegregation of the region as a whole. Part of the problem is that journalists and scholars from the Bay Area and around the world fueled this self-centered approach by obsessing over a small and beautiful city while largely ignoring the vast metropolis around it.

At least San Francisco tried. Even with its troubling racial history, it was a diverse city which tried to stay that way, in both race and class terms. A similar thing cannot be said for the county immediately to the north, facing the Presidio and its Yoda statue. As Silicon Valley grew dramatically and San Francisco struggled to do the right thing, Marin County, where Yoda was born, simply built a wall.

THE HYPOCRISY OF MARIN COUNTY

In the 2012 presidential election, Barack Obama won eight of the ten richest counties in the United States (Toscano 2012).[23] Six of those eight are suburbs of major cities—three suburbs in three states surrounding New York City (Westchester, New York; Somerset, New Jersey, and Fairfield, Connecticut), two Virginia suburbs of Washington, DC (Loudon and Fairfax), and Marin County.

None of the six supported Obama with a fervor to match Marin County's. At 74.3 percent of the vote, Obama won a higher percentage of the vote than in either Cook County (Chicago), Illinois, or Honolulu County, Hawaii, his two homes. Marin gave him the second-highest percentage of any suburban county of a major city in the United States.[24] In doing so, Marin was just like its neighbors. As noted in the introduction, the Bay Area was the only major region in the county where every county voted 60 percent or more for Obama.

Of these six wealthiest metropolitan Obama-voting counties, Marin is also the whitest. It is more than 15 percentage points whiter than the county is it most often compared to—Westchester County, New York. It is the least African American by a longshot—2.7 percent, versus 7.2 percent for the second lowest and a 9 percent average for all six. In terms of income and poverty, it is not radically different than its peers, but the fact that its per capita wealth is so much higher should be a clue to a key difference. Its median age is almost four and a half years older than the second oldest county, almost ten years older than the youngest.[25] This is an enormity in statistical terms.

It is also by far the least populated, both in overall terms and in terms of density. Westchester County has almost four times the population on barely 80 percent of the land area. Only Loudon County, Virginia, comes close to those numbers, all while being younger and more diverse (and barely pro-Obama). Marin County, California, is by far the whitest, richest, oldest, and least populated Democratic stronghold in any major metropolitan area in the United States. In demographic terms, it has more in common with Morris County, New Jersey, its fellow member of the top ten that is 75 percent white and almost as old, and where Mitt Romney beat Obama by 10 percent.

The extreme exclusion that is Marin County is the final piece of what could be regarded as the West Bay Wall. For all that Santa Clara County's wealthy Silicon Valley cities gorged on job growth and failed to build adequate housing, for all that San Francisco failed to do what it and the region needed it to do, nothing compares to Marin. Despite being geographically central to the region, it is has the second smallest population of any county in the nine-county Bay Area, roughly half the size of Sonoma County to the north. From 1970 to 2010, during a time when the nine-county region added more than 2.5 million people and San Joaquin and Stanislaus counties absorbed another three-quarters of a million, Marin County grew by only

46,371 men, women, and children. That is less that 1.8 percent of the nine-county total. Antioch alone added more people between 1980 and 2000 than Marin did over a period twice as long.

Ironically, this entrenched exclusion received the attention of the federal government in the early days of Obama's presidency. A 2009 fair-housing audit by HUD expressed concern at two facts that in the words of one local journalist are "common knowledge" in the county (Seidman 2015: n.p.): there are few people of color in general, and there are two communities, Marin City and San Rafael's Canal District, which are both low-income and overwhelmingly nonwhite. Marin City was the county's version of shipyard-induced diversity. African Americans came during the war to work in the often-forgotten local shipyard, and this spot of land hidden behind a hill from Sausalito was the only place in the county they were allowed to live (Dornheim 2011a). It is now the only majority nonwhite place in the county, and remains 37 percent African American. The Canal District of San Rafael was built as a rare zone of apartments in the postwar era, for white families saving to buy a home. It became home to significant refugees from the wars in Southeast Asia and Central America, and is now one of the few areas in the county with significant housing for the many low-wage workers who basically run the county on a daily basis (ibid.).

As I have tried to show throughout this book, the resegregation of the region was produced through a complex set of dilemmas, some due to legitimate barriers and challenges, others to greed, absence of foresight, and political myopia. The broad political fragmentation that goes far beyond jurisdictional politics comes from many sources, and was constantly reproduced and often exacerbated throughout the neoliberal era. But no single factor fragmented the region like the ghosts from the earlier era—the echoes and memories of a modernist, postwar growth machine and planning apparatus that was as environmentally destructive as it was racist. Marin County became a national leader in pushing back against many of the excesses of the growth machine, fighting freeways and habitat destruction in a 1960s political rebellion that would forever alter county politics. This strong environmental streak would help to flip the county from Republican to Democrat, and make it a pioneer in open space preservation and park-building. But along the way, this deep opposition to one sin of the modernist era also led it to become one of the worst reproducers of the other cardinal sin of the very same era.

Marin's Rebellion

[B]y the end of the 1950s policy and plans at every level—local, state, and federal—encouraged the continuation and even acceleration of Marin's development.

—LOUISE NELSON DYBLE (2007: 40)

As the 1950s turned into the 1960s, Marin County was not all that different from most of the other suburban parts of the Bay Area.[26] It was almost exclusively white, but so were San Mateo and Santa Clara counties and most of the "white noose" communities that made up Contra Costa and Alameda counties. Like the other counties immediately surrounding San Francisco, it had grown rapidly during the 1950s, almost doubling in size. It had a faster growth rate (71 percent) than both Contra Costa and Alameda counties (Bay Area Census n.d.), part of a typical wave of suburbanization in which San Francisco lost population for the first time. This process, as we know so well in the United States, was driven by that heady mix of federal- and state-supported home- and highway-building. Car registrations doubled in the same decade (Dyble 2007).

Marin, like San Jose and Contra Costa and so many other places at the time, was also run by a county growth machine that embraced suburbanization for what it was—the center of the county's economy. Real estate brokers, businessmen, landowners, and newspaper publishers acted as a coordinated set of boosters of the county's suburban aspirations. They ran the local councils and the county's board of supervisors, advocated for state investment in local freeways through local representatives in Sacramento and various established associations and networks, and otherwise worked to grow Marin as a slightly more exclusive yet nonetheless somewhat typical Californian suburban county. The county leaned Republican, but just slightly—it supported Eisenhower in 1956 and Nixon in 1960, but voted for Johnson in 1964, a time in which registered Republicans outnumbered registered Democrats in the county by 92 voters.[27]

County leaders, led by local state senator John F. "Jack" McCarthy, had a direct line to Governor Earl Warren. The county featured heavily in the state's ambitious freeway development plans, the *California Freeway Program,* published in 1959. This plan would detail not only a major widening and expansion of the historic 101 Freeway that ran north–south through the county, but it proposed two major new interventions. The first was a series of new highways crisscrossing the county from east to west to open up the massive and rural western portion of the county to development. The second was a new bridge to San Francisco, barely two decades after the construction of the famed Golden Gate Bridge (Dyble 2007).

Based on these proposals, the Army Corps of Engineers issued projections for what these developments would do to the county. Its 33 square miles of residential land use (out of 521) would grow to 166 square miles, much of it newly opened by freeways in West Marin or on landfill and "reclaimed" wetlands in the southern and eastern portions of the county. The population of roughly 150,000 was estimated to double by 1990 and reach 780,000 by 2020 (ibid.).

The visions were a mix of populist grandiosity and postwar developmental logic. The coast would become a massive recreation and tourism zone, a "Jones Beach on the Pacific." Suburban housing units would fill in virtually any developable land in a hilly and mountainous county. It was part of an era that thought nothing of proposing massive landfills, including the proposal to bulldoze portions of the Tiburon hills in 1949 to fill in Richardson Bay (Marin Conservation League n.d.). The sheer absurdity of some of the development plans in Marin was matched throughout the region, and helped launch organizations like Save the Bay and much of the region's and even the nation's contemporary environmental movement (Walker 2007).[28]

By the early 1960s, the state's bridge and highway plans had become more developed, and the county's growth machine was firmly behind them. But challenges began to come from all sides. San Francisco's board of supervisors and local activists had already revolted against freeway development, making the prospect of a second crossing more difficult. This second crossing would have gone through Angel Island, which the increasingly powerful Marin Conservation League (MCL) wanted to turn into a state park. The MCL, founded in 1934 amidst the construction of the Golden Gate Bridge by "four Marin women in lives of comfortable circumstance" (Marin Conservation League n.d.), and a key force behind preventing the Richardson Bay fill, was a leading force behind the park. Slowly but surely, an emerging network of conservationists, preservationists, and what would become environmentalists emerged to push back at the grandiose designs of state highway planners and their local boosters.

Both the bridge crossing and the West Marin plans would come to a head in the late 1960s. Even as the bridge proposal crumbled, the push for the east–west route continued. But in a series of public meetings in 1966, a wide array of county residents came out to push back. This was not solely local residents impacted by the proposed route, or the "conservation elite," but civil society more broadly. This shook the very foundations of the local political structure. Without a local vote, the state pulled out. Governor Ronald Reagan was already beginning to slash infrastructure spending; the building boom was over. But Marin was left forever changed. As Louise Dyble (2007: 49) argues, "For the first time, opposition to a major transportation project represented the entire spectrum of interest groups and localities in the county .... Under tremendous public pressure, mayors and city council members had abandoned the growth machine, and soon county-level politics would be transformed, as well."

By the early 1970s, the growth regime had been replaced by a growth-control one. Party registration flipped to make the county majority Democratic. The growth control and environmental measures that had been sweeping the region and the state would also find their place in Marin County and its cities and towns.

But as Dyble so trenchantly points out, one of the most critical aspects of Marin's rebellion had little to do with land preservation, open space, or park building. It was not about wetlands or streams or ecosystems, or even primarily about housing. The rebellion against growth remained focused on what had been seen as growth's primary enabler—transportation. As Dyble (2007: 50) notes, "the ascendance of Marin's new growth control regime did much more than stop state freeway construction; it transformed the purpose of transportation policy, precluding any significant increase in infrastructure or mass transit capacity in the county indefinitely .... It marked the public rejection of all new transportation in the county in the interest of growth control."

Rejecting Transit, Rejecting Growth

The events of the late 1960s would presage a long struggle with questions of transportation, and in particular mass transit. Arguably the most important event occurred before the growth rebellion, and is the one major decision in which Marin County and its leaders were largely not responsible. In 1962, following the 1961 withdrawal of San Mateo County from BART (as noted earlier, Santa Clara decided not to participate in 1957), Marin County was forced to withdraw as well. Without San Mateo, Marin's "marginal tax base could not adequately absorb its share of BART's projected cost" (BART n.d.). There was also a brewing controversy about whether the

Golden Gate Bridge could support the engineering work required to accommodate trains.

But from this point forward, especially with the constantly shifting state and federal landscapes, the decisions made were largely local.[29] In the early 1970s, this new regime in the county officially put an end to the speculative ventures of the growth machine in the western party of the county via a countywide plan that limited growth to a "city-centered" corridor which ran along Highway 101, largely preserving the coastal and agricultural lands of the West Marin coasts and its inland valleys. The plan, which had drafts published in 1971 and was adopted in 1973, was a logical response both to the existing pattern of urban development and to the clear threats that had only just been averted. This decision would be reinforced by a series of decisions at multiple scales. Lobbying efforts by local preservationists led to the establishment of Point Reyes National Seashore and the Golden Gate National Recreation Area in 1972. As tax revenues dried up following Prop. 13, local farmers and conservationists developed the innovative Marin Agricultural Land Trust to further preserve agricultural land and open space in the western part of the county (Dyble 2007).[30] At virtually every turn, efforts to combat the unnecessary urbanization of West Marin were innovative, aggressive, and progressive.

The problem is that the progressive innovation that implemented the West Marin portion of the plan was utterly missing in the "city-centered" corridor. The 1973 plan specifically attempted to "diversify the housing supply, increase jobs in Marin, and provide transportation that will support these development objectives," alongside its open space goals (Marin County Board of Supervisors et al. 1973: 1–1). Moreover, it explicitly recognized that "Marin is an integral part of the Bay Area, physically, socially and economically" (1–10). The plan, in Dyble's (2001: 69) words, "was clearly intended to promote and realize a vision of regional planning and decision making that would transcend local and individual interests." But, as Dyble also points out, "While goals of environmental preservation and growth control in West Marin were realized, goals for housing, density, mixed-use development and community diversity and were not" (56).

Any real hopes for the full implementation of the 1973 plan went downhill almost immediately. Cities along the supposed growth corridor began implementing growth controls of all kinds, from downzonings to protect existing neighborhoods to density restrictions and much more. The already limited growth essentially ended, at least in most towns. This early period also began decades of toggling back and forth between transport and housing, with one common theme: The inability or unwillingness to support or fund transportation improvements made traffic worse, which in turn furthered the argument against housing. The failure to invest in the 1970s and 1980s, combined with continued growth farther up the 101 in Sonoma County—which had a growth politics more akin to East County than its southern neighbor—meant that traffic became brutal. This led to an even harsher set of housing moratoriums in the mid-1980s in Sausalito, Mill Valley, Corte Madera, Tiburon, and even previously pro-growth San Rafael—essentially the entire southern and central portions of the county. At the same time, NIMBYism against affordable housing proposals grew more intense and more open (Butler 1986).

Part of the problem was that Marin County and its cities had followed increasingly familiar strategies. Corridor cities like Corte Madera epitomized the fiscalization of land use in the Prop. 13 era, welcoming major commercial developments on either side of 101. Driven by the job-housing balance push from regional agencies and by underlying fiscal concerns, cities like San Rafael began to be major job centers. Commuting patterns began to shift, with Marin becoming a destination. By 2010, more workers would come into Marin County from Contra Costa, Alameda, and Sonoma counties than would go from Marin County to San Francisco.

The foot-dragging on transportation continued throughout this period. Three tax measures to fund transport had already been defeated between 1973 and 1983 (Dyble 2007). A 101 corridor commission set up in the 1980s to study solutions—including a potential revival of running BART across the Golden Gate Bridge—spent seven years working toward a tax measure on the 1990 ballot to fund a light rail. The measure, similar to Contra Costa's and other counties who had slowly but surely been trying to fund transport, gained the support of every city council except Sausalito, the unanimous support of the board of supervisors, the endorsement of the once powerful League of Women Voters, and of course the backing of business and labor. But there would be no grand bargain in Marin. The local Sierra Club chapter, MCL, and various environmental groups fought the bill, even as groups like Greenbelt Alliance worked regionally to convince greens to think differently about development. The environmental groups stated their opposition in the voters' pamphlet: "After careful study, all of Marin's major environmental groups have concluded that the growth management component of Measure A is too weak. It will be no match for the growth which the trolley system will unleash on Marin" (quoted in Ingram 1990).

In a reversal of the dynamics in Contra Costa County, greens outspent the pro-transit coalition by more than 50 percent, and the measure was trounced, getting barely 40 percent of the vote. And also unlike Contra Costa, no further grand bargain would occur. Another set of measures made it to the 1998 ballot. By this point, Prop. 218 had passed, requiring two-thirds majorities for the approval of tax measures. The measure to build a light rail passed, but the measure to pay for it—and the various other transport programs—failed. A failed 2006 ballot measure tried to do the same thing.

Meanwhile, most places in Marin kept their growth policies tight, and with skyrocketing land prices, development of anything but mansions became exceedingly difficult and rare. Corte Madera added less than 1,000 people between 1970 and 2010. Mill Valley also added less than 1,000, Larkspur less than 2,000, Tiburon less than 3,000. The only cities that grew significantly were San Rafael and Novato, adding roughly 20,000 housing units and about twice that in population in 40 years. It is not a coincidence that these are the only two incorporated cities in the county that are less than 80 percent non-Hispanic white.

While the backlash against growth was happening in many other parts of the region, in Marin there was no effective political counterbalance to insist that some growth was necessary, that Marin had some sort of obligation to house the region in which it lived and upon which it had made the vast wealth it was now investing in building a wall. There were no Fortune 500 companies, few major developers, no real union presence, no major presence of communities of color or low-income people and their organizations. Environmental organizations like MCL remained strong but stuck in a conservationist mentality reminiscent of the era in which they were founded. Groups like Save Marin came and went, but the profound inertia they helped to create remained. The county's relative lack of political complexity helped make the anti-growth rebellion virtually a complete reversal of the previous era. Marin gradually became home to both increasingly well-off individuals who did not object to the increasing exclusivity their actions were producing, and people who were rapidly becoming house-rich as prices escalated but who remained middle-income. For these latter residents in particular, preservation seemed a lifeline. With Prop. 13, they were protected from property tax increases on their suddenly valuable homes, and could stay as long as they liked in a home few, including themselves were they in the market, could afford to purchase.

It is thus no accident that Marin—and the smaller cities of Silicon Valley like Palo Alto—would become a key case study in academic debates about the impact of land use controls on housing. Much of the early debate focused on whether what cities were doing was driving up house prices (Frieden 1979; Dowall 1984). Like so many issues in the neoliberal era, the issue of local housing regulation became an ideological football. Right-wing anti-planners would use some of this work to justify broad attacks on "planning," even if these rules were clearly driven by populist revolts and not by the desires of planning departments (O'Toole 2007). This was exactly the opposite of the modernist era when planners and planning did decide.

Some, like Frieden (1979), did little to acknowledge the gains of the environmental movement or the reasons why the rebellion against growth-machine-led suburbanization was needed. Some progressives attempted to defend the environmental regulations, arguing that they had little to do with the high cost of housing in Marin, all the while ignoring the utter lack of housing production and diversity in these communities (Walker 2007). Scholars produced volumes and volumes of studies about the pros and cons of land use regulation in various forms, including what became a niche field in its own right—understanding NIMBYism (cf. Dear 1992). Both free-market economists and anti-discrimination progressives argued that the local regulatory system was making places like the Bay Area more expensive, worsening inequality and segregation, and contributing to sprawl and environmental degradation. Smart-growth groups and affordable housing advocates pushed for changes in how we live and build, but to little avail. Despite rising talk of reconciling economic, social, and environmental goals through sustainability (Campbell 1996), it never happened in the West Bay.

Forward or Backward?

It was not until 2008, more than 50 years after the rejection of the state highway plan, that Marin passed a countywide measure to fund transportation improvements. The major provision of the bill was to fund a commuter train, the Sonoma-Marin Area Rail Transit (SMART), between San Rafael and northern Sonoma County. It would further connect Sonoma and Marin, which are increasingly important to each other economically. But even with the planned extension to the Larkspur ferry, it did not end the isolation of the North Bay from the far more diverse communities to the south and east.

Nor did it put an end to affordable housing problems. In the aftermath of the vote, as routes were being finalized and station area plans were being developed, affordable housing advocates saw an opportunity for transit-oriented development in the station areas. It would be an opportunity to pursue some of the "city-centered" density and development called for in the 1971 plan. After years of focusing primarily on one part of that earlier vision, perhaps the other part of the plan—the one that could potentially make an exceptionally exclusive place more inclusive, and bring ridership to an new and expensive train—could happen. Instead, the Marin supervisor who chaired the SMART board helped a local assemblymember to pass special state legislation targeting only Marin County. The legislation *reduced* the default densities from 30 units per acre to 20 by reclassifying Marin and its cities as suburban.[31]

This disconnect would be one of many that seemingly defines Marin County growth policies. It finally approved transit, but then moved to avoid density vital to the transit's utility and economic well-being. It prided itself on being one of the most environmentally progressive places on earth, but its housing and transportation politics had exacerbated polluting traffic and made no small contribution to millions of regional residents being forced farther out from the core in search of housing.

There was no greater disconnect than the supposedly super-progressive Marin and its long history of race and class exclusion. In 2011, in response to questions related to the HUD segregation audit regarding Marin's lack of diversity, the same supervisor who was active in SMART and in changing the housing law summed up what many in the county thought: "The first reaction from many people . . . was, 'What do you mean they've [HUD] come in? Seventy-three percent of this county voted for Barack Obama, one of the most liberal counties in the United States!'" (Arnold quoted in Dornheim 2011b).

At least she was being honest. Moreover, the supervisor, Judy Arnold, was one of the few elected officials in the county actively talking about race and discrimination, and advocated for affordable housing even as she pushed against density. At risk in the HUD audit were federal funds, including CDBG (Community Development Block Grant) monies that were a lifeline to the small amount of affordable housing actually being built. Some prominent voices advocated giving up federal funds rather than make any real commitment to diversification (Spotswood 2011).

But the HUD case has exposed what can only be called Marin County's hypocrisy. This hypocrisy would get blasted onto the front pages of the national news, when George Lucas would be involved in yet another land use controversy, this time in Marin County, where he lived. After failing to get permits to expand Skywalker Ranch, his legendary studio in unincorporated Lucas Valley, Lucas threatened to build affordable housing on the site.[32] He was then accused of class warfare by a member of the local advocacy group. When the financial deal to build the housing became difficult for a local nonprofit to finance, Lucas decided to finance it himself.

The case attracted national attention, with articles in the *New York Times, Washington Post*, and NPR's *Marketplace*, on internet sites like Reddit and CNET, and even in the *Daily Mail*. As Matthew Yglesias (2012) wrote in response to the controversy, "The story of Lucas' squabble with his neighbors has attracted national attention because it's funny, Star Wars is popular, and the affordable housing denouement is an amusing way to skewer limousine-liberal hypocrisy."

But there is another, lesser-known story involving George Lucas that is even more symbolic for Marin, for it gets to the environmentalism versus segregation dilemma which is even deeper. Lucas owned an old storefront in downtown San Anselmo that was somewhat dilapidated. He wanted to build much-needed housing on the site, which is in the heart of the historic downtown. The town refused. So Lucas razed the building, donated the land to the town, and helped turn it into a park, which opened in 2013.

Standing in a fountain in what is now known as Imagination Park is another statue of Yoda, this one with the inscription "Star Wars, created in San Anselmo, 1973." Like the Presidio, Imagination Park is a beautiful place, and it was likely the right land-use decision. But in her dedication letter for the park, San Anselmo Chamber of Commerce president Connie Rodgers (n.d.) unwittingly exposed the problem. She quotes an unnamed study which claims that the new park showed how "the ability and willingness to work together to create such community assets defines 'stable, prosperous places where people want to live and work.'"

Over and over, much of the West Bay chose its own community assets over the region's collective right to stable and prosperous places. It wanted and largely got one critical portion of the progressive agenda—environmental protection and preservation, parks and open spaces. They did incredible work channeling their political and financial capital into undoing the horrible environmental legacy of the postwar era.

But in doing so, they failed in the even more difficult task of addressing the human questions of social justice or race and class discrimination, both of which have also been part of the Democratic Party platform for a generation. Their attention to one sin of the postwar era came at the expense of the other, an almost classic example of racism through neglect (Bonilla-Silva 2017). And while their communities overwhelmingly became nicer over the past 40 years, the social and racial aftermath of this hypocrisy would grow to megaregional proportions.

SIX

The Altamont Line and the Planning Dilemma

LONG BEFORE GREEN ENERGY BECAME A BUZZWORD, and alternative energy solutions became familiar sights, the wind turbines that cover the hills east of Livermore were an iconic Bay Area symbol. Conceived in the late 1970s in response to the oil shocks, the almost 5,000 windmills of the Altamont Wind Farm sit starkly on the barren and generally beige hills of the Diablo range, sprawling in quasi-psychedelic patterns up and down the hillsides and into the Central Valley. Decades after they were built, Altamont remains one of the largest wind farms in the world.

The windmills also epitomize the Bay Area's success and failure. The region was ahead of the curve in some vital environmental areas, like renewable energy from wind, and the preserved open space upon which it stood. But these advances were never matched by the more politically and socially difficult decisions about transportation, land use, and housing. Just underneath the windmills, along Interstate 580, 135,000 polluting cars travel each way every day, mostly carrying workers from the cities and towns of the Central Valley into the workspaces of the nine-county region. The Altamont is not just a wind farm, but a gateway between the valley and the Bay Area, a 741-foot-high pass through the grassy hills that separates two regions and unifies a megaregion simultaneously.

For most of Northern California history, you knew you had left the Bay Area when you traveled over the Altamont Pass. It was as stark a line between two neighboring regions as one can find in the United States. The Altamont is still striking and stark, but the question of whether or not it is a border is now much more difficult to answer. The limited regional political structure would say that the line still holds; commute patterns would say that it does not. Questions of identity, religiosity, politics, and local culture make the picture even murkier. But few would argue with the fact that whatever the relationship between the two sides of the pass had been, it now is both quantifiably larger and qualitatively more complex.

In the breaking down of the once clearly imagined line between Bay Area and Central Valley one can see the *physical* location of sprawling growth and ultimately foreclosure. Here, East County's postindustrial garden was written on a much larger scale, incorporating whole cities—Modesto and Stockton—that are central cities in their own right. It now includes dozens of formerly small farm towns like Patterson, Manteca, Tracy, and Lathrop, places that are now simultaneously small city and suburb. In a roughly 100-mile arc running from East County down to Merced, the rapid growth, lost homes, and fiscal uncertainty were enormous and extensive, impacting not only individual towns and subdivisions but the overall economic future of a territory the size of Rhode Island.[1]

This is the scale at which the 50 / 5000 club is most clearly seen, the scale at which the Bay Area's diverse out-migration is most evident. This is the heart of chapter 1's Zone 4, that outer edge of the region which added more than a million people between 1970 and 2009, the majority of whom were people of color. This is the home of San Joaquin County, whose growing African American population mimicked the decline of San Francisco's (see chapter 1, figure 1). This is the scale at which broader questions about twenty-first-century mobile segregation and the production of foreclosure are most evident.

THINKING MEGAREGIONALLY

This massive scale of development is challenging in virtually every way. To speak of a 12-county "megaregion" is to consider a place thousands of square miles in size, home to more than ten million people and hundreds of separate jurisdictions and authorities. It is not only hard to plan for and plan in, it has been a challenge to describe, analyze, and critique.[2]

One way of dealing with this outsized complexity is to focus on what I consider the key spaces of the megaregion, as opposed to the larger megaregional space (Schafran 2014). The massive geography of the megaregion can serve to mask inequality as much as ferret it out (Benner and Pastor 2008, 2011; Jones 2007; Blackwell and Duval-Diop 2008). Especially when considering the spaces between older regions, one cannot simply view them as "spillover" between metro regions (Teitz and Barbour 2007: 15), but rather as the physical and social glue that binds places together, even if they remain politically apart. These "spillovers" in many ways are the megaregion, as this is where the fusion of previously "separate" regions matters, or at least matters far more than in the more stable spaces in the core or in outer peripheries on the far side of the connecting zones.

Although a megaregion is formed by the coming together of multiple regions, the dynamics of this formation are not necessarily evenly distributed across space. Both San Francisco and Stockton are part of the megaregion, but the production of the megaregion is happening in and to Stockton much more than San Francisco.[3] All this growth, all these houses, and all these people did not just spread out amorphously on the wide-open plains of the Central Valley, even if it may seem that way when you drive over the Altamont or gaze down on the valley from the Diablo range or the Sierra foothills. They "sprawled" into specific places, as part of plans, zoning maps, and generally legal if at times dubiously conceived and executed land-use decisions. Without making the key error this book is keen to avoid—rooting the problems evident in geography in those specific geographies—it is worth pushing down in scale rather than up to see the actual places and spaces of the megaregional growth corridor: the Interstate 205 / 5 / 99 triangle of Lathrop and Manteca, Patterson on Stanislaus County's west side, Los Banos farther down Highway 33 in Merced County, Modesto's north side and Stockton's Weston Ranch, Tracy's growth at the foot of the Altamont, and Mountain House's appearance right next door.

In the words of one longtime valley leader, "the valley has always been the poor cousins" of the Bay Area, a familial inequality which meant that the formation of a megaregion is in part the expansion of one region into the spaces of another.[4] The dynamics that helped to produce growth throughout these spaces are similar to the story of East County, at least at the most basic level. There was intense demand for land from developers. Local officials facing economic need and fiscal uncertainty saw urbanization as a way to solve problems. A deeply entrenched political economy of land geared toward manipulating land and water was transformed to grow houses like they grew crops. There was an intense demand for affordable homeownership from a diverse generation of Bay Area out-migrants, people employed but not housed by the core Bay Area. Residents of the still struggling parts of the inner core had the additional need for safety and security, decent schools, and safe streets.

Unlike East County, which has always been part of the formal Bay Area politically and as such was part of many unrealized grand plans to better integrate it, the Central Valley and its fast-growing cities have always been seen as fundamentally different.[5] The Altamont is both a major psychogeographic border and a real one.

Yet like East County, what was built is woefully incomplete. The "problem" with megaregionality is not that it wove together these massive geographies, but that it was done in unsustainable and unequal fashion. The Netherlands and Germany have integrated large regions and woven together the economies and commute-sheds of previously separate cities without courting economic or environmental disaster or endangering the middle-class status of an entire generation (Schafran 2015a). Joining together large areas does not have to be part of a megaregional-scale resegregation.

Documenting this fusion of bay and valley and how and why they came together is relatively straightforward. The numbers are clear and overwhelming, even if too many scholars and analysts remain stuck in older census geographies. In this chapter, I briefly sketch how the megaregion was put together in numbers, how the San Joaquin Valley became a bedroom community for Bay Area workers, and why local leaders consistently approved development that further tied them to their richer neighbors in an unequal way. The cities and counties of the northern San Joaquin Valley were very much players with agency in this massive, spatial barn dance, even if as in East County they were making decisions in the face of massive pressure and using a highly stacked deck. Valley cities did not all take the same path. Instead, they faced yet another "damned if you do / damned if you don't" dilemma—what I call the planning dilemma. Those that enacted reasonable planning rules became more expensive and more exclusive; those that did not faced more foreclosure.

The Altamont Pass is not just a line between the traditional, formal Bay Area and the Central Valley, but a key marker of a more troubling frontier—the line between Democrat and Republican, between red and blue. Party affiliation predicts little in terms of whether your city embraced exclusion or unhealthy growth. But the stark political divide between the two sides of the pass was just another barrier working against a more equal fusion of two proud regions. This inability to weave together an already fragmented social and political geography is less a question of ghosts, as I have argued in previous chapters for smaller scales. There is so little to report in terms of concerted efforts at making the megaregion work politically or infrastructurally that a single on-the-ground effort is reduced to a small section at the end of this chapter. There has never been a truly concrete plan or proposal for the larger problem 40 years after people began to notice what was happening, and the few "solutions" offered were always inadequate. Unlike East County, the valley counties had their own COGs (council of governments) and MPOs (metropolitan planning organizations), influential members of the Assembly and Senate, and a freeway system that was part of the Eisenhower system and integral to the state's powerful agricultural economy. There is little like the 1956 BART plan that aimed to expand over the pass and never did. In the valley, unlike Brentwood and East County, development was done without the promise of higher-scale investment that never came—they were always on their own, and they knew this from the beginning.

THE PRODUCTION OF THE
NORTHERN CALIFORNIA MEGAREGION

The northern San Joaquin Valley has long been central to the story of the transformation of Northern California. The original point of centrality was economic, as capital from the gold and silver rushes in the mid-nineteenth century was plowed by San Francisco–centric capitalists into the large-scale agriculture that would bring fame, wealth, and poverty to the whole of the "Great Central Valley." If commodity-chain analysis is one's criteria for determining megaregional status, Northern California was essentially founded as a megaregion (Walker 2004a; Brechin 2006).

The northern valley's main cities, Stockton and Modesto, have never been massive, but they are very much cities in their own right, with all the trappings of modern American and California civic life—downtowns and class politics, urban boosterism and symphonies and sports teams, posh neighborhoods of stately Victorians, skid rows and Chinatowns, single-family homes and small apartments. The cities have their own dynamics of suburbanization and sprawl independent of the Bay Area. Race, immigration, urban renewal, freeway-building, decline and abandonment, and deindustrialization are part of their stories as well, even if their economy is far more agriculture- and land-based than their more metropolitan cousins on the other side of the Altamont Pass. If their role in the larger restructuring of Northern California was primarily to provide suburban-style homes for Bay Area commuters and out-migrants, it is nonetheless a critical error to ignore and deny the urbanity of the cities at the center of economic and political life in the valley.

Stockton and San Jose were founded in the same year, 1850, and remained roughly the same size until 1960, when the postwar boom came to the Bay Area much more intensely than it did to the Central Valley. Stockton's 2010 population of 291,707 people made it the 65th largest city in the United States, sandwiched between Anchorage and Toledo, larger than Salt Lake, Baton Rouge, and Buffalo. It has much in common with cities like Toledo—small cities that struggle with poverty and an image problem, losing many of its brightest children to the bigger and more vibrant economic zones nearby—and it must wage a public relations battle to be seen as more than a one-dimensional place.

Modesto is not far behind Stockton in either size or history. Legend has it that the city was to be named in honor of San Francisco capitalist Billy Ralston, he of Palace Hotel and Comstock Lode riches. He declined the honor of having it named Ralston, and thus they named it after his modesty. Modesto is the 107th largest city in America, a few thousand souls shy of Des Moines, and it too has long toiled in the shadow of its larger, wealthier, and more famous trading partner by the bay. Long before Modesto talked about BATs (Bay Area Transplants)—"ghost neighborhoods" where people making long-distance commutes left before daylight and came home after dark—and a sprawling northside that seemingly could continue forever, it grappled with a bitter irony. Its most famous native son is arguably George Lucas, who not only found fame and fortune in the Bay Area, but became a linchpin of an industry and economy that helped the Bay Area further dominate the valley and helped spur the out-migration in the first place.

There is no lack of nostalgia in the valley for the postwar era that Lucas made famous in the 1973 film *American Graffiti,* the small-town feel in what was still a city of less than 50,000 people when Lucas was growing up. Agriculture and ag-related industries dominated the Stanislaus County economy, and although San Joaquin's economy was more industrial and had the benefit of a port—again, primarily for agricultural goods and break-bulk—poverty was always a significant factor, as it has been in the Central Valley since before the Depression-era migration from the Dust Bowl to California depicted in Steinbeck's 1939 classic *The Grapes of Wrath* (Walker 2004a; McWilliams [1937] 2000; Mitchell 1996). In 1970, none of the nine core Bay Area countries had a poverty rate above 10 percent; San Joaquin (10.8%), Stanislaus (11.8%), and Merced (14.2%) all did.

But the acceptance by the valley's capitalist and middle / working classes of a high level of poverty—often hidden in unincorporated zones near factories or in labor camps tucked behind almond orchards and along dusty farm roads far off the beaten path—did not mean that they would stand by as the overall economy stagnated. By the time *American Graffiti* debuted in 1973—shot not in Modesto but in Petaluma (Sonoma County)—the farm economy was in an employment holding pattern. Between 1969 and 2000, farm employment flatlined in all three counties, while nonfarm jobs more than doubled in each county.

This did not necessarily mean that farming was not profitable—mechanization helped remove the need for certain types of labor, water remained artificially cheap for many farmers, and rising commodity prices at times have meant boons for some growers. But the number of humans involved shrunk, and there was strong impetus for local leaders and local landowners—mostly farmers and ranchers—to diversify the economy. Change did not come to the 150-year-old political economy of the valley, where those who control the land and water are those who rule; rather, change came with regard to what could be done with that land and water. Regardless of whether one aimed to protect the employment base (i.e., labor unions, some elected officials), the tax base (city officials), or land values (owners, county officials), (sub)urbanization was an unmatchable economic balm.

The end result was the growing domination of a construction and building industry that took hold of an increasing portion of each county's political economy. What began as a few subdivisions here and a few strip malls there saw the total annual construction wages in San Joaquin County alone go from $270 million in 1990 ($400 million adjusted for inflation) to over $700 million by the height of the boom in 2005.[6] And like Contra Costa County, San Joaquin's businesspeople got into the real estate credit game—17 establishments in 1990 became 52 in 2005 and generated almost 10 times the revenue, even when adjusted for inflation.[7] Stanislaus County was much the same on a slightly smaller scale. It is no wonder that one former elected official in Stanislaus County commented, "I cannot overstate just how much influence the development community has over local elected officials."[8] It was as if the economy and opportunity of East County met the full force of Contra Costa's real estate industry head on, without the distraction of edge-city building, the anti-growth politics of a strong environmental movement, or even the physical challenges of hillside development. It was, at least initially, a much simpler equation focused on transforming fields into subdivi-

TABLE 7 San Joaquin County Commuting, 1970–2000

	1970	1980	1990	2000
Total Out-of-County Commuters	4,637	9,364	31,192	49,329
% Bay Area	40.70	45.40	65.10	68.80
% Sacramento	21.80	19.90	12.70	14.40
% Stanislaus	27.50	27.10	16.50	13.50
Total Population	292,085	350,186	484,131	568,023
% Bay Area Commuters	1.60	2.70	6.40	8.70
In Labor Force (Census)	96,792	131,295	214,969	244,516
% Bay Area Commuters	4.80	7.10	14.50	20.20
Internal Commuters	85,604	123,118	159,413	163,450
Total Commuters	90,241	132,482	190,605	212,779
Out of County as % of Total	5.10	7.10	16.40	23.20
Bay Area as % of Total	2.10	3.20	10.70	15.90
Commuters to San Joaquin County	5,617	10,067	21,182	31,612
From Bay Area	899	1,132	2,656	3,772

SOURCE: U.S. Census journey to work data. Compilation by Census Bureau; calculations by author.

sions, and it did far more than transform the political economy of the valley—it made it part of the Bay Area. That would not have been possible without the human dimension: not just the demand for housing, but the emergence of a new type of economic actor from the perspective of the valley—the commuter.

Commuters

Table 7 captures much of the critical detail in the transformation of San Joaquin County from an urbanized agricultural region into a key space in a larger megaregion. In 1970, only 5 percent of the people who commuted to work left the county to do so—by 2000 it was almost 25 percent. Of that 5 percent in 1970, less than half went over the Altamont Pass to the Bay Area—by 2000, more than two-thirds of the out-of-county commuters went to the Bay Area.

We are talking serious numbers: the number of out-of-county commuters grew more than tenfold from an area where the population essentially doubled. Almost 50,000 people commuted out of the county by 2000, while only 31,612 commuted to the county, making it "suburban" in the sense that it was a major bedroom community for somewhere else's economy. This was 20 percent of its entire labor force, four times the rate from 1970.

As much as the farm economy was stagnant, this growth in megacommutes for a megaregion was not driven by locals looking for jobs, but by people with jobs coming over the hill to live. In the 2000 census, more than 40,000 San Joaquin residents reported living in the Bay Area in 1995, almost 30,000 from Alameda and Santa Clara counties alone, almost five times the number that made the reverse migration, despite the vastly superior economy. Stanislaus County's numbers were closer—22,000 in-migrants and 13,000 out-migrants—but still imbalanced. Merced County took in more than 10,000—more than 8,000 from Santa Clara County alone—and sent back 3,300.[9]

This data only captures a fraction of the incessant churning that saw ample movement in both directions. There is a tendency to conceptualize the above as a one-way migration like refugees from a flood, but people moved both ways, just like immigrants often go back to their home countries; that said, the result was still a constant net gain of Bay Area residents in the Central Valley over the course of decades. Merced, Stanislaus, and San Joaquin counties all more than doubled in size between 1970 and 2010, far outstripping the growth rates of the counties of San Francisco (12.5%), San Mateo (29.2%), and even Santa Clara (67.3%). It is not just a question of percentages—the combined growth of Merced, Stanislaus, and San Joaquin counties, an area that only partially includes outer-ring growth, added more actual humans (862,614) than San Francisco and Santa Clara counties combined (806,489) during this period.

This is the demand that helped provide the market for most of those homes and most of that bad debt. Map 11 shows the distinct geography of "high-cost mortgages," with its clear emphasis on the places that should by now be familiar—Richmond and Oakland, East County and the Cities of Carquinez, and these spaces of the megaregion out in the Central Valley.

All these people with all these homes driving long distances to work also brought profound challenges to local and regional infrastructure, to local social and political culture, and to the identity of valley towns. But one of the most important challenges came from a need that fed the growth machine itself and its tendency to borrow unwisely from unscrupulous financial actors. It was a self-perpetuating logic of growth even more basic than the development fee paradigm—these new residents had to shop somewhere.

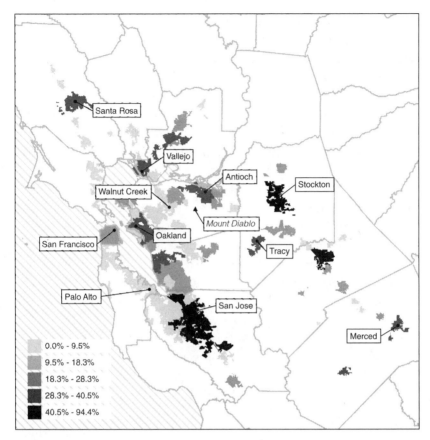

MAP 11. High Cost Mortgage Map, 2004–2006. Source: 2007 HMDA.

Rooftops, or the Logic of Corporate Retail Math and the Question of Amenities

Academic discussion of both exurban development and amenities often focuses on resort locations, small towns being gentrified by second home-owners or plowed under by "a complex nexus of global processes." Critical scholarship aims at understanding "the consequences of the residential side of the amenity-seeking behaviour of exurbanites colonizing the countryside," whereby amenities are golf courses or other luxury development, and big-box stores are somehow alien to the "natural" landscape of small communities (Taylor 2011: 326).[10] Northern California certainly has examples of this type, from the Diablo Grande development outside Patterson to increasingly bourgeois towns in the Sierra foothills.

But there is a decidedly more middle-class, suburban, American, and small-town Californian question of "amenities" that cannot be reduced to "global processes" or "colonization." New homes and new residents bring needs and desires for more basic amenities like supermarkets and public swimming pools, and they feed into a self-perpetuating logic of growth, one driven by the intersection of three different logics, all of which demanded more rooftops. This is the amenities question, a decidedly unsexy and mundane aspect of everyday life in consumerist America, but one that drives growth enormously.

In talking with people who relocated to the Central Valley, many refer to the "small-town atmosphere," to the sense of community, safety, and quiet, an idea that this "is how it used to be," even if many came from places where it was never quite like this. But few seemed nostalgic for old-time retail, small local stores with limited selections and often higher prices. They wanted their Targets, their large-scale supermarkets, their Home Depots or Lowe's, and they did not want to have to drive miles and miles to find them. After all, they drove enough every day on their way to work.

Local government also looked favorably upon this retail growth, for it meant tax dollars. They needed money to pay for new infrastructure demanded by new and old residents alike—public swimming pools, new or refurbished and expanded schools, sports facilities for high school teams— pieces of generally public infrastructure that provided both services and community pride to small towns where pride and local identity are critical currency.

This push for both retail and public amenities—consistently cited in interview after interview with local officials, planners, and citizens— was subject to an increasingly quantitative corporate retail math. The decision to open a specific store of a specific type is determined in the United States not by the hunch of an entrepreneur but because the demographic equation calculated by someone sitting in corporate headquarters adds up. Race, income, education levels, ethnicity, and a host of other data points factor in, but nothing matters more than rooftops. If you want a full-service supermarket, you need a minimum of 5,000 houses. Patterson in 1990 had only 2,703 housing units, and no major supermarket. As the population began to grow, people wanted a large market—there was only so much small-town they could take, despite the fact that there were two old-style markets downtown, one generally serving the Latinx community and the other the white community.[11] Once you have a supermarket, the next step is something like a Target, a Lowe's, or undoubtedly the most controversial—a Walmart.

To see the growth of major retail chains as primarily colonization—the trappings of metropolitan life brought with or demanded by newcomers— not only strips local towns of agency and responsibility but misreads how this all came about in the first place. Again, old-time Central Valley residents continued to dominate politics in virtually every city, town, and county in the valley, despite rapid growth and change. Some farmers were fighting to preserve the old ways of life and farming, while others couldn't wait to sell. Old–time residents may have bemoaned the cultural habits of the newcomers, the noise, or above all the traffic, yet they voted in favor of growth by consistently electing pro-growth politicians. And many wanted the new stores themselves—to shop in, to profit on as developers or landowners or accountants or lawyers, or to work in as employees in an always fragile economy.

This trajectory of "progress" is best conceived of as a small-town Americana example of Gramscian hegemony. Unlike the development fee paradigm discussed in chapter 2, where growth becomes a Faustian bargain, the amenities question reaches deeper into the American model of suburban lifestyle and consumption. We buy lifestyles when we buy homes, even if that lifestyle is not formally built into the community. We will then support, or at least consent to, further political decisions to allow more growth, as long as it brings amenities which we see as convenient. For all that some people warned of its unsustainability, for all the local dissent and hand-wringing over lost culture, or buyer's remorse from former urbanites and continued economic, fiscal, and political struggles, the unreal growth of the spaces of the Northern California megaregion was not possible without wholesale buy-in from virtually every major segment of political and social economy. Major *local* opposition to development in these spaces of the megaregion grew only after there had been enough growth to attract amenities—in Tracy in the 1990s, or more recently in Brentwood. Then it becomes more of a question of whether *further growth* will overtax those amenities, making traffic worse or the swimming pool more crowded. In many ways, it is no different than Silicon Valley, multiple generations later.

This consent enabled the commercial development industry and their corporate retail partners to grossly exploit the consumption desires of new residents and the fiscal needs of fast-growing towns. For every story of amenities-driven growth you hear in the valley, you also hear stories of crass corporate exploitation—Walmart insisting on a 50 percent sales tax rebate in Modesto, Home Depot pitting three cities against each other in a bid for services, corporate site plans and locational desires that reflect internal company policies designed in Minneapolis or Bentonville rather than the traffic, consumption, and community needs of Patterson or Manteca.[12] As one longtime valley planner put it, citizen demand for amenities and fiscal demand for sales tax revenue "fundamentally changed the nature of the power relationship between cities, citizens, and corporations." Corporate actors and their developer allies exploited this double form of demand as much as they could during this entire era, even as the fiscal and economic wheels were coming off the bus.

The Planning Dilemma

In the face of this restructured power relationship, not all cities reacted precisely the same way. Unlike Contra Costa County, where significant growth occurred in unincorporated areas and where the county was a major player in development, much of the growth in the northern San Joaquin Valley took place in incorporated cities, or at times on the edge of cities in anticipation of annexation—with a few noteworthy exceptions.[13] The smaller cities and towns share much in common with East County, and even more with Brentwood, which unlike the industrial towns of Pittsburg and Antioch is itself an old Central Valley railroad town not too different historically from Ripon, Patterson, and Manteca. In the conversion of old farm towns into postindustrial garden, one sees a slightly different dynamic, a shift from an agricultural to an urban economy without passing through a major industrial era.

Although many of the key Central Valley towns were members of the 50 / 5000 club, and all have struggled to some extent with growth and foreclosure, the places of the northern San Joaquin are not all the same. The differences between them can be massive, i.e., between the large cities of Stockton and Modesto and the smaller former farm communities. Or they can be quite subtle—a matter of a few miles' difference in commute, a cultural variation in the approach to development established years before, a few decisions of major landowners or city councils. They all did not take the same approach, and one of the key questions emerging in the valley post-crash was why some places like Ripon and Lodi emerged *relatively* unscathed, especially when compared to neighbors like Manteca and Lathrop that garnered national attention as part of the crisis.

In Lodi's case, it largely resisted the siren call of rampant growth, building more slowly and avoiding the 50 / 5000 club. It "benefitted" from a location just beyond the primary commute-sheds, too far north of Silicon Valley to "compete" for commuters—Stanislaus and Merced county towns would always win out for the Silicon Valley folks, while Tracy, Lathrop, Manteca, Mountain House, and Stockton were all closer to the 580 / 680 corridor. But Lodi, Ripon, and the Stanislaus County city of Oakdale specifically tried to aim for a wealthier class of new resident, using planning controls to push prices just a bit higher than surrounding communities.

The differences are subtle. Per square foot housing prices were not radically different, but Ripon insisted on bigger houses. Bigger houses on bigger lots equal higher prices, and towns have known this for generations. This was not gross exclusion as practiced in the San Ramon Valley or Marin, nor anything that would remotely make the historical record of suburban exclusionism, not with the myriad examples throughout Californian and American history.

Again, like the almost normal rates of growth in some Silicon Valley communities, one could also argue that this was "good planning." The cities would simply demand that developers build more amenities for residents, such as better quality streets, parks, and lighting. They insisted that developers conform to locally produced plans rather than accepting stock subdivision design from corporate headquarters. Brentwood planners made similar arguments, and believed that some of their relative success vis-à-vis Antioch in terms of foreclosure rates has to do with the higher planning standards. If such an approach chased away some developers—for instance, KB Homes, one of the major national corporate builders, pulled out of Ripon because it found the costs and standards too exacting—there were always other developers willing to build. And Ripon certainly grew, almost doubling in size in two decades.

These subtle strategies pursued by towns like Ripon and Lodi are just part of a long tradition of American planning where the link between good planning—sound fiscal judgment, good design, maximizing benefits from a development community dedicated to minimizing cost—and exclusion runs deep. All the towns in the Central Valley eventually adopted some form of more controlled and better regulated planning, especially after having gotten burned in initial rounds. But one of the many tragedies of this crisis is that it is seen to vindicate those who advocate subtle exclusion as sound planning practice at the local level—chances are that the more your housing stock remained affordable to "the masses" during the boom years, the more your town is now struggling.

The most troubling story evident in the question of the uneven transformation of the San Joaquin Valley is the ongoing relationship between foreclosure and race. Ripon, Lodi, and Oakdale had three of the four lowest foreclosure rates in 2008 of cities and towns in the three counties. They were also three of the four whitest places in the three counties, all with a white majority at a time when the rest of the valley's fast-growing cities and towns became majority-minority. Like the wealthier communities of the West Bay and parts of Contra Costa County, they were economically rewarded for being economically and racially exclusive, while cities that did not try to make their housing more expensive were punished.

This perverse math created yet another set of "damned if you do, damned if you don't" choices for northern San Joaquin Valley towns. Good planning equaled exclusion, bad planning equaled racialized foreclosure. This is what I call the planning dilemma, yet another set of either / or choices that drove the production of a new map of segregation. Towns that opened their doors did so by keeping standards too low; towns that raised standards raised walls. Quality development with reasonable levels of growth, good design, and solid foundations made things more expensive in the absurd political economy of development that had evolved in the neoliberal-era Bay Area. Although this dilemma is clearest in the differences between valley towns, it has long plagued planning and development everywhere in the region. Building quality places slowly became reserved only for one class of people rather than another, a differentiation with deeply racial manifestations. This dilemma fed more ideological battles about regulation versus markets, arguments that offered great headlines but few solutions. The application of tired twentieth-century economic ideologies to the questions of how a region provides quality environments for all its residents turned the debate into a Dougherty Valley–type argument where everyone loses regardless of who "wins."

The question of ideology goes even deeper than just the planning dilemma or Dougherty Valley, for there is another set of divisions, intersecting with black and white and brown and green in complex ways, that are also most evident when one crosses the Altamont. The pass is now the line between red and blue.

A DIFFERENT COLOR OF FRONTIER

Etched into the grasslands at the base of the Altamont windmills is another symbol visible from 580, a large cross cut into the brown hill proclaiming

"Jesus Saves." Fittingly, it is greeting you as you leave the Bay Area and head into the Central Valley, not the other way around. As you head down the eastern side of the Altamont, Christian radio outnumbers NPR in roughly the reverse ratio as on the western side of the pass. Spanish-language radio is omnipresent, as is country music and classic rock, announcing in no uncertain terms that you have crossed a cultural line.

No matter how much one marshals economic and demographic data to argue for the formation of a megaregion, the feeling that one is crossing a line when going over the Altamont is powerful, a psychogeographic sense which is more than myth or outdated perception. When you cross the Diablo range, the climate changes, the air changes, the smells and horizons and points of reference all undergo a transition. One gets a muted version of the same feeling crossing over the Kirker Pass, the line between the 680 corridor and East County, a physical extension of the massive Diablo range that separates the Bay Area and the Central Valley and a baby cousin to the Altamont. The eastern part of East County is part of the Central Valley geographically, connected to its vast farm- and land-based economy, and very much part of the frontiers that are part of the often unspoken backstory to megaregional Northern California.

For all that the core of the Bay Area has become a Democratic stronghold over the course of the past 40 years, when one zooms out to the scale of the megaregion one begins to see shades of purple and red. The arc formed by the Diablo range was a growth frontier and a demographic frontier, a line between high foreclosure and low foreclosure. It was the periurban frontier, where the metropolis met the rural lands, where the transition was from an agricultural to an urban economy. It was also a critical political frontier, not inborn but produced over the past half century.

It is hard to imagine that Berkeley was once a Republican stronghold, but in the 1950s it had a Republican city council majority. This soon changed, and by the 1970s San Francisco and Berkeley were at the heart of a growing progressive empire. Yet Republicans and conservatives existed in relative numbers, even in San Francisco. Almost a third (32 percent) of San Francisco's registered voters in 1964, the year Barry Goldwater ran for president and the contemporary conservative movement in America began to crystallize, were Republicans (McGirr 2001). Contra Costa, San Joaquin, and Stanislaus counties were only a few percentage points higher. During that era, the line between red and blue was not constituted at the Altamont, but between neighborhoods in San Francisco, between the wealthy and Republican towns of central Contra Costa like Danville and the blue-collar and Democratic cities like Pittsburg.

But over the past 40 years, this core of the Bay Area has grown more blue, while the Central Valley and its extensions in East County have grown increasingly red. Analyzing party affiliation data from 1964 through 2008 for all cities and counties in the 12-county region shows important trends. San Francisco in 2008 was 10 percent Republican, with Democrats outnumbering Republicans 5 to 1. In San Joaquin and Stanislaus counties, the percentage of Republicans grew during an era when California as a whole shifted from red to blue, and the ratio of Democrats to Republicans (D2R) went from roughly 1.6:1 to 1:1.

Taken as a whole, the emergence of the Altamont as a political divide is part of the wholesale separation of California politically along east/west lines, as opposed to the historical north/south division. This is what Douzet, Kousser, and Miller (2008) call the "new political geography of California," and it is a phenomenon one can see up and down the Central Valley and into the foothills. Like the rest of California before the New Deal, the Central Valley was a Republican stronghold, famous for brutal labor conditions and violent confrontations over workers' rights (Walker 2004a; McWilliams [1937] 2000; Mitchell 1996). The New Deal changed this, and by 1940, only a third of the registered voters across the entire Central Valley were Republican. But throughout the neoliberal era, as the coast became more liberal, the valley became more conservative (Miller and Levitt 2008).

At first glance, there seems to be a clear correlation between high-growth places and becoming Republican. There will undoubtedly be readers who take this data and the chapter on Marin and wave it as a clear example of how the Republican Party treats the working class better by removing barriers to economic growth. But the actual data shows that the divides in party affiliation are a result of what occurred, not the cause. Republicans controlled Piedmont, Danville, and Lamorinda at the height of the exclusionary era, and were no more welcoming to the masses than their Democratic counterparts in Marin and Silicon Valley. They have become more blue over the years as the cultural politics of Silicon Valley and environmentalism have become hegemonic, but their exclusionary nature was built when they were still red.

Moreover, the most exclusionary of the Central Valley towns—Lodi, Ripon, and Oakdale—were also the most Republican. Oakdale had more Democrats than Republicans in 1964 and became more Republican during the neoliberal era. Stockton, which embraced growth as much as any city, had more Democrats than Republicans. Same with smaller Patterson. While one can point to the hypocrisy of certain Bay Area Democrats, there is no evidence that Republican majority places acted any better.

What is evident is that the transformation of the region did occur alongside political shifts. As the Central Valley grew more diverse, parts of it also grew more conservative, and it is impossible to ignore the racialized nature of the subtle lines between towns.

The Central Valley towns have always had a strong conservative presence, but the increase in Republican registration points to the relationship between the redness (or purpleness) of the valley and the larger restructuring of the region. Some of those new valley Republicans were former Bay Area residents who are part of a Brentwood-era version of white flight, or perhaps just as accurately a version of red flight—conservatives fleeing the hegemonic blue-statism at the core of the Bay Area.[14]

The argument that people moved because of their political beliefs, seeking to live among others of a similar ilk, is made by Bill Bishop in his 2008 book *The Big Sort*. Bishop asserts that the polarization of America is geographic—we are increasingly opting to live in communities with people who are similar to us politically, a phenomenon he contends explains the more extremist views possible by politicians representing geographies that are more like San Francisco (i.e., overwhelming majority of one party) rather than frontier spaces like San Joaquin County. *The Big Sort* was immediately attacked by the political science establishment, both for the inadequacy of its statistical methods and for what they called "pop sociology" (Bishop and Cushing 2009; Abrams and Fiorina 2012: 203).

Much of the debate about the propriety of certain measurements centered around the "neighborhood effects" debate in sociology, the extent to which the isolationism asserted by Bishop impacts political discourse, tolerance of other issues, etc., or around whether a red / blue dualism for America was really a valid description of polarization in the first place. Yet lost in these debates is any consideration of whether some type of sorting along political lines is really happening, or whether there are purple places, frontiers where a mixing is happening and where new lines are being drawn, questions about whether where people move has anything to do with regional restructuring and the politics of the local. Academic critics attacked the methodological foundation and the totality of Bishop's arguments rather than going out to the town and cities of places like the Central Valley to see if there is any validity to his arguments. There is simply no denying that the political shifts now evident across the Altamont were very real, and sorting had something to do with it.

Yet if the relationship between party affiliation and growth is not straightforward, adding a party divide to an already deep set of cultural and social fissures did not make planning across the Altamont any easier. Just like with East County, just like with Silicon Valley's housing crisis, leaders, planners, and citizens saw the creation of this megaregion and could not mount a plan to make it less unequal. So immense were the barriers, and so grand the scale, that a real plan to alter the dynamics was unthinkable from the start.

THE LIMITS OF THE MEGAREGION

Legend has it that in the mid-1980s, during a period of growing concern in Modesto about the impact that Bay Area migration was having on the city, then-mayor Carol Whiteside stormed into ABAG (Association of Bay Area Governments) and demanded that Modesto be admitted to the regional body. It makes for a beautifully theatrical image, but alas, the story is not true.[15] What is true is that Whiteside and other Central Valley leaders had long been aware of the restructuring under way, as subdivisions that began sprouting in Tracy in the 1970s and early 1980s started mushrooming throughout San Joaquin, Stanislaus, and Merced counties.

Although it may not have been at the forefront of their minds, Bay Area leaders knew what was happening as well. Traffic patterns on the Altamont had picked up, often at ungodly hours. Bay Area real estate developers and brokers saw the flow of people and capital and were part of the migration. Anecdotes about "megacommutes" began to circulate, stories about this engineer who commuted to Cupertino from Modesto, about that teacher who came in from Tracy.

Part of the problem is that the anecdotes were just that—anecdotes. The 1980 census did not show a flood of long-distance commuters, as the process was just beginning.[16] In 1980, San Joaquin and Stanislaus residents ranked near the bottom in terms of percent of long commutes (60+ minutes) in the region. Marin County, with its mounting traffic problems and not yet aged workforce, had the highest percentage of long commutes in the 12-county region (12.3%). More than twice as many Marinites traveled long distances to work as did the residents of San Joaquin and Stanislaus counties combined.

Long commutes were also a much greater problem in the more heavily populated parts of the region like Contra Costa and Alameda counties, as the Bay Area became a massive traffic bottleneck. With Prop. 13 having severely constrained local finances, with cutbacks in state and federal support, and with local sales tax referendums not yet legal, it is not clear what could have been done in the early 1980s about the emerging commute-shed on the other side of the Altamont, other than attempting to prevent it by building more housing in the Bay Area.

This lack of true options was partly driven by a structural factor in the political economy of the Central Valley. Unlike the Bay Area, which is "united" by regional agencies (chapter 7), each county in the Central Valley has its own metropolitan planning organization (MPO) and / or council of government (COG). Each of the cities of Modesto, Merced, and Stockton is its own metropolitan statistical area (MSA) according to the census, despite their proximity and similarities. But similarity does not mean integration— they have parallel economies, each producing agricultural goods for markets elsewhere, rather than more codependent urban economies. The Bay Area did not become connected to a unified agro-metropolis, but to three different ones operating under similar conditions.[17]

It was not until the turn of the millennium that formal planning cooperation emerged, and even that was short-lived. Buoyed by a state planning grant, planners from the Bay Area's COG (the aforementioned ABAG), the Central Valley COG, and Alameda, Contra Costa, Santa Clara, San Joaquin, and Stanislaus counties helped set up the Interregional Partnership (IRP) to address the clear and present challenges of growth. Begun with much enthusiasm, the partnership met regularly, developed some new projections, and tried to identify ways of intervening in the jobs-housing mismatch. Despite having state support, the IRP did not even pretend that strong policy measures were possible. Instead, they used the language of innovation that was emerging at the time to talk in terms of being "a laboratory to determine whether or not the location of jobs and / or housing can be influenced through the use of focused incentives."[18]

The IRP ended in 2004, not long after it began, having accomplished little relative to the scale of the problem. By that time, the numbers had changed dramatically. Reflecting the rise of long commutes throughout the country, the census added a new category of 90-plus-minute commutes in 1990, what became known as megacommutes. Already in 1990, Stanislaus jumped to the top of the 12-county chart in this most ignominious of categories, almost three times that of Marin. By 2000, more than 25,000 people traveled more than 90 minutes each way from San Joaquin and Stanislaus counties to work every day.

Relative Accomplishments

Perhaps most emblematic of the situation is that the clearest "success" story in the midst of four decades of economic and social integration is the development of a single train line, the Altamont Commuter Express (ACE). The ACE train is the product of a political-business coalition that in 1990 was able to pass a transportation sales tax measure similar to Contra Costa's Measure C. In ACE's own words, "In 1989, passenger rail service across the Altamont was considered only a pipe dream that might be worth discussing in twenty years."[19] While the Northern California–worthy florid language is surely a bit of gamesmanship to play up their accomplishment, it is a fair reflection of just how limited the planning possibilities and horizons were despite the massive, unequal, and unsustainable megaregional fusion that was occurring in full view of citizens and leaders alike.

Opened in 1998, the service has gone through multiple iterations of governance, from an initial Joint Powers Agreement that required deeper cooperation between Santa Clara, Alameda, and San Joaquin transit agencies to the current agreement whereby Santa Clara County largely pulled out of the agreement—as they pulled out of BART—and Alameda County played a limited role. ACE is now essentially operated by San Joaquin County, with some funding from Alameda and Santa Clara counties and a myriad of other sources.[20]

The "Express" in the train's title is used loosely. In 2010, the train ran three times each day in each direction, leaving Stockton at 4:20, 5:35, and 6:40 a.m., taking more than two hours to reach its final destination in San Jose and an hour just to reach the first major job center on Vasco Road in Livermore. There were three similar return trips back in the afternoon, at 3:35, 4:35, and 5:35 p.m. By 2015, a fourth train each way had been added, but there was still no weekend service, no holiday service, and no reverse commutes. The distances are significant—it is roughly 80 miles between Stockton and San Jose, with a thousand-foot pass in between—but nothing that similarly wealthy countries around the world have not been able to handle.

ACE for the most part is not like BART, a potential solution to a larger problem that was undone by ghosts. ACE, like the SMART train in Marin, is a classic example of the diminished expectations that permeated planning in a post-Babylon world, where such a limited service is all one can hope for despite decades of need, thousands of hours of hard work by dedicated professionals and politicos alike, and clear examples from around the world as to how to integrate regional spaces that are larger than the "traditional" metropolis. A true solution was never even a remote possibility, and there is no Dougherty Valley paradigm to blame here. What makes it even more egregious is that these broader failings have only helped exacerbate some of the problems of segregation—both mobile and traditional—that helped spur growth in the first place.

There is one ghost that hangs over ACE, one of the true original sins of Californian urbanization, the Golden State's other version of primitive accumulation alongside gold. ACE's limited service is driven in large part because it is dependent on tracks that it does not own, but merely uses under an agreement with Union Pacific (Monger 2008).[21] This severely limits capacity, especially with regard to expansion and timetables. It is a similar story in Antioch, which is blessed with an Amtrak station but cursed by the fact that the San Joaquin branch line is also leased from these same freight operators who were one of California's original power brokers. BART's initial eBART route for East County was originally planned to use the moribund Mococo right-of-way, which had not been operational since the 1970s, a path that would have brought trains much closer to the downtowns and would not have taken up valuable median space in Highway 4. But the train operators cut off negotiations after initial plans had been released, and now the region is stuck with a less than ideal route that runs along a freeway median rather than near hoping-for-revitalization downtowns.

This is the deepest and saddest irony of the structure of urbanization in megaregional space. Virtually every one of these towns exists alongside a railroad track, a reminder that the original development of the megaregion was made possible by the fact that the state urbanized largely through the use of rail. But the power of the train operators to ignore the changing needs of a growing population for more diverse forms of connectivity remains a major impediment, even if they possess the needed infrastructure that could weave together the sprawling region which the trains helped to build.

Sad irony becomes historical farce if one digs slightly deeper. Omaha-based Union Pacific was the eastern partner to San Francisco–based Central Pacific on the transcontinental railroad, which united in Promontory, Utah, in 1869, one of foundational moments in the history of the American West. Central Pacific began to fuse with Southern Pacific not long after the "golden spike" was driven home, and by 1901 Southern Pacific and Union Pacific had begun a merger process that would take almost a century to complete (Orsi 2005).

That same year, Frank Norris ([1901] 1986) published *The Octopus: A California Story*, a fictionalized account of the Mussel Slough tragedy in which seven people were killed during a land dispute that involved Southern Pacific. The Octopus of the title referred to how Southern Pacific's "tentacles" reached down to every level of government. Calls for reform saw Hiram Johnson elected governor in 1910 on an explicitly anti–Southern Pacific platform. In 1911, Johnson and his progressive allies installed the initiative, referendum, and recall systems, at the time unprecedented in the United States.

This populist / Progressive Era solution to the control of the state government by a single powerful company helped lessen the power of Southern Pacific, but the Octopus never truly went away—its tracks remained, and the state never truly challenged its power over this invaluable land. Rights-of-way, which in many cases were acquired through land grants and government bonds, were now entirely private, and the fact that they no longer served the late twentieth- and early twenty-first-century transportation needs of Californians was ignored.[22]

Moreover, the medicine that California took to kill the Octopus would prove just as dangerous as the original problem, especially to the urban fabric. The initiative system would become arguably the most critical and destructive venue for the divisive development politics of neoliberal-era California, begetting the famed Proposition 13 in 1978 that laid the foundation for much of the preceding story.

Despite the dreams of some megaregionalists, the Altamont line was never going to be bridged by some 12-county governance structure or a beefed-up version of the IRP. One can sense, in the minutes and documents from the IRP's brief life span, the clear limits they set for what they did. From talking to those who participated, it is clear—they knew their hands were tied before they sat down together. At best, they could publicize and understand the problem more clearly, even if it was likely too late, and hope that local, regional, or state actors would intervene. The megaregion is increasingly a critical scale for analyzing and understanding problems, but it was never going to be an important scale at which to intervene in them (Schafran 2014a). Overcoming the problems of the Altamont line could perhaps have been done with the full efforts of the state government, but as I will show in chapter 8, this help was not forthcoming during an era in which the state was ripping itself apart politically.

Preventing the problems of the Altamont line perhaps could have been done with a more successful effort at bringing together actors in the nine-county Bay Area before 12-county analysis became necessary. For more than a century, planners, reformers, and business leaders have talked about "regionalism" as the only true solution to what are clearly regional problems. If only the Bay Area had had stronger regional governance, or so the argument goes, the sins and errors recounted in the first six chapters of this book could have been avoided. Perhaps this is true, but just like every other scale and geography examined in this book, regional leadership failed, and political fragmentation of the deepest kind was at the root of the problem.

SEVEN

The Regionalist Dream

THE ONE THING THAT THE NORTHERN CONTRA COSTA SHORE-
LINE, Mount Diablo, Edwards Park, and the Presidio have in common is a
clear view of either the San Francisco Bay or the San Joaquin delta that forms
the bay's eastern arm. The bay is and has always been the central organizing
principle of the area, the region's "defining feature" in the words of both
business and progressive leaders.[1] Part of why the Altamont remains an
important line is that one is literally leaving the area defined by the bay.

The bay has long been a critical unifying force in building a regional sense
of identity that few areas in the country can match. Perhaps because the
region has always been sprawling, always been fragmented into innumerable
jurisdictions, always been spread out along the bay and its various foothills,
always been more than San Francisco, residents often think of themselves as
part of a region. Perhaps it is the relative isolation of the region from other
places, or a rivalry with Southern California that makes the "Bay Area" or
"NorCal" something to claim or be proud of. Perhaps it is the fact that the
region's hip-hop scene, as much about Vallejo as it is about Oakland and San
Francisco, has become the "Yay Area" (Chang 2016). Or perhaps it is simply
the majesty of this "defining feature," such that being from "the Bay"—
always capitalized—means something.

One of the cruelest ironies of the resegregation of the Bay Area is that the
political fragmentation which was unable to prevent it occurred despite such
a strong sense of collective belonging to a region. The Bay Area is not greater
New York, spread out across three states, where nobody writes songs or gets
tattoos about the "tri-state area." It had both a collective sense that there was
a region, and a single-state legal and policy structure whereby strong regional
action was at least theoretically possible. The Bay Area may have been able to

do little to change decisions on the eastern side of the Altamont Pass, but much more could have been done on the western side to lessen the pressure.

Like their counterparts at the local level, regional leaders, regional organizations, and regional agencies saw the restructuring of the region and knew what was happening from the very beginning. From the troubling development trajectory of East County to Contra Costa's edge cities, from the ongoing struggles of Richmond and Oakland to the stagnation of the military base redevelopment, from San Francisco's creeping gentrification to Silicon Valley's unwillingness to build enough housing to Marin County's refusal to build virtually anything at all, few parts of the story I have told thus far were mysteries to those with a regional perspective during this period.

This chapter focuses on trying to understand why effective regional action on segregation and resegregation never materialized. Part of the issue is that the hope for regional intervention is an old one. Regional or metropolitan governance has been a dream of political reformers in the United States for a century, and the Bay Area has long been at the center of this particular political imagination.[2] Regionalism—as the effort to make political reforms and institution at the regional level is known—has ghosts dating back to San Francisco's post-1906 dream of annexing much of the inner Bay Area, much as New York City had done to most of the surrounding boroughs barely a decade previously. An important failed attempt also occurred in 1960, during the height of postwar modernism. Efforts to build a more effective regional governance structure during the 1990s were hampered by these ghosts and made the mistake of not learning from them. The major reform effort of this period, Bay Vision 2020, repeated the top-down, elite-driven process that so characterized postwar planning. It ended up as a conversation all too typical during this era, one between environmentalist and business groups, largely excluding communities of color and social justice actors from the negotiating table.

Even with Bay Visions' failure, regional planning efforts kept materializing. A steady stream of academic and policy work from different disciplines increasingly saw more collaborative forms of regionalism as the answer, including to problems of regional segregation. In the Bay Area, new initiatives were started, new planning processes begun. State mandates to plan regionally for housing would be supplemented by a national mandate for more regional transportation planning and a later state mandate to plan for greenhouse gas reduction.

Yet even with improved planning and cross-sectoral cooperation during the latter half of this period, major interventions that could possibly have changed the direction of the region did not occur. The game-changing housing and transportation interventions were never even on the table, part of a regionalism increasingly hamstrung by limited possibilities. Imagining an effective regional politics capable of solving the regions' segregation and equity problems was considered a political impossibility almost from the beginning, so deep were the divisions even amidst increasing collaboration, so heavy were the ghosts of past failures.

Regionalism in the aftermath of foreclosure showed important signs of hopes. A landmark planning process seemed to strike a balance between open space conservation and transit-oriented development, and even paid attention to displacement, if somewhat after the fact. A federal grant to study economic prosperity brought together social justice and more mainstream actors as never before. But these moments of post-crisis regionalism, while boding some hope for the future, also showed how far the region was from truly understanding the problem and from building the type of grand coalition needed to combat it. Most troubling was the fact that decades after the production of this new map of segregation had begun, there was nary a hint of any regional effort to ensure that the places where communities of color had increasingly *migrated to* were on the road to receiving increased regional support and attention. Actors from all sides of the sustainability puzzle— economic, environmental, and social justice—acted as if the map had not already been profoundly and irrevocably changed.

Post-crisis regionalism also highlighted what by now has become a too obvious trope. The one policy arena where the region was able to overcome its broad fragmentation and political inertia was the one area where it has long been a world leader—environmental protection. In 2016, virtually the entire region, its voters and its leaders, voted in a historic fashion to tax themselves to pay for much-needed wetlands restoration. Overcoming segregation and spatial inequality was another matter.

THE EARLY DAYS OF BAY AREA REGIONALISM

In 1898, New York City accomplished one of the most grandiose political maneuvers in urban history. Cities had long expanded by annexation, including taking over small towns and cities on their outskirts. Paris's Montmartre seems so integral to contemporary Paris, yet it was once a separate village outside the city walls. Mexico City is made up of numerous old villages that have been slowly urbanized. But nothing like New York had been seen before. When Manhattan and Brooklyn were joined together that year, it represented the combining of the largest and third-largest cities in the nation.

This consolidation was not lost on Bay Area leaders at the time, especially in San Francisco. The 1906 earthquake had devastated the city, but by the 1910 census the numbers were already rallying. San Francisco had largely escaped abandonment; instead, the region saw its population grow by more than 40 percent between 1900 and 1910. Much of that growth went to newly expanded Oakland, which almost tripled in both population and land area during the same period. Oakland had arrived, and the *relative* waning of San Francisco vis-à-vis the region discussed in chapter 5 had begun.

Government officials and powerful civil society actors in San Francisco reacted to this regional restructuring by devising a plan for a New York–style consolidation. Promoted by the Greater San Francisco Association and the San Francisco Chamber of Commerce—the first of what would be many forays into regionalism by elite, business-driven civil society institutions—the idea of Greater San Francisco emerged (Scott 1985; Barbour 2002; Dyble 2009).

The vision incorporated less people than New York, but was even more ambitious in terms of territory. It would have amalgamated not only San Francisco and Oakland, but East Bay cities from San Leandro to Richmond and Marin's Sausalito, Mill Valley, and San Rafael (Scott [1959] 1985). San Francisco leaders pushed the proposal for a consolidated city all the way to the state legislature, where it was soundly defeated. Opposition came in part from Southern California cities like Pasadena, anxious about Los Angeles's growing hunger, and from an increasingly powerful Oakland.

What is most important about the failure of Greater San Francisco is that the aggressiveness with which San Francisco leaders acted undermined forms of regional cooperation that had been brewing. A regional water district had been proposed simultaneously, and that too became a victim of the amalgamation plan. In the words of historian Mel Scott ([1959] 1985: 134), the "movement for a supermunicipality . . . would antagonize Oakland officials and generate sectional bitterness which would long retard the economic development of the entire Bay Area."

Additional murmurings for regionalism would continue, including a short-lived attempt at creating a Regional Plan Association for San Francisco, following the one in New York (Scott [1959] 1985). One thing working against regionalism was the constant expansion of the region itself and its subsequent incorporations. Between Progressive Era political reforms that encouraged incorporation and a development industry quickly establishing itself at the center of the state's political economy, there were more and more organized municipalities to deal with (Barbour 2002).

But certain forms of cross-jurisdictional cooperation did occur. After the failure of the regional water system, East Bay cities formed the East Bay Municipal Utility District (EBMUD) in 1923. They would do the same thing for parks in the 1930s. In 1928 San Francisco would join with North Bay counties extending to the Oregon border to finance and build the Golden Gate Bridge. Subregional-scale special-purpose districts like EBMUD would end up becoming the foundation of regional cooperation, and one could argue that they remain so to this day. That does not mean the more grandiose visions for regional government would not return; a few governance trends come back in style more regularly than regionalism, especially in the Bay Area.

POSTWAR REGIONALISM

Every 20 years or so in the Bay Area, regionalists link arms, find the biggest brick wall they can find, and then run straight into it.

—Longtime Planning Researcher, Bay Area, 2009

I foresee—and I advocate—the gradual development of a two-level system of local and metropolitan government for the Bay Area. Twenty or thirty years from now, the local municipal governments will have become more numerous as a result of the formation of new cities in the outlying areas. These governments will also have become more powerful. Like the Swiss, the people of the Bay Area will have decided in favor of all-purpose, home-rule cities. Also like the Swiss, they will have created a unified, limited-function federation of local governments, largely controlled by the cities, to handle area-wide problems.

—T. J. KENT, *City and Metropolitan Planning for the Metropolitan San Francisco Bay Area* (1963: 3)

The creation of special-purpose districts continued after the war, at different scales. Air pollution was gradually becoming a major problem even before mass freeway-building, and the state of California began creating air pollution control districts. Originally set up at the county level, the regional nature of air pollution soon mandated a new geography. The Bay Area set up the first regional air district in the nation in 1955, eventually named the Bay Area Air Quality Management District (BAAQMD) (Scott [1959] 1985). BAAQMD would prove to be truly regional, but focused on a single issue.

It was soon followed by BART, the epitome of special-purpose regionalism. It was designed to do just one thing—build a new, state-of-the-art transit system. When formed in 1957, BART represented the first major new regional-scale mass transit system in the United States in a half century (Barbour 2002). It eventually became fundamentally different from the other regional-scale agencies: it was funded through a direct vote, and remains the largest regional agency with a directly elected board.

Close on the heels of BART the revival of big-idea regionalism, this time named the Golden Gate Authority (GGA). Like Greater San Francisco, the GGA was first and foremost the brainchild of an organized business elite. This time it was the Bay Area Council (BAC), formed at the end of the war to bring together major corporate leaders on different sides of the bay. BAC had been integral in pushing BART, and they now set their sights on a more multipurpose regional government. Their primary political partner was none other than Jack McCarthy, he of the Marin County growth machine. BAC at the time was led by Edgar Kaiser, Henry Kaiser's son (Dyble 2012). This proposed Authority was also patterned after New York—this time the Port Authority of New York and New Jersey, which required an act of Congress to create—with its dedicated revenue to come from the region's bridge tolls (Scott [1959] 1985). It would focus on major transportation investments and infrastructure, a regional powerhouse built at the height of modernist growth-oriented planning.

The design of the organization was almost a caricature of the growth machine, and anti-democratic in the extreme. It would intentionally be insulated from local politics. Like Robert Moses's Triboro Bridge Authority in New York, it would rely on the cash cow of bridge tolls to fund its projects. It would be run in a corporate fashion like a business, with professional experts accountable only to the Authority directors. These Authority directors would in turn have been nominated by county chambers of commerce, for approval by county supervisors (Dyble 2008).

Local governments and the powerfully connected special district that ran the Golden Gate Bridge both opposed the GGA, for different reasons. Fearing the future imposition of regionalism by the state, local officials proposed a voluntary association of local governments to discuss regional matters. It was purposefully toothless, and like the U.S. Senate, gave undo power to smaller jurisdictions by giving each municipality a vote. This version of regionalism would have little power to intervene in regional problems.

But it would also have little power to create them. In a close vote, the measure to create the GGA failed in the state legislature, dying for good in 1961 (Dyble 2012). With GGA no longer a possibility, the BAC eventually threw its support to a new organization, the Association for Bay Area Governments (ABAG), a council of governments (COG) in which cities and counties joined voluntarily. Regionalism would continue—BART was funded by a historic vote in Alameda, Contra Costa, and San Francisco counties in 1962. Progressive organizing by environmentalists determined to stop the filling of San Francisco Bay led to the creation of the Bay Conservation and Development Commission (BCDC), the first coastal management agency in the nation and the first nine-county agency with real powers granted to it by the state (Walker 2007). Federal frustration with ABAG's inability to plan for transportation led the state to create the Metropolitan Transportation Commission (MTC) in 1970, which became the region's official federally designated metropolitan planning organization (MPO), with statutory power to redistribute federal transportation monies in the region. Four separate agencies, all with separate remits covering the same territory and with no true mandate for cooperation or coordination, were set up within the span of 15 years.

As many have noted, both the foundational structure of ABAG and the divisions between different regional agencies meant that regionalism was purposefully set up to fail (Pincetl 1994; Barbour 2002; Dyble 2012). As one regional leader active in regionalism debates in the 1980s put it, "When the regional organizations were created back in the late 1960s and 1970s . . . they were really created to thwart regionalism. They were really created to protect local jurisdictions' authority and protect local control" (Diridon 2011, quoted in Thibert 2016: 124).

ABAG would change and transform over time, and to view the organization, even in its relatively early days, as solely an impediment is a misreading of history. ABAG instead internalized the tensions and struggles between ardent regionalists, many of whom were also local elected officials, and classic localists (Innes and Booher 2010; Thibert 2016). ABAG produced a visionary, "city-centered" regional plan in 1966 that was essentially smart growth before smart growth. The 1966 plan tried to combine greenbelts and open space preservation with denser, transit-oriented development. It saw the future growth in "edge cities" and technology jobs, and regarded transit-connected housing growth in East County as a potential solution to mounting affordability problems. Although not particularly explicit about injustice and racial discrimination, the plan did see regional inequality as an issue, and even called for institutional reforms to make these changes more possible (Association of Bay Area Governments 1966). The political and bureaucratic structure to realize great visions had not been put in place, but the agency and many of those who worked with and for the organization produced plans that combined the spirit of modernist progress with lessons learned during this era regarding environmentalism and social justice.

More important than any critique of early ABAG or a bemoaning of what could have been is the historical lesson of how the choice presented during the GGA versus ABAG debate was yet another Dougherty Valley. On the one hand a too-powerful regional behemoth controlled by a very small elite intent on development at all costs, on the other an ineffectual regional club controlled by decidedly localist locals; that is, modernist-era growth and machine-style overdevelopment versus localist protectionism and inertia. Much has been made about the intransigence of localism over the years, and the home-rule obsession has been disastrous in so many ways for so many places. But the elite-driven regionalism was not necessarily better. As in Dougherty Valley, no matter which side won, the region lost. Low-income people and people of color in particular were going to lose no matter how this turned out—neither a truly transformative nor truly democratic option was ever on the table.

Despite numerous state bills being pushed in the early 1970s to fuse regional agencies, work supported by emerging statewide groups like California Tomorrow, not a single one passed (Barbour 2012).[3] The Bay Area would not become cantons like the Swiss, nor would it federate. It would remain a patchwork and an archipelago, and regionalist reform would die down for the moment. Such reform would return again in the late 1980s, and although this new effort was unique for a certain reason, it repeated one of the most critical errors of past failures.

A CONVERSATION BETWEEN TWO GROUPS

In the late 1980s and early 1990s, as Babylon remained entrenched while Antioch and Brentwood emerged with breathtaking speed despite growth control and anti-sprawl efforts, regionalists in the Bay Area started pushing a new vision of regional governance. Bay Vision 2020, as the broader effort would be called, sought to combine MTC, ABAG, and BAAQMD into a single regional agency.

The Bay Area Council once again took center stage with this new effort; it was one of the three primary co-conveners of the Bay Vision committee, which drafted the Bay Vision Plan. The other major nongovernmental partner in the "blue-ribbon commission" behind Bay Vision—alongside local politicians—was the Greenbelt Alliance, fresh from its transformation from People for Open Space and its critical battles in Contra Costa County (Barbour 2002: 128; Lydon 1993; Innes et al. 1994). In forming the commission, chaired by UC Berkeley chancellor Ira Michael Heyman, organizers involved elected officials, especially from increasingly powerful and historically anti-regionalist Santa Clara County.

The heavy involvement of environmental organizations was a major change from the GGA effort, and from the more bureaucratic and legislative efforts from the late 1960s and 1970s. The new agency would certainly not be simply a tool of the growth machine. But little effort was made, especially at the beginning, to include communities of color or social and environmental justice organizations in a discussion partly taking place in their name.

As one prominent environmentalist put it, Bay Vision 2020 was largely "a private conversation between two groups."[4] With Heyman out in front and the region's long history of liberal ideals, their vision "echoed all the classic themes of the planning visionaries: The greenbelt, housing justice, regional governance, city-centered development, higher density housing, and better transit. But Heyman and [former BCDC director Joe] Bodovitz did most of the work themselves, and the commission failed to mobilize broad support" (Walker 2007: 141).

As the vision moved from plan to legislative proposal, the commission grew to include a handful of representatives from communities of color, including East Bay Asian Local Development head Lynette Lee. Yet despite the mandate to "adopt a general vision for the Bay Area in the year 2020," issues of stratification, inequality, segregation, and exclusion were treated as "social issues," outside the primary purview of the commission. In the words of Peter Lydon, the commission gave "steady if somewhat mechanical respect to regional social issues," but when the few commissioners who recognized their importance "tried to raise the intensity of economic stratification and the needs of the inner city poor as ills central to a metropolitan agenda, they did not get far" (Lydon 1993: 33–34). Ultimately, the regional agencies themselves soured on the proposal, and despite its elite support, the bill to merge the agencies fell two votes shy in the state legislature (Walker 2007; Lydon 1993).

While there may have been some representation of minority groups, there was no true representation of their broader concerns. There was certainly no representation by low-income communities. In a caricature of post–civil rights tokenism, esteemed professors from UC Berkeley—one black, one Asian, and one Latinx—were invited to give papers about the state of "their communities." With that box officially checked, commissioners were free to continue planning for land use and transportation governance as if they were completely detached from the social reality of the region. In theory, the plans of Bay Vision were inclusive, but like classic modernist, top-down, expert-driven efforts, in practice and formation they were not.[5] In the words of one consultant, "How could you expect major social proposals from a group created by stakeholders from the environmental, business and local-politician communities?" (McCreary quoted in Lydon 1993: 34).

One longtime environmental justice advocate put it much more bluntly. Bay Vision 2020 was just the most regional version of a broader problem within the environmental movement, a movement he describes as "reinvented racism," in part by subverting the social justice gains of the 1960s by "allowing for militancy without justice or race."[6] Environmentalists had worked hard to get themselves a seat at the table, and once they were there they behaved similarly to other regional elites when it came to issues of justice, race, and segregation.

Bay Vision 2020's failure is informative because it illustrates more than just the age-old story of home-rule advocates defeating regionalists. Surely, as Elisa Barbour argues, Bay Vision 2020's regional reform "met with the same fate in the 1990s as it had in the 1970s . . . because of continuing resistance to reforms calling for institutional change" (Barbour 2002: 128). But it also failed because it repeated the top-down, elitist form of modernist planning born in the early days of planning, a style that had in part produced the problem in the first place. In its elitist nature, Bay Vision 2020 was simply a continuation of a historic regional planning tradition, from the Greater San Francisco Association and the Commonwealth Club through the Golden Gate Authority and many others. Unlike the push for BCDC, there was no clear crisis, no terrifying maps of a filled-in bay to generate popular interest (Thibert 2016). As Jonas and Pincetl (2006) make clear, regionalism in Northern California has long been a social movement, but not a grassroots one. It has been by and large for elites from the outset.

The contours of this elitism were new, and what was happening in Dougherty Valley at that time only partially altered the political economy of development in the region. In Dougherty Valley it was war, whereas at the Bay Vision 2020 table it was a partnership, but either way one absence was clear. Two powerful and elite actors, one in favor of environmental restraint and one pushing development, both of which claimed to plan *for* the disadvantaged communities of the region but were not willing to make the efforts to plan *with* them. During Bay Vision, when this tag team ran up against the age-old opposition of the home rulers, they were economically comfortable and politically powerful enough to fold. They lacked any true sense of urgency, for both had the resources to cope without effective region politics. They may have wanted cooperation at times, but did not need it, and those who needed it were not invited to the discussion. These needs were never made central problems. The grand regionalist vision was once again abandoned, and so environmentalists and developers fought battle after battle in town after town, often drawing rival regional agencies into the fray.

THE NEW REGIONALISM

By the mid-1990s, with memories of Bay Vision's demise still fresh, regionalism itself was being promoted throughout the United States. Two politicians turned authors, Myron Orfield and David Rusk, each wrote passionate pleas for regionalism. Rusk was the former mayor of Albuquerque, which gave him a certain standing, and his 1993 *Cities without Suburbs* remains very influential (cf. Troutt 2014). Orfield ([1997] 2002), both a law professor and a state legislator in Minnesota, developed a data-driven method of analyzing regional inequity that would be utilized heavily by a new generation of academic regionalists.[7]

At the same time, there began to be talk of a "new regionalism," one that was more about collaboration and coalition-building and less about creating a new agency or regional government (Jonas and Pincetl 2006). The new regionalism emphasized less formal collaborations over new agencies and structure, collaborations that were not meant to last forever.

In the Bay Area, this took the form of the Bay Area Alliance for Sustainable Communities (BAASC).[8] The alliance came together in 1997, not long after the demise of Bay Vision. It was funded by a major California foundation, the James Irvine Foundation, which had become interested in new regionalism and decided to fund a series of initiatives across the state. Representatives from the Sierra Club and Pacific Gas & Electric (PG&E), fresh from service on President Clinton's Council on Sustainable Development, worked to bring a regional coalition together where each of the three e's of sustainability—environment, economics, and equity—would be represented. This time, equity would not just be discussed, but would get an actual seat at the table.

In the wake of the Bay Vision failure, this alone was progress. The alliance built a membership that eventually included almost 50 leading organizations. The Bay Area Council joined with longtime regional powers like Bank of America and PG&E; Greenbelt Alliance and the Sierra Club were joined by other national and regional greens, some of whom had a stronger environmental justice profile than old-guard groups like the Sierra Club. Numerous local, county, and regional government agencies participated, including ABAG and MTC.

The equity caucus was represented first and foremost by Carl Anthony, founder of Urban Habitat. Urban Habitat had been created a decade earlier specifically to help progressive environmental justice organizations in the Bay Area work at a more regional level, in part out of frustration with the historical blindness toward racial injustice in "progressive" urban development and planning organizations. Anthony took up a leadership position in the alliance against the objections of his own staff, who were not convinced that the environmental organizations had fully divorced themselves from their racist past (Innes 2004).

The steering committee included Van Jones, who was beginning to develop a national profile. Established social service agencies like Building Opportunities for Self-Sufficiency in Oakland and Legal Aid of Marin represented the service side of the equity caucus. The Greenlining Institute was a well-respected racial justice organization specifically focused on reversing the effects of redlining and segregation.

But although present, the equity caucus was small, at least relative to the others. It included Jones but not his organization, the Ella Baker Center for Human Rights, which was more connected to grassroots organizing than Urban Habitat. As the alliance went about its projects—developing a set of regional indicators, developing a compact on smart growth and sustainability that members would present to local governments, and developing a fund to invest in low-income communities in the inner core—the deeper involvement of equity issues or by equity groups did not materialize.

Some of this had to do with skepticism from environmental and racial justice groups themselves, who were suspicious of the Bay Area Council and the big banks. Urban Habitat was itself repeatedly accused of being a sellout by other environmental justice organizations (Walker 2007). The investment fund quickly got locked behind the opaque walls of fund managers, becoming a small-scale Bay Area Council project with fuzzy equity goals rather than a game-changing investment tool (Innes and Rongerude 2006). Some participants felt that in general the alliance was too business dominated. Others simply saw it as too hasty in seeking lowest-common denominator consensus rather than pushing for more radical compromise (Innes 2004).

While few concrete policies or programs came out of the alliance, and while it did little to move the indicators that it had developed to analyze the problem, it did effect some subtle changes. Equity was now officially a bigger part of the conversation; smart growth was essentially establishment policy. The plans and visions and reports from the 2000s were more collaboratively developed, especially from ABAG's side, which had been a full participant in the initiative. Regional collaboration seemed to be building slowly; agencies were working more collaboratively, including the 2006 Focus program that would be the foundation for a new regional plan.

This era of "new regionalism" also saw the development of other regional or subregional collaborations.[9] Urban Habitat developed the Social Equity Caucus, which would work to strengthen the regional voice of an increasingly diverse and increasingly active set of environmental, racial, and social justice actors. The Great Communities Collaborative emerged out of the San Francisco Foundation, also with Urban Habitat and Greenbelt, this time to push specific campaigns around affordability and inclusivity in transit-oriented development at specific locations around the region. Hybrid groups like the Transportation and Land Use Coalition, which would become Transform, attempted to integrate environmental and social justice goals through better planning and development.

New regionalism was now established alongside the continuing forms of old regionalism—the regional agencies, BART, etc.—a back-and-forth governance structure that in many ways was simply a more open and honest version of what had long been a complex dance between powerful civil society actors and regional agencies and authorities. Increasingly, equity and social justice advocates were either invited to be part of the regionalist club, or organized themselves to demand a seat at the table.

But this engagement of social and racial justice organizations was well after the fact, far too late to impact regional restructuring. Without permanent funding, and with an overreliance on too few leaders and voices, the Bay Area Alliance for Sustainable Communities folded in 2008, just as the foreclosure crisis was at its peak. Despite decades of regionalism in many forms, despite almost a half century of knowing that a different form of region-building was needed, effective action did not occur. By the end of 2008, the 10 Cities of Carquinez, with a population of more than 600,000 residents that was more than 60 percent nonwhite, had suffered 10,000 foreclosures that year alone.

PERSISTENT DIVIDES AND LIMITED IMAGINATIONS

In 2006, just before the foreclosure crisis hit, the state of California passed AB 32, a historic piece of legislation aimed at cutting greenhouse gas (GHG) emissions. For planning and urban development, the more critical act occurred two years later, as foreclosure signs dotted front lawns from Antioch to Stockton and down into Southern California's Inland Empire and Antelope Valley. SB 375 was the planning and land-use enforcement for AB 32, mandating that regions develop a joint land-use and transportation plan, one that specifically sets targets for reducing GHG, primarily through reducing automobile dependency.

Responsibility for developing the plan fell to ABAG and MTC. Despite its relative lack of power, ABAG had long been involved in one area of state-mandated regional planning—the Regional Housing Needs Assessment (RHNA). California had been concerned about housing for lower-incomes groups for a half century, and beginning in the late 1960s tried to convince and even force cities to plan for housing in general and low-income housing in particular. After various attempts at enforcing this more directly from Sacramento, what evolved by 1980 was a system in which the COG would work with its members to forecast population growth and "allocate" housing units that each municipality needed to build. Units were divided by income strata, and in theory municipalities were expected to alter the housing element in their general plan and their local zoning code to ensure that at least from a regulatory perspective all of this new housing could be built (Baer 2008).[10] This process would occur in cycles—the first lasted a decade (1980–90), followed by seven-year cycles which at times overlapped (1988–95, 1999–2006, 2007–14).

TABLE 8 RHNA Allocations Versus Units Permitted / Built, by County,
All Four Cycles

	Total Allocations	Total Permits	Above or Below Allocation	Percent Permitted	Number of Cycles Meeting Allocation for Total Units
Alameda	191,477	140,898	−50,579	73.6	1
Contra Costa	168,755	151,933	−16,822	90.0	2
Marin	32,431	18,273	−14,158	56.3	0
Napa	29,164	14,605	−14,559	50.1	0
San Francisco	81,231	57,942	−23,289	71.3	0
San Mateo	79,041	46,227	−32,814	58.5	0
Santa Clara	279,841	178,738	−101,103	63.9	0
Solano	95,530	67,092	−28,438	70.2	1
Sonoma	104,003	76,271	−27,732	73.3	1
Bay Area	1,072,817	751,979	−320,838	70.1	0

SOURCE: ABAG, U. S. Census; calculations by author.

Research at the state level is inconclusive as to whether the RHNA process has been effective.[11] But an analysis of regional performance in the Bay Area reveals the obvious—the region did not come close to meeting the goals it had set, following the contours described in previous chapters.[12] During the four cycles that can be analyzed, the Bay Area came up short by 320,838 total units (Table 8). Alameda County met or exceeded its housing allocation once, during the first cycle in the 1980s, when Solano, Sonoma, and Contra Costa counties did as well. Since that first cycle, only one county has met the mark—Contra Costa during the 1999–2006 cycle. Santa Clara, Marin, San Mateo, and San Francisco counties—the West Bay Wall—have failed to meet their agreed-upon targets all four times.

The numbers are equally disheartening when broken down by income level, as the RHNA process demands (Table 9). For very low income units (<50% Area Median Income [AMI]), only San Francisco in the 1988–95 cycle built what was said to be needed, and the region came up short by more than 100,000 very low income units between 1988 and 2014. Marin and Santa Clara met their RHNA goals only once, in low-income (51–80% AMI) units during the 1999–2006 cycle, and were the only counties ever to do so. No county ever built enough moderate-income housing (80–120% AMI). Only in "above moderate" <120% AMI) did counties hit their mark, and even then less than half the time cumulatively, and still with an almost 50,000-unit deficit cumulatively. No matter how you cut the data, no matter the era, the region's cities and counties did not meet the goals that they collectively set. The need simply kept mounting.

Plan Bay Area and the Economic Prosperity Strategy

In theory, Plan Bay Area, as the process became known, would be different. This time, the RHNA allocations were being done together with MTC's periodic allocation of transportation money. This was real money—$289 billion over the 28-year life of the plan, with updates every four years. Housing goals and transport goals could be aligned, and some of that lower-income housing and transit-oriented housing dreamed of in past RHNA cycles could be both planned and realized. The plan revolved around Priority Development Areas (PDAs) and Priority Conservation Areas (PCAs), both chosen by local jurisdictions, a détente between the two needs. Plan Bay Area created the One Bay Area Grant (OBAG) to incentivize municipalities who hit their RHNA targets with added monies for transit. An affordable housing fund was created to ensure that some of the new transit-oriented development was affordable, as the increasing emphasis on transit-oriented housing was putting serious displacement pressures on low-income residents near existing transit.[13]

Although the planning process began in 2011 and a draft plan was issued in 2013, the process did not end there. The more than thousand page EIR for the plan included four alternatives, all of which were tweaks to the existing plan. Environmental groups, the Building Industry Association, and right-wing anti-regional planning organizations would file four lawsuits against the plan.[14] But organizing around the initiative also continued. Many members of the Social Equity Caucus reformed under the banner of the 6 Wins for Society Equity Network, specifically to push regional agencies "to ensure that the Bay Area's transit, housing, jobs, and sustainability policies break the patterns of segregation, sprawl, and pollution that have disadvantaged low-income communities and communities of color for generations."[15]

Many in the 6 Wins network would participate in a "new" regionalist effort sponsored by HUD, whose goal was to develop an Economic Prosperity Strategy (EPS) aimed both at Plan Bay Area and beyond. It furthered the new regionalist tradition of putting different sides of the debate in the same

TABLE 9 RHNA Performance by Income Categories by County, Cumulative for Cycles 2 (1988–95), 3 (1999–2006), and 4 (2007–14)

County	Very Low (<50% AMI)		Low (50–80% AMI)		Moderate (80–120% AMI)		Above Moderate (>120%)	
	% of Allocation Permitted	Units above or below allocation	% of Allocation Permitted	Units above or below allocation	% of Allocation Permitted	Units above or below allocation	% of Allocation Permitted	Units above or below allocation
Alameda	1.03	–20,679	1.038306	–13,741	1.296495	–18,077	2.630648	–6,769
Contra Costa	1.12	–13,347	1.747567	–6,282	2.425634	–4,205	3.386994	1,010
Marin	0.92	–3,036	1.959192	–1,300	1.398479	–2,330	1.887183	–4,083
Napa	0.51	–3,855	0.793544	–2,320	1.292139	–2,432	2.578229	–901
San Francisco	2.56	–2,970	1.722897	–5,246	0.584388	–12,621	2.651958	518
San Mateo	1	–7,235	1.113578	–5,150	0.816461	–8,755	2.375206	–6,757
Santa Clara	1.03	–27,913	1.665534	–16,044	0.672913	–33,984	2.979879	–8,829
Solano	0.41	–12,206	1.109195	–6,413	1.572884	–6,377	2.499514	–6,773
Sonoma	1.13	–10,022	1.868801	–4,216	1.819352	–5,321	1.900869	–11,026
Bay Area	1.1	–105,113	1.411633	–63,044	1.231551	–95,894	2.756176	–46,980

SOURCE: ABAG; calculations by author.

room. It included longtime regionalist advocates like SPUR and the Bay Area Council (participating through its economic institute), both with strong connections to business and developers in different ways. Labor was represented, as were academics. Urban Habitat, Transform, and Greenbelt Alliance each represented different components of the environmental justice / smart growth spectrum. What made this effort unique was that the plan "deliberately focused on the inclusion of the smallest, most progressive CBOs" (Frick et al. 2015). Not only were grassroots, membership-based, community-based organizations at the table, they had been funded to do their own research, organizing, and outreach. Publications like Causa Justa / Just Cause's *Development without Displacement* came from the first stages of the grant, and made an impact on their own, let alone as part of collective learning. The final EPS document was not nearly as progressive as documents produced by some participants, but this seeming contradiction is not one—rather, it is a process whereby opposing viewpoints are assumed to be the case, a recognition of what political philosopher Chantal Mouffe (2005) called "agonism." Contrary to Frick et al. (2015), the "interagency conflicts" that were part of the EPS process were not just "background drama," but a sign that diverse voices had actually been brought to the table and thus real political solutions were technically possible. New regionalism had clearly taken the next step from BAASC, and it was light years removed from Bay Vision 2020.

But the increasing attention to social justice did not sit well with the business community. Despite record corporate profits and rising inequality and a housing and gentrification crisis that made international headlines, helping low-income workers was apparently too much. In two letters written to the head of the steering committee of the prosperity plan, business leaders united in objecting to the inclusion of a goal for the EPS to improve conditions for low-wage workers.[16] The original goals of the plan involved producing more middle-class jobs and improving economic growth overall, both of which the business community of course supported. But the letters, coming from a relatively new coalition—the Bay Area Business Coalition (BABC), headed by the BAC with various other business-oriented membership organizations, including the Building Industry Association—not only objected to some of the measures that would support low-income workers. They objected to the inclusion of the goal in the first place.

These letters were just the beginning. Jim Wunderman, head of the Bay Area Council, wrote another letter about the EPS, this time to the head of

MTC, which had been a sponsor and participant.[17] He felt that the business community was being attacked unfairly, blamed for causing the problem, particularly at the launch event for the plan. In the end, after three years of working toward compromise with as diverse a group as had ever participated in a regional-scale exercise with official backing, the final report was released without the official sponsorship of either major regional body—MTC and ABAG—due to these objections by the business community.

At no point in these letters, in their publications or pronouncements, did the Bay Area Council or any major leaders of the business communities act with any contrition over what had occurred. They maintained the clichéd rhetoric against regulation, even as they supported various forms of state action and alternative regulation. There was no acknowledgment of past errors or failures, of BAC's involvement in the Golden Gate Authority or any of the top-down modernist schemes that had undermined public trust and in part set off the wave of localist, defensive politics. There was no recognition of how long and hard some of the people who participated in the EPS had fought for a seat at the table.

If the Bay Area Council or major leaders of the business communities felt their organizations and sector were being blamed, the thing to do in the name of furthering regional cooperation would have been to look in the mirror, to understand where the anger was coming from and why. After all, the second BABC letter came barely a month after the Dropbox workers incident with kids in the Mission, amidst Airbnb controversies and Google Bus protests and rising tensions, amidst rising evictions and much more. For all their wealth, education, and supposedly good ideas, the BAC and business community leaders did not have the courage to fundamentally change the tone of the conversation by admitting that they were part of the problem.

Doing so could have let other actors do the same. For Wunderman and BAC were only part of the problem. Gabriel Metcalf's (2015) aforementioned international essay attacking San Francisco's progressives would come just a few months after the final Wunderman letter in 2015. Progressive and even radical organizations that have long hated or distrusted SPUR because of its past involvement with urban renewal and / or its continued relationships with major developers had sat in a room and planned with SPUR as part of the EPS process. This nascent trust was then partially undone, and "common purpose" would be kicked down the road yet again.

Unfortunately, throughout this time, one could not look to the regional agencies for leadership on how to get along, or to the state representatives who funded them, because they were fighting among themselves. First it was over a decision to move the regional agencies from Oakland to San Francisco, then a battle over a takeover of ABAG by MTC.[18] As one of the few regions in the country where the MPO and COG were separate, a merger was long overdue. But the acrimonious nature of how it was done did not reduce tensions at an already tense time. With the debates and public name-calling and political maneuvering around this old regionalist fight occurring at the same time the business-led revanchism undermined a historic new regionalist collaboration, the Bay Area once again showed why regionalism was never able to intervene effectively to stop what had happened. It remained fragmented, both jurisdictionally and politically, and every step forward seemed to have a similar step backward. Worse yet, these fights, which occurred in the wake of the Plan Bay Area draft, also served to obscure one important fact: Plan Bay Area did not seem to even recognize the new geography of the region, nor did it take steps to intervene.

The Dream of a Region That Never Was

Buried on page 46 of the 2013 Plan Bay Area, among the many maps in a 108-page document, is one entitled "Resource Lands."[19] Areas in red are "critical habitat," whereas the white parts are essentially the urbanized zones, including urban parks. Two things are worth noting. Marin County has no critical habitat along the 101 corridor running north / south on its eastern half. And East County, now home to a quarter of a million people, is entirely covered in red.

The map seems to contradict other parts of the plan. East County is also home to multiple PDAs. The four incorporated cities of East County have been "allocated" more than 5,400 homes, almost two and a half times that of Marin County as a whole. It would seem the plan, one in which Greenbelt Alliance played a central (and controversial—see Frick 2013) role, is putting housing in sensitive areas and ignoring housing opportunities in less-sensitive areas closer to the core.

This seeming contradiction illuminates some of the fundamental political and geographical limitations of regional planning in the Bay Area during this entire period. Places in which housing should go are not possible because of pure NIMBYism, with no real environmental case against them. And places where housing perhaps should not have been built but was anyway are still imagined as if somehow this "mistake" can be forgotten or ignored.

Marin County, which had finally approved the SMART train and would be connected to another county by rail for the first time in almost a century, got transport investment under the plan, but still avoided any real housing and any real density. Sonoma County was scheduled for more than three and a half times the amount of housing as Marin, even though the latter has more jobs, is closer to the region, and has so obviously underperformed over the last 40 years, never once hitting its overall RHNA targets as a county, even when those targets were absurdly low.

East County, which for all its sins and all its poor decisions had at least opened the door to communities of color, is still planned for as if it should never have happened in the first place. Instead, in the plan's own words;

> Plan Bay Area's focus on [a] "fix it first" [strategy] ensures that we maintain existing transportation assets, primarily concentrated in the region's core, which reinforces the plan's focused growth strategy. In total, Plan Bay Area dedicates 87 percent of all available funding (committed and discretionary) to sustaining the existing transportation network. Given the age of many major assets—BART turned 40 last year and San Francisco Muni turned 100—this should come as no surprise. (ABAG 2013: 13–14)

The overwhelming focus of the plan is to try and undo some of major push factors described in this book. It tries to invest in Oakland and parts of Richmond. It tries to build more transit-oriented housing in San Francisco, San Mateo, and Silicon Valley. Massive attention has been paid to the region's gentrifying core, and much of the politics leading up to and in the aftermath of the plan has focused on doing this equitably. More money for affordability, more protections against displacement.

This core-oriented strategy would be an equitable one had it been suggested in 1970. In 2013, it was not. None of the proposed alternatives to Plan Bay Area—neither the equity plan proposed by Transform and Public Advocates, nor the Building Industry Association–favored developer plan, nor the adopted plan itself—dared to propose the type of serious public investment in transit and urbanism in places like East County and the Cities of Carquinez that could have intervened in resegregation *where it is actually occurring.* Throughout the entire history of this major demographic shift, too many organizations of all kinds thought they could prevent change by ignoring it, or by underinvesting in the communities to which people of color were relocating.

The only regional plans that have ever really considered what might happen if the area truly invested in the Cities of Carquinez were written a half century ago. As I have tried to make clear, these cities are old, deeply rooted places, with historic cores, dormant or underused rail lines, and wide flat roads that dream of being retrofitted for cycling. They have planned but languishing ferry terminals, ample brownfields for redevelopment, and the largest decommissioned military base right at the point where the two sides of the river come together. And of course, these happen to be the areas in need, where poverty is suddenly a major issue, where lost housing equity has not recovered, and where segregation is being remade on a larger scale.

Why visionary planning did not happen for Marin should be obvious by now. Development there has become so unthinkable that few are crazy enough to even broach it. Part of the reason visionary planning for the Cities of Carquinez does not occur is that neither capital nor the environmental movement wants it. The former sees more risk than reward, especially because something different from cheap and easy suburban sprawl would need to take place. And they know the environmental community would largely oppose it, as so many still see it as the red area on the map.

An aspect of this lack of vision comes from the social justice community itself. There is a sad corollary to the gentrification dilemma. Gentrification intensely targeted core inner-city neighborhoods with deep historical meaning for communities of color. There are places in close proximity to downtown San Francisco, Oakland, and Berkeley—San Francisco's Mission, Hayes Valley, and Fillmore districts, the South of Market (SoMa) area, the North Oakland and South Berkeley corridor so critical to the formation of the Black Panthers and the black Left, and eventually West Berkeley, West Oakland, and Bayview–Hunters Point. These were the places where many communities of color first established a foothold in the region and first developed collective cultural and political institutions, creating more than just a physical or laboring presence.

The tragedy of gentrification in these spaces is that it forced these communities to adopt a defensive stance once again. Rather than being able to turn the hard-won political gains made for neighborhood politics during the Babylon era into broader regional power for the reconstruction of a truly regional metropolis, they were forced to defend territory. Faced with the gentrification dilemma—either the onslaught of new capital designed to transform the community for someone else, or the ongoing hardships of abandonment and exclusion—many chose to stand and fight. This is especially true of civil society organizations, almost in tautological fashion. The very presence of equity advocates at the table of the EPS, the recognition of the need to seed affordable housing and prevent displacement that is being contested in the face of Plan Bay Area—all are testimony to the vast network of civil society actors who chose to stay and fight for an equitable core. What was true about preservation in San Francisco is true in parts of Oakland and San Mateo and Silicon Valley and even Marin. Activists fought long and hard and often successfully to mitigate displacement and create at least some long-term affordable housing.

The problem is that many actual members of these communities followed a different path. They chose breathing space, safety for their children, the American dream, or just to follow a friend or relative. Unfortunately, racial and social justice-oriented politics was never able to make the same move to the Cities of Carquinez, at least not in time, and not with full commitment. In general, equity activists saw suburbia as the problem, and often they were right. Public Advocates led a critical and now famous victory in 2010 in Pleasanton, whose long-standing cap on housing units was one of the most egregious examples of suburban exclusion and one of the grossest abuses of regional infrastructure in the history of the Bay Area.

When community of color organizations sued MTC in 2005, following clear evidence that AC (Alameda County) Transit riders in poorer Oakland received a much lower subsidy from the region than higher-income BART and Caltrain users, Oakland still had more poor people than East County (Mayer and Marcantonio 2005). But the larger demographics of race and poverty had already shifted seismically. Rather than focus on making BART work for the poor, or work for the exurban black and brown middle classes by forcing MTC and BART to bring true BART service to East County, this stance reinforced the core versus periphery dynamic.

This core-centric strategy, necessary to defend low-income communities still hanging on, fit together with the smart-growth consensus and made allying with longtime opponents easier. But it ignored the fact that in the current era of mobile segregation, the right to a fiscally sound, transportation-enabled and viable suburb must be considered alongside the right to the city as a critical social and racial justice issue. This is the right to the metropolis, a right that has never been truly represented by either attempts to preserve, defend, or enhance the right to the city or efforts to "open up the suburbs" (Downs 1973). Had equity activists been able to convince the region to plan this way a generation ago, perhaps the core-oriented strategy that became the Plan Bay Area consensus could have worked. But what was planned for in Plan Bay Area was not the region that actually happened; it was the region that many powerful actors—including the equity caucus—wished had developed a generation earlier.

In interviews following the EPS process, some equity advocates recognized that Plan Bay Area "largely focuses on the Bay Area's urban core with little attention directed towards the suburbanization of poverty in the outer areas, especially those that experienced numerous housing foreclosures and significant declines in property values" (Frick et al. 2015: 18). In 2016, groups like Urban Habitat truly began studying the suburbanization of poverty for the first time.[20] The Anti-Eviction Mapping Project in San Francisco is regionalizing its perspective, and more and more organizations are waking up to the megaregional scale of the problem and the reality of resegregation. But grand visions for true intervention in the Cities of Carquinez remain largely unthinkable.

The absence of grand visions to intervene in the spaces of resegregation is once again made clear by grand environmental visions that did occur. In a historic June 2016 election, Bay Area voters in all nine counties voted more that 70 percent in favor of taxing each parcel of land to pay for wetlands restoration. They created yet another regional agency to distribute the estimated $25 million per year for 20 years to restore wetlands and prepare for the inevitability of sea-level rise and climate change. Measure AA, as it was known, was backed by full-page adds listing seemingly every major elected official, every regional and local agency, and every environmental and business group in the region.

Like the Presidio, like Imagination Park, like so many other green initiatives over the years, this was the right thing to do. But it once again showed how the region's elite and its leaders can build common purpose for unprecedented action for environmental initiatives, but not for the type of more difficult but just as necessary efforts to combat segregation and rising spatialized inequality. That would require a true sustainability coalition, a true bringing together of economic, environmental, and equity actors, something which has not happened at the regional level in the Bay Area. This is why the region has never been able to intervene effectively as resegregation occurs on a megaregional scale, and why most of the plans that are made cannot envision true solutions to the problem. Part of the problem of course is that this is a reflection of similar divides at the most important scale of them all—the state of California.

EIGHT

The Unrealized Coalition

THE POINT OF CONVERGENCE OCCURS ROUGHLY ten miles east of Livermore, on the eastern side of the Altamont Pass and the edge of the Central Valley. This is the point where California's federally and state-financed highway system intersects its federally and state-financed water system, the latter in the form of the state-run California Aqueduct and the federally managed Delta-Mendota Canal. If you head south along I-5, the aqueduct is a regular companion. It weaves in and out of view for almost 300 miles, until you ascend the famed "Grapevine" and then head into Los Angeles. Pumped through giant pipes over 2,000 feet up the Tehachapi mountains, the water travels in even more spectacular fashion than the cars.

This convergence is an apt symbol for the California of this book. Both freeways and aqueducts represent an earlier era, a politics of space and place that has so fragmented as to render the contemporary production of these colossal and grandiose pieces of infrastructure unthinkable. Both are symbols of a type of growth and development that is challenging to evaluate. Moving large quantities of humans and goods via "freeways" and large quantities of water via a cement-laden engineering marvel has engendered new ways of life and means of economic production that made the state of California a global economic wonder. Yet in their historic form they are not environmentally, economically, or fiscally sustainable, at least not in the current era. One reason they are not fiscally or economically sustainable is the political backlash against funding them, a backlash with complex roots.

So dyspeptic were Californian politics during the neoliberal era that asking how and why California never came to the rescue of a restructuring and growing megaregion like Northern California marks the asker as ignorant or naive in the eyes of many: of course the state did not intervene more effectively in the internecine battles in the Bay Area, of course it did not provide a more functional infrastructural base upon which neoliberal-era suburbs could be built, and of course it did not take seriously the challenge of the most diverse wave of suburbanization in American history. California politics became so sclerotic during this era that one becomes reticent to ask questions that to an outsider seem logical to ask.

Yet ask we must. What happened so that the state government largely got "out of the infrastructure construction business" (Landis 2000: 39), with the exception of prisons and schools? Why did California, the world's greatest urban project during the first three quarters of the twentieth century, decide that it no longer needed to collectively invest in its urban future? Why did it not develop a more functional system of urban and regional politics that could have dealt with the sins of the postwar era? Why could it not wean itself from an overreliance on certain forms of infrastructure without constructing an entirely new map of inequality?

A common recent explanation for this inaction reaches beyond development politics to basic governance. California's political dysfunctionality during this era grew to new heights. Only the most doe-eyed of political actors could have imagined California stepping up in the way that was needed given the challenges. California reached a nadir with the 2003 recall of Governor Gray Davis, an act that garnered international headlines because of who replaced him (Arnold Schwarzenegger). It exposed how the combination of political animosity, a broken and overused system of "direct democracy" (Schrag 2004), and a generalized loss of political faith left many inside and outside of California wondering whether the state was in fact "ungovernable" (Greuner 2011; *Economist* 2009a). It is not a coincidence that this latter trope emerged in the wake of the foreclosure crisis, as the state's notoriously sensitive finances once again took a nosedive.

A second set of reasons for inaction fits squarely within the focus on neoliberalism and Reaganite revanchism. California, and particularly Southern California, was the 1960s birthplace of the neoconservative wave that swept Reagan into the presidency (McGirr 2001).[1] What occurred in California starting with Proposition 13 and the tax revolt of 1978 and culminated in 16 years (1982–98) of increasingly conservative Republican control of the governor's mansion meant that California politics was hopelessly neoliberal right from the start. Not investing in publicly funded infrastructure becomes a tautology.

A related explanation focuses on the red / blue divide that became increasingly virulent during this time. The California of the postwar era had been fairly centrist. Earl Warren, who was governor before he became chief justice of the U. S. Supreme Court and one of the central progressive figures of the civil rights era, was a Republican. Pat Brown, a Democrat at the heart of the infrastructure boom and the landmark California Master Plan for Higher Education, also gave the order for mass arrests of students during the Free Speech movement in Berkeley in 1963. With the emergence of California as both the center of the new Right and the radical Left, polarization should be expected.

A fourth explanation focuses on the role of the environmental movement, which built enough power to replace Reagan with Jerry Brown, ushering in a "progressive" environmentalist skeptical about infrastructure to replace an arch-conservative who despised it. All four explanations add value to what can only ever be a partial understanding of a state with a population larger than Canada and an economy the size of Italy, all squeezed into a history shorter than electricity and a territory thrice the size of England. All four explanations similarly find a place in a fifth explanation, one centered on the single most influential product of the state's infamous initiative system, an act referenced throughout this book—Prop. 13.[2] This is where right-wing politics and dysfunctionality come together in a single political act so powerful that it established a new path dependency which has laid waste to any subsequent political machinations.[3]

While containing important truths, both generalized political explanations and the mire of Prop. 13 ignore too deeply a key factor this book has sought to highlight: the intersection of the very specific politics of growth and development and just as specific politics of race.[4] It is the way these two politics, and those who practiced them, did and did not come together during this era that helped allow California to step away from the "infrastructure business" and effectively underwrite the foreclosure crisis that would sweep the exurbs of both Northern and Southern California. Like the Bay Area, California as a whole has long possessed two key ingredients of the "Obama coalition": white, middle- and upper-middle-class environmentalists and working- and middle-class communities of color. Both worked hard during this era to build power for their causes, but were not able to find common cause in the "common purpose" that was the making and remaking of California.

Rather than realize that the political hope for environmental protection lay in coalition-building with an increasingly diverse (and organized)

California populace, environmentalists helped construct a statewide version of the Dougherty Valley dilemma. Growth politics from the 1970s and 1980s culminated in a pitched battle over sprawl between powerful environmentalists and powerful developers and their assorted allies. This fight was crystallized in the controversy surrounding a 1995 report entitled *Beyond Sprawl: New Patterns of Growth to Fit the New California* (Fulton 1995), a well-meaning document that sparked a vicious debate which symbolized the futility of development politics, for a "victory" by either side would have accomplished little.

Beyond Sprawl was also a repeat of Bay Vision 2020—its small coalition of elite financial, environmental, and state actors who saw the need to eventually "forge a constituency to build sustainable communities" and which included "inner-city community activists" in its language, yet did not work to include them in the creation of the report. They went at it alone, ended up in a massive fight with developers who paid for their own report, and the state as a whole went nowhere. Moreover, environmentalists lost the opportunity to prove that their dark past, with connections to eugenics and blatant anti-immigrant sentiment, was behind them, and that theirs was not simply a white, affluent, and elitist cause.

The absence of communities of color, social justice groups, and others at the *Beyond Sprawl* table is not simply a result of exclusion. Communities of color as a whole faced a statewide version of the gentrification dilemma during this era—a generalized existential attack from all sides. Whether coming from an upsurge in anti-immigrant sentiment or a globally unprecedented wave of prison-building, the very right of many communities of color to exist in California was under constant threat during this entire period, not for the first time in the state's history. Their collective focus turned to building power, and to specific fights over education and prisons, immigration and integration, leaving little space, time, or resources for broad coalition-building around the building and rebuilding of the metropolis.

This view of a failure of coalition politics necessitates a certain perspective of (sub)urban development as a potential center around which a coalition could have been built, as opposed to the hyper-divisive political football it became. This is not just twenty-first-century idealistic hindsight. It draws inspiration from the below-mentioned 1978 *Urban Strategy* report, drafted just months before California's white middle-class suburban voters drew a line in the sand from which the state has never recovered.

They say that nothing is forever. Except, perhaps, Proposition 13.

—JACK CITRIN (2009: 1)

The passage of Proposition 13 in 1978 was one of the foundational moments in contemporary California history, a moment whose reverberations in both American history and the built environment of California are profound. Prop. 13, as it is commonly known, ushered in similar "tax revolts" throughout the United States. Right-wing populist movements fought to cap property and other taxes, limiting government funding and presaging the Reagan revolution and the true beginnings of the neoliberal era. In the case of California, it amended the state constitution to freeze property taxes at 1 percent of full cash value, limit increases in assessed value to 2 percent per year, roll taxes back to 1975 values, and prohibit reassessment to cases of new ownership or new construction. Just as critically, it codified in the state constitution the requirement for a two-thirds majority vote by either the state legislature or local elections for *any* tax increase (Coleman 2005).

Robert Self, in what is functionally a coda to *American Babylon,* argues that we must see its passage in the broad historical light of the postwar era. The passage of Prop. 13 was not simply a question of tax policy or even the ascendancy of the New Right, but a white, suburban, middle-class, populist revolt against the "breakdown of a decades-old 'compact' between homeowners, industry and city governments that dated back to the 1940s" (Self 2006: 147). The property tax was central to the fiscal system that undergirded this political compromise surrounding the production of space. As the entire model began to fall apart, with skyrocketing home prices and subsequent property tax hikes amidst the stagflation of the 1970s, California voters chose the nuclear option.

There was another important "event" in 1978 that has largely been reduced to the dustbin of history, but which in many ways represents the well-trodden path that Californians did not take. In February of that year, the State Office of Planning and Research (OPR) issued a 44-page report entitled *An Urban Strategy for California.*[5] In the cover letter to the document, Governor Jerry Brown, then nearing the end of his first term in office, noted that 94 out of 100 California residents lived in cities and suburbs, that its population was going to continue to grow dramatically, and that the state faced a challenge of how to meet its needs given both environmental and fiscal constraints. The plan was a series of ideas and strategies to give "focus" to "thousands of individual decisions which will affect California's cities and suburbs by directing state and local governments toward a *common purpose:* the revitalization of existing cities and suburbs and the sound management of new urban development" (California Office of Planning and Research 1978: iii).

The fourth of 45 ideas in the "urban action program," ideas which included everything from reducing intrajurisdictional conflicts to renting out houses owned by CalTrans, from waterfront development to building codes, local general plan reform to urban forestry, stated: *"Property Tax Relief.* As one means of reducing the cost of housing, the Administration and the Legislature will continue their efforts to provide property tax relief for homeowners and renters" (24). The efforts referred to were the 22 different reform plans discussed by the legislature in 1977, as rising home prices and subsequent property tax increases had become a major problem over the course of the 1970s. The average home value in the state went from $34,000 in 1974 to $85,000 in 1978 (Schrag 1998). Particularly in Southern California, increases were exponential. Tax bills quadrupled in that same period in some places, leaving older and retired residents—many part of the white wave of migrants from the Midwest who were the demographic backbone of Southern California's mid-century population explosion—fearful of losing their homes.

But when the legislature adjourned in the fall of 1977, they had not passed anything. Instead, Proposition 13, then known as the Jarvis-Gann proposition, hastily gathered enough signatures for the June ballot. A counter-reform by the legislature also qualified for the ballot, but in June 1978, four months after the release of the *Urban Strategy* report, Prop. 13 passed and the legislature's reform did not.

Few pieces of law-making—after all, Prop. 13 is not legislation, but rather populist constitution rewriting—have had as widespread effects, and as robust a debate about those effects, as Prop. 13. Not only is Prop. 13 at the heart of the fiscalization of land use (Schwartz 1997; see chapter 2), it has had other unintended consequences, including the growth of overly complex finance mechanisms to deal with the infrastructure finance deficit, and has actually increased state power over localities in certain ways (Chapman 1998; Sexton, Sheffrin, and O'Sullivan 1999).[6] In the words of Jack Citrin (2009: 8), who has studied Prop. 13 as intensely as anyone, "the fiscal constraints on the legislature unleashed a mad scramble for money that has produced an incoherent, dysfunctional system of budgeting that makes it harder to react in times of fiscal stress."

The end result has been a "fiscal shell game" (McCubbins and McCubbins 2010), one that has been regularly exacerbated by additional layers of voter- and legislature-sponsored activity (Barbour 2007).[7] Building much of anything as a state—except prisons—became harder and harder. Tax base became everything. In the language of social theory, Prop. 13 structured the agency of local agencies.

It also structured the politics of the possible in California. Passing Prop. 13 required and enabled a coalition of anti-tax groups, libertarians, and neoconservatives who used the proposition to build a stronger movement, one which wielded significant power despite its minority status (Self 2006). Regardless of its clear injustices, unintended consequences, and unnecessary evils—for instance, it covers commercial properties as well, handing corporate landlords hundreds of millions of dollars in benefits overnight (Schrag 2004)[8]—reforming the law even in the slightest has proven to be near impossible, despite both politics and demographics that have changed significantly in the almost *four decades* since the vote in question.[9]

Part of the problem with Proposition 13 was how it seemingly destroyed any hope of a different politics, ushering in an era of neoliberal ideology, suburban revanchism, and (renewed) racial anxiety, not to mention ballot box governance that extended the power of a certain white minority long after its demographic majority ended.[10] We must also ask whether its power and obvious centrality obscure a more complex politics that may have been possible, allowing an easy excuse for some organizations to pursue a more isolationist politics.

Prop. 13 may have immediately jettisoned *Urban Strategy* as a functional policy document, but it did not render irrelevant some of the possible politics that the document sets out. *Urban Strategy* actually originated as part of an update to the state-mandated 1973 Environmental Goals and Strategy Report (EGPR), itself part of a wave of 1970 environmental legislation.[11] In its 45 action points, 14 goals, and two study areas, this product of environmental politics is radically "urban" in its content and progressive in its recognition that urban and suburban (and the rural bits connected to the metropolis) are in this together.

The goals alone discuss tax levels and schools, health care and hospitals, freeways and public transit. It is anti-sprawl and pro-city without being anti-suburb; it discusses affordable housing and clean air, policing and public participation. Deeper in the action points and study areas it raises issues like tax base sharing, urban art, community mental health, community-based crime prevention, apprenticeships, and much more that would not be out of place in a contemporary set of "progressive" planning documents. In the fairly tragic words of a 2012 OPR document (Office of Planning and Research 2012), part of an attempt to revive the EGPR and update it after 34 years:

> The 1978 Urban Strategy, adopted via Executive Order by Governor Brown, is the only EGPR to have been prepared and adopted. The Urban Strategy laid out an action plan to address issues facing the state's urban areas. The action plan was broad and inclusive and included steps to address environmental quality, resource protection, land use, infrastructure, financing, safety, and health.

This inclusivity included an environmental agenda that had urbanism at its core, which addressed the three e's of sustainability—economics, equity, environment (Campbell 1996)—long before the concept was elucidated in those terms. The strategy provided a chance for the environmental movement to signal a radically more pro-human and pro-equity shift, a chance to be at the center of a new coalition that saw a more just and equitable metropolis as central to conservation and environmental protection. It was also a chance to signal clearly that its participation in some of the darkest days of race and class discrimination was a thing of the past, and that it recognized its growing power and racialized, class-based privilege. It didn't happen.

THE LIMITATIONS OF BEING GREEN

> For most white environmentalists, the key problem is too much growth, not too much inequality, and the central threat to their way of life is too little breathing space, not too little justice. Worse yet, there are not a few who feel that it is other people—especially dark-skinned immigrants—who are the greatest threat to their golden lands.
>
> —RICHARD WALKER (2007: 240)

Californians rightly celebrate the state's role as the "cradle of the modern environmental movement" (Stern 2005: 119). As I have repeatedly stated throughout this book, there is much to be proud of in terms of lands protected, open spaces made public and accessible, progressive legislation drafted, technical and social innovations that have helped to make environmentalism mainstream. For all that this book is critical of the failure of the environmental movement as a whole to recognize its privilege and power and do a better job of being a bulwark in the coalition required to realize *Urban Strategy,* the accomplishments in the face of enormous challenges should never be underestimated (Walker 2007).

Nor should past successes be overly valorized, considering the reality of two intertwined threads of racism that have been part of the foundation of the green movement. The most conspicuous racism was the link to eugenicists, in which California was similarly in the vanguard. As Alexandra Minna Stern (2005: 120) argues in her disturbing book on the history of eugenics:

> From the outset, eugenic guidelines of selective breeding and species endangerment were central to these three organizations [Sierra Club, Sempervirens Club, Save-the-Redwoods League], especially Save-the-Redwoods League. Indeed, hikers passing through Madison Grant Forest and Elk Refuge in Prairie Creek Redwoods State Park or climbing Mount Jordan in Sequoia National Park might be surprised to learn that they are enjoying places named in honor of two of the most prominent eugenicists in the first half of the twentieth century.

This was no innocent foray into bad ideas by misguided intellectuals. As Stern documents, California was responsible for one-third of the involuntary sterilizations in the United States between 1909 and 1979.

If eugenics is the skeleton in the closet, connections to anti-immigrant ideologies is a living, breathing pathology hiding in plain sight. The origins are similar, for the social and quasi-scientific Darwinism of eugenics was generally connected to a neo-Malthusian worldview with its concern about "overpopulation," with its obvious link to what would become one of the central dividing lines in late twentieth-century California—immigration. In the 1960s and 1970s, the publication of books such as Paul Ehrlich's (1968) *Population Bomb*—written at the suggestion of legendary Sierra Club director David Brower (Ehrlich and Ehrlich 2009)—heavily influenced groups like the Sierra Club and the National Audubon Society (Bhatia 2004), both important actors in California. The Sierra Club adopted an official policy position arguing for limited immigration on environmental grounds in the mid-1960s, only voting to change it in 1996.[12]

This link between environmental groups like the Sierra Club and controversies over immigration would dog the organization and the environmental movement as a whole throughout the post–Prop. 13 era. The 1996 reversal came only after the state voted in yet another plebiscite—1994's infamous

Proposition 187—to deny undocumented immigrants basic services like education and health care. It took until 2004 for the organization to start speaking up in earnest, publishing a heartfelt polemic from director Carl Pope (2004) entitled "The Virus of Hate" and highlighting its work on environmental justice with pieces like "Why Race Matters in the Fight for a Healthy Planet" (Hattam 2004). The latter expressly addresses both the notion of environmentalists "as wealthy, white tree-huggers who don't care about people of color and the poor" and the poor and people of color as people who don't care about the environment.

Even with this relatively recent push to change its image, the link between environmentalism and either overpopulation-based anti-immigrant stances or outright racism remained strong throughout the entire post-1978 period. Some of its more recent strains cannot be blamed on the mainstream environmentalist movement, but rather on the increasing adoption of environmentalist themes by the Far Right and hate groups (Bhatia 2004; Mix 2009). Yet others are simply stubborn hangovers of the Ehrlich / Brower connection, otherwise very good works of ecological economics and new environmental politics undermined by a continued adherence to anti-immigrant rhetoric (cf. Dietz and O'Neill 2013).

Yet the ultimate problem with California's green movement during this period was not entirely about its inability or unwillingness to acknowledge or move beyond its racist past. Nor was it about an ignorance of the environmental justice movement, whose arguments eventually—and very slowly— "altered those of the larger conservation movement" (Walker 2007: 12). It was the fact that as a collective movement they were slow to embrace the "common purpose" outlined in *Urban Strategy*, a document whose origins are in the movement itself.

One problem was a general anti-urban stance and an obsessive focus on green spaces and conservation. Greenbelt Alliance, which was one of the first mainstream and powerful environmental organizations to have a pro-active and progressive stance on affordable housing and city-building, was not set up until the late 1980s.[13] Even then they remained somewhat of the rebel within the larger environmental community, the first environmental organization in the region to actually promote "the right development in the right places."

In this stance, they became part of the growing "smart growth" community, and fell into a trap similar to what was discussed in chapter 7. From its early days in the "California Tomorrow Plan" (Heller 1971; Hart 1984),

California's visionaries of a greener urbanism largely ignored the reality of communities of color, or their role as potential partners in a greener future. Lengthy tomes about California's problems (Durrenberger 1971; Heller 1971), collections that are very forward thinking in terms of the urbanization-environmental linkage, nevertheless relegate race, racialized inequality, and the entire legacy and reality of postwar segregation to the margins, if they discuss it at all.

This general willingness to neglect and ignore is part of the casual racism so pervasive in the Bay Area and throughout the state, part of the supposedly "unintentional" nature of racism highlighted throughout this book. Yet it was also politically foolish. The green movement as a whole largely neglected the political reality that to win any deep and meaningful changes, they needed to build bridges across racial lines, rather than simply ignore "social" issues, or more importantly, those political actors who fought for them. Nothing epitomizes how far California fell from the dreams of *Urban Strategy* than the controversy surrounding another strategic report almost two decades later—the innocuously titled *Beyond Sprawl*.

BEYOND SPRAWL

Times Change—California Growth Issues Don't.
— *San Francisco Chronicle* headline, March 9, 2009
(King 2009)

Aside from one major fact, *Beyond Sprawl* was a fairly standard 1990s-era report from the smart-growth community. Greenbelt Alliance and the California Resources Agency were two institutions long involved in the sprawl question, two of the main actors actively engaged with metropolis-building in the positive sense, as opposed to simply opposing growth. The Low Income Housing Fund (now the Low Income Investment Fund) was a national organization based in San Francisco and a major community development finance player. The report was essentially authored by Bill Fulton, a widely respected planner and author (and future mayor of Ventura) who was functionally a centrist in California politics.

It contained ideas that are relatively innocuous to a contemporary reader, and which partially channel some of the ideas of *Urban Strategy*. It recognized both a changing economy and changing demographics, and paid close attention to job creation. It was not entirely anti-suburb (only "distant" suburbs), identifying a need for regional patterns of growth, albeit ones with more critical density. It pointed out the limits of politics at the time, the general lack of quality state intervention, and the need for a new trajectory. And like *Urban Strategy*, its origins were in high-level politics, this time a 1991 cabinet-level council formed by *Republican* Governor Pete Wilson to build consensus around growth-management practice (Fulton 1995).

What made it unusual was that the sponsor and lead author was none other than Bank of America. Bank of America's presence at the front of the report helped produce significant press coverage, high-level meetings with the governor and state officials, and in general caused a stir during a time when Dougherty Valley and other skirmishes in the development wars were raging.

Unfortunately, what got covered was the debate over the report, not the ideas within it. Displeased with the report, the development community struck back with a barrage of letters to the editor, op-ed pieces, and eventually a report of its own. Authored by USC planning academics Peter Gordon and Harry Richardson (1996), two authors whose strident articulation of conservative principles has enshrined them as conservative archetypes in planning theory, *The Case for Suburban Development* summarily attacked *Beyond Sprawl* piece by piece. It argued that suburban development does not impinge on agricultural land, does not make traffic worse, can accommodate transit, is more efficient, is better economically, and people like it. And while they were at it, Gordon and Richardson channeled David Harvey, reminding readers that cities were corrupted by rent-seeking corporations living off the public dime.

The Building Industry Association, which paid for Gordon and Richardson's report, did everything in its power to paint *Beyond Sprawl* as an extreme text, when it is only extreme in its vagueness and its attempts to please all sides. One development industry representative called the controversy "the low water mark" in planning politics, one which "caused a lot of damage," damage that would not be repaired for close to a decade.[14] He undoubtedly sought to cast blame on the *Beyond Sprawl* side, but the validity of the "low water mark" holds true—this was the epitome of dysfunctional California development politics, a cheaper statewide version of Dougherty Valley.[15]

As in Dougherty Valley, real issues got lost in the hysteria of two well-armed sides battling it out for a "solution" that would not solve problems. The *Beyond Sprawl* report epitomized many of the problems with the sprawl discourse—"distant suburbs" became the enemy, with little or no recognition of the sprawling, fragmented geography virtually inborn in this state. The report talked of California as a place that had recently emerged as one of the most urbanized states in the union, when it had held that status for a century. It talked of cities and suburbs in a generic sense, which may work in other places but which has never held true in California. Its core-centered mentality played into the hands of those who would accuse anti-sprawlers of being obsessed with city centers (as Gordon and Richardson do), when a close reading of the report indicates that what they really want is densification around already urbanized areas. By propping up sprawl as a bogeyman and refusing to deal with true California geography, *Beyond Sprawl* played into the hands of those who would misuse the report to maintain the status quo.

Beyond Sprawl also recognized that "edge cities" have been built, but does not set forth ways to work *with* this new geography. It recognized that these were radical interventions in regional geography, but did not argue for a radical change in approach to growth and development to deal with decentralized job bases. It merely argued that this was another indication that what California was doing did not work, and it should be stopped.

The Achilles heel of the report was the way that it dealt with demographic change, and the politics it knew needed to come together. The emergence of California as a majority-minority state is well acknowledged (Maharidge 1996), but what the authors seem to have misunderstood is that the suburbanization of communities of color was already well under way by the time this report was issued. Antioch, Tracy, Manteca, Southern California's Lancaster and Palmdale, Fontana and Rancho Cucamonga were already diverse by this time, and already being built on shaky fiscal and economic foundations. There was certainly much that could have been done to prevent problems from getting worse, starting with lead author Bank of America not jumping into the subprime fiasco with both feet in an incredible display of hypocrisy. But by 1995, the restructuring of the California's largest regions, including the Bay Area, was already under way.

Moreover, the report, focused as it was on the sins of sprawl, ignored the reproduction of the problems in the core, or simply implied that they were caused exclusively by sprawl-induced abandonment. The report ignores the beginnings of gentrification en masse, a factor already at play in San Francisco at the time and starting to surface in Oakland. The fact that many suburban areas were safer, cheaper, and had better schools is treated as a "perception," when in fact it was a reality.

More troubling than the content, and evident in some of its missteps, was the lack of participation of "inner–city community advocates" in the drafting. Everything about the report reads as if it was written *for* the "changing demographics" but not *with* them, a failure we have seen all too often from planning elites. While developers are consciously—and of course unrealistically—excluded from the "broad-based constituency" that the report envisions, communities of color are included in name but not in the production of the ideas. It was a literal microcosm of Bay Vision 2020 extended to the statewide level, minus the actual legal proposal.

As I discussed in the introduction, part of the problem is the very question of sprawl and growth management. It can be a myopic view of urban and regional development, one that is ontologically rooted in opposition, often to communities which are already built, with little to offer on how to help them retrofit and transform. The ghosts of the Babylon era were also clear—the whole report seemed intent on merely putting an end to the development patterns of the 1950s and 1960s, instead of coming to terms with solutions for what was already a very different map.

Beyond Sprawl epitomized the vastly curtailed horizons of *Urban Strategy*, and a stubborn unwillingness to form coalitions capable of moving the political needle on major regional development and infrastructure reform. Despite attempts by environmental organizations and environmentally minded "smart growth" advocates to convince communities of color that sprawl was their issue too—based on the idea that it drains resources from inner cities, the nominal geography of the nonwhite—it never caught on as a discourse beyond the opposition to specific proposals like the lawsuit about BART versus buses discussed in the last chapter.

Sadly though, the problems run deeper. Communities of color in California are as old as the state itself, as are attempts to undermine their very right to live there. Perhaps no single fact helped undermine the "broad-based constituency" needed to push forward a "common purpose" than that, instead of exorcising the ghosts of a racialized past, Californians in the 1980s and 1990s decided to rip the wounds open even wider. The growing power of greens and other white progressives was not brought to bear with any real effectiveness, and in the tragic words of Dale Maharidge (1996: 145), "progressive groups' complacent disregard of California's rising xenophobia would prove catastrophic."

In 1991, the Pulitzer Prize–winning journalist Maharidge began doing interviews across racial lines for a book about the various reactions to the growing diversity of California. As he notes sadly at the end of the book, which was published in 1996, between the time he started and the time he finished, California's racial ghosts exploded. The 1992 Los Angeles riots highlighted the deep anger and inequality that still affected Babylon, represented now by questions of policing and justice more than old-fashioned segregation. The populist, ballot-box-driven anger of 1994's anti-immigrant Proposition 187 and "anti-crime" Three Strikes law and 1996's anti-affirmative action Proposition 209 were a cavalcade of revanchism that drew global attention to California. It was a series of events that moved at such a "stunning pace . . . [they were] comparable in some ways to the anti-Chinese tumult in the 1870s and the anti-Japanese eruptions early in the century, when the state's racial outbursts affected the nation" (Maharidge 1996: 280).

The Three Strikes law, which would disproportionally affect blacks and Latinxs, was itself part of an unprecedented prison-building boom, both for California and the industrialized world.[16] Between 1982 and 2000, the California prisoner population grew nearly 500 percent, and the 162,000 prisoners by that point were two-thirds African American and Latinx. To house them, California built 23 major prisons, costing $280–$350 million apiece, almost twice the number (12) of prisons built between 1852 and 1964. General fund expenditures quadrupled from 2 to 8 percent of the budget; the Department of Corrections became the largest state agency (Gilmore 2007: 7).

This massive increase in capital expenditures from Sacramento came during an era when the overall trend of state-building had been reversed. As Dowall and Whitington (2003) make clear, the decline in capital spending by the state is a trend that did not start with Proposition 13. The 1966 election of Ronald Reagan as governor replaced the state-building of Pat Brown with the most important skeptic of public spending in the nation's history. Jerry Brown's election in 1974 was aided by a newly empowered environmental movement also skeptical about the physical impacts of state spending, especially on infrastructure. During the 1950s, *per capita* capital spending never dropped below $100 per person (in 1996 dollars). By 1975, it was less than $40 (ibid.).

When Proposition 13 came along, it merely reinforced and codified a general trend more than a decade under way, sending per capita capital spending down to less than $20 per person. This was not simply the right-wing, suburban populism that led from Reagan to Proposition 13. There was a conservatism to the conservation movement as well. Yet as argued at the beginning of this chapter, what this type of analysis often misses, as do many of the more apolitical analyses of infrastructure, is the critical importance of race.

The election of Reagan in California was preceded by an earlier version of the Proposition 187 and 209 battles—the 1964 debate over Proposition 14, a ballot measure aimed at overturning the state's historic 1963 Rumford Fair Housing Act. The 1963 act, named after its sponsor Byron Rumford, who in 1948 became the first black elected official from Northern California, was specifically designed to undo the housing discrimination that so defined the postwar era. The only thing more bruising than the political fight to pass the act was the battle over its repeal. The California Real Estate Association sponsored Proposition 14—which codified in the state constitution the right of property owners to discriminate on racial (or any other) grounds—and it quickly gained the support of the rising John Birch Society and growing conservative movement, whose trip to the polls that November was buoyed by the presidential campaign of arch-conservative Barry Goldwater. Proposition 14 passed overwhelmingly, gaining 65 percent of the vote throughout the state and close to 75 percent in the "white noose" of southern Alameda County and similar suburbs throughout the state (Self 2003).

Both the Johnson administration in Washington and the Brown administration in Sacramento were irate about Proposition 14—Washington responded by cutting off funding to California, and Governor Brown supported the lawsuit that would eventually result in the law's nullification by the United States Supreme Court. But the damage was done. Brown lost to Reagan in 1966, and as Lisa McGirr (2001) shows so clearly, the Proposition 14 battle helped galvanize the California Right and send Reagan, and his distaste for state-building and public investment in urban development, from the statehouse to the White House.

Yet the legacy of Proposition 14 goes deeper. This was the bridge between the anti-Chinese legislation of the nineteenth century and Propositions 187 and 209, and more critically, it specifically targeted efforts to undo the ghosts of the Babylon era. A major coalition was built around the Rumford Act, which was damaged by the repeal. This was the one and only time when the state of California explicitly attempted to undo the racialized legacy of postwar and even prewar metropolis-building, and it was then attacked by the white and the suburban and the conservative. It was Proposition 14, not Proposition 13, which was the most critical shot across the bow from a suburban white majority. It was a clear message that they would not open up the California metropolis to those who were not white, even if they had been there for generations, and even if their labor had been integral to the production of California's wealth and the nation's security.

When outright racism became less and less possible, the majority began to show their distaste for those who were different by rolling up the urban carpet. Proposition 13 is simply a fiscal version of Proposition 14—if you cannot codify discrimination in housing, then undermine the fiscal foundation upon which a more equal and less segregated California would have to be built.

This is the argument put forth by Peter Schrag (2004) and others (cf. Myers 2007; Pastor and Reed 2005) when it comes to the divides in California. An older generation of Californians, raised during the heyday of the "white republic," simply refused to pay for the schools, roads, sewer systems, transit agencies, and other aspects that make metropolis-building work.[17] There was no "common purpose" to be found in the building of the metropolis—a fact made even more pertinent by the opening of U.S. immigration policy in 1965, barely a year after the passage of Proposition 14. Just as the United States was turning a brave new corner when it came to immigration and multiculturalism, California's voters were attempting to undo the metropolitan foundations that it would have to be built upon and lived in.

This is in essence the purpose of Propositions 187 and 209—to continue this process of cutting off access by people of color and the undocumented to core state institutions, facilities, and services. But they were only part of the larger onslaught that saw Californians use the ballot box for a steady stream of attacks—some overtly racist, some merely racist in their application—part of the transformation of the initiative system into a "catalyst for racial politics" (Christensen and Gerston 2008).

There is no other way to describe it than relentless. A 1972 measure to ban school busing (63 percent in favor) was part of the bridge between Propositions 14 and 13. But the real activity began in the 1980s. Amidst a generalized uptick in ballot measures—the 52 measures in the 1980s were more than the previous three decades combined, a pace which continued throughout the period this book covers—race, or race combined with immigration, was a driving force in measure after measure. The first issue was language. Proposition 38 (71 percent yes) in 1984 required the governor to petition the president to amend federal law in order to require that election ballots be printed only in English. Proposition 63, two years later (73 percent yes), established English as the official language of the state. Although back-and-forth court rulings and the lack of enforcement made the measure "primarily a symbolic statement" (*Gutiérrez v. Municipal Court* [1988]), the decision by state officials to largely ignore Proposition 63 merely "stoked the flames of those who felt believed that California was not confronting racial issues" (Christensen and Gerston 2008: 127). Eight years later in 1994 came Proposition 187 (no services for undocumented migrants), followed by 209 in 1996 (banning affirmative action), 227 in 1998 (restricting bilingual education), and 54 in 2003, which would have prevented the state and local governments from collecting information on race. Only this latter bill failed.

Yet these are only the propositions that are formally about race, not the bills that are functionally racialized. In the same year as Proposition 187 (1994), California passed the harshest "Three Strikes law" (Proposition 184, 72 percent yes) in the country, mandating life sentences for a third felony (Chen 2008).[18] This came just two years after two Northern California Democrats, one a centrist, one a progressive, both heavily supported by the environmental community, were elected to the U.S. Senate in a historic election that saw California vote for a Democratic presidential candidate for the first time since 1964. By 2005, 70 percent of second- and third-strike prisoners were African American or Latinx, roughly the same percentage as the prison system overall. As mentioned above, African Americans made up 45 percent of third strikers (Brown and Jolivette 2005).

The Three Strikes law came after a dozen years of Republican governorships and a decade of Reagan / Bush in the White House. This era saw politicians elected by a still-white electorate expand the criminal justice system dramatically, one that would be occupied primarily by young men of color. And it would get worse. In 2000, over 60 percent of voters passed Proposition 21, a bill whose title, the "Gang Violence and Juvenile Crime Prevention Act," did little to hide its racial coding (Espiritu 2004). The bill used the fear of juvenile crime, and the highly racialized notion of gangs, to once again mobilize a white electorate, despite the fact that youth crime was falling (Twomey 2001, cited in Espiritu 2004). It is any wonder why Espiritu (2004: 198) reaches for "Propaganda" by Dead Prez (2000) when trying to explain the "racialized construction" of Proposition 21:

> When he be speaking in code words about crime and poverty
> Drugs, welfare, prisons, guns and robbery
> It really means us

The response to these measures, and to the general sense of insecurity, was to build power along racial and ethnic lines, and to focus on what was directly at the time under attack—education, public services like welfare benefits and public health—or ways in which the state was directly targeting minority communities, as through policing and the criminal justice system.[19] It is hard to fathom the amount of political and activist energy that went into opposing the above agenda, from immigrant rights organizing to a steady stream of criminal justice system reformers working to combat California's drive to create one of the great human rights disasters of late twentieth-century America (Gilmore 2007).[20]

Latinx and Asian communities in particular worked to build new coalitions and gain greater electoral power during this time, building on their growing demographic strength. Los Angeles saw a historic shift when Antonio Villaraigosa was elected mayor in 2005, followed ultimately by Oakland and San Francisco's first Asian American mayors in 2010.[21] Basic power and basic survival had to become the focus, and the issues fought over were largely the ones politicized at the state level—schools, prisons, basic services. There was little time or energy for the "common purpose" of regional development or for coalition-building with a progressive white environmentalist community that was not there for them in their time of need.

As in the case of Bay Area regionalism, more attention was paid to urbanization in the latter period. The environmental justice movement, one of the most important movements with regard to racialized space since the fight over fair housing in the 1960s, slowly built up power during this time, and as noted earlier began to penetrate the conservationist agenda. The new regionalist initiatives discussed in chapter 7 occurred in every major metropolitan area in the state, and the aforementioned greenhouse gas bills, AB 32 and SB 375, marked a distinct change from the dark days of *Beyond Sprawl*. The negotiating table for SB 375 in particular was a lot more diverse than during the drafting of *Beyond Sprawl*, Bay Vision 2020, or much previous legislation.[22] This was partly a result of the new power built by communities of color during this period. This time, they could not be ignored by a two-party set of talks.

Yet just like at the regional level, this newfound focus on California's role in urban development and new attempts to be more inclusive were not enough to overcome decades of dysfunctionality and inaction. The postwar ghosts were never fully exorcised, and the fact that in the 2000s planners, activists, developers, environmentalists, policymakers, and thinkers slowly began to find more common purpose in some ways makes the lost decades of the 1980s and 1990s particularly bitter. When Manuel Pastor (2007) talked about innovative racial coalitions and the construction of a new California, he was talking about an imagined and necessary future, not the California of the neoliberal era.

Even more so than in the battles over gentrification and displacement, communities of color in California during the neoliberal era—and in particular the progressives among them—were forced into a near constant politics of opposition. Environmental and smart-growth advocates at least had a choice, one granted by privilege of every kind—including the steady rise of a more green-focused version of Silicon Valley as the cornerstone of the state's economy. Rather than realize that the possibilities of a "sustainable" state depended on the "common purpose" of urban development, and that this common purpose had to be built with communities of color and with the question of segregation at its center, many held onto an outdated oppositional environmentalism that largely reinforced privilege and failed to make the state sustainable. Key voices in the business and development community also thought they could just continue with business as usual, never admitting their institution's or sector's roles in Proposition 14, never acknowledging the harm that the *Beyond Sprawl* "debate" caused and its role in perpetuating the lack of real vision and effective politics.

Conclusion

RESEGREGATION AND THE PURSUIT
OF COMMON PURPOSE

The next generation of middle-class Americans is destined to enjoy the unprecedently rich life that the post-industrial, national urban society will offer. Our central domestic task now is deliberately to invent ways of extending those opportunities to those groups that future history threatens to exclude.

—MEL WEBBER, "The Post-City Age" (1968: 1109)

Forget about intentions . . . . "Good intention" is a hall pass through history, a sleeping pill that ensures the Dream.

—TA-NEHISI COATES, *Between The World And Me* (2015: 33)

IN THE DECADE THAT HAS PASSED since the first foreclosure signs began popping up in East County and around the country, the intertwined questions of race and segregation have only grown more visible in the United States. Attention to the violence of dispossession and lost homes morphed into deep concern about the direct and even more racialized violence against black lives. Activists and scholars wasted no time in connecting these different forms of violence to the profound and ongoing legacy of postwar racial segregation (cf. Chang 2015; Coates 2015; Taylor 2016).

No single place has been as important to this recognition as Ferguson, Missouri. Ferguson's racialization began not as a place where Michael Brown was killed, but as a place where Michael Brown would not have been welcome. The first African American homeowner would not be allowed to live there until 1968, and even then not without a struggle (Rothstein 2014). While we may imagine "white flight" as something that happened from central cities to suburbs, it also happened *from* suburbs like Ferguson, only a decade (or two or three) later.

When we look at the underlying structure of Ferguson—a city where two-thirds of the residents are black but where the city council and police force at the time of Brown's death were overwhelmingly white—we must see it as the coming together of different eras of segregation and urban change, not simply the legacy of redlining and suburbanization. While certainly no excuse for its actions, it is important to understand part of the reason why Ferguson's council used its police force and its courts to target its own citizens—it was caught in an even worse fiscal bind than many California cities. Right-wing ideology in the Missouri state house starved cities of needed resources, a racialized legacy of the Reagan doctrine that typified the neoliberal era.

We must also recognize that at no point in its postwar history was racialized segregation absent from Ferguson. It may have changed form, changed location, changed structure and impact and even meaning, but it was always there.

The necessity of understanding segregation as both an ongoing process that never ended and one that is produced by complex historical interactions holds true throughout the San Francisco Bay Area. As I have tried to make clear throughout this book, new forms of geographic inequality and new forms of racialized space are not just a result of redlining, racial covenants, and disinvestment in inner cities, but of the many decisions that have been made in the aftermath of that era, often as a reaction to that era. Subprime lending may have been a poison manufactured by the financial industry, but it was allowed and even encouraged to flourish in part because it was seen as the long-awaited arrival of mass credit to communities of color who were denied it in an earlier era (Wyly et al. 2009). The fact that the terms of the deal were invariably worse than for white borrowers (Chiteji 2010) was seemingly less important than the intention behind it.

In the years since the crisis began, one of the most important contributions that contemporary scholars of race and segregation have made is to foreground the question of intent. Writers like Ta-Nehisi Coates and Nikole Hannah-Jones have worked to confront the combined myths that contemporary segregation is either unintentional, or simply the result of trying and failing by a well-meaning public. In the pithy words of Hannah-Jones, "We didn't try very hard for very long" (quoted in Misra 2017: n.p.).[1]

For all that this book attempts to emphasize the ways that segregation has changed in places like the San Francisco Bay Area, and how this new form of mobile segregation is now as prevalent or more prevalent in Northern California than older forms of ghettoized segregation, the question of intent is more important. Yes, scholars and activists and policymakers and citizens would do well to better appreciate the constant mutations of racialized segregation, to see how these different forms represent different eras coming together and appear differently in different places. It is vital for people to recognize that achieving the American Dream only to realize it was built on a bad foundation is different than being told from the outset that this dream is not for you, and that both can be products of segregation. It is important to understand that having to move far away for an affordable home, decent schools, and safe streets is not the same as being trapped in a disinvested neighborhood, but that they are two sides of the same coin and both can be forms of segregation.

But misunderstanding segregation is not the same as pretending it is not constantly being reproduced, not the same as imagining that "we tried really hard . . . and it just didn't work" (ibid.). This is particularly important in a place like the San Francisco Bay Area, a region that prides itself on being "progressive." Few places have taken Coates's "hall pass" through history quite like the Bay Area, mostly in the form of excuses.

One excuse that is too easy and too convenient is that the resegregation of the Bay Area was the unwitting consequence of reactions to the environmental sins of the postwar era, the end result of rebelling against top-down, "growth machine"—style politics that would have gladly paved over most of the Bay and anyone and anything in its way. A related excuse comes from the other "side"—the Bay Area is simply too expensive to build because of all these regulations, and if only developers had been given free rein everyone would have a nice house in a nice place. One can also look at earlier eras of California history and argue for path dependency, that inequality was so ingrained in the landscape that little could be done. It is also too easy to look outside the region for excuses, to powerful ideologies and agencies and industries and political parties and presidents, which certainly did make a bad situation worse.

Like others who criticize historical inaction, I fully recognize that hindsight is 20/20 vision. I have tried in this book to offer clear *empirical evidence* that had political leaders and a broad coalition of interest groups truly wanted to heal *both* wounds from the postwar era—racialized segregation and environmental destruction—far more could have been done. All told, the utterly broken politics of urbanization and development in the Bay

Area became and *remain* a useful excuse from varying political sides, a way of abdicating responsibility in the face of history. Not only did the Bay Area largely fail Mel Webber's above-quoted challenge to extend benefits of a wealthy region and wealthy nation "to those groups that future history threatens to exclude," it failed to even properly acknowledge just how deeply the region was constructed upon past exclusions, and to fully include those already excluded.

STUCK IN DOUGHERTY VALLEY

As I have also tried to make clear over the course of this book, leaders and activists in the region have known about the problems of segregation and resegregation, unaffordability and exclusion, inequality and injustice for two generations now. They have had plenty of good policy ideas and plenty of good plans with which to potentially fix them, but the deeply fragmented politics of urbanization and development derailed them from the start. Actually changing the course of history was never considered truly feasible, because the increasingly combative and sclerotic politics of region-building predetermined fundamental limits on what was considered possible. In the sadly apt language of Judith Butler (2002), alternative histories were "foreclosed" from the outset.

Instead, the region has been trapped in a series of either / or dichotomies—no matter which way you turned, the problem got worse. Dougherty Valley symbolizes what happens when two powerful forces collide and the greater good loses regardless of who "wins." The gentrification dilemma symbolizes the fact that low-income communities and communities of color generally have a choice between investment that won't help them and will likely produce displacement, and disinvestment that makes things worse. The planning dilemma means that virtually any decision by a municipality to make a place nicer to live in (and less vulnerable to foreclosure) also makes it more expensive and thus more exclusive.

But these dilemmas are not inherent, even if they seem inborn. They were created and perpetuated, in part by a collective political imagination that is similarly limited. For Californians of my generation, we have never known anything different.

As touched on in previous chapters, the decade since the crisis does offer more hope for Northern California politics than earlier decades. Equity organizations have grown stronger and more diverse, and are now able to insist on a seat at the table, not simply be granted one. The environmental justice movement has built some bridges with the mainstream environmental movement. The newest round of regionalism has a very wide base of institutions.[2] The affordable housing crisis has reached such a crescendo that more political attention is being paid. Housing has become a greater priority at the statewide level, and state government now represents a major opportunity for rebuilding common purpose.

But two recent developments suggest that many voices in the Bay Area and California are content to let Dougherty Valley remain the dominant political paradigm. At the statewide level, instead of trying to build a more effective politics, powerful actors decided that the problem is the California Environmental Quality Act. In a caricature of a growth-machine reunion party, the Bay Area Council, developers, banks, and many government agencies banded together to push CEQA reform. This spurred a "Save CEQA" movement by environmentalists, who this time have environmental justice organizations on their side. CEQA became the problem, not the lack of common purpose or California's dysfunctional development politics that allow CEQA to be both a political weapon and the only defense against terrible projects simultaneously. The CEQA debate is Dougherty Valley and *Beyond Sprawl* 3.0, with little to be gained for most of California no matter what happens.

In the Bay Area, YIMBY groups have emerged to supposedly oppose NIMBYs. Groups like the San Francisco Bay Area Renters' Federation (SFBARF) and others claim to represent pro-development renters fighting for more development and denser housing.[3] They have quickly developed a statewide presence and gained national and international media coverage (Dougherty 2016; McCormick 2017).

While it may be disrupting San Francisco politics, the emergence of YIMBYs has drawn more lines in the sand, and in some ways has furthered the either / or divides that are the grist for California's excuse-making mill. The problem is often now portrayed as anti-development forces aligned with anti-system activists, versus the supposedly more practical YIMBYs who would work with developers (Johnson 2017). This twenty-first-century version of Dougherty Valley is summed up by a UCLA researcher (ibid.): "You could say we need to blow up the system, but it doesn't strike me as being particularly realistic. I think the YIMBY movement is right to work within that system and work with developers."

But neither working within the system nor blowing up the system is going to actually change anything. The "build build build" slogan popular with journalists covering the rise of YIMBYs is seemingly at odds with similarly loud cries for rent control, which have also grown in recent years throughout the region, as even suburban cities react to widespread displacement and insecurity (White 2017). But to imagine *both* widespread rent control and a massive uptick in home-building is seen as an impossibility, a violation of market rules based upon deeply ingrained understandings of economics, and more importantly, an acceptance of business-as-usual politics. Imagining a true solution to the gentrification dilemma so that vulnerable communities do not feel compelled to fight development is not the fundamental goal, as it needs to be. True fiscal and economic reform that changes the underlying rules for municipalities remains outside of most political imaginations, as does game-changing financing, ownership, and tax structures that would fundamentally fix the system for producing housing, transportation, and other foundational systems.

The YIMBY debates also typically offer very little to places like East County. As discussed in chapters 5 and 7, even as some groups sue or threaten to sue elitist suburbs, they still epitomize a San Francisco–centered or urban core–centered politics that obscures the lived reality of resegregation. The debates spurred by the rise of YIMBYism largely forget about the communities that already built a lot of housing, but lack the transportation infrastructure or fiscal stability to make them complete communities. "Build build build" is a slogan, not a solution.

The limited geographical imagination of so many people in power and even more people who write about power continues to hamstring any possibility of real reform. Any solution that is not fundamentally about the spaces of the megaregion that have borne the brunt of multiple generations of racialized inequality is not a solution at all. This is not simply a moral argument but a practical one. No amount of new housing on a few strips of buildable San Francisco and Oakland will change the story of the region, even if were 100 percent affordable and maximally dense. To imagine so is to ignore the full extent of the transformation described in this book, to once again plan for a region as we imagined it should have become or once was, not the region it most certainly has become. Sprawl and resegregation are the realities for the overwhelming majority of Californians, not a future to be avoided or a reality to be ignored, no matter what happens on any given street corner in San Francisco.

IMAGINING A NEW POLITICAL ECONOMY OF
URBANIZATION AND DEVELOPMENT

Instead of drawing lines in the sand on CEQA reform, or arguing the merits of "build build build," what is needed is to make more possibilities possible. The questions of housing affordability and segregation, transportation infrastructure and fiscal crisis, environmental sustainability and climate change adaptation cannot be addressed for the 10 million residents of the Bay Area or the 40 million residents of California until bigger ideas become thinkable.

Neither policy ideas nor new plans can fundamentally change the broken system, nor can we afford to operate in a break-the-system / preserve-the-system dichotomy. This is not to say that policy and plans do not matter, but they matter in the ways in which they can contribute to a stronger political foundation in the future. The pathway forward must be a long-term vision for constructing a new, more *effective* political economy of urbanization and development.

Focusing on the political is not without its pitfalls. Given the political logjams documented in this book, it is tempting to take any number of problematic stances that may seem justified, but which do not offer real possibilities for change. Some would focus on a single enemy, be it regulators or tech or developers or unions or environmentalists or NIMBYs or YIMBYs or the poor themselves. Choose an ideology, and it will give you a seemingly clean and clear picture of *who* is the problem. But as this book has attempted to show, this stance would be empirically wrong. Responsibility should be viewed as a formula based on power, and there were many different institutions that wielded and continue to wield their power in problematic ways. Instead, an operating philosophy for a new political economy of urbanization and development must start with T. L. Marrow's (1999) famous maxim: "Don't hate the play[er], hate the game."

Some would just keep pushing for "more participation" or "more democracy," furthering important political advances in how the public is involved in planning and decision-making. While participation is certainly important, there is little proof that simply adding more voices will result in better housing and better transport. There must be a qualitative change, a new means of giving not only effective voice but ensuring that our collective voices produce an effective politics, i.e., one that actually builds and preserves and enhances the urban systems we need to survive.

Others would focus *exclusively* on building power for the powerless. While this is absolutely vital, it is not enough. While I too look to grassroots organizations and activists for inspiration, and those in power should be humbled by the work that people have had to do just to hang on over the past generation, the Bay Area is simply too big and too diverse to build any sort of coalition of the powerless that can fundamentally change the game. Even in the face of mounting inequality, the region is not made up simply of haves and have-nots, but a vast spectrum of people and communities with various degrees of power, wealth, and privilege. Only a coalition among actors across the power spectrum can make fundamental change.

Still others would choose an anti-political stance with regard to urban development. More than a few dedicated urbanists look to Chinese authoritarianism with envy. Every time NIMBYism, endless lawsuits, dysfunctional political meetings, and contentious and time-consuming politics appear to delay needed development, people in the development community wish that everyone would shut up, and in the British parlance, let the experts "just get on with it." But depoliticizing development is neither possible nor desirable. Tip O'Neill's famed maxim that "all politics is local" has long had a planner's addendum that "all local politics is about development." This is not going to change, but what can change is the nature of this politics.

Finally, there is cynicism. The very act of imagining a different politics of development in the Bay Area and California seems absurd to anyone who engages with it. Even to suggest the possibility of a grand bargain, a new coalition, a major political compromise, or new ideas leaves one open to being branded as naïve, as a romantic, or as some depoliticized centrist. Many who have spent their lives in the "trenches" will dismiss this conclusion as an academic's fantasy. But cynicism is just a tautology, reinforcing its own truth, and is often perpetuated by those in relatively comfortable positions of power. They claim the game can't be changed because they don't want the game to change; after all, they have invested a lifetime in learning how to play it.

EIGHT PRINCIPLES FOR BUILDING
COMMON PURPOSE

No matter how warranted any of the above approaches may feel, they are either inadequate to change the game or a pathway to further dysfunctionality and inequality. In what follows, I sketch out a series of principles around which a new political economy of urbanization and development can be built. These principles are imagined as a pathway forward for the specific politics of development that helped resegregate the San Francisco Bay Area, but it is my hope that they are useful outside of the region.

1. Embrace an Urbanization-Centered Politics

As crazy as it may sound, the Bay Area needs to first embrace urbanization and development as the very center of politics.[4] The saddest truth of the resegregation of the Bay Area and the generalized crisis of metropolis-building is that it actually does not get enough political attention. Our political system is not organized around the building of regions. Our education system is not organized to ensure that all citizens know how things get built or could be built. Our leaders are generally not trained to understand sewerage and housing costs, transportation and park development.

In order to change the game, we must begin to see that systems like housing, transport, public space, education, food, water, health care, etc.—what my colleague Stephen Hall and I call *foundational urban systems* (Hall and Schafran 2017)—should be the primary purpose of twenty-first-century politics. How to build, maintain, strengthen, and expand access to these systems must become the heart of basic debates between human beings as to how to act institutionally and collectively. In the language of the 1978 *Urban Strategy* document, discussed in chapter 8, it is our "common purpose." Building better systems is why we need to be talking to our neighbors, why we need complex arrangements of organizations and institutions, why we need differently scaled systems of *governance*. Note that I did not say government, but politics and governance. In the state of California, as in most places, government is only one set of institutions out of many that are engaged in these conversations.

This is what I call *urbanization-centered politics,* one where we refocus collectively around these core parts of our collective life that matter. It is a real challenge to think this way. As political theorist Warren Magnusson (2010, 2014) has so eloquently written, politics since the days of the Greeks has been obsessed with issues of sovereignty, with the "state," with ideological debates about power and markets and the public and the private. For thousands of years, we have imagined political structures and then applied them to the systems we need to govern. This is what I call a politics-centered urbanization, or a politics-centered politics. It becomes about the shouting, not the systems, or about war, social issues, and false narratives. This has to change.

Instead, we need to start "seeing like a city" in Magnusson's words, to begin treating the seemingly mundane debates about transit systems and affordable housing as "high politics." The systems are what matters, and we need a bespoke political economy for each of them. Housing is not food. Transport is not health care. We must start with the system, and build the politics (and governance structures) that help deliver what people want and need.

In an urbanization-centered politics, how to make homes, schools, and transport systems is what gets debated on television and on what elections are won or lost, not political ideology about states and markets, quasi-religious beliefs about the role of government, toxic discourses driven by xenophobia or anger, or political power games played by increasingly useless political parties. Who people are sleeping with becomes less important; how to provide everyone with a place to sleep becomes more important. Instead of debating "the economy," we discuss different *economies,* for the economy of housing is different than the economy of water which is different from the economy of food or education or public space. An urbanization-centered approach recognizes that public safety is an economy as well, with its own institutions and logics, not just an arena of policy only discussed when there is a problem. An urbanization-centered approach recognizes that metropolis-building always requires complex mixes of institutions, capital, labor, and materials, and starts from this point. It does not start from an ideological viewpoint about states, markets, certain types of institutions, or scales of engagements.

Truly embracing an urbanization-centered politics is the foundation for building a new social contract based on urbanization and development. As I discuss in more depth in forthcoming work with Stephen Hall and the philosopher Matthew Noah Smith (Schafran, Smith, and Hall 2019), this new social contract—what we call the *Spatial Contract*—focuses on developing a general political agreement between individuals and institutions with regard to the building and rebuilding of the core systems upon which we all rely for survival.

This broader commitment to a more effective politics of urban systems, to more debates about housing, transport, water, and food, to a "common purpose" defined through foundational urban systems, is the first of many steps toward reconstructing the political economy of urbanization. In a twenty-first century where history will be written through how we deal with urbanization and its challenges, and how we use urbanization to meet the combined challenges of poverty, climate change, and disaster, this is the only way forward.

In the Bay Area in particular, this new social contract must be developed as a coalition, a true sustainability coalition that binds together equity, environmental, and economy actors in ways which this book has shown has never truly happened. Institutions of every shape, size, and sector in the San Francisco Bay Area need to redouble their commitment to making these politics effective so they produce, protect, and govern the systems we depend on for survival. And it must begin by accepting the diversity of institutions that plan and make the metropolis.

2. Demand Broad Institutional Responsibility for Urban Development

In her deeply unsettling book on the construction of California's prison complex during the same era as this story, Ruth Wilson Gilmore (2007: 178) discusses the involvement of local activists in the small Central Valley towns that became sites of incarceration as engaging in "the tarnished practice of planning." These were not government officials, but activists and NGOs, developing their own alternative plans in the hopes of building their communities on something other than one of the great human rights disasters of late twentieth-century America.

Further on in the same section she refers to the planning practice of yet another nongovernmental institution, namely the corporate and banking forces she sees as integral to the construction of land and property markets (and deconstruction of industrial labor markets), which form an underlying pillar in her explanation for prison-building. The way these entities determine "the movement of capital across the land feature[s] central planning as a fundamental activity of their institutions and organizations" (ibid., 179).

Her purpose in discussing planning in this context is to elicit the ways in which prison-building was a form of anti-development, to use the language of James Ferguson (1990), a way that plans are sold to or forced upon poorer regions in the name of development, but where the end result is the opposite. But in doing so, she defines planning in a way that renders the state as but one of many actors involved in the production of our urban region.

This is a perspective that is historically unassailable in California. In a book I have repeatedly referenced, Mark Weiss (1987) shows how almost every aspect of the planning system we think of as government was put in place by the development industry. Planning commissions were designed to help developers self-regulate, weeding out unscrupulous actors who were tarnishing an industry just getting off the ground.

In the years that followed, other institutions—unions, environmental organizations, community groups of different sizes, shapes, and political orientations—found their voice. As this book has tried to show, the political system that governs how we build regions in California and the Bay Area does not originate from government. We are not France or the UK or a centralized nation. Ours is a system born fragmented, where every type of institution is involved—for better or for worse—in the production of our cities and towns, in our economies of urbanization.

Again using housing as an example, this book has worked to show how at different points in history, virtually every type, size, and sector of organization has contributed to the region's failure to build enough housing at affordable prices in an accessible location. This is the fault of "planning," but not only of those with planning in their title. Developers need to accept collective responsibility that they too are "planners" in this sense, and are part of both success and failure. The same is true for all other institutions where humans band together in an institutional form in a way that attempts to determine what gets built where, or how foundational urban systems function, expand, or are sustained.

This is not a value judgment, but a fact. There is no future political economy of development in California without diverse actors, without bankers and developers and environmentalists and tech industry players and unions and civil rights groups and local block associations and grassroots organizations and universities and innumerable other institutions. The first step toward building an effective urbanization-centered politics is thus to ensure that *all institutions* involved in the production of urban systems and the urban sector *accept responsibility* for what occurs. Urban planning is not something done by governments or by experts, but by all institutions involved in the production of space, place, and structures. We are most of us planners, and we need a broader acceptance of responsibility for making it work. Ideological viewpoints that see problems in urbanization as the responsibility or fault of any one sector are just empirically wrong. All institutions have a role, from all sectors—the greater the institution's power, the greater the responsibility. But as long as "planning" is viewed as a governmental activity—whether by those who are ideologically for or against it—the system will not produce.

This acceptance of responsibility must come before any formal restructuring of the political process. The project in the Bay Area that comes closest to taking a step toward common purpose is not Plan Bay Area, nor anything in San Francisco, Oakland, or Silicon Valley, but rather Vallejo's experiment with participatory budgeting.[5] Barely four years after becoming the largest municipal bankruptcy in California history in 2008, the city garnered national attention as the first city in the country to adopt participatory budgeting citywide.[6]

What makes this project important is not "participation," nor is it a suggestion that this is the only way to budget—Vallejo, like most cities engaged in participatory budgeting, only distributes a small percentage of its budget this way. What makes the project important is that it is built on a wildly diverse group of civil society actors from across a very diverse city—one which has suffered as much as any in the process described in this book—banding together *and accepting responsibility in new ways for how the city is built*. It has also produced a new environment in which people can learn about city-building, and can see the sources and flow of ideas and how they are discussed.

What also makes participatory budgeting in Vallejo important is that it was a political decision, not a policy one. It can only be seen as a step toward somewhere, not a "solution." It does not engage with "solutionism" so popular in Silicon Valley, nor is it entirely about reinventing or technology. It is about taking steps toward a new political compromise. If the Bay Area wants to solve its growing social and environmental problems, it needs to embrace the *political spirit* behind participatory budgeting in Vallejo, one that can potentially make possible the actual policy fixes like tax base sharing, statewide tax reform, major investments in transportation and housing and education, etc., that are needed over the next two generations.

3. Restorative Justice

Accepting institutional responsibility must be followed by accepting historical responsibility. Most of the institutions involved in making California have been involved in doing so for a long time, and bear responsibility both for the successes and failures across history. The most fundamental obstacle in building any new social contract around urbanization and development is that trust in virtually all of the institutions engaged in building, repairing, and governing our urban systems has been severely undermined by both the history told in this book and that which came before.

This lack of faith comes in many forms. For many communities of color, it is taken as common knowledge that the game is rigged, that the disinvestment in the inner-city Bay Area was just part of a larger plan to gentrify those places. People don't trust developers, local government, state government, national government, transit agencies, "planners," NIMBYs, YIMBYs, politicians, bankers, "experts," or most any other institution in which they do not play a role. As one longtime Contra Costa environmental advocate told me, "NIMBYism was the lack of faith that anyone would follow through with what they were promising."[7]

In 2016, San Francisco approved one of the largest residential complexes in the history of the Mission district, roughly 300 units, of which 35–42 percent will be affordable. Even by San Francisco standards, that is a high percentage of affordable housing. Yet it was still very controversial, with opposition from a number of sources. In response to this opposition, the project's developer was quoted in a local newspaper, arguing that "Fundamentally, it is a shame that a Mission project with unprecedented affordability faced such opposition" (Green 2016: n.p.). Whether or not the "Beast on Bryant" proposal is "good" or "bad" is not the point. The point is that any developer working in the Mission should be able to understand why so many are upset, why faith is so low.[8] More importantly, no developer should fail to understand the ways in which the development community—a group that has built many wonderful and needed structures—has contributed to this lack of faith.

Like the cases discussed in chapter 7, a more productive response would have been for the developer to use this moment to recognize their industry's role in creating such a poor political climate for development, to call for *more contrition by institutions in positions of power.* This is what is needed throughout the region. It is impossible to build an effective system of housing, transport, etc., without the major for-profit, nonprofit, and public sector organizations that have historically been part of their development. But building a better politics means making a concerted effort to build faith and build trust, and this can only happen when institutions make it clear that they recognize why trust is so low.

The notion of restorative justice provides a pathway toward this acknowledgment. Developed as an alternative means of reconciliation between offenders and victims, it has famously been used in South Africa in the aftermath of apartheid. There is a large restorative justice community in the Bay Area, with trained leaders and an ethos that appeals broadly across a variety of Bay Area subcultures.[9] The region is well prepared to apply restorative justice principles and techniques toward a collective and institution-focused acknowledgment of what has been done—intentionally or not—to further resegregation and the unequal and unsustainable restructuring of the region.

Restorative justice provides a proven and established set of practices that can help major organizations in the Bay Area begin to acknowledge mistakes, to acknowledge the ghosts that they helped nurture, ghosts which continue to undermine the possibility of a new politics, no matter how much water has flowed under the seven bridges. They can do so in a way which demands that others do the same, but do it they must. The only way forward in an era of great tension is to admit what has been done, to be contrite in the face of irrefutable history. As I have tried to make clear throughout this book, any organization or institution with the guts to come forward can find some solace in knowing they are just one of many.

4. Exploitation and the Duty to Protect

Restorative justice and institutional honesty not only can begin building faith in the institutions made to make the region, but it can help isolate those only motivated by exploitation. One critique that can and perhaps should be leveled at this book is that it does not spend enough time showcasing the ways in which the resegregation of the Bay Area was profitable or the result of corruption. Subprime lending is a classic example of the way in which segregation is and always has been a system of exploitation for economic gain. As Matthew Desmond (2016) reminds us, poverty remains endemic in the United States in part because poverty is profitable.

If restorative justice is a means to address the past, developing a basic yet concrete institutional commitment to opposing exploitation in the provision of foundational urban systems is critical for the present and future. Exploitation is not as simple as profit, for history has shown that exploitation can come from all forms of power, and that all forms of profit are not exploitative.

The question needs to become: how much profit and on what type of system? Earning a 7 percent return on housing development and a 30 percent return are not the same thing. Systems cost money to build and maintain. But what percent goes to real costs, and what percent to speculation, or the demands of capital far away, to asset managers and various betters who are investing in exploitation, not housing?

In the aftermath of foreclosure, one of the most troubling developments has been the steady acquisition of foreclosed homes by Wall Street investors, particularly large hedge funds that have set up massive corporate structures to own and rent homes (Schafran, Fields, and Taylor 2017). The problem is not that families are renting single-family homes, but that under the current system, they are vulnerable to exploitation. Wall Street landlords have now organized themselves politically to ensure that regulations do not impede their attempts to profit or their launch of new forms of securitization based on rental streams rather than mortgages.[10]

Part of the reason why the politics of urbanization and development around the world are getting more and more contentious is the recognition that housing, transportation, public space, energy, water, and even schooling are increasingly targets for exploitation. The pursuit of yield in an era of historically low interest rates has attracted investors of all kinds into infrastructure, real estate, and urban systems, pushing these vital systems to operate more according to Wall Street logics and the demands of capital than the needs of those who consume them.

All this money sloshing around urban systems has not gone unnoticed by Bay Area tech giants. "Smart cities," driverless cars, hyperloops, and many other technological innovations are spurring a massive investment by technology corporations and their venture partners into all aspects of city-making. As I discuss in more detail below, these technical interventions are vital. We must be able to imagine a future metropolis where technology (and technology corporations) make a major contribution, as they have since the invention of the wheel and the sewer and the toilet. As I argue above, all institutions are needed for the future of city-making, and technology corporations are vital participants.

But all institutions, and especially for-profit ones, must take clear and concrete steps to show that they recognize the contemporary and historical injustice of exploitation when it comes to urbanization. Profit margins on housing and transport cannot be the same as profit margins on space exploration or whiskey or gambling. We must develop a system by which profit on urbanization systems is minimized in exchange for greater political certainty and the social assumption of risk.[11]

A firm and concrete stance against exploitation is also the only way to escape the gentrification dilemma, the only way to convince those not in power that somehow development, new technology, and new and renewed systems—all of which we need—are worth supporting politically because one has faith that what is made will support rather than exploit.

But solving the gentrification dilemma also means committing to *protection* as a collective value.[12] This is both a moral and a political necessity. The moral component should be obvious, as homeless encampments increasingly dot the landscape, as racialized inequality cuts too many lives short and reduces too many others to a daily struggle to survive.

The political question should also be obvious, but it is not. The combination of increasing exploitation and the broken politics of urbanization has left many people uncertain and fearful, and rightly so. Even Proposition 13, with its clear racial undertones, was based in part on legitimate fear by lower-income homeowners that they would lose their houses to rising property tax. Lost in the constant stream of neoclassical economic attacks on rent control is the fact that rent regulation is not about housing economics, but about protecting people, and about *making people feel protected.*

In Bay Area affordable housing circles, there is increasing talk about the three p's—preservation, protection, and production. Everyone knows that all three are needed to solve the housing crisis. But what needs to be clearer is that protection is the first step. If we do not make people feel safe from displacement, secure in their homes and communities, they will not support the massive uptick in production that is needed.

5. Reconstruct the Growth Machine

Exploitation has long been a problem in the economies of urbanization like housing. Exploitation does not just happen in fields and factories, but in the basic social reproductive functions. Sometimes this happens in the economy itself through low wages, other times when those low wages prevent people from consuming these vital economies. Part of the reason why these economies are currently a major focus of exploitation is not just interest rates, but size—more and more, the economies involved in producing California, in building its houses and staffing its schools and hospitals and moving its people and its goods, are a greater and greater component of our overall economy.

Figure 11 shows the size of the transportation, construction, and real estate economies in the state of California between 1963 and 1998 relative to the manufacturing and extractive (agriculture and mining) industries. Even as the latter two industries declined, the making of California did not. These sectors form the heart of what I like to talk about as the *economies of urbanization.*[13] These are the industries common to all regions that construct and provision the metropolis. Construction, real estate, and transportation are clearly part of this process. But what about utilities, schools, and hospitals?

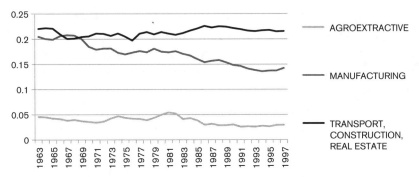

FIGURE 13. Economic sectors as percent of total California GDP, 1963–97. SIC codes. Source: BEA; calculations by author.

What about the basic services we all depend on to live—the markets and shops, the logistics and wholesalers?

If we expand our notion of urbanization economies to the basic economies that we all depend upon to survive, it is more than half of the economy of California. Yet economic thinking has historically not been concerned with these economies (a) that we all need and (b) which employ the majority of workers. Urban development is traditionally viewed as an input into a larger and more important "real economy," or as a by-product, a result of the "multiplier effect," something that just naturally happens. But as we can see from this text, it does not. Demand for homes, schools, and transport networks may arise from economic growth, but the homes, schools, and transport networks themselves do not. How else would a region continue to grow wealthier and fall behind in housing production by hundreds of thousands of units, and largely fail to build a sustainable and humane transport network?

Even before David Dowall's (1984) *Suburban Squeeze,* there has been this idea that the region's lack of affordable living threatens its livelihood. Both equity and business advocates have made similar arguments, even if their agreement on this fact has not been enough to forge compromise on how to do it. Clearly, this is not the case. No matter how absurd the resegregation of the region has become, no matter how unaffordable most housing is to most people, the Bay Area's heady mix of an innovative culture, a highly trained workforce, strong economic institutions, and the largest venture capital pool on the planet has kept the economic machine humming.[14]

Fundamental to developing an effective urbanization-centered politics is to better understand these economies of urbanization. Increasingly, people are realizing that these overlooked sectors of our economy are more than just the "multiplier effect," more than an automatic by-product of the "real" economy. Some have called these important sectors "maintainers," to distinguish from the emphasis on "innovators" (Bliss 2016). While it is vital to better integrate the high-paying corners of the economy—a fact that is increasingly getting recognition throughout the region—a diverse tech industry only solves part of the economic problem. Somebody will always have to clean the building.

Maintainers are undoubtedly the sectors that sustain our society, the sectors which take the fruits of economic innovation and translate them into basic life. These sectors are the purpose of economic activity in the first place, of all that innovation and company-building. This push for recognition of the value of all kinds of labor and industry, from the most informal labor in the global South to more formal versions of the same in the global North (Chen, Roever, and Skinner 2016), is a growing call in economic thinking. These are part of what colleagues in Manchester would call "foundational economies" (Bentham et al. 2010). Increasingly, the millions of people who contribute their labor to these industries cannot afford to consume the core product of these industries, especially housing and transportation.

The Bay Area is proof that we cannot take the existence of these economies for granted, assuming they will automatically appear because the economy is growing, or that the product of these economies will be affordable to those who make them. Yes, these are economies ripe for abuse and exploitation, as we all depend on them. But they are also excellent arenas for alternative economies, new institutional and organizational structures that attempt to produce and provide differently.[15] These industries also represent vast networks of companies, labor markets, supply chains, and other institutions, with powerful corporate and labor alliances alike.

These industries, even in their alternative form, are fundamentally part of the growth machine, and for all of their sins, the growth machine is integral to the economy of the state and to the provision of basic life. It must be reconstructed, invested with new life and ideas and ways of doing business, not simply opposed or destroyed. The growth machine must embrace more equitable forms of land ownership, must embrace political peace and more guaranteed if smaller profit margins, and must wean itself from predatory capital and speculative greed. Instead of build build build with the old ways or blowing up the system, we must be able to imagine and demand a smarter, less exploitative urbanization industry that combines some of the best innovations from both radical grassroots organizations and social entrepreneurs, while respecting the skill and effort involved in creating these vital systems.

6. Develop a Vision for All People and Places

Few institutions in the Bay Area would admit to not being inclusive. It is one of the many buzzwords of contemporary progressivity, for good reason. But when it comes to urban geography, few truly practice what they preach. Our politics of urbanization and development are still mired in imaginations of the right way to live, of the good place and the bad, the right scale and the wrong scale. This twentieth-century mentality only furthers fragmentation, and prevents the formation of a true twenty-first-century social contract of space and place.

A new politics can only occur if we stop the long tradition of devalorizing and denigrating how and where other people live. This includes currently "unsustainable" or even some unsanitary ways of living. History has shown that one group vilifying another group's way of life and place of living only furthers political fragmentation, only undermines common purpose. Calling a place names never helped that place change.

Some of this devaluing occurs in brutal, derogatory fashion, such as "slum talk" and other forms of overt discrimination (Schafran 2013). But it often occurs through more subtle forms of disinvestment. In the postwar era, this was famously done in inner-city areas. In the current era, it is just as likely to occur in faraway regions on the metropolitan edge, areas like East County and the Cities of Carquinez, like Patterson and Manteca and Lathrop and Stockton. These are places that, as I have argued, must be viewed as incomplete, not inherently problematic.

If we see the new zones of segregation as incomplete rather than inferior, it enables us to work to weave in all the places of the metropole, even ones that perhaps should not have been built in the first place. We cannot erase history or turn back time. Building East County in the way it was built was a mistake, but it is now home to a quarter of a million people, and it can only be included. This is both a practical and a political statement. But common purpose has to be just that—common.

This applies not just to East County but to all the spatial divisions that fragment metropolitan space—cities versus suburbs, rural versus urban, etc. We can only build common purpose if we commit to working on the map as we have built it, not as different parties wished it to have been built.

One barrier to this, one which is most evident in the anti-sprawl literature and in the Tea Party backlash to smart growth, is how different groups regard their way of living as the best way. The existing politics of urbanization especially needs to move on from its obsession with different types of places, and more specifically, different types of housing tenure. In recent work with colleagues Jake Wegmann and Deirdre Pfeiffer (Wegmann, Schafran, and Pfeiffer 2017), we try to push American housing politics and policy away from the tired debates between renting and owning, and away from those who focus exclusively on alternatives like community land trusts or accessory dwelling units. These are great policy ideas, but in housing, as in all urbanization politics, one size never fits all. We need an agreement where the full range of housing choices is supported, made less risky and less exploitative, where people have real choice in how and where they live at different times in their lives. We need to recognize that different people want different degrees of control over their homes, and different degrees of equity risk. Debating housing on ideological terms is one of the many reasons why housing has never become common purpose.

Part of the Tea Party–esque backlash against Plan Bay Area is the belief that planners are involved in a conspiracy to "stack and pack," i.e., to force everyone out of their homes and into high-density apartments around transit. It is an absurd proposition—the goal has only been to make these types of living a choice, when low-density, transit-inaccessible housing has long been the only choice. But the constant mantra of density, density, density has clearly failed to engage in what we call 100 percent housing politics—making people feel that no matter their housing desires, the housing system is designed to meet it.[16] We can and always will have a system of different densities, tenures, types, sizes, etc., of housing, and we need to focus on (a) making the choice between different lifestyles a real choice, and (b) making sure that risks that come from each tenure are minimized.

This is not Shangri-la, have-your-cake utopianism. Not only are urban, suburban, and rural lives compatible, all three and various hybrids are needed and can be woven together in a sustainable and equitable way, but only through a new social contract that explicitly recognizes the totality of the region, not just the lifestyle choices of millennials or some other favorite group. The reverse is also true—no new social contract is possible based on a political alliance of similarly living households, a return to the dark ages of postwar division.

The sheer diversity of place types, lifestyle approaches, housing tenures, and landscapes that characterize hyper-diverse places like the Bay Area must become a political strength, not an unending source of political conflict. This can only happen if people in all types of environments learn how they are connected through the systems we depend upon to survive.

7. Teach Urbanization Widely

Developing an effective political economy of urbanization and development also means building a body politic that knows more about the systems involved. Our education systems are designed around the old conception of politics. Children in public schools learn more about how Congress "works" and how the Constitution was formed and why, than about how housing gets built, or sewers, or roads, or hospitals. We learn little or nothing about taxes, fiscal issues, or most every issue discussed in this book. Learning about the economies and systems that sustain our communities is often absent from formal education in American society. Yet somehow, we expect our politicians to know how things work, and in California, we regularly vote on incredibly complex taxes and bonds that determine what gets built where. This is madness.

If we are going to build a better political economy of urbanization by making the politics of urbanization more central to politics in general, all of us need to know more about how urban systems and sectors work, and how they could work. This learning needs to be a formal part of education, starting in elementary school and continuing all the way through graduate school. This learning needs to be considered integral to being a true citizen of any place in the country.

This does not mean "teaching" in the old-fashioned sense, nor necessarily employing more people like me. Learning also needs to come through the political process itself, and not just when a developer, politician, or official makes a proposal. This is the second major accomplishment of Vallejo's participatory budgeting—they have changed how and where and when people learn about the city. The wonderful thing about urban systems is how spread out the knowledge is in actual society; teaching and learning is not just about formal degrees. We certainly need degree programs to build experts, but as part of those programs students need to be teaching their new expertise in public education settings (Schafran 2015b), and citizen experts need to train professional experts at the same time.

Our educational institutions also represent a massively underutilized resource for building new and immediate places of political debate and engagement. As I have mentioned throughout this book, every aspect of the standard approach to how urbanization is done politically is a modern invention, from who proposes ideas to how and where they are discussed and debated to how they are decided upon and implemented. Schools and universities can play a much larger role in two key areas of urbanization politics—how we learn and where we discuss and debate.

As media is transformed across the landscape, universities in particular need to play a much greater role as the primary way through which citizens learn and engage with urban change. The decline of local newspapers is both a problem and an opportunity. As great as local journalism has been, newspapers have long been the key voice of the powerful more than the powerless.[17] Working with civil society of all kinds, universities can fundamentally reconstruct and dramatically increase the ability of people to engage with and understand what is happening around them in terms of urbanization and development.

Universities and educational institutions can also play a much greater role in trying to rebuild trust. While universities in particular are fully implicated in many of the problematic features of history, and certainly need to engage in some restorative justice of their own, they also represent a relatively neutral party in the complex political dynamics of urbanization. They thus make excellent venues for beginning the process of having a new kind of conversation, of doing the restorative justice work that is foundational to any new politics. In the Bay Area, universities can and should develop a multiyear commitment by every public and private college and university in the Bay Area to host a series of conversations and debates focused on how to build a more effective political economy of urbanization and development in the Bay Area.

8. Rebuilding the Possibility of Progress

Just north of central San Rafael sits one of the most fascinating and symbolic buildings in Northern California (Figure 14). Designed by Frank Lloyd Wright, the Marin County Civic Center is an icon of futuristic modernism. The building, completed in 1962, was so ahead of its time that it was the setting for the future in the 1997 film *Gattaca*. It was the last building designed by Wright, who died before it began construction. It is now a state and national historic landmark, and was included as one of ten Wright buildings submitted to UNESCO for consideration of World Heritage Status.

FIGURE 14. Marin Civic Center. Photo collage by Ruth Schafran, 2005.

Wright's building represents a grand, supposedly future-thinking act of building that would become impossible in Marin not long after it was completed. It symbolizes in so many ways the problems of the modernist era and the reaction to it. It stands out in part because it sits right in the heart of the "city-centered" corridor that Marin in theory was going to develop and never truly did. The Marin Civic Center should be harder to see, but instead it is surrounded by a sea of parking in a supposed environmental stronghold. It is a beautiful building that shows both what can be done and how little was done simultaneously.

Wright's Civic Center, like the BART system that opened this book, is one of many potent symbols of both the hubris and lost hope of the postwar era. BART may not have been built ideally, but it was a vision that tried to get ahead of the curve, that saw the region for its size and complexity and tried to meet a dire need. Surely, its failings, like the failings of so many institutions in the Bay, can be pointed out ad nauseum. It is a good thing we have moved beyond some of the elitist and racist failures of the modernist era. There should be no mourning the old growth machine, especially not in the ways even today it tries to regain power in an unreconstructed way.

But the sins of the past era do not mean we should not "mourn the end of the hard-edged idealism" (Walker 2007: 142) that defined the modernist era, the belief in the possibility of large-scale betterment. We must look back at some of the spirit of the modernist, postwar era, and find a way to recapture the possibility of a collective belief in progress. This does not mean losing track of the hard lessons learned over the past few decades from rebellions against the postwar mentality that underlay so many of the issues in this book.

What is needed instead is what I like to think of as the paramodern spirit, an attempt to combine the idealism of modernism and the belief in the possibility of progress while abandoning the one-size-fits-all mentality, the worship of expertise, or the belief in top-down power. A paramodern spirit is not the techno-fetishism of neomodern Silicon Valley, but one that is able to see the possibility of new technology and how it can be used for good, yet knows when to put the smartphone down. It is a spirit which recognizes that disruption can be part of the process, but building something new is the goal.

When it comes to urban development, we need to be able to think and act in large- and small-scale fashions alike, and recapture the possibility that progress can be envisioned in a more inclusive way. Accessory dwelling units are a popular new housing policy in part because they are small-scale, a micro-intervention in the suburban and urban fabric without major redevelopment. But the region also needs to be able to build large housing projects, and even consider New Towns for a growing region. The major base redevelopment projects need to be far more ambitious. The Bay Area must be able to build truly rapid transit from Marin to Vallejo, truly high-speed connections to the Central Valley, a true ferry system or even hyperloop-type projects without running the risk of being dismissed as naive, crazy, or technofetishistic, and must be able to see how this vision is not only compatible with biking and walking and the protection of the old and the natural, but that they go together. The region must build vast amounts of new units and protect millions of existing ones. It needs bike lanes and driverless cars, new forms of modular building and old-fashioned hammers and nails. It needs to invest energy and capital and ideas in some places, and leave other places alone. This both / and type of thinking is at the heart of what I mean by a paramodern spirit, and is the only solution to the constant either / or dilemmas that have plagued the region for generations.

These eight principles—embracing an urbanization-centered politics; demanding broad institutional responsibility for planning; embracing restorative justice; protection not exploitation; understanding the economies of urbanization; developing a vision for all people and places; teaching urbanization widely; embracing the paramodern spirit and the possibility of progress—can become the foundation for making common purpose out of urban and regional development. They would set a baseline for all institutions, accepting the basic agonism that is politics but agreeing to focus political energy in effective ways on foundational urban systems.

The region needs to get to the point where a radical grand bargain is possible. A grand bargain is where a reconstructed and reimagined development industry gets permission to build the units that need building, in exchange for rent control and other important neighborhood and environmental protections, where major investments in affordable housing are agreed upon in exchange for agreements to clamp down on predatory finance, where new transportation plans are envisioned at the radical scale needed, and include the automobile, often without a driver or as part of a sharing economy model. In a grand bargain, any sharing economy company that is part of this deal must agree to proper wages, protections, and standards, agree to end their exploitative practices, as do all others who want a seat at the table. The region can find a way to get the good out of sharing homes, while ensuring taxes are paid, neighbors are respected, and longtime tenants are not evicted in the name of profit. California can develop a plan to reform Proposition 13, reform CEQA without gutting it, share tax base and merge agencies when needed. The region can turn places like the Concord Naval Weapons Station into the grand example of what a new Bay Area planning can do.

But these are only possible if a new political economy of urbanization and development is imagined in the first place, and if all institutional actors accept responsibility for what has happened and what will happen. This has never been more necessary than now, as California and the Bay Area struggle to define what it means to resist in the face of racist demagoguery. Being a progressive in the twenty-first century means putting an end to excuses, embracing a new politics of urbanization, and redoubling efforts to put an end to the racialized segregation that has marked this region and all regions in the United States from the beginning. Only then can the Bay Area become the equitable and sustainable region it wants to be but has never been.

NOTES

INTRODUCTION: GHOSTS IN THE MACHINE

1. This is the combined growth approved by two separate specific plans in late 1981 and early 1982 respectively.

2. Some of these units may have been foreclosed multiple times. Foreclosure is from RAND California via DataQuick. Data for Bay Point, an unincorporated area on the western edge of East County, was not available. Housing unit data are from the 2010 U.S. Census.

3. See inset map for regional geography. The North Bay is generally considered the counties of Marin, Sonoma, and Napa. The East Bay is Contra Costa and Alameda counties.

4. Trulia, an online real estate information site owned by Zillow and the source of the data in McLaughlin (2016), relies on the smallest definition of metro areas used by the census, one which divides the Bay Area up into multiple regions.

5. Throughout this book, I use urbanization to refer to the full set of processes involved in producing human settlements, including rural development. Urbanization does not refer only to people moving to large cities. Suburbanization, exurbanization, gentrification, and other processes are part of urbanization.

6. Similarly, Michelle Alexander's (2012) argument that mass incarceration is the "new Jim Crow" does not imply that the old forms of spatialized racism which formed the heart of Jim Crow have disappeared.

7. As opposed to David Harvey's notion of "spatial fix" to describe the use of the built environment by capitalism.

8. The Bay Area does have two of these "brand-new cities"—Discovery Bay in eastern Contra Costa County and San Joaquin County's Mountain House. Mountain House in particular is fascinating and a potent symbol, but it is hardly representative. See the underappreciated Paul Lewis (1998, 2000) on the virtually inborn nature of California's fragmentation.

9. As Walker (1996) points out, this historical misreading also plagues students of globalization, which is also far from a late twentieth-century phenomenon.

10. This book explicitly does not engage deeply with theories of urban political power, largely because the goal is to explain inaction rather than rule, and because these theories are often limited geographically to cities. As an operating intellectual framework, my approach blends aspects of Logan and Molotch's (1987) notion of the "growth machine" and its attention to the interaction of seemingly opposing actors, Richard DeLeon's (1992) version of racial politics, and Mike Davis's (1990) historical approach to power and city-building, particularly those drawn from Carey McWilliams ([1949] 1973).

11. This notion is influenced by the ideas of regulation theory (see Painter 1995 for a good review). Fragmentation in this sense is the tearing apart of a particular mode of development, and its replacement by more of an anti-regime (see DeLeon 1992) than a new mode of development. This notion of fragmentation is also about the prevention of a new, more functional and effective mode of development from adhering.

12. The Bay Area is the bluest place in the country by a long shot. In 2008, it was the only major metropolitan region where Barack Obama won more than 60 percent of the vote in *every* county. Obama won a higher percentage of the vote in Marin County, a vastly wealthy county just across the Golden Gate Bridge from San Francisco whose 2010 population was 2.8 percent African American, than his former home base in Chicago's Cook County, which is 25 percent African American (http://elections.nytimes.com/2008/results/president/map.html).

13. This historical viewpoint of neoliberalism, less as a set of policies or transformations and more as an epoch where the push for those changes occurred, is the fundamental use of neoliberalism in this text. As Peck and Tickell (2002) note, it can be difficult to separate out the era of neoliberalism (generally accepted to begin in the mid-1970s) from the policies themselves. For the purpose of this text, the "neoliberal era" is the period from the mid-1970s to the foreclosure crisis, the "postwar era" from 1945 to the mid-1970s. This does not mean I believe neoliberalism to be over, nor does my analysis neatly fit into these categories. But it is a basic framework that helps understanding.

14. This historical math owes an intellectual debt to Ed Soja's (1996) interpretation of Los Angeles history from the Watts riots of 1965 to the Los Angeles riots of 1992.

CHAPTER ONE: THE SUBURBANIZATION
OF SEGREGATION

1. See the preface for a discussion as to why this book does not address these vital questions.

2. Moreover, Hall, Crowder, and Spring (2015) find a link between the foreclosure crisis and *increasing* segregation.

3. Californio is the Spanish term for people of Spanish or Mexican descent who lived in California, first under Spanish, then Mexican, and eventually American rule.

4. See Kruse and Sugrue (2006) and Nicolaides and Weise (2006) for the revisionist historiography that has now found this form of historical altersuburbanity in most regions of the United States.

5. Asian and Latinx geography reflects a much longer tenure in the region and in the agriculture economy of the area, which persisted up through the development of Silicon Valley in the 1960s and continues in Brentwood, throughout parts of Napa, Sonoma, and Marin counties, and in pockets around the region.

6. A year after the big earthquake and fire sent hundreds of thousands of refugees streaming to the East Bay, and two years before the city of Oakland would triple in size and take all of the land between downtown and San Leandro, this wealthy neighborhood in the hills—where many of Oakland's decision-makers lived—incorporated. Piedmont is now one of the few island cities in America, surrounded entirely by Oakland, a la West Hollywood, California, and Hamtramck, Michigan.

7. Based on the 1970 census. Piedmont had almost no Latinx population, while San Leandro's Latinx population was over 10 percent.

8. Inner-ring suburbs are now the center of a burgeoning literature on suburban poverty. See Murphy (2010) for an excellent review.

9. This book accepts the link between where you live and life outcomes. See, for example, Newburger, Birch, and Wachter (2011). There is a vast sociological debate on "neighborhood effects" with which this book does not engage. See Sampson (2011) for a review.

10. For an excellent review of these debates, see Teitz and Chapple (1998).

11. See also Steinberg (2010).

12. There is a tinge of what I have referred to as "the ecology of the proper place"—an unspoken assumption that certain groups of people belong in certain places.

13. Orfield (2002), Dreier, Mollenkopf, and Swanstrom (2001), and many of the key regionalists fall into this category as well.

14. The consolidated metropolitan statistical area (CMSA), with micropolitan statistical area (μSA) used for smaller regions.

15. See, for example, Lopez, Snipp, and Camarillo (2001).

16. In no small part because academic studies and ideas underpinned this regime.

17. Incorporated cities and towns primarily but also census-designated places (CDPs), a category for unincorporated areas with some "place-like" feature—generally historical, often based on the location of a post office and an address. See Lichter, Parisi, and Taquino (2015) for a discussion of the need for segregation research to become more place-focused. This analysis was limited to incorporated cities and census-designated places with more than 10,000 residents in 2010.

18. The nine-county Bay Area—Alameda, Contra Costa, Marin, Napa, San Francisco, San Mateo, Santa Clara, Sonoma, Solano—plus Monterey, Santa Cruz, San Benito, Merced, Stanislaus, and San Joaquin counties. Total 2010 population: 9,338,999.

19. Median foreclosure rate refers to foreclosures per 100,000 people.

20. Keep in mind that some high-growth, high-foreclosures cities like Stockton and Modesto, whose numbers did not quite grow by 50 percent because they were already major cities, are counted in the non–50 / 5000 groups. Stockton, for example, grew by 38 percent, significant for a city so large. Had they been included, the differences would be even more extreme.

21. Research by Hugo Lefebvre (2013) on foreclosure in San Joaquin and Stanislaus counties alone shows similar strong correlations between growth and foreclosure.

22. Mountain House, which does not yet have 10,000 residents but is planned for 40,000, would also qualify in this category. But these are the outliers, not the rule.

23. This is based on calculation of before and after populations, not migration patterns. All race data for whites, blacks, and Asians is Non-Hispanic. I use the term Latinx except when directly reporting census data, in order to reflect their terminology.

24. The Asian American story is much more complicated, given the incredible diversity of the Bay Area's Asian community and the geographic range of the term "Asian." Nevertheless, if one parses the Asian community into four main categories based on country of ethnic origin—East Asian (Chinese, Taiwanese, Japanese, Korean), South Asian (Indian, Sri Lankan, Pakistani, Bangladeshi), Southeast Asian (Vietnamese, Lao, Cambodian, Hmong, Thai, Indonesian, Malaysian), and Filipino—a stark pattern emerges. While South and East Asian communities are clustered in the wealthy and low-foreclosure zones of San Francisco, Silicon Valley, and the transformed industrial belt of Fremont and Milpitas, the outer foreclosure zones are heavily Southeast Asian and Filipino.

25. Schafran and Wegmann (2012) includes a more complex analysis, using a regression model developed by Wegmann. This meshed real estate data from DataQuick (via UC Data lab) that was at the zip code scale with census data converted to zip code scale.

26. As noted earlier, the Asian story is more complicated when broken down into subgroups.

27. The research on youth violence was conducted as part of the Youth Violence and Neighborhood Change project of the UC Berkeley Institute for the Study of Societal Institutions. The main dataset was collectively compiled by a team of researchers and ultimately included 38 interviews with young adults (ages 20–24) who had been youth in the year 2000. An additional 37 interviews involved a mix of adults active in the neighborhood, from teachers to real estate agents to parents. The youth roughly reflected the significant diversity of the young people in neighborhood in terms of race / ethnicity, gender, and level of academic attainment. The interviewees included 18 women and 20 men and consisted of 13 Asian Americans (Cambodian, Vietnamese, Mien, and Chinese), 15 Latinxs (all Mexican American except for two of Salvadoran and Guatemalan heritage), 8 African Americans, and 2 youth who identify as mixed race: African American / Asian American. Five

interviewees were at the time attending a four-year college or university full-time; 26 finished high school (a majority of whom attend or have attended community college part-time on an intermittent basis); and six did not complete high school. Since 2000 some of the interviewees have not moved, while others moved both within and out of the neighborhood.

Data was collected in recorded, semi-structured interviews that typically lasted between 45 and 120 minutes. Interviews addressed what was it like growing up in the neighborhood, how and why the neighborhood has changed, and whether the changes in the neighborhood have affected commonly mentioned issues, such as violence. Interviewees received a $25 gift card for participating in the study. Interviews were transcribed, and each sub team on the project did their own coding.

A parallel project was built by LeConte Dill, PhD, in the Elmhurst neighborhood of East Oakland using similar methods and questions. The question of youth geography and the link between risk-avoidance strategies at the neighborhood level and similar strategies at the regional level produced a collaboration that would ultimately include Yvonne Hung, PhD, an expert on youth geography. I developed a coding system using Adobe Acrobat to identify place references upon which the data presented is based. This information was combined with Dill's research on local strategies in an unpublished paper.

28. Based on averaged values of monthly data over three years (2003–05): San Antonio, $312.6; Antioch, $241.4 (94509) and 222.7 (94531).

29. Marcuse (1997) has further explored the link between segregation and ghettoization, creating a typology of ghettos that includes spaces of the very rich, and acknowledging the complex lines between ghettos as segregation and ghettos as enclave.

30. These places still exist, and have been partially reproduced (chapter 4). As I have tried to make clear, the development of this new form of segregation does not necessarily mean the old version has been completely replaced.

31. Regional differences are one of the reasons it is difficult to understand contemporary segregation (Flippen 2016). It is not simply that the "basis" for segregation is changing, incorporating class and complex demographics like never before (Massey, Rothwell, and Domina 2009), but that it is changing in different ways in different places.

CHAPTER TWO: THE POSTINDUSTRIAL GARDEN

1. Proposition 13 capped property taxes for all properties, including commercial and industrial lands, and mandated a two-thirds majority at the state and local level for most new taxes and revenue streams. See Barbour (2007) and Citrin (2009). This book will return to Prop. 13 repeatedly.

2. *Antioch Daily Ledger* (1981a, 1981b, 1981c), Cunniff (1981), Crittenden (1981), Ginsberg (1982a), Cuff (1982).

3. Walker also points to the critical role that labor played in the out-migration. By this time, San Francisco already had the beginnings of a powerful labor move-

ment, and capital sought the friendlier confines of the company towns in isolated Contra Costa County. Also critical in this movement was the search for unincorporated space, impossible in the City and County of San Francisco. Most of Antioch's industrial waterfront remained outside of city limits for the first half of the twentieth century, in order to keep taxes and fees low (Bohakel et al. 2005). Antioch's industry ran plant employees for city council positions to keep it this way, and much of northeast Antioch remains unincorporated and underdeveloped to this day, despite its waterfront location and the city's massive growth to the south and east. Isolated pockets of intentionally unincorporated industrial land remain an issue throughout the region.

4. http://energyalmanac.ca.gov/powerplants/index.html. Calculations by author. This is not what is consumed, as the region imports electricity.

5. For more on the concept of the economic hinterlands of the Bay Area, see Brechin (2006). The population estimate for Brentwood and Oakley comes from the U.S. Census 1960 population for Brentwood (2,186) and the 1970 California Department of Finance estimate for Oakley (1,306). It is highly unlikely that Oakley lost 500 people in the decade of the 1960s. Likely, the combined population was closer to 3,000.

6. Even today, most old-timers you meet in East County worked at some point in the canneries or factories or had a relative who did. Cannery work was particularly prevalent among women, many working seasonally to provide for extra income during harvest season.

7. Interview, transportation planner, resident, East County, 2011. (Note: All interviews are with author unless otherwise specified. Description indicates subject(s) of expertise, not complete expertise.)

8. Fights between the city and developers over improvements continue to this day. Seeno and its partner Discovery Builders (owned by Albert Seeno III) and the city are embroiled in a dispute over road improvements to a subdivision that will now go to court (www.ci.antioch.ca.us/Community/announcements/Pressrelease-041111.pdf).

9. There is no doubt Gentry used a helicopter to get around to his developments (http://biahawaii.org/displaycommon.cfm?an=1&subarticlenbr=402).

10. Ibid.

11. When Gentry began building, Highway 4 was a four-lane freeway only as far east as A Street, just past Gentrytown. The portion from A Street to the Antioch Bridge would not be completed until 1971.

12. Interview, transportation planner, resident, East County, 2011.

13. Many had humble roots like the old East County developers, and cannibalization was common—Garro and Vetrano, for instance, sold out to Seeno, as did other local developers, and Seeno played the role of a more sophisticated outside developer in cities and towns throughout the Central Valley in later years of the boom.

14. See Arieff (2011) on changing the suburban paradigm and just how tenaciously suburban developers are holding onto the model.

15. To get a sense of just how connected developers were to the process, the City of Antioch was one of six of the formal sponsors of the plan; the other five—Broadmoor Development Company, Bren Company / Antioch Investors, D.L. Nelson Corporation, Gordon Gravelle, Dave Dobrich / Emerald Cove Mobile Home—were developers.

16. Work began on widening this stretch in 2010. The only point of contention at the celebratory groundbreaking for the Highway 4 widening was whether this project was three decades late or five.

17. www.cahighways.org/001–008.html#004.

18. Santa Clara County famously went at it alone in completing some of its freeway network during this period (Walker 2007). The difference is they had a much larger tax base and were filling in gaps, not trying to build the primary connection.

19. Oakley would join the agreement in 1999 following incorporation.

20. http://sr4bypass.org/Information/Projectinfo_general.htm.

21. To make things even more complicated, disagreements between Pittsburg and the rest of the East County cities led the ECCRFFA board to create a new Joint Exercise of Powers Authority, the East County Transportation Improvement Authority (ECTIA), to raise additional fees for projects of interest to the three cities but not Pittsburg. Fees were lower for multifamily units, and commercial, office, and industrial uses paid per square foot. Again, Pittsburg's were a fraction of the other cities. Source: East Contra Costa Regional Fee and Financing Authority, and East County Transportation Improvement Authority reports, 2002 and 2008.

22. This point was made by multiple interviewees.

23. These districts, known as Mello-Roos districts in California, became a critical tool for towns and developers.

24. The sad irony is that a fee-based system has long been supported by opponents of growth. Some forms of fees are mandated by the county-wide sales tax funds that go to transportation projects. The idea is it will "make development pay for itself" and at the same time deter growth. Instead, it creates dependence, because the new fee regime is implemented not to be layered atop strong capital funding for infrastructure from higher up the governmental food chain, but to replace it.

25. Interview, transportation planner, government, Contra Costa, 2010.

26. This story is told on a plaque outside the building commemorating the building's placement on the National Register of Historic Places. It is now home to the Antioch Historical Society and the Antioch Sports Legends.

27. Data from the 1950 and 1960 U.S. Census via bayareacensus.gov. Keep in mind that although Spanish-surname data was collected in those days, it was not separated out as it is today.

28. Interview, resident, East County, 2010. This wasn't Antioch's first foray into racial discrimination. A small Chinese community had developed in the low-lying neighborhood of Prosserville, just west of downtown in the 1850s and 1860s, but was driven out by residents in 1876 (http://sundown.afro.illinois.edu/sundowntownsshow.php?id=1038).

29. Interview, elected official, resident, East County, 2010.

30. Precise data on specific intracity moves is very limited. This claim is based on multiple references by interviewees, from realtors to city officials. It is well known in local circles that whites moved east, in part because of diversity. Brentwood is also considered by some as higher in the class scale, and does consistently maintain higher property values. This "upward" move has been reported in nonwhite communities as well. No single or simple explanation holds, but the fact of internal migration and the establishment of an imagined hierarchy of value in East County is important.

31. As one real estate developer with local roots in East County told me in an interview: "I've watched Brentwood use Antioch as the antithesis, just like Antioch used Pittsburg."

32. The cities had been meeting in an attempt to band together to convince the county to pursue a different routing option for Highway 4 in Brentwood, but negotiations fell apart over Deer Valley.

33. The sphere of influence (SOI) is the unincorporated area outside of the formal municipal boundaries that is considered under the control of a local jurisdiction, and a possible candidate for future annexation. Land inside one city's SOI cannot be annexed by another jurisdiction, unless the Local Area Formation Commission (LAFCO) removes it from one city's sphere and places it in another. In the words of one LAFCO member, "The sphere is the engagement, the annexation is the marriage."

34. The urban growth boundaries and its link to transportation funding are part of the "grand bargain" negotiated in Contra Costa County starting in the 1980s. See chapter 3.

35. I was a resident of Brentwood for the month leading up to the election and the immediate aftermath.

36. LAFCOs were set up by the state to decide on all jurisdictional boundary changes. They operate at the county level and usually consist of a mix of county supervisors and other representatives from local authorities, with voices from real estate, environmental, and other civil society interests.

37. Initial reports in the press had a 46 to 1 ratio based on May 27, 2010 numbers (Vorderbrueggen 2010; Coetsee 2010). This figure is from Save Mount Diablo, one of the opponents (http://savemountdiablo.org/lands_landuse_measure_f_brentwood.html/). Ordinarily it would be less trustworthy than a more independent source, but since it cites a lower ratio at a later date, I would argue it is more reliable. There is little dispute that the Yes on F forces dramatically outspent the No forces.

38. Interview, government planner, transportation, East County, 2010.

39. Interview, journalist, resident, East County, 2011.

40. Whether this has been a "success" depends on how you view redevelopment in general, whether you benefitted, etc. Large areas of low-income housing were bulldozed over the years, and the city had to take control of the Vidrio complex after the foreclosure crisis. Public monies have had to be pumped in continuously, and it is far from what one would call vibrant all of the time. But in East County, it cer-

tainly amounts to something, and it is viewed as a success by many leaders in Antioch who wished they had done the same thing when it was possible.

41. Antioch's portion of James Donlon Boulevard was built by Seeno under an agreement with the city. One of Antioch's complaints is that Pittsburg is not willing to make Seeno build needed infrastructure, necessitating the use of limited ECCRFFA dollars.

42. *Transplan Committee and East Contra Costa Regional Fee and Financing Authority v. City of Pittsburg,* Contra Costa County Superior Court Case No. N11–0395.

43. Interview, government planner, East County, 2010.

44. Figure for residents over five years of age. Form QT-p16.

45. U. S. Census Form QT-P13.

46. Informal conversation, local minister / activist, East County, 2010.

47. Interview, government planner, East County, 2010.

48. This is a phenomenon that has been confirmed by research done by Ehrlich (2010). One woman I met from Hercules (West County) who was looking to buy a new condo in Pittsburg reports that after moving to Virginia for work, she flew home *every weekend* to go to church.

49. Section 8 is the colloquial name for the Housing Choice Voucher program, a federally funded program designed to give low-income households choices in their housing, particularly in terms of location. It is the principal program in the attempt to move from place-based affordable housing—i.e., public housing projects—to people-based programs. It is also specifically imagined with the idea of breaking up concentrated poverty and enabling low-income people to live in the resources-rich suburbs. The theory of the program has been attacked by Imbroscio, Goetz, and others who critique poverty deconcentration (chapter 1).

50. Antioch Quality of Life Forum #9 (February 26, 2010), Deer Valley High School.

51. Quote from QOL speaker in defense of the name. TBA folded a few years after this event.

52. The educated guess is that the street was named for a former planning commissioner at the time, Rosemary Lefebvre.

53. This is counting only homes with a Lefebvre Way address.

54. This is based on a total of 6,308 foreclosures from July 2006 to December 2010 (source: RAND California) in 34,459 housing units (ACS 2005–09). Granted, some houses could have gone through foreclosure twice, resulting in double counting, but this has not been widely reported.

55. The 94531 zip code is the wealthier part of southeast Antioch, whereas few neighborhoods are much poorer than Lefebvre Way, but many are wealthier. This figure, calculated from monthly sales data from DataQuick, is conservative, given that comparative data from Lefebvre Way in 2000 are closer to $175,000.

56. What makes this particularly tragic is the link we saw in the last chapter between race and real estate values—for many residents of the Lefebvre Ways of East County, this was their chance to escape the use value / transfer value bind of the

gentrifying but still unequal core (expensive homes but unsafe streets and bad schools), only to be left with neither. The latter bind I discuss as part of the gentrification dilemma in chapter 4.

57. Zillow shows the tragedy of those who tried to bail but were too late. One house that went from $252,000 in 2000 to $550,000 in 2005 was listed in 2007 for $365,000, only to be ratcheted down slowly until being sold at auction for $199,000 in 2009.

58. The house showed a foreclosure notice in 2013. It was purchased in 1997 for an affordable price, leading to the assumption that this was about job loss or lack of income rather than debt load.

59. Although the current wave of *global* competition is clearly unprecedented, we tend to ignore the pre-Keynesian roots of Harvey's (1989) managerial-entrepreneurial city shift. See for instance Cronon (1991), McWilliams ([1946] 1973), and Brechin (2006) on the entrepreneurialism responsible for the establishment of Chicago, Los Angeles, and San Francisco, respectively, as major metropoles.

60. Source: U.S. Census via California Department of Finance.

61. See Harvey (2000) regarding the inner harbor in Baltimore.

62. Strengths, Weaknesses, Opportunities, Threats (SWOT), a common analysis done by planning firms.

63. See Berman (1983) for one of many critiques.

CHAPTER THREE: THE DOUGHERTY VALLEY DILEMMA

1. www.mdshs.org/article.html. The gold in "them thar hills" was plentiful enough to help the North win the Civil War and seed an economic engine that would one day produce a GDP the size of France.

2. The Metropolitan Transportation Authority estimates that in 2007 the nine-county region saw 154,172,000 miles of vehicular travel, projected to grow to more than 200 million miles by 2030 (www.mtc.ca.gov/maps_and_data/datamart/stats/vmt.htm).

3. "Edge cities" is a term coined by Chris Leinberger and popularized by Joel Garreau (1991). Edge cities are generally defined as major suburban job centers, typically offering white-collar work, with more jobs than residents.

4. Only Alaska and Louisiana do not call their county-like jurisdictions counties, but they function similarly enough. The overwhelming majority of Americans live in a county, save the residents of St. Louis, Baltimore, Carson City, Nevada, and the 39 independent cities of Virginia.

5. See Benton (2005) and Menzel et al. (1992) for excellent summaries of this literature at two points in time.

6. Compare this to England, where counties are much older and far more important culturally, but have had their powers and geographies changed regularly.

7. Lamorinda is local parlance for the towns of Lafayette, Moraga, and Orinda.

8. www.forbes.com/2010/09/27/most-expensive-zip-codes-2010-lifestyle-real-estate-zip-codes-10-rank.html. 2010 list based on median home price.

9. See Nelson's (1986) brilliant study of the gendered nature of the new suburban workforce and its role in attracting new corporations to places like Bishop Ranch.

10. According to Bishopranch.com.

11. Including 1.1 million square feet in 1984 alone.

12. Contra Costa general plan from ABAG 2002 projections (www.abag.ca.gov /planning/interregional/pdf/projections/IRP_Projections.pdf).

13. Source: U. S. Census Bureau, ACS 2006–08 three-year estimate, Special Tabs for CTPP, calculated using CTPP interactive software (http://gis.ctpp.transportation.org/ctpp/ctpp.aspx).

14. Data from RAND California via BEA.

15. California Regional Economies Employment (CREE) Series from QCEW data. Calculation by author from NAICS codes 522292 (Real Estate Credit), 522231 (Mortgage and Nonmortgage Loan Brokers), 52593 (Real Estate Investment Trusts), 23 (Construction), 53 (Real Estate and Rental and Leasing). This is a low estimate that does not include industrial sectors dependent on the real estate industry and integral to the political economy such as utility companies, transportation and logistics, wholesalers of construction materials, consulting services (planning, environmental, architecture) and local manufacturing of building products.

16. Interview, planner, real estate professional, Contra Costa, 2009.

17. The "real estate credit" subsector generated roughly $200 million in total wages per year from 2003–07, more than San Francisco and Santa Clara combined.

18. The city of San Ramon would not exist until 1983, part of an early 1980s wave of incorporation (Danville 1982, Orinda 1985) in South County largely in reaction to the pro-growth stances of the county government and the exclusionary tendencies of its well-heeled residents.

19. Construction permit data via RAND California.

20. A friend of Albert Seeno, Lesher was accused of turning a blind eye to Seeno's shoddy workmanship, squashing a follow-up story about a lawsuit filed by East County homeowners against the developers after an angry visit by Seeno.

21. www.savemountdiablo.org/about_history.html.

22. Weir had barely held on to his seat in a challenge by a slow-growth candidate.

23. Thanks to Phelps, Wood, and Valler (2010) for reminding me of this passage.

24. The extensive research of Todd Goldman (2003, 2007; also Goldman and Wachs 2003) into Contra Costa's Measure C and other local-option transportation taxes has been critical in both filling the gaps in my knowledge of the county's decisions and providing critical context within the broader literature and history of transportation finance. I am grateful to him for sharing his data and his ideas many years after the fact. He also provides a much more detailed history that I summarize here, one which is fascinating in its small details.

25. The plan, "sketched out on a napkin" by an elected official and a business leader, was pushed through with near unanimous support from public officials and the backing of a tech industry just beginning to find its ground politically (Goldman 2007: 11).

26. Interview, transportation planner, government, Contra Costa, 2011.

27. There was some shifting of monies from capital projects to maintenance, which benefitted Central County, as it already had capital investment made during the postwar era.

28. Despite grumblings in East County that they never get a fair shake, an analysis of Measures C and J showed a relatively fair and balanced geographic distribution of funds, with the majority of monies in Measure C actually going to East County because of the high cost of BART and Highway 4.

29. http://sanramon.patch.com/articles/iron-horse-trail-a-brief-history.

30. A huge aspect of the environmental objections was around water, but this was part of a larger statewide controversy about water and development, in which the Dougherty Valley project was as much a pawn as anything else. This aspect of the case will come back at the regional / state scales, where it is more appropriate.

31. Demographics in Dougherty can be tough to calculate, as it is bisected by multiple census tracts. Only the smallest wedge of census territory west of Bollinger Canyon is more than 20 percent black and Latinx, with the remaining tracts evenly split between slightly more white and slightly more Asian.

32. Developer contributions to elected officials were a major source of controversy in this era.

33. Contra Costa's notable Republican presence will often get blamed for its generally staunch pro-development stance, and that surely matters to some degree. The Republican Party remains strong in parts of the county, and both East County and the Tri-Valley area have noticeable and at times notable Tea Party presences. Yet the 1992 vote to approve Dougherty Valley came on the heels of a Democratic sweep of the board of supervisors, whose stable Democratic majority of Sunne McPeak, Tom Powers, and Tom Torlakson presided over most of the 1980s growth, supported by labor unions and Democratic politicians up and down the political food chain. The "redness" of Contra Costa County surely matters in local development fights and in questions of race, poverty, and crime in places like Antioch. But the developed future of the core of the county was decided by green versus white, with brown and black largely not a part of the conversation.

CHAPTER FOUR: THE REPRODUCTION OF BABYLON AND
THE GENTRIFICATION OF DILEMMA

1. Silicon Valley has grown to include southern portions of San Mateo and Alameda counties.

2. I lived in Oakland for four years, but was rarely at any real risk of ending up in the statistics that I quote below. It would have been very different if I had been a

young black man living in a different neighborhood. I worked on a project in Richmond during this same period and spent a good deal of time there and was not at any real risk of either homicide or environmental illness.

3. As discussed in the preface in more detail, among the many reasons why this project became less about the social science of this new geography and more about the structural conditions that produced it and into which newcomers found themselves, is that focusing too much on the suburbanization of people of color—especially from my perspective—risks casting it as a problem or as something odd or unusual. What makes it important is that it was done under certain inequitable conditions that have fueled foreclosure and that this book argues represents a new form of segregation.

4. For the Shortened Lives series, see www.mercurynews.com/life-expectancy /ci_13919297.

5. Data in this section comes from the FBI via randstatetstats.org.

6. Sources: openjustice.doj.ca.gov; author's own calculations.

7. Interview, real estate professional, nonprofit planner, policy, Bay Area, 2010.

8. The data is very similar for West Oakland and other parts of East Oakland and Richmond. San Francisco's Bayview–Hunters Point experienced a slight dip in the mid-1990s, before exploding with the dot-com boom.

9. Data on rents is notoriously unreliable (especially historically), very difficult to use at the smaller geographies of zip codes or even cities, and often proprietary.

10. FMR is used to set rents and subsidy levels for housing vouchers and public housing. It is often criticized for underestimating local rents as it is a larger-scale estimate. But for the purposes of this section, it is useful.

11. Alameda and Contra Costa are combined in HUD FMR data.

12. Interviews: government planner, Oakland / Emeryville, 2010; real estate professional, Oakland / Emeryville, 2009; real estate professional, Oakland / Emeryville, 2010; nonprofit planner, academic, policy, Oakland / Emeryville, 2010.

13. This project was in many ways emblematic of Oakland's difficulty. The historic site of the Black Panthers meeting and manifesto, it was 12 years before a development agreement could be reached (DelVelcchio 1995).

14. Interview, real estate professional, Oakland / Emeryville, 2009.

15. The immortal words of former California governor and Supreme Court Chief Justice Earl Warren during his days as Alameda County district attorney (www.ci.emeryville.ca.us/index.aspx?NID=660).

16. Interview, government planner, Oakland / Emeryville, 2010.

17. RAND California data, www.californiacityfinance.com from State DOF and Controller Data.

18. Emeryville did build more than its formal regional share of affordable housing, but that was based on its prior population, not based on the workforce it employed.

19. This is a far greater problem in Los Angeles County.

20. Portions of this section are drawn from Schafran and Feldstein (2013).

21. When it comes to "firsts," much depends on how you define city and whether

direct election matters. Stokes and Hatcher are widely considered the first African American mayors because Gary and Cleveland are larger cities and they were directly elected, unlike Carroll, who was elected as a councilmember and appointed by the council under the system employed at the time. Richmond now elects the mayor directly, although it remains a weak mayor system with the mayor functionally the president of the council rather than a true executive.

22. Although Browning, Marshall, and Tabb (1984) characterized Richmond's African American incorporation as one of co-optation—it did coincide with a white Democratic takeover from a previous Republican majority, and whites maintained an outsized presence in the powerful bureaucracy at the time—it was never tokenism, as black Richmond was well organized and asserted its influence in and on the all-important bureaucracy much as it did in and on elected office.

23. One local newspaper, *Richmond Confidential*, runs a section, "Company Town," exclusively devoted to Chevron-related news.

24. Interviews (all conducted for Schafran and Feldstein [2013]): elected official, longtime activist, Richmond, 2010; elected official, social services, Richmond, 2010; elected official, social services, Richmond, 2010; activist, organizer, Richmond, 2010.

25. Katz and Stern (2006), in a brilliant study of a century of census data, show that the link between African American poverty and deindustrialization is not as strong as argued by scholars like Wilson (1987). Rather, above all it was neoliberalism and the decline of the Cold War that affected the military and public sector jobs and thus impacted the black middle class. Integration of the bureaucracy in Richmond was one of the first major impacts of black political power.

26. Like Oakland, Richmond' s leaders sought government buildings to stem the hemorrhaging, allowing the Social Security Administration to build a regional office in the heart of its downtown. It is a virtual fortress, barely generating lunchtime traffic for the strip mall across the street.

27. Richmond went from a prewar population of 24,000 to almost 100,000—roughly its current population—after the war (www.cr.nps.gov/nr/travel/wwIIbay area/ric.htm).

28. www.visitvallejo.com/about-vallejo/mare-island-history.php/.

29. Dillon also points to a study done by community members in the aftermath of the 1966 Bayview riots—sparked by the killing of a young black man by a white police officer—which points to growing economic instability and the lack of jobs as key sources of frustration, rather than the "subculture" argument being promoted in the media and the academy at the time.

30. The combined opportunity cost to the state is staggering—more than 100,000 jobs, 23,000 housing units, 6,600 affordable units, and almost $400 million in state and local government revenue on $21 billion in real estate value.

31. Richmond tracts: Tracts 3760, 3770, 3790, 3800. Poverty rate of 31 percent is cumulative for all four tracts. In tract 3770, it was as high as 41 percent. All data via Neighborhood Change Database; census data normalized to 2000 census tract boundaries. Courtesy UC Data Lab. Oakland Army Base / Alameda NAS Tracts: 4013, 4014, 4015, 4017, 4018, 4019, 4020, 4021, 4022, 4023, 4024, 4025, 4026,

4028, 4031, 4275, 4276, 4277. Hunters Point Tracts: 0230.01, 0230.02, 0230.03, 0231.01, 0231.02, 0231.03, 0232, 0233, 0234, 0606, 0609, 0610

32. Bayview–Hunters Point signed a community benefits agreement (CBA) in 2008, and a jobs- and industry-focused CBA was signed at the Oakland Army Base in 2012. The latter was put together by some of the same coalition partners that were part of Oak to Ninth. The Oak to Ninth project itself stalled amidst the 2008 crash, but was reborn in 2013 and broke ground in 2015.

CHAPTER FIVE: SILICON SAN FRANCISCO
AND THE WEST BAY WALL

1. Lucasfilm and its subsidiary, Industrial Light and Magic, eventually created what would become Pixar, with early investment from Steve Jobs. When discussing the tech economy of the region, one must expand from early roots in military and semiconductors and include the full range of biotech, media, internet, and other technology companies, and the financial apparatus that funds them.

2. See Saxenien (1983, 1994) for a more complete history of the Silicon Valley.

3. California Air Resources Board.

4. Data for this section comes from U.S. Census data accessed through the Bay Area Census (1950, 1960) and NHGIS (1970–2010). Calculations are based on increases in housing units. These numbers are imperfect, as annexations did continue in some places, meaning that cities could add units to their totals without adding housing; but such numbers were relatively small. Santa Clara County largely discouraged further growth in unincorporated areas during this period, and the overall number of units in unincorporated areas only decreased by an average of 429 units per year for the entire county from 1970–2010.

5. This imbalance is even worse when you consider the megaregion, including San Joaquin and Stanislaus counties.

6. One could add to this the focus the tech giants place on housing themselves. Apple's new corporate campus is estimated to cost $5 billion (Burrows 2013).

7. There was even an internal version of offshoring in the postwar Bay Area, as industry left the heavy industrial belt of the northern part of the East Bay for the wide-open spaces of the southern part. The Bay Area's two major auto factories, Ford and General Motors (GM), each moved during the postwar era. The Ford plant moved from the Richmond waterfront south to Milpitas in the 1950s. The GM plant went from the heart of East Oakland to Fremont, in Alameda County just north of the Santa Clara County line.

8. San Ramon, the heart of Contra Costa edge-city wealth, is itself more than one-third Asian American, primarily households of Chinese or Korean descent.

9. 17 percent versus 6.2 percent (2010–14 American Community Survey).

10. See Silk's excellent dataset on diversity in tech, which also examines major gaps at venture capital firms (http://ethnic-diversity-in-tech.silk.co/).

11. Source: Census 2010, Redistricting Data (Public Law 94–171) Summary File, California Department of Finance, generated on March 8, 2011.

12. San Francisco's 49 square miles have had more books written about them than the rest of the region combined. See Hartman ([1984] 2002), DeLeon (1992), Brechin (2006), Craddock (2000), and Solnit (2002) among others. See also Chris Carlson's excellent Shaping San Francisco project (www.shapingsf.org/).

13. This is one of the many brutal facts documented by the Anti-Eviction Mapping Project (http://antievictionmappingproject.net/evictionsurge.html).

14. Fourteen of the top 20 zip codes for venture investment were in the Bay Area. No other region had more than three in the top 20.

15. This is based solely on calculations made from Florida and King's (2016) top 20 data. It does not assume that this gap would exist for the entire San Francisco / Silicon Valley comparison, as the latter remains much larger in every sense.

16. I will discuss rent control more in the conclusion.

17. Source: U. S. Census. By 2010 the numbers had declined precipitously (Causa Justa n.d.), with white households and white homeowners in particular increasing dramatically amidst a Latinx decline.

18. In all three of the discussed cases, I recognize that this is a difficult claim to make. The numbers mask many things. But some aspects of San Franciscans' political fight to protect vulnerable communities were successful, and that does not get enough attention. Without this politics, it would have been much worse.

19. Nancy Hellman Bechtle, longtime Presidio Trust board member and chair, speaks of playing as a child in the Presidio, which was across the street from her house (Wallechinsky 2010). She is the great-granddaughter of Isaias Hellman, one of wealthiest and most important bankers in post–Gold Rush California history, and the sister of Warren Hellman, a private equity titan who founded and funded a major music festival in Golden Gate Park that has become an institution. He also helped to fund a very controversial 2002 ballot measure that ended cash support to the homeless and played a role in ushering Gavin Newson into the mayor's office.

20. This figure is based on the campaign goal, which includes $245 million for an endowment (www.sfmoma.org/read/expansion-faq/#section-how-much-will-the-project-cost).

21. The major exception being Oakland / Alameda County's deal with the Oakland Raiders, who are now leaving for Las Vegas. The stadium issue was also a missed opportunity for regionalism (Schafran 2012c).

22. And that is only if you cut the line at the nine-county region.

23. Morris and Hunterdon counties in New Jersey voted for Romney. Pitkin County, Colorado, home to Aspen, and Nantucket County, Massachusetts, are the two nonsuburban wealthy counties that supported Obama. This calculation is based on mean household income from the 2006–10 ACS. Most scholars use median household or per capita income, as means can be skewed by high earners. In the former, Marin ranks seventeenth nationally. Yet if one extends the same analysis to the Obama voting counties above Marin in median income (Charles, Howard, and Montgomery, Maryland; Nassau, New York; Arlington and Prince William, Vir-

ginia; and Santa Clara), similar patterns emerge. Marin is the whitest and oldest. Only Charles County and Arlington County are smaller in population; the latter is 16 times denser, the former is 41 percent black.

24. Prince George County, Maryland, was the highest. Essex County, New Jersey, was also higher, but in addition to being a suburb of New York City it includes the city of Newark.

25. With the exception of Florida counties, Marin is the second-oldest county in terms of median age in the country with a population greater than 250,000. Only Westmoreland County, Pennsylvania, a suburb of Pittsburgh, is older. Marin is the oldest county in California that is part of the major metropolitan regions.

26. This section and the work on Marin in this book owe a great deal to Louse Nelson Dyble, one of the few scholars to really examine Marin and its growth policies in depth. Whereas any failings in this chapter are mine, much of this section draws from her 2007 article cited repeatedly here.

27. California Secretary of State Voter Registration Statistics 1964, U.S. Election Atlas (uselectionatlas.org).

28. In addition to the highway plans described here, two other major plans were critical in galvanizing the conservationist movement in Marin. The first was a proposed nuclear power plant in Bodega Bay, on the Marin-Sonoma county border, opposition to which would be foundational in the national push against nuclear energy (Wellock 1998). The second was Marincello. In 1964, Pennsylvania real estate promotor Thomas Frouge had managed to get backing from Gulf Oil for one of the most grandiose development schemes in the nation, a new town of 30,000 residents perched on the Marin Headlands, replete with 50 apartment towers, acres of suburbs, and even light industrial space (Hart 2003).

29. This does not mean they were not heavily constrained. See Gerald Frug (1980, 2001a, 2001b) on the illusion of home rule.

30. See also Walker (2007) for a more complete history of trusts and land preservation in the Bay Area.

31. This is only for the purposes of the Regional Housing Needs Assessment, a state-mandated requirement that cities plan for housing at all income levels. Marin County has never built or permitted its allocation under any of the previous four cycles dating back to 1980. See chapter 6 for further discussion.

32. The valley was named after a nineteenth-century rancher, not the filmmaker.

CHAPTER SIX: THE ALTAMONT LINE
AND THE PLANNING DILEMMA

1. The broader question of Sacramento and its massive urban growth can also be tied to this larger process, but for the sake of analytical clarity and the author's sanity, this chapter deals with this "inner" ring of the northern San Joaquin Valley and not with the Sacramento Valley and its sprawling foothill suburbs. Greater

Sacramento is fully part of the Bay Area's diverse out-migration, but its complexities are beyond the scope of this book.

2. The language of the outer edge of the metropolis has been subject to the same "name game" that produced "edge cities," and the debates and discussion overlap. There are two terms that seem to have settled into regular use—the megaregion and exurbia. "Exurbia" was coined by Spectorsky (1955) to refer to a certain type of sub-urbanite moving farther and farther out to escape an urbanizing suburbia. Academics have worked to define "this amorphous concept and its land use in a way that can be quantified and mapped," but as with every urban concept there is little consensus (Travis 2007: 114; Berube et al. 2006). A common working definition involves economic relation to a metropolitan region, low population density, and population growth. Megaregions are massive regions of interconnected cities and previously "independent" regions that have emerged throughout the country (Dewar and Epstein 2007). This parallels the growing and older recognition in Europe of interconnected cities forming conurbations that defy traditional conceptions of the metropolis. See Schafran (2014a, 2015a) for a review of thinking on megaregions and a more academic discussion of some of the concepts used in this chapter.

3. That is, unless you are one of the San Franciscans making that move.

4. Interview, former elected official, longtime resident, policy, Central Valley, 2010. (With regard to interviews, Central Valley indicates Merced, San Joaquin, and Stanislaus counties.)

5. In a 2012 article on population loss in the Bay Area (Glantz 2012), a local newspaper treated the fact that people were moving to San Joaquin County the same as people moving to Henderson, Nevada—even if they were likely to keep their Bay Area job in one case but not in the other, and even though San Joaquin County is connected to the Bay Area by 150 years of history.

6. California Regional Economies Employment Data, San Joaquin County, section 23.

7. Ibid., sector 522292.

8. Interview, former elected official, longtime resident, policy, Central Valley, 2010.

9. U.S. Census 2000 county to county migration data.

10. See also Cadieux and Hurley (2011) on exurbia. One reason for this divide is the myriad definitions of exurbia pointed out by Taylor, some that include suburbanized fast-growing small towns at a previous metropolitan edge and others that do not.

11. As Susan Strasser (2006) makes clear in a brilliant history of American consumption, we have a tendency toward nostalgia for small business relationships which ignores that they are just as capable of exploitation. With captive audiences, small-town merchants were often able to artificially inflate prices and use their money and influence to control small-town politics.

12. Interviews: government planner, planning consultant, Central Valley, 2010; government planner, Central Valley, 2010; government / planning, Central Valley, 2010.

13. Mountain House, wedged into a corner of San Joaquin County at the intersection of the Alameda–Contra Costa border, is the only major "new town" to be built in Northern California since Discovery Bay in the 1970s. In 2010 it had just under 10,000 residents, severely stalled development, and high rates of foreclosure and underwater borrowers. Delhi (Merced) and Salida (Stanislaus) are both towns in the cultural-identity sense but are officially unincorporated. Diablo Grande is a combination resort-residential community high in the Diablo range west of Patterson, but despite grand plans and major water infrastructure had only a few hundred permanent residents in 2010.

14. Some of it even occurred internally in East County. Brentwood became almost evenly Democrat/Republican during this period, down from a more than 2:1 ratio of Democrats in 1964. Brentwood was also the center of East County Tea Party activity following the election of Obama.

15. Carol Whiteside, interview with author, 2010.

16. NHGIS—Minnesota Population Center, 1980, 1990, and 2000 STF-3 Sample Data.

17. Interview, former elected official, longtime resident, policy, Central Valley, 2010.

18. www.abag.ca.gov/planning/interregional/brochure3.htm.

19. www.acerail.com/AboutUs/HistoryofACE.aspx.

20. ACE expansion did receive monies in the 2013 Plan Bay Area allocation from the Metropolitan Transportation Commission (MTC).

21. Union Pacific now controls Southern Pacific, the Octopus of California fame and the reason why California has an initiative system—itself a disaster.

22. Additionally, a major court battle during this era, *Santa Clara County v. Southern Pacific Railroad* (1886), was the first Supreme Court ruling which established that the equal protection clause of the Fourteenth Amendment applied to corporations (Horwitz 1985).

CHAPTER SEVEN: THE REGIONALIST DREAM

1. Words used by progressive San Francisco leaders John Avalos, David Campos, and Aaron Peskin and Bay Area Council president Jim Wunderman in their separate statements in support of the historic Measure AA in 2016.

2. Regions in many ways are the antithesis of counties. Whereas the county is politically real yet often forgotten, the region is the object of much political and scholarly fascination and very limited institutional reality, the two most famous exceptions being Portland and to a more limited extent the Twin Cities. For excellent reviews of regionalism from the broad perspective of American political science see Weir (2004), and from the broad intellectual perspective of planning see Wheeler (2002). For California regionalism from a planners' perspective see Barbour (2002), and from the political geography/scalar theory perspective see Jonas and Pincetl (2006). For comparative work on regional collaboration see Thibert (2016). For the intersection of regionalism and equity see Pastor, Benner, and

Matsuoka (2009). See also Mildred Warner's excellent web resource on regionalism that includes many of the most salient debates, including those who favor home rule and fragmentation (www.mildredwarner.org/restructuring/regionalism).

3. In part because of resistance from Southern California conservatives anxious to prevent such a development in Greater Los Angeles (Barbour 2002).

4. Interview, nonprofit planner, activist, Bay Area, 2009.

5. This exclusiveness is not unique to the Bay Area, nor is my argument that racial blindness helped undermine regional efforts. See Pastor (2001) and Rast (2006) for examples of similar failings in Los Angeles and Milwaukee respectively.

6. Interview, activist, academic, policy, Bay Area, 2009.

7. Orfield also became a key voice in the de-concentration of poverty debate, and as such has been a target of Imbroscio's (2012a, 2012b) critique, as regionalism for Orfield is expressly considered as a means of enabling the poor to move.

8. Also known as the Bay Area Alliance for Sustainable Development.

9. See Pastor, Benner, and Matsuoka (2009) and Benner and Pastor (2015) for a positive spin on the interaction between equity and new regionalism. See Lester and Reckhow (2012) for a more skeptical take. Innes and Rongerude (2006) review the Irvine Foundation's efforts in California at that time.

10. This was classic neoliberal-era thinking—rather than incentivize housing through subsidy, or through a better fiscal deal for cities, or any other more creative approach, it assumed that removing regulatory barriers would induce "the market" to build. And since developers knew that many municipalities would be recalcitrant, it gave them a built-in political excuse if it didn't work—the lack of housing remained the fault of the cities. Neoliberalism as an exclusive analytical framework leaves much to be desired, but at times it is spot on.

11. Lewis (2003, 2005) is somewhat skeptical about the effectiveness of the RHNA process, based on local noncompliance. Ramsey-Musolf (2016) has a more mixed view, and indicates some unintended consequences in terms of tradeoff between low-income housing production and overall housing production. Some of the divisions between the two perspectives are methodological, and Ramsey-Musolf does not analyze the Bay Area. No comprehensive evaluation of the relationships between RHNA allocations and actual housing production seems to have been done.

12. There have been four RHNA cycles completed. The first, 1980–90, was not analyzed by ABAG for performance. As it matches up with the census year, data on housing units was used, and analysis is only available for total units. For cycle 2 (1988–95), ABAG did follow up, and results were self-reporting, and often spotty. Nevertheless, I combined this data with the allocation data. For cycles 3 and 4 (1999–2006, 2007–14) ABAG produced a report with both allocations and performance. These data have been combined. This is an inexact analysis due to variations in data sources and lack of reliability in earlier years. Additionally, there is some overlap in cycles. Finally, cumulative numbers are reported with the recognition that ABAG recalculates need in every cycle, thus new cycles in theory account for unmet goals in the previous cycle. It should be noted that the small analysis done here is the first cumulative analysis I have found.

13. Chapple (2009) found evidence before Plan Bay Area even began that while Transit Oriented Development (TOD) was important, proximity to major transit stations carried a displacement and gentrification risk. With the gradual acceptance of TOD as a development strategy, there seems to be new emphasis on research into potential links between TOD and displacement (Zuk et al. 2015; Rayle 2015).

14. The environmental and BIA lawsuits were settled out of court, both for promises of a different process for the 2017 update. The lawsuits by the conservative Pacific Legal Foundation on behalf of a group called Bay Area Citizens was dismissed by the Alameda County Superior Court and upheld on appeal. The lawsuit by the post-sustainability institute was dismissed as well.

15. Like the Social Equity Caucus, 6 Wins is organized through Urban Habitat (http://urbanhabitat.org/campaigns/6-wins-social-equity-network).

16. Letters of April 18, 2014, and November 14, 2014, from the Bay Area Business Coalition to Pilar Lorenzana-Campo Chair, Bay Area Regional Prosperity Plan Steering Committee.

17. Letter of May 11, 2015, from Jim Wunderman to Dave Cortese, chair of MTC. Wunderman was a co-signator on the previous two letters.

18. https://oaklandliving.wordpress.com/2011/09/29/mtc-approves-move -to-san-francisco-triggering-senator-desaulnier-to-commit-to-drastically-overhaul -the-agency/.

19. This map can be viewed in color at www.planbayarea.org/previous-plan and in a visual appendix to this book at alexschafran.com.

20. Full disclosure: I was involved in this process as an advisor.

CHAPTER EIGHT: THE UNREALIZED COALITION

1. McGirr's brilliant work shows how in some ways Orange County in the early 1960s was equally as revolutionary as Berkeley, albeit in a reactionary way, as it built grassroots support for Barry Goldwater and ultimately helped to propel Reagan into the governor's office in 1966.

2. A variation on this explanation is one that focused on the general dysfunctionality of the initiative system (Schrag 2004).

3. Dowall and Whittington (2003), writing as part of a wave of infrastructure reports from the Public Policy Institute of California and others in the 2000s, during a time when political shifts and a generalized infrastructure crisis seem to make new investment both more possible and more needed, argue Reagan + Environmentalism + Prop. 13.

4. My argument builds on the work of Schrag (1998), Pastor and Reed (2005), Myers (2007), and Gilmore (2007), scholars who wisely refuse any explanation of California's unwillingness to invest in its future that ignores the question of who that future looks like, or in the case of Gilmore, the "alternative" forms of infrastructure that California did build during this time—prisons.

5. It made a comeback on the website of the State Office of Planning and Research website, as the state attempted to update the document with a new Environmental Goals and Policy report with the return of Jerry Brown as governor.

6. See for instance Mello-Roos districts (Barbour 2007).

7. Barbour (2007) is an excellent review of the fiscal issue post–Prop. 13. There is a vast Prop. 13 literature, both in terms of its origins and impacts at every scale.

8. Major business groups—substantial beneficiaries of the proposition—actually opposed it (Schrag 2008), out of fear of a subsequent hike in corporate taxes that theoretically should have followed.

9. Nalder (2010) and others often refer to Prop. 13 as California's "third rail," a common metaphor whose use accidentally says a lot about the problems of funding infrastructure. Surely touching the rail will kill a person—hence the metaphor—yet it seems to ignore the fact that the electrification of subway trains through this technology fundamentally changed urban transport. The Prop. 13 problem is that it prevents California from building the new third rails it needs.

10. A common argument is that initiatives measure voters, who are whiter, older, and wealthier than the population as a whole (Schrag 1998; Maharidge 1996).

11. The EGPR was mandated in the same 1970 bill (AB 2070) that created the State Office of Planning and Research (OPR). AB 2070 was a product of the Assembly Select Committee on Environmental Quality, which also produced an "Environmental Bill of Rights" and the California Environmental Quality Act (CEQA), which established the environmental review process in the state (Calavita 1995).

12. This decision so angered anti-immigrant Sierra Club members that some formed a splinter group called Sierrans for U. S. Population Stabilization (SUSPS). It is worth noting that while the webpage on the Sierra Club's website that explained the organization's controversial history on the issue has been erased, SUSPS's webpage (www.susps.org/) has a very detailed examination going back to 1961. See King (2009) for an interesting analysis of how population and environmentalism are linked discursively by organizations, including SUSPS. A recent text that I hope to see in print one day and which has an excellent and subtle discussion of these issues is Hultgren (2012).

13. www.greenbelt.org/about/history/.

14. Interview, real estate professional, policy, Bay Area / California, 2010.

15. In a postmortem of the controversy, the California Planning Roundtable (1995) noted that few reports had caused such rises in blood pressure and so many accusations of hidden agendas.

16. According to a 2004 study, African Americans and Latinxs were imprisoned under the Three Strikes law at a higher rate than whites. Blacks made up 6.5 percent of the state population but 45 percent of those convicted of a third strike (Ehlers, Schiraldi, and Lotke 2004).

17. Pastor and Reed (2005) provide clear evidence for Schrag's hypothesis, showing that there is a statistical relationship between the ethnic gap separating older and younger residents in a state and the state's willingness to pay for infrastructure.

18. Only California at the time allowed the third offense to be minor. This allowed some people to be jailed for life when a petty theft was raised to felony petty theft because of prior convictions, leading to international press about teenagers imprisoned for life for stealing socks (*Economist* 2009b). Less than half of "strikers" are imprisoned for serious / violent offenses (Brown and Jolivette 2005). The law costs roughly half a billion dollars annually to enforce.

19. It is not a coincidence that the two policy-oriented papers in Bass and Cain's (2008) edited volume *Racial and Ethnic Politics in California* are on education and criminal-justice reform.

20. Ruth Wilson Gilmore's *Golden Gulag* is in many ways a parallel sequel to *American Babylon,* as it follows a related race- and class-based restructuring and migration tied to land and labor—in this case, the movement of primarily men of color from inner-core neighborhoods to prisons in the Central Valley. It is a monumental book.

21. Amazingly for a state made famous for anti-immigrant sentiments in the 1990s, it would be hard to imagine that type of politics in contemporary California.

22. Interview, real estate professional, policy, Bay Area / California, 2010.

CONCLUSION: RESEGREGATION AND THE
PURSUIT OF COMMON PURPOSE

1. Hannah-Jones's work is primarily about education and schooling, one of the most critical parts of segregation and a topic for which this book is woefully inadequate.

2. https://mtc.ca.gov/our-work/plans-projects/casa-committee-house-bay-area /casa-membership-roster.

3. The YIMBY movement is a complex and global phenomenon, even if the Bay Area gets the most attention. Much has yet to be researched and written about YIM-BYs. One challenge in the Bay Area is that older YIMBY groups like Oakland's ULTRA, which is a neighborhood group that emerged to argue for densification in Oakland's Temescal district and to specifically counter a NIMBY group, get drowned out by the more ideological and politically savvy SFBARF, and by the din of San Francisco development politics in general. This section deals with the general debate that has emerged around YIMBYs, not the specific politics of individual YIMBYs.

4. My talk of political compromise should not be confused with centrism, for like Mouffe (1998), I share the view that centrism often seeks to depoliticize, even the supposed radical center. I am speaking about the creation of a new center around which a more functionally agonistic politics can form.

5. www.ci.vallejo.ca.us/city_hall/departments___divisions/city_manager /participatory_budgeting/

6. The year 2016 marked its fourth cycle of funding, with almost $10 million distributed through the first three cycles.

7. Interview, elected official, nonprofit planner, policy, Solano, Contra Costa, 2011.

8. All development in San Francisco is a political football, used by many different institutions as leverage. But opposition cannot simply be chalked up to the game—displacement is real.

9. http://rjcenterberkeley.org/bay-area-rj-organizations/.

10. See KCRA's recent report on rental prices in the Sacramento region that reveals a disturbing trend of post-foreclosure ownership by Wall Street (Manoucheri 2017).

11. The foreclosure crisis is a classic example of where society bore the risks as Wall Street gambled with people's homes.

12. Doctors take an oath to first "do no harm," a principle that should extend to bankers, engineers, architects, planners, developers, police officers, and anyone else involved in the production of cities and regions. After all, just as with health care, interventions can build healthy lives or cause grievous harm depending on how they are carried out.

13. See Schafran et al. (2018) for a fuller account. At the heart of this work is a reconfiguration of economic activity, jettisoning the concept of the service sector and replacing the World War II–era three-sector theory with a new configuration that recognizes urbanization economies as an economic sector.

14. Research has shown that the relationship between urban development and economic development is not a chicken-and-egg question anymore, but a cart-and-horse one. We know that urban development is the cart, and industrial development the horse. But the only reason to have a horse, in this scenario, is because you have a cart that needs pulling. See Storper et al. (2015) and Cheshire, Nathan, and Overman (2014), in contrast to Florida (2002). Moreover, Storper et al. show clearly that the region's growing inequality did not spur economic growth. The wealth grew despite the housing situation, not because of it. But he also functionally rejects the notion that fixing the housing situation matters to wealth creation.

15. This includes efforts like land trust and cooperatives that emerged from progressive civil society, for-profit start-ups, and many hybrids. See for instance Oakland Community Land Trust (oakclt.org) and Kendall (2017) for the start-ups and hybrids.

16. For instance, many would point to single-family zoning as the root of the problem. And while single-family zoning is overly ubiquitous, often exclusionary, and certainly in need of reform, positioning single-family zoning as the enemy and the problem leads too many to believe that single-family homes themselves are under attack, and they thus defend boundaries rather than build common purpose. A different approach is needed.

17. This has continued to be an issue in the internet age. See the shuttering of Gothamist and DNAinfo by its billionaire owner as they attempted to unionize (McKenzie 2017).

REFERENCES

Abbas, A. 2000. "Cosmopolitan De-Scriptions: Shanghai and Hong Kong." *Public Culture* 12(3): 769–86.

Abbott, C. 1981a. *Boosters and Businessmen: Popular Economic Thought and Urban Growth in the Antebellum Middle West* (No. 53). Westport, CT: Greenwood Press.

———. 1981b. *The New Urban America: Growth and Politics in Sunbelt Cities.* Chapel Hill: University of North Carolina Press.

Abrams, S. J., and M. P. Fiorina. 2012. "The Big Sort That Wasn't: A Skeptical Reexamination." *PS: Political Science and Politics* 45(2): 203.

Adams, D., and S. Tiesdell. 2010. "Planners as Market Actors: Rethinking State–Market Relations in Land and Property." *Planning Theory and Practice* 11(2): 187–207.

Adelman, R., and C. Mele, eds. 2014. *Race, Space, and Exclusion: Segregation and Beyond in Metropolitan America.* New York: Routledge.

Alameda County Public Health Department. 2008. *Life and Death from Unnatural Causes: Health and Social Inequity in Alameda County.*

———. 2013. *How Place, Racism, and Poverty Matter for Health in Alameda County: Our Local Data on Health and Social Inequities.* (An update of the 2008 report cited above.)

Alexander, M. 2012. *The New Jim Crow: Mass Incarceration in the Age of Colorblindness.* New York: New Press.

Ambruster, A. 1995. "Pact Ends Dougherty Dispute." *Contra Costa Times,* October 12.

Anderson, M. 1964. *The Federal Bulldozer: A Critical Analysis of Urban Renewal, 1949–1962.* Cambridge, MA: MIT Press.

Angelo, H., and D. Wachsmuth. 2015. "Urbanizing Urban Political Ecology: A Critique of Methodological Cityism." *International Journal of Urban and Regional Research* 39(1): 16–27.

Antioch Daily Ledger. 1981a. "Prop 13. Caused Fiscal Crisis." Editorial, November 10.

———. 1981b. "Layoffs Slated for Two Area Plants." November 10.

———. 1981c. "Reagan Forecasts Hard Times." November 10.

ARCADIS and City of Antioch. 2006. *Rivertown Waterfront Master Development Plan.*

Archer, J. 2005. *Architecture and Suburbia: From English Villa to American Dream House, 1690–2000.* Minneapolis: University of Minnesota Press..

Archibald, K. 1977. *Wartime Shipyard.* New York: Arno Press.

Arieff, A. 2011. "Shifting the Suburban Paradigm." *New York Times,* accessed on October 4, 2012, at http://opinionator.blogs.nytimes.com/2011/10/02/shifting-the-suburban-paradigm/.

Arnold, J. 2016. "Barriers to Fair Housing." *Novato Advance* 93(16) (April 20). Accessed at www.fairhousingmarin.com/in-the-news/county-connections-novato-advocate-by-judy-arnold.

Associated Press. 2002. "Privately Built Pacific Bell Park a Curse to Other Teams." October 22. Republished and accessed via ljworld.com on August 26, 2016 at www2.ljworld.com/news/2002/oct/22/privately_built_pacific/.

Association of Bay Area Governments (ABAG). 1966. *Preliminary Regional Plan for the San Francisco Bay Region.*

——— and the Metropolitan Transportation Committee. 2013. *Plan Bay Area: Regional Transportation Plan and Sustainable Communities Strategy for the San Francisco Bay Area 2013–2040.*

Atkinson, R. D., and G. Bridge. 2005. *The New Urban Colonialism: Gentrification in a Global Context.* London: Routledge.

Atkinson, R. D., and P. D. Gottlieb. 2001. *The Metropolitan New Economy Index: Benchmarking Economic Transformation in the Nation's Metropolitan Areas.* Washington, DC: Progressive Policy Institute.

Avila, E. 2004. *Popular Culture in the Age of White Flight: Fear and Fantasy in Suburban Los Angeles.* Berkeley: University of California Press.

Badger, E. 2016. "The Divided American Dream." *Washington Post,* April 28.

Baer, W. C. 2008. "California's Fair-Share Housing 1967–2004: The Planning Approach." *Journal of Planning History* 7(1): 48–71.

Bagwell, B. 1982. *Oakland: The Story of a City.* Oakland: Oakland Heritage Alliance.

Banham, R. 1971. *Los Angeles: The Architecture of Four Ecologies.* Berkeley: University of California Press.

Barbour, E. 2002. *Metropolitan Growth Planning in California, 1900–2000.* San Francisco: Public Policy Institute of California.

———. 2007. *State-Local Fiscal Conflicts in California: From Proposition 13 to Proposition 1A.* San Francisco: Public Policy Institute of California.

Bardhan, A. 2009. "Housing and the Financial Crisis in the US: Cause or Symptom?" *Vikalpa: The Journal for Decision Makers* 34(3): 1–7.

——— and R. A. Walker. 2010. *California, Pivot of the Great Recession.* Berkeley: UC Berkeley Institute for Research on Labor and Employment.

Barron D. J. 1999. "The Promise of Cooley's City: Traces of Local Constitutionalism." *University of Pennsylvania Law Review* 147(3): 487–612.

———. 2003. "Reclaiming Home Rule." *Harvard Law Review* 116(8): 2255–386.

Bass, S., and B. E. Cain, eds. 2008. *Racial and Ethnic Politics in California: Continuity and Change, Volume 3*. Berkeley: Berkeley Public Policy Press.

Bauer, C. 1934. *Modern Housing*. Boston: Houghton Mifflin.

Bauer Wurster, C. 1963. *Housing and the Future of Cities in the San Francisco Bay Area*. Berkeley: Institute of Governmental Studies, University of California.

Bay Area Census. N.d. "Selected Census Data from the San Francisco Bay Area: Provided by the Metropolitan Transportation Commission and the Association of Bay Area Governments." www.bayareacensus.ca.gov.

Bay Area Rapid Transit District. 1976. *Pittsburg Antioch Bay Area Rapid Transit (BART) Extension Project, Final Summary Report*. Prepared for Pittsburg-Antioch Extension Project Board of Control by Parsons-Brinkerhoff Tudor Bechtel (March).

———. N.d. *A History of BART*. bart.gov/about/history.

Bay Area Regional Health Inequities Initiative. 2008. *Health Inequities in the Bay Area*.

Beauregard, R. 1990. "Bringing the City Back In." *Journal of the American Planning Association* 56(2): 210–15.

———. 1993. *Voice of Decline: The Postwar Fate of US Cities*. Oxford: B. Blackwell.

Benner, C., and M. Pastor. 2008. "Fractures and Fault Lines: Growth and Equity in California's Megaregions." Paper presented at the America 2050 Research Seminar on Megaregions, March 19.

———. 2011. "Moving On Up? Regions, Megaregions, and the Changing Geography of Social Equity Organizing." *Urban Affairs Review* 47(3): 315.

———. 2015. *Equity, Growth, and Community: What the Nation Can Learn from America's Metro Areas*. Berkeley: University of California Press.

Bentham, J., A. Bowman, M. de la Cuesta, E. Engelen, I. Ertürk, P. Folkman, J. Froud, S. Johal, J. Law, A. Leaver, and M. Moran. 2013. *Manifesto for the Foundational Economy*. Manchester: Centre for Research on Socio-Cultural Change. www.cresc.ac.uk/sites/default/files/Manifesto%20for%20the%20Foundational.

Benton, J. E. 2005. "An Assessment of Research on American Counties." *Public Administration Review* 65(4): 462–74.

Berg, N. 2016. "Oakland's Housing Crisis: 'I'm the Last One Here. I Don't Know if I Can Stay or Go.'" *The Guardian*, April 21.

Berman, M. 1983. *All That's Solid Melts into Air: The Experience of Modernity*. London: Verso.

Bernard, S. 2012. "Henry Clark and Three Decades of Environmental Justice." *Richmond Confidential*, December 6.

Bernstein, D. E. 1999. "Lochner, Parity, and the Chinese Laundry." *William and Mary Law Review* 41(1): 211–94.

Berube, A., A. Singer, J. H. Wilson, and W. H. Frey. 2006. *Finding Exurbia: America's Changing Landscape at the Metropolitan Fringe*. Washington, DC: Brookings Institution.

Bhatia, R. 2004. "Green or Brown? White Nativist Environmental Movements." In *Home Grown Hate: Gender and Organized Racism*, edited by A. Ferber, 194–214. Hove: Psychology Press.

Bishop, B., and R. G. Cushing. 2009. *The Big Sort: Why the Clustering of Like-Minded America Is Tearing Us Apart*. New York: Mariner Books.

Blackwell, A. G., and D. Duval-Diop. 2008. "The Quest for Megaregion Equity: The Gulf Coast and Beyond." Presented at the America 2050 Research Seminar on Megaregions, March 19–21.

Blakely, E. J., and M. G. Snyder. 1997. *Divided We Fall: Gated and Walled Communities in the United States*. New York: Princeton Architectural Press.

Bliss, L. 2016. "How 'Maintainers,' Not 'Innovators,' Make the World Turn." *Citylab*, April 8. www.citylab.com/design/2016/04/how-maintainers-not-innovators-make-the-world-turn/477468/.

Bohakel, C., P. Hiebert, E. Rimbault, and C. A. Davis. 2005. *Antioch*. Mount Pleasant, SC: Arcadia.

Bonilla-Silva, E. 2017. *Racism without Racists: Color-blind Racism and the Persistence of Racial Inequality in America*. Lanham, MD: Rowman & Littlefield.

Bonus, R. 2000. *Locating Filipino Americans: Ethnicity and the Cultural Politics of Space*. Philadelphia: Temple University Press.

Bourne, L. S. 1996. "Reinventing the Suburbs: Old Myths and New Realities." *Progress in Planning* 46(3): 163–84.

Boyer, M. C. 1986. *Dreaming the Rational City: The Myth of American City Planning*. Cambridge, MA: MIT Press.

Bradshaw, T. K. 1993. *Is Growth Control a Planning Failure?* Berkeley: Institute of Urban and Regional Development, University of California.

Brahinsky, R. 2014. "Race and the Making of Southeast San Francisco: Towards a Theory of Race-Class." *Antipode* 46(5): 1258–76.

———, M. Chion, and L. M. Feldstein. 2012. "Reflections on Community Planning in San Francisco." *Justice Spatiale / Spatial Justice*, no. 5.

Brechin, G. 2006. *Imperial San Francisco: Urban Power, Earthly Ruin*. Berkeley: University of California Press.

Brenner, N. 2013. "Theses on Urbanization." *Public Culture* 25(1): 85–114.

———. 2014. *Implosions / Explosions: Towards a Study of Planetary Urbanization*. Berlin: Jovis.

——— and C. Schmid. 2014. "The 'Urban Age' in Question." *International Journal of Urban and Regional Research* 38(3) (May).

——— and C. Schmid. 2015. "Towards a New Epistemology of the Urban?" *City* 19(2–3): 151–82.

——— and N. Theodore. 2002. "Cities and the Geographies of Actually Existing Neoliberalism." *Antipode* 34(3): 349–79.

Briggs, X. de S., ed. 2005. *The Geography of Opportunity*. Washington, DC: Brookings Institution Press.

Brody, J. G., R. Morello-Frosch, A. Zota, P. Brown, C. Perez, and R. A. Rudel. 2009. "Linking Exposure Assessment Science with Policy Objectives for Environmental Justice and Breast Cancer Advocacy: The Northern California Household Exposure Study." *American Journal of Public Health* 99(S3): S600.

Broussard, A. S. 1981. "Organizing the Black Community in the San Francisco Bay Area, 1915–1930." *Arizona and the West* 23(4): 335–54.

———. 1993. *Black San Francisco: The Struggle for Racial Equality in the West, 1900–1954.* Lawrence: University Press of Kansas.

Brown, B., and G. Jolivette. 2005. *A Primer: Three Strikes—The Impact after More Than a Decade.* California Legislative Analyst's Office, October.

Brown-Saracino, J. 2010. *The Gentrification Debates: A Reader.* New York: Routledge.

Browning, R. P., D. R. Marshall, and D. H. Tabb. 1984. *Protest Is Not Enough: The Struggle of Blacks and Hispanics for Equality in Urban Politics.* Berkeley: University of California Press.

Bruegmann, R. 2005. *Sprawl: A Compact History.* Chicago: University of Chicago Press.

Brunet, R. 1989. *Les Villes Européenes: Rapport Pour la DATAR.* Montpellier: RECLUS.

Bullard, R. D. 1996. "Environmental Justice: It's More Than Waste Facility Siting." *Social Science Quarterly* 77(3): 493–99.

——— and J. Lewis. 1996. *Environmental Justice and Communities of Color.* San Francisco: Sierra Club Books.

Burkhalter, L., and M. Castells. 2009. "Beyond the Crisis: Towards a New Urban Paradigm." Paper presented at the 4th International Conference of the International Forum on Urbanism (IFoU), Amsterdam / Delft, November 26–28.

Burrows, P. 2013. "Inside Apple's Plans for Its Futuristic, $5 Billion Headquarters." *Bloomberg,* April 5. Accessed at www.bloomberg.com/news/articles/2013-04 -04/inside-apples-plans-for-its-futuristic-5-billion-headquarters.

Butler, J. 2002. *Gender Trouble: Feminism and the Subversion of Identity.* London and New York: Routledge.

Butler, K. 1986. "A Marin Housing Problem: Too Costly for Municipal Employees." *San Francisco Chronicle,* July 7.

Cadieux, K. V., and P. T. Hurley. 2011. "Amenity Migration, Exurbia, and Emerging Rural Landscapes: Global Natural Amenity as Place and as Process." *GeoJournal* 76(4): 297–302.

Calavita, N. 1995. *California Environmental Goals and Policy Report, Part I: Legislative History of the Environmental Goals and Policy Report.* Faculty Fellows Program, Center for California Studies, California State University, San Diego.

California Office of Planning and Research. 1978. *An Urban Strategy for California.*

California Planning Roundtable. 1995. *Beyond Beyond Sprawl: Work in Progress by the Members of the California Planning Roundtable,* edited by Val Alexeef and Roberta Mundie (September).

Campbell, S. 1996. "Green Cities, Growing Cities, Just Cities?: Urban Planning and the Contradictions of Sustainable Development." *Journal of the American Planning Association* 62(3): 296–312.

Castells, M. 1983. *The City and the Grassroots: A Cross-Cultural Theory of Urban Social Movements.* Berkeley: University of California Press.

Castillo, E. N.d. "California Indian History." California Native American Heritage Commission. Accessed June 20, 2016, at http://nahc.ca.gov/resources /california-indian-history/.

Causa Justa / Just Cause. N.d. *Development without Displacement: Resisting Gentrification in the Bay Area.* Accessed at http://cjjc.org/wp-content/uploads/2015/11 /development-without-displacement.pdf.

Cavin, A. I. 2012. "The Borders of Citizenship: The Politics of Race and Metropolitan Space in Silicon Valley." PhD dissertation, University of Michigan.

CBS Films. 1971. *The Suburban Wall.* Accessed May 2, 2011, at www.briancopeland .com/e-press/media/video/suburban_wall.mov.

Center for Responsible Lending. 2010. *Dreams Deferred: California Foreclosure Report.* Accessed July 7, 2011, at www.responsiblelending.org/california/ca-mort-gage/research-analysis/dreams-deferred-CA-foreclosure-report-August-2010.pdf.

Cervero, R. 1986. *Jobs-Housing Imbalances as a Transportation Problem.* Berkeley: Institute of Transportation Studies, University of California.

———. 1989. "Jobs-Housing Balancing and Regional Mobility." *Journal of the American Planning Association* 55(2): 136–50.

———. 1994. "Making Transit Work in Suburbs." *Transportation Research Record no. 1451.* Berkeley: Department of City and Regional Planning, University of California.

———. 1996. "Jobs-Housing Balance Revisited: Trends and Impacts in the San Francisco Bay Area." *Journal of the American Planning Association* 62(4): 492–511.

——— and J. Landis. 1992. "Suburbanization of Jobs and the Journey to Work: A Submarket Analysis of Commuting in the San Francisco Bay Area." *Journal of Advanced Transportation* 26(3): 275–97.

——— and K. L. Wu. 1997. "Polycentrism, Commuting, and Residential Location in the San Francisco Bay Area." *Environment and Planning A* 29: 865–86.

———, T. Rood, and B. Appleyard. 1995. "Job Accessibility as a Performance Indicator: An Analysis of Trends and Their Social Policy Implications in the San Francisco Bay Area." Working paper (April). Berkeley: Department of City and Regional Planning, University of California.

Chang, J. 2016. *We Gon' Be Alright: Notes on Race and Resegregation.* New York: Macmillan.

Chapman, J. I. 1998. "Proposition 13: Some Unintended Consequences." San Francisco: Public Policy Institute of California.

Chapple, K. 2009. *Mapping Susceptibility to Gentrification: The Early Warning Toolkit.* Berkeley: Center for Community Innovation.

Charmes, É. 2007. "Carte Scolaire et 'Clubbisation' Des Petites Communes Périurbaines." *Sociétés Contemporaines*(3): 67–94.

———. 2011. *La Ville Émiettée: Essai Sur La Clubbisation De La Vie Urbaine.* Paris: Presses Universitaires de France.

Chen, E. Y. 2008. "Impacts of 'Three Strikes and You're Out' on Crime Trends in California and throughout the United States." *Journal of Contemporary Criminal Justice* 24(4): 345–70.

Chen, M., S. Roever, and C. Skinner. 2016. "Urban Livelihoods: Reframing Theory and Policy." *Environment and Urbanization* 28(2): 331–42.

Cheshire, P. C., M. Nathan, and H. G. Overman. 2014. *Urban Economics and Urban Policy: Challenging Conventional Policy Wisdom.* Cheltanham, UK: Edward Elgar.

Chinitz, B. 1961. "Contrasts in Agglomeration: New York and Pittsburgh." *American Economic Review* 51(2): 279–89.

Chiteji, N. S. 2010. "The Racial Wealth Gap and the Borrower's Dilemma." *Journal of Black Studies* 41(2): 351–66.

Christensen, T., and L. N. Gerston. 2008. "Initiatives as Catalysts for Racial Politics." In *Racial and Ethnic Politics in California*, edited by Bruce Cain, Jaime Regalado, and Sandra Bass. Berkeley: University of California Press.

Citrin, J. 2009. "Proposition 13 and the Transformation of California Government." In *After the Tax Revolt: California's Proposition 13 Turns 30*, edited by J. Citrin and I. W. Martin. Berkeley: Public Policy Press.

City of Antioch. 1976. *Using Air Rights for Urban Waterfront Development.* Report prepared by John Keilch and Shirley Langlois under the supervision of the City of Antioch Planning Division (September).

———. 1982. *Southeast Antioch Specific Plan.*

City of Fremont. 2010. *City of Fremont, California Comprehensive Annual Financial Report, for the Year ended June 30, 2010.*

Clark, C. 1940. *The Conditions of Economic Progress.* London: Macmillan.

Clavel, P. 1986. *The Progressive City: Planning and participation, 1969–1984.* New Brunswick, NJ: Rutgers University Press.

Coates, T. N. 2015. *Between the World and Me.* Melbourne: Text.

Cobbina, J. E., J. Miller, and R. K. Brunson. 2008. "Gender, Neighborhood Danger, and Risk-Avoidance Strategies among Urban African-American Youths." *Criminology* 46(3): 673–709.

Coetsee, R. 2010. "Brentwood Urban Limit Line Proponents Attribute Defeat to Confusion, Apathy." *Contra Costa Times,* June 9.

Coleman, M. 2005. "A Primer on California City Finance." *Western City,* March.

Coleman, W. 1966. "Science and Symbol in the Turner Frontier Hypothesis." *American Historical Review* 72(1): 22–49.

Contra Costa County. 1992. *Dougherty Valley Draft Specific Plan,* April.

Copeland, B. 2006. *Not a Genuine Black Man, Or, How I Learned to be Black in the Lily-White Suburbs.* New York: Hyperion Books.

Costa, H. 2009. "ACLU, Antioch File Expert Arguments in Discrimination Case." *Contra Costa Times,* November 21.

Craddock, S. 2000. *City of Plagues: Disease, Poverty, and Deviance in San Francisco.* Minneapolis: University of Minnesota Press.

Crittenden, A. 1981. "House Loans Risky." *Antioch Daily Ledger* (AP wire story), November 15.

Cronon, W. 1991. *Nature's Metropolis: Chicago and the Great West.* New York: W.W. Norton.

Crump, J., K. Newman, E.S. Belsky, P. Ashton, D.H. Kaplan, D.J. Hammel, and E. Wyly. 2008. "Cities Destroyed (Again) for Cash: Forum on the US Foreclosure Crisis." *Urban Geography* 29(8): 745–84.

Cuff, D. 1982. "Area's BART Plans Derailed." *Antioch Daily Ledger,* February 7.

Cunniff, J. 1981. "The Lender Is Foreclosing—Debt Is on Everyone's Mind." *Antioch Daily Ledger,* November 10.

Cutler, K.M. 2014. "How Burrowing Owls Lead to Vomiting Anarchists (or SF's Housing Crisis Explained)." *TechCrunch,* April 24, at https://techcrunch.com/2014/04/14/sf-housing/.

Daly, H.E., and J. Farley. 2011. *Ecological Economics: Principles and Applications.* Washington, DC: Island Press.

Davis, M. 1990. *City of Quartz: Excavating the Future in Los Angeles.* New York: Verso Books.

Dayrit, I., R. Arulanantham, and L. Feldman. 2002. "Successful Redevelopment and Risk Management in Emeryville, California." In *Brownfield Sites: Assessment, Rehabilitation and Development,* edited by C.A. Brebbia, D. Almorza, and H. Klapperich. Southampton, UK: WIT Press.

Dear, M. 1992. "Understanding and Overcoming the NIMBY Syndrome." *Journal of the American Planning Association* 58(3): 288–300.

DeBolt, D. 2012. "Google Housing Axed in City's General Plan." *Mountain View Voice,* July 13.

DeLeon, R.E. 1992. *Left Coast City: Progressive Politics in San Francisco, 1975–1991.* Lawrence: University Press of Kansas.

De Leon, G., and H. Greenwich. 2006. "Local Residents Benefit from Oak to 9th Plan." *Berkeley Daily Planet,* September 1.

Deluca, S. 2012. "What Is the Role of Housing Policy? Considering Choice and Social Science Evidence." *Journal of Urban Affairs* 34(1): 21–28.

DelVecchio, R. 1995. "Oakland Finally Sells Old Merritt College: Restoration of Blighted Campus Set." *San Francisco Chronicle,* March 2.

Desmond, M. 2016. *Evicted: Poverty and Profit in the American City.* New York: Broadway Books.

Deverell, W. 2004. *Whitewashed Adobe: The Rise of Los Angeles and the Remaking of Its Mexican Past.* Berkeley: University of California Press.

Devine-Wright, P. 2009. "Rethinking NIMBYism: The Role of Place Attachment and Place Identity in Explaining Place-Protective Action." *Journal of Community and Applied Social Psychology* 19(6): 426–41.

De Vries, J.R. 2009. "Trust as a Central Concept in Planning Research and Practice." Paper presented at the 23rd Congress of the Association of European Schools of Planning, July 15–18, Liverpool, UK.

Dewar, M., and D. Epstein. 2007. "Planning for Megaregions in the United States." *Journal of Planning Literature* 22(2): 108.

Dietz, R., and D. O'Neill. 2013. *Enough Is Enough: Building a Sustainable Economy in a World of Finite Resources.* San Francisco: Berrett-Koehler.

Dillon, L. 2011. *Redevelopment and the Politics of Place in Bayview-Hunters Point.* Berkeley: Institute for the Study of Societal Issues, University of California. http://escholarship.org/uc/item/9s15b9r2.

——— and J. Sze. 2016. "Police Power and Particulate Matters: Environmental Justice and the Spatialities of In/securities in U.S. Cities." *English Language Notes* 54(2): 13–22.

Diringer, E. 1985a. "Walnut Creek Council OKs Growth Measures." *San Francisco Chronicle,* August 8.

———.1985b. "Growth Vote Sends Message to Politicians." *San Francisco Chronicle,* November 7.

Donato-Weinstein, N. 2015. "9,100 Housing Units Next to Google? Mountain View Council Signals Support for Sweeping North Bayshore Housing Plans." *Silicon Valley Business Journal,* November 11.

Dornheim, R. 2011a. "Marin City and the Canal: Two Brief Histories." *KQED,* November 30. kqed.org/news/bayarea/affordablehousing/timeline.jsp.

———. 2011b. "Marin Struggles to Meet Fair Housing Laws." *KQED,* November 30. kqed.org/news/bayarea/affordablehousing/timeline.jsp.

Dougherty, C. 2016. "In Cramped and Costly Bay Area, Cries to Build, Baby, Build." *New York Times,* April 16.

Douzet, F. 2007. *La Couleur Du Pouvoir: Géopolitique de L'immigration et de la Ségrégation À Oakland, Californie.* Paris: Belin.

———. 2008. "The Geopolitical Transition of Oakland." In *The New Political Geography of California,* edited by Frederick Douzet, Thad Kousser, and Kenneth P. Miller. Berkeley: Berkeley Public Policy Press, Institute of Governmental Studies.

———. 2009. "Revisiting Black Electoral Success: Oakland (CA), 40 Years Later." *Journal of Urban Affairs* 31(3): 243–67.

———, T. Kousser, and K.P. Miller. 2008. *The New Political Geography of California.* Berkeley: Institute of Governmental Studies, University of California.

Dowall, D.E. 1984. *The Suburban Squeeze: Land Conversion and Regulation in the San Francisco Bay Area.* Berkeley: University of California Press.

——— and J. Whittington. 2003. *Making Room for the Future: Rebuilding California's Infrastructure.* San Francisco: Public Policy Institute of California.

Downs, A. 1973. *Opening Up the Suburbs: An Urban Strategy for America.* New Haven, CT: Yale University Press.

Dreier, P., J.H. Mollenkopf, and T. Swanstrom. 2001. *Place Matters: Metropolitics for the Twenty-First Century.* Lawrence: University Press of Kansas.

Dunham-Jones, E., and J. Williamson. 2011. *Retrofitting Suburbia: Urban Design Solutions for Redesigning Suburbs.* New York: Wiley.

Durrenberger, R. W. 1971. *California: Its People, Its Problems, Its Prospects.* National Press Books.

Dyble, L. N. 2001. "North of the Golden Gate: A Historical Perspective on Land Use Policy in Marin and Sonoma Counties." Unpublished manuscript prepared for the Northern California Project Group, UC Berkeley College of Natural Resources.

———. 2007. "Revolt against Sprawl Transportation and the Origins of the Marin County Growth-Control Regime." *Journal of Urban History* 34(1): 38–66.

———. 2008. "The Defeat of the Golden Gate Authority: A Special District, a Council of Governments, and the Fate of Regional Planning in the San Francisco Bay Area." *Journal of Urban History* 34(2): 287–308.

———. 2009. *Paying the Toll: Local Power, Regional Politics, and the Golden Gate Bridge.* Philadelphia: University of Pennsylvania Press.

———. 2012. "The Defeat of the Golden Gate Authority: Regional Planning and Local Power." *ACCESS Magazine* 1(40).

Dymski, G. A. 2009. "Racial Exclusion and the Political Economy of the Subprime Crisis." *Historical Materialism* 17(2): 149–79.

Dyson, E. 2012. "Competition Can Make Cities Better." *Slate.* Accessed April 1, 2012, at www.slate.com/articles/business/project_syndicate/2012/03/cities_need_competition_and_intelligent_design_to_thrive_.html.

East Bay Alliance for a Sustainable Economy. 2007. *Growing with Purpose: Residents, Jobs and Equity in Richmond, CA.*

——— and UC Berkeley Center for Labor Education and Research. 2003. *Behind the Boomtown: Growth and Urban Redevelopment in Emeryville* (May).

Economic and Planning Systems. 2007. *Economic Impact Analysis of Delayed Military Base Reuse in California.* January update, EPS #17002.

Economist. 2009a. "California: The Ungovernable State." May 14.

———. 2009b. "Criminal Law in California: A Voice for the Forsaken." June 11.

Egan, T. 2010. "Slumburbia." *New York Times,* February 10.

Ehlers, S., V. Schiraldi, and E. Lotke. 2004. *Racial Divide: An Examination of the Impact of California's Three Strikes Law on African-Americans and Latinos.* Washington, DC: Justice Policy Institute.

Ehrenhalt, A. 2012. *The Great Inversion and the Future of the American City.* New York: Borzoi.

Ehrlich, P. R. 1968. *The Population Bomb.* New York: Ballantine.

——— and A. H. Ehrlich. 2009. "The Population Bomb Revisited." *Electronic Journal of Sustainable Development* 1(3): 63–71.

Ehrlich, S. 2010. "The Disappearance of Black San Franciscans: 1970–2010." Unpublished senior honors thesis, University of California, Berkeley.

Espiritu, N. 2004. "(E)Racing Youth: The Racialized Construction of California's Proposition 21 and the Development of Alternate Contestations." *Cleveland State Law Review* 52: 189.

Etzkowitz, H., and J. Dzisah. 2008. "Unity and Diversity in High-Tech Growth and Renewal: Learning from Boston and Silicon Valley." *European Planning Studies* 16(8): 1009–24.

Faludi, A. 2005. "Polycentric Territorial Cohesion Policy." *Town Planning Review* 76(1): 107–18.

Farley, R. 2011. *The Waning of American Apartheid?* Accessed May 2, 2012, at www .psc.isr.umich.edu/pubs/pdf/rp617.pdf.

Farooq, S. 2005. "Light Rail Said to Be a Stretch." *Oakland Tribune*, March 30.

Ferguson, J. 1990. *The Anti-Politics Machine: Development, Depoliticization, and Bureaucratic Power in Lesotho.* Cambridge: Cambridge University Press.

Fisher, A. G. B. 1939. "Production, Primary, Secondary and Tertiary." *Economic Record* 15(1): 24–38.

Flippen, C. A. 2016. "The More Things Change the More They Stay the Same: The Future of Residential Segregation in America." *City and Community* 15(1): 14–17.

Florida, R. 2002. *The Rise of the Creative Class: And How It's Transforming Work, Leisure, Community and Everyday Life.* New York: Basic Books.

———. 2009. "How the Crash Will Reshape America." *Atlantic Monthly* 303(2): 44–56.

———. 2013. "Why San Francisco May Be the New Silicon Valley." *Citylab,* August 5. Accessed at www.citylab.com/work/2013/08/why-san-francisco-may -be-new-silicon-valley/6295/.

———, T. Gulden, and C. Mellander. 2008. "The Rise of the Mega-Region." *Cambridge Journal of Regions, Economy and Society* 1(3): 459.

——— and K. M. King. 2016. *Rise of the Urban Startup Neighborhood Mapping Micro-Clusters of Venture Capital-Backed Startups.* Martin Prosperity Institute, University of Toronto.

Fogelson, R. M. 1993. *The Fragmented Metropolis: Los Angeles, 1850–1930.* Berkeley: University of California Press.

Freire-Gibb, L. C. 2012. "Vallejo, California: A Case for Promoting a City Region Innovation System?" *International Journal of Innovation and Regional Development* 4(2): 180–95.

Frey, W. H. 2003. "Melting Pot Suburbs: A Study of Suburban Diversity." In *Redefining Urban and Suburban America: Evidence from Census 2000,* edited by B. Katz and R. E. Lang, vol. 1, 159–79. Washington, DC: Brookings Institution Press.

Frick, K. T. 2013. "The Actions of Discontent: Tea Party and Property Rights Activists Pushing Back against Regional Planning." *Journal of the American Planning Association* 79(3): 190–200.

———, K. Chapple, E. Mattiuzzi, and M. Zuk. 2015. "Collaboration and Equity in Regional Sustainability Planning in California: Challenges in Implementation." *California Journal of Politics and Policy* 7(4).

Frieden, B. J. 1979. *The Environmental Protection Hustle.* Cambridge, MA: MIT Press.

Frug, G. E. 1980. "The City as a Legal Concept." *Harvard Law Review* 93(6): 1057–154.

———. 1984. "The Ideology of Bureaucracy in American Law." *Harvard Law Review* 97(6): 1276–388.

———. 1993. "Decentering Decentralization." *University of Chicago Law Review* 60(2): 253–338.

———. 1996. "The Geography Of Community." *Stanford Law Review* 48: 1047–108.

———. 2001a. *City Making: Building Communities without Building Walls.* Princeton, NJ: Princeton University Press.

———. 2001b. "Beyond Regional Government." *Harvard Law Review* 115: 1763.

Fujita, M., and P. Krugman. [2004] 2013. "The New Economic Geography: Past, Present and the Future." In *Fifty Years of Regional Science,* edited by R. Florax and D. Plane, 139–64. New York: Springer.

Fullbright, L. 2007. "San Francisco Moves to Stem African American Exodus: Critics Say Effort to Reverse Longtime Trend May Be Too Late." *San Francisco Chronicle,* April 9.

Fulton, W. 1995. *Beyond Sprawl: New Patterns of Growth to Fit the New California.* San Francisco: Bank of America.

——— and P. Shigley. 2005. *Guide to California Planning.* Point Arena, CA: Solano Press.

Gallagher, L. 2013. *The End of the Suburbs: Where the American Dream Is Moving.* New York: Penguin.

Gans, H. J. 1967. *Levittowners: Ways of Life and Politics in a Suburban Community.* New York: Penguin.

Garreau, J. 1991. *Edge City: Life on the New Frontier.* New York: Doubleday.

Geluardi, J. 2006. "Measure T Loses Big In Richmond." *Contra Costa Times,* November 8.

Gilmore, R. W. 2007. *Golden Gulag.* Berkeley: University of California Press.

Ginsberg, M. 1981. "Commission Backs 3,000 Acre Plan." *Antioch Daily Ledger,* November 5.

———. 1982a. "Feisty Wilhelmina Won't Run." *Antioch Daily Ledger,* February 5.

———. 1982b. "Huge City Growth Plan OK'd." *Antioch Daily Ledger,* February 24.

Ginwright, S. A. 2010. *Black Youth Rising: Activism and Radical Healing in Urban America.* New York: Teachers College Press.

——— and A. Akom. 2007. *African American Out-Migration Trends Initial Scan of National and Local Trends in Migration and Research on African Americans.* Prepared for Mayors Office of Community Development Task Force on African American Out-Migration, College of Ethnic Studies and Public Research Institute, San Francisco State University.

Glaeser, E. L. 1996. "Why Economists Still Like Cities." *City Journal* 6(2): 70–77.

———. 2011. *Triumph of the City: How Our Greatest Invention Makes Us Richer, Smarter, Greener, Healthier and Happier.* New York: Pan Macmillan.

——— and Harvard Institute of Economic Research. 2007. *Do Regional Economies Need Regional Coordination?* Harvard Institute of Economic Research, Harvard University.

——— and J. D. Gottlieb. 2008. "The Economics of Cities." Harvard University.

Glantz, A. 2012. "Bay Area Residents Leaving in Droves: Without Immigration, the Region's Population Would Shrink." *Bay Citizen,* March 30. Accessed May 4, 2012, at www.baycitizen.org/census-2010/story/bay-area-residents-leaving-droves/.

Godfrey, B. J. 1988. *Neighborhoods in Transition: The Making of San Francisco's Ethnic and Nonconformist Communities.* Berkeley: University of California Press.

Goetz, E. G. 2003. *Clearing the Way: Deconcentrating the Poor in Urban America.* Washington, DC: Urban Institute Press.

Goldman, T. 2003. *Local Option Taxes and the New Subregionalism in Transportation Planning.* Berkeley City and Regional Planning. Berkeley: University of California.

———. 2007. "Transportation Tax Ballot Initiatives as Regional Planning Processes." *Transportation Research Record: Journal of the Transportation Research Board* 1997(41): 9–16.

——— and M. Wachs. 2003. *A Quiet Revolution in Transportation Finance: The Rise of Local Option Transportation Taxes.* Berkeley: University of California Transportation Center. http://escholarship.org/uc/item/2gp4m4xq.

Goonewardena, K. 2003. "The Future of Planning at the 'End of History.'" *Planning Theory* 2(3): 183–224.

Gordon, P., and H. Richardson. 1996. *The Case for Suburban Development.* Lusk Center Research Institute, University of Southern California. Report prepared for the Building Industry of Northern California and the Home Ownership Advancement Foundation (March).

Graham, S., and S. Marvin. 2001. *Splintering Urbanism: Networked Infrastructures, Technological Mobilities and the Urban Condition.* London: Routledge.

Green, E. 2016. "SF Supervisors OK Mission District's Largest Residential Complex." *San Francisco Chronicle,* September 13.

Greenbelt Alliance. 2003. *Contra Costa County: Smart Growth or Sprawl? An In-Depth Analysis of the County's Sprawl Threats and Opportunities for Smarter Growth.* San Francisco: Greenbelt Alliance.

Greuner, G. 2011. "An Endless Array of Minor 'Reforms' Made California Ungovernable; A Few Major Reforms Could Fix It: A Review of *California Crackup: How Reform Broke the Golden State* by Joe Mathews and Mark Paul." *California Journal of Politics and Policy* 3(1).

Gross, J., 2007. "Community Benefits Agreements: Definitions, Values, and Legal Enforceability." *Journal of Affordable Housing and Community Development Law* 17(1–2): 35–58.

Gutiérrez v. Municipal Court, 838 F.2d 1031 (9th Cir. 1988).

Hackworth, J. 2007. *The Neoliberal City: Governance, Ideology, and Development in American Urbanism.* Ithaca, NY: Cornell University Press.

Haeseler, R. 1985. "Walnut Creek Wants Growth Limits, Poll Says." *San Francisco Chronicle,* May 22.

———. 1995. "Big East Bay Water Fight May Dry Up: Tentative Pact on Dougherty Valley to Be Revealed." *San Francisco Chronicle,* June 26.

Hall, M., K. Crowder, and A. Spring. 2015. "Neighborhood Foreclosures, Racial/Ethnic Transitions, and Residential Segregation." *American Sociological Review* 80(3): 526–49.

Hall, P. G. 1982. *Great Planning Disasters, Volume 1.* Berkeley: University of California Press.

———. 1988. *Cities of Tomorrow.* Oxford: Blackwell.

Hall, S., and A. Schafran. 2017. "From Foundational Economics and the Grounded City to Foundational Urban Systems." Working paper, March. https://foundationaleconomy.com.

Hallissy, E. 1992. "Contra Costa OKs Huge Home Project—Cities, Water District Threaten to Sue over 11,000-Unit Development Near San Ramon." *San Francisco Chronicle,* December 23.

Hart, J. 1984. *The New Book of California Tomorrow: Reflections and Projections from the Golden State.* Los Angeles: William Kaufmann.

———. 2003. "Saved by Grit and Grace: Wild Legacy of the Marin Headlands." *Bay Nature Magazine,* July 1.

Hartman, C. W. [1984] 2002. *City for Sale: The Transformation of San Francisco.* Berkeley: University of California Press.

Harvey, D. 1973. *Social Justice and the City.* Baltimore: Johns Hopkins University Press.

———. 1989. "From Managerialism to Entrepreneurialism: The Transformation in Urban Governance in Late Capitalism." *Geografiska Annaler* 71(1): 3–17.

———. 2000. *Spaces of Hope.* Berkeley: University of California Press.

———. 2005. *A Brief History of Neoliberalism.* Oxford: Oxford University Press.

———. 2009. "World Social Forum: Opening Speech at the Urban Reform Tent." Belém, Pará, Brazil, January 29.

———. 2012. *Rebel Cities: From the Right to the City to the Urban Revolution.* London: Verso Books.

Hattam, J. 2004. "Why Race Matters in the Fight for a Healthy Planet." *Sierra Magazine.* http://vault.sierraclub.org/sierra/200405/diversity.asp.

Haughwout, A., D. Lee, J. Tracy, and W. van der Klaauw. 2011. *Real Estate Investors, the Leverage Cycle, and the Housing Market Crisis.* Staff Report no. 514, September, Federal Reserve Bank of New York.

Hayden, D. 2003. *Building Suburbia: Green Fields and Urban Growth, 1820–2000.* New York: Vintage/Random House.

Healey, P. 2009. "The Pragmatic Tradition in Planning Thought." *Journal of Planning Education and Research* 28(3): 277–92.

Heller, A. 1971. *The California Tomorrow Plan.* Sacramento: California Tomorrow.

Hendrix, A. 2001. "Up and Out: More Blacks Leaving Inner Cities for Suburbs." *San Francisco Chronicle,* April 17.

Heredia, C. 1998. "Brentwood Fastest Growing City in State: Many Worry Area Is Losing Rural Character." *San Francisco Chronicle,* October 15.

Hirschman, A. O. 1970. *Exit, Voice, and Loyalty: Responses to Decline in Firms, Organizations, and States.* Cambridge, MA: Harvard University Press.

Hollander, J. B. 2011. *Sunburnt Cities: The Great Recession, Depopulation and Urban Planning in the American Sunbelt.* New York: Routledge.

Horwitz, Morton J. 1985. "Santa Clara Revisited: The Development of Corporate Theory." *West Virginia Law Review* 88: 173–224.

Hultgren, J. 2012. "American Environmentalism, Sovereignty and the 'Immigration Problem.'" Unpublished PhD dissertation, Colorado State University.

Hwang, J., M. Hankinson, and K. S. Brown. 2015. "Racial and Spatial Targeting: Segregation and Subprime Lending within and across Metropolitan Areas." *Social Forces* 93(3): 1081–108.

Hyra, D. S., G. D. Squires, R. N. Renner, and D. S. Kirk. 2013. "Metropolitan Segregation and the Subprime Lending Crisis." *Housing Policy Debate* 23(1): 177–98.

Imbroscio, D. 2012a. "Beyond Mobility: The Limits of Liberal Urban Policy." *Journal of Urban Affairs* 34(1): 1–20.

———. 2012b. "The End of (Urban) Liberalism." *Journal of Urban Affairs* 34(1): 35–42.

Immergluck, D. 2011. *Foreclosed: High-Risk Lending, Deregulation, and the Undermining of America's Mortgage Market.* Ithaca, NY: Cornell University Press.

——— and G. Smith. 2004. *Risky Business: An Econometric Analysis of the Relationship between Subprime Lending and Neighborhood Foreclosures.* Chicago: Woodstock Institute.

———. 2005. "The External Costs of Foreclosure: The Impact of Single-Family Mortgage Foreclosures on Property Values." *Housing Policy Debate* 17(1): 57–79.

———. 2006. "The Impact of Single-Family Mortgage Foreclosures on Neighborhood Crime." *Housing Studies* 21(6): 851–66.

Indian Institute of Human Settlements. 2015. Accessed June 25, 2015, at www.iihs.co.in.

Ingram, E. 1986. "Building Bans, Marin Traffic Crisis: Cities Fight Back." *San Francisco Chronicle,* January 22.

———. 1990. "2 Measures Would Overhaul Marin-Sonoma Transit: Environmental Groups Fighting $1 Billion Package." *San Francisco Chronicle,* October 31.

Innes, J. 2004. *Taking the Three 'E's Seriously: The Bay Area Alliance for Sustainable Communities.* Berkeley: Institute of Urban and Regional Development, University of California.

——— and D. E. Booher. 1999. "Metropolitan Development as a Complex System: A New Approach to Sustainability." *Economic Development Quarterly* 13(2) (May): 141–56.

———. 2010. *Planning with Complexity: An Introduction to Collaborative Rationality for Public Policy.* New York: Routledge.

——— and S. Di Vittorio. 2010. "Strategies for Megaregion Governance." *Journal of the American Planning Association* 77(1): 55–67.

——— and J. Rongerude. 2006. *Collaborative Regional Initiatives: Civic Entrepreneurs Work to Fill the Governance Gap.* Berkeley: Institute of Urban and Regional Development, University of California.

———, J. Gruber, M. Neuman, and R. Thompson. 1994. "Coordinating Growth and Environmental Management through Consensus Building." Paper presented at Policy Research Program Report, California Policy Seminar, University of California.

Izadi, E. 2015. "George Lucas Wants to Build Affordable Housing on His Land Because 'We've Got Enough Millionaires.'" *Washington Post,* April 17.

Jackson, K. 1985. *Crabgrass Frontier: The Suburbanization of the United States.* New York: Oxford University Press.

Jacobs, A. B. 1978. *Making City Planning Work.* Chicago: American Society of Planning Officials.

Jacobs, J. 1961. *The Death and Life of Great American Cities.* New York: Random House.

———. 1984. *Cities and the Wealth of Nations: Principles of Economic Life.* New York: Random House.

Johnson, N. 2017. "Enviros and Developers: A Love Story—Is the Future of Environmentalism Build, Build, Build?" *GRIST,* October 30.

Jonas, A. E. G., and S. Pincetl. 2006. "Rescaling Regions in the State: The New Regionalism in California." *Political Geography* 25(5): 482–505.

Jones, C. 2007. *Economic and Equity Frameworks for Megaregions.* Washington, DC: Regional Plan Association.

Judge, D., G. Stoker, and H. Wolman. 1995. *Theories of Urban Politics.* Thousand Oaks, CA: Sage.

Kain, J. F. 1992. "The Spatial Mismatch Hypothesis: Three Decades Later." *Housing Policy Debate* 3(2): 371–460.

Kaplan, D. H., and F. Douzet. 2011. "Research in Ethnic Segregation III: Segregation Outcomes." *Urban Geography* 32(4): 589–605.

Kaplan, D. H., and K. Woodhouse. 2004. "Research in Ethnic Segregation I: Causal Factors." *Urban Geography* 25(6): 579–85.

———. 2005. "Research in Ethnic Segregation II: Measurements, Categories and Meanings." *Urban Geography* 26(8): 737–45.

Katz, B., and J. Bradley. 2013. *The Metropolitan Revolution: How Cities and Metros Are Fixing Our Broken Politics and Fragile Economy.* Washington, DC: Brookings Institution Press.

Katz, M. B., and M. J. Stern. 2006. *One Nation Divisible: What America Was and What It Is Becoming.* New York: Russell Sage Foundation.

Kendall, M. 2017. "Meet the Startups Fighting Bay Area's Soaring Housing Costs." *San Jose Mercury News,* November 6.

Kent, T. J. 1963. *City and Regional Planning for the Metropolitan San Francisco Bay Area.* Berkeley: Institute of Governmental Studies, University of California.

Kim, J., H. Chung, and A. G. Blanco. 2013. "The Suburbanization of Decline: Filtering, Neighborhoods, and Housing Market Dynamics." *Journal of Urban Affairs* 35(4): 435–50.

Kim, Q. 2016. "As Our Jobs Are Automated, Some Say We'll Need a Guaranteed Basic Income." *National Public Radio,* September 24.

King, J. 2009. "Times Change—California Growth Issues Don't." *San Francisco Chronicle,* March 9.

King, L. 2007. "Charting a Discursive Field: Environmentalists for US Population Stabilization." *Sociological inquiry* 77(3): 301–25.

Kinnaird, L. 1966. *History of the Greater San Francisco Bay Region.* New York: Lewis Historical.

Kirkpatrick, L. O., and C. Gallagher. 2013. "The Suburban Geography of Moral Panic." In *Social Justice in the Diverse Suburb: History, Politics, and Prospects,* edited by C. Neidt. Philadelphia: Temple University Press.

Kling, R., S. C. Olin, and M. Poster. 1995. *Postsuburban California: The Transformation of Orange County since World War II.* Berkeley: University of California Press.

Kneebone, E. 2009. *Job Sprawl Revisited: The Changing Geography of Metropolitan Employment.* Washington, DC: Brookings Institution, Metro Economy Series for the Metropolitan Policy Program.

——— and A. Berube. 2013. *Confronting Suburban Poverty in America.* Washington, DC: Brookings Institution Press.

KQED. 2011. "Oakland's Black Flight." *KQED Forum,* July 7. Accessed January 5, 2012, at www.kqed.org/a/forum/R201107071000.

Kroll, C. 1986. *Suburban Squeeze II: Responses to Suburban Employment Growth.* Working Paper 86–110 (April). Berkeley: Center for Real Estate and Urban Economics, University of California.

Kruse, K. M., and T. J. Sugrue. 2006. *The New Suburban History.* Chicago: University Of Chicago Press.

Lamb, J. O. 2013. "Tech Job Growth Is Booming in SF, but Other Industries Still Dominate." *San Francisco Examiner,* November 19.

Landis, J. D. 1992. "Do Growth Controls Work? A New Assessment." *Journal of the American Planning Association* 58: 489–508.

———. 2000. "Growth as Density: Understanding California's Postwar Growth Patterns and Trends." In *Metropolitan Development Patterns: 2000 Annual Roundtable.* Cambridge, MA: Lincoln Institute of Land Policy.

———. 2006. "Growth Management Revisited." *Journal of the American Planning Association* 72(4): 411–30.

Lang, R. 2003. *Edgeless Cities: Exploring the Elusive Metropolis.* Washington, DC: Brookings Institution Press.

——— and D. Dhavale. 2005. *Beyond Megalopolis.* Metropolitan Institute Census Report Series.

——— and J. LeFurgy. 2006. *Boomburbs: The Rise of America's Accidental Cities.* Washington, DC: Brookings Institution Press.

——— and Paul Knox. 2009. "The New Metropolis: Rethinking Megalopolis." *Regional Studies* 43(6): 789–802.

Laurian, L. 2009. "Trust in Planning: Theoretical and Practical Considerations for Participatory and Deliberative Planning." *Planning Theory and Practice* 10(3): 369–91.

Ledger Dispatch (California). 2000. "Antioch Taxpayers Deserve the Discount." February 4.

Lee, B. A., S. F. Reardon, G. Firebaugh, C. R. Farrell, S. A. Matthews, and D. O'Sullivan. 2008. "Beyond the Census Tract: Patterns and Determinants of Racial Segregation at Multiple Geographic Scales." *American Sociological Review* 73(5): 766–91.

Lees, L., T. Slater, and E. K. Wyly. 2007. *Gentrification.* London: Routledge.

Lefebvre, Henri. 2003. *The Urban Revolution.* Minneapolis: University of Minnesota Press.

——— and K. Goonewardena. 2008. *Space, Difference, Everyday Life: Reading Henri Lefebvre.* London: Psychology Press.

Lefebvre, Hugo. 2013. "Croissance urbaine, fragmentation politique et crise économique dans la Vallée Intérieure de la Californie." In *Ségrégation et fragmentation dans les métropoles: Perspectives internationales,* edited by M. Carrel, P. Cary, and J. M. Wachsberger, 191–215. Paris: Presses Universitaires du Septentrion.

Leinberger, C. B. 2008. "The Next Slum? Tomorrow's Suburban Decay." *Atlantic Monthly,* March.

———. 2011. "The Death of the Fringe Suburb." *New York Times,* November 25.

Lemyre, R. 2010. "Measure F's LAFCO Link." *Brentwood Press,* June 4.

Lester, T. W., and S. Reckhow. 2012. "Network Governance and Regional Equity: Shared Agendas or Problematic Partners?" *Planning Theory* 12(2): 115–38.

Levine, N. 1999. "The Effects of Local Growth Controls on Regional Housing Production and Population Redistribution in California." *Urban Studies* 36(12): 2047.

Lévi-Strauss, C. 1966. *The Savage Mind.* Chicago: University of Chicago Press.

Lewis, O. 1966. *San Francisco: Mission to Metropolis.* Berkeley: Howell-North Books.

Lewis, P. G. 1996. *Shaping Suburbia: How Political Institutions Organize Urban Development.* Pittsburgh: University of Pittsburgh Press.

———. 1998. *Deep Roots: Local Government Structure in California.* San Francisco: Public Policy Institute of California.

———. 2000. "The Durability of Local Government Structure: Evidence from California." *State and Local Government Review* 32(1): 34–48.

———.2003. *California's Housing Element Law: The Issue of Local Noncompliance.* San Francisco: Public Policy Institute of California.

———. 2005. "Can State Review of Local Planning Increase Housing Production?" *Housing Policy Debate* 16(2).

Leykam, J., and Concord Chamber of Commerce (Calif.). 1989. *Contra Costa County: A Chronicle of Progress.* Northridge, CA: Windsor.

Lichter, D. T., D. Parisi, and M. C. Taquino, M. C., 2015. "Toward a New Macro-Segregation? Decomposing Segregation within and between Metropolitan Cities and Suburbs." *American Sociological Review* 80(4): 843–73.

Living in the O. 2011. "MTC Approves Move to San Francisco, Triggering Senator DeSaulnier to Commit to Drastically Overhaul the Agency." Accessed June 30, 2015, at http://oaklandliving.wordpress.com/2011/09/29/mtc-approves-move-to-san-francisco-triggering-senator-desaulnier-to-commit-to-drastically-over-haul-the-agency/.

Logan, J. R., and H. Molotch, H. 1987. *Urban Fortunes: The Political Economy of Place*. Berkeley: University of California Press.

Lopez, A. M., M. Snipp, and A. Camarillo. 2001. *Racial / Ethnic Diversity and Residential Segregation in the San Francisco Bay Area*. Stanford, CA: Center for Comparative Studies in Race and Ethnicity.

Lotchin, R. W. 2002. *Fortress California, 1910–1961: From Warfare to Welfare*. Champaign: University of Illinois Press.

Los Angeles Department of City Planning. 1971. *The Visual Environment of Los Angeles*.

Lovejoy, J. 1981. "Two Cities Seek Growth in Area of Deer Valley." *Antioch Daily Ledger*, October 5.

Low, S. M. 2003. *Behind the Gates: Life, Security, and the Pursuit of Happiness in Fortress America*. New York: Routledge.

Lucy, W. H., and D. L. Phillips. 2000. "Suburban Decline: The Next Urban Crisis." *Issues in Science and Technology* 17(1): 55–62.

Luhmann, N. 1979. *Trust and Power*. Chichester, UK: John Wiley and Sons.

Lung-Amam, W. 2015. "Malls of Meaning: Building Asian America in Silicon Valley Suburbia." *Journal of American Ethnic History* 34(2): 18–53.

Lydon, M. 2011. "DIY Urbanism: One Block, One Shipping Pallet at a Time." *Planetizen*, April 28. Accessed April 28, 2010, at www.planetizen.com/node/43991.

Lydon, P. 1993. *San Francisco's Bay Vision 2020 Commission: A Civic Initiative for Change*. Institute of Governmental Studies, University of California at Berkeley.

Magnusson, W. 2010. "Seeing Like a City: How to Urbanize Political Science." In *Critical Urban Studies: New Directions,* edited by J. Davies, 41–53. New York: SUNY Press.

———. 2011. *Politics of Urbanism: Seeing Like a City*. London: Routledge.

———. 2014. "The Symbiosis of the Urban and the Political." *International Journal of Urban and Regional Research* 38(5): 1561–75.

Maharidge, D. 1996. *The Coming White Minority: California's Eruptions and America's Future*. New York: Times Books.

Maly, M. T. 2005. *Beyond Segregation: Multiracial and Multiethnic Neighborhoods in the United States*. Philadelphia: Temple University Press.

Manoucheri, D. 2017. "How One Company Affects Rent Prices in Northern California: Blackstone Group Owns Multiple Subsidiaries That Bought Thousands of Homes." *KCRA,* November 6. www.kcra.com/article/how-one-company-affects-rent-prices-in-northern-california/13440089.

Marcuse, P. 1978. "Housing Policy and the Myth of the Benevolent State." *Social Policy* 8(4): 21–26.

———. 1997. "The Enclave, the Citadel, and the Ghetto: What Has Changed in the Post-Fordist US City." *Urban Affairs Review* 33(2): 228–64.

Marin Conservation League. N.d. "About Us / History." marinconservationleague.org.

Marin County Board of Supervisors and the Marin County Planning Commission. 1973. *Marin Countywide Plan*.

Marrow, T. L. (Ice-T). 1999. "Don't Hate the Playa." *Seventh Deadly Sin*. Distributed by Roadrunner Records.

Marshall, H. H., and J. M. Stahura. 1979. "Determinants of Black Suburbanization: Regional and Suburban Size Category Patterns." *Sociological Quarterly* 20(2): 237–53.

Martínez-Alier, J., U. Pascual, F. D. Vivien, and E. Zaccai. 2010. "Sustainable Degrowth: Mapping the Context, Criticisms and Future Prospects of an Emergent Paradigm." *Ecological Economics* 69(9): 1741–47.

Massey, D. B. 1984. *Spatial Divisions of Labour: Social Structures and the Geography of Production*. London: Macmillan.

Massey, D. S., and N. A. Denton. 1993. *American Apartheid: Segregation and the Making of the Underclass*. Cambridge, MA: Harvard University Press.

Massey, D. S., J. Rothwell, and T. Domina. 2009. "The Changing Bases of Segregation in the United States." *Annals of the American Academy of Political and Social Science* 626(1): 74–90.

Mathiopoulos, M. 1989. *History and Progress: In Search of the European and American Mind*. New York: Praeger.

Mayer, G., and R. Marcantonio. 2005. "Bay Area Transit: Separate and Unequal." *Race, Poverty and the Environment* 17(1): 30–33.

McCarthy, A. 2008. "Big Oil in Little Richmond." *East Bay Express,* July 9.

McCormick, E. 2017. "Rise of the YIMBYS: The Angry Millennials with a Radical Housing Solution." *The Guardian,* October 2.

McClymont, K. 2011. "Revitalising the Political: Development Control and Agonism in Planning Practice." *Planning Theory* 10(3): 239–56.

——— and P. O'Hare. 2008. "We're Not NIMBYs! Contrasting Local Protest Groups with Idealised Conceptions of Sustainable Communities." *Local Environment* 13(4): 321–35.

McCubbins, C. H., and M. D. McCubbins. 2010. "Proposition 13 and the California Fiscal Shell Game." *California Journal of Politics and Policy* 2(2).

McDaniel, J. 2015. "The Progressive Ideological Coalition and the Crisis of Housing Affordability in San Francisco." *The New West: The Official Blog of the Western Political Science Association,* August 9.

McGirr, L. 2001. *Suburban Warriors: The Origins of the New American Right*. Princeton, NJ: Princeton University Press.

McGovern, P. 1998. "San Francisco Bay Area Edge Cities: New Roles for Planners and the General Plan." *Journal of Planning Education and Research* 3(17): 246–58.

McKenzie, E. 1994. *Privatopia: Homeowner Associations and the Rise of Residential Private Government*. New Haven, CT: Yale University Press.

McKenzie, G. 2017. "What's the Best Thing Local Publications Like DNAinfo Have Done for Your City?" www.citylab.com, November 2.

McLaughlin, R. 2016. "Million Dollar Creep: Where Seven-Figure Homes Are the New Normal." www.trulia.com/blog/trends/million-dollar-homes-2016/.

McNeill, D. 2016. "Governing a City of Unicorns: Technology Capital and the Urban Politics of San Francisco." *Urban Geography* 37(4): 494–513.

McWilliams, C. [1946] 1973. *Southern California: An Island on the Land*. Layton, UT: Gibbs Smith.

———. [1949] 1999. *California: The Great Exception*. Berkeley: University of California Press.

———. [1937] 2000. *Factories in the Field: The Story of Migratory Farm Labor in California*. Berkeley: University of California Press.

Menzel, D. C., V. L. Marando, R. B. Parks, W. L. Waugh Jr., B. A. Cigler, J. H. Svara, M. M. Reeves, J. E. Benton, R. D. Thomas, and G. Streib. 1992. "Setting a Research Agenda for the Study of the American County." *Public Administration Review* 52(2): 173–82.

Mercury News. 2005. "History of BART to the South Bay." August 8. www.mercury news.com/ci_5162648.

Merrifield, A. 2012. "The Politics of the Encounter and the Urbanization of the World." *City* 16(3): 269–83.

———. 2013. "The Urban Question under Planetary Urbanization." *International Journal of Urban and Regional Research* 37(3): 909–22.

Meronek, T. 2015. "Affordable Housing in San Francisco Affordable Only for Upwardly Mobile." *Al-Jazeera*, February 3. http://america.aljazeera.com/articles /2015/2/3/san-francisco-affordable-housing-is-unaffordable.html.

Metcalf, G. 2015. "What's the Matter with San Francisco? The City's Devastating Affordability Crisis Has an Unlikely Villain—Its Famed Progressive Politics." *Citylab*, July 23. www.citylab.com/housing/2015/07/whats-the-matter-with -san-francisco/399506/.

Meyers, A. A. 1998. "Invisible Cities: Lewis Mumford, Thomas Adams, and the Invention of the Regional City, 1925–1929." *Business and Economic History* 27(2): 292–317.

Michaels, L., D. Reid, and R. Scheer. 1989. *West of the West: Imagining California*. Berkeley: University of California Press.

Miller, K. P., and J. Levitt. 2008. "The San Joaquin Valley: Republican Realignment and Its Limits." In *The New Political Geography of California*, edited by Frederick Douzet, Thad Kousser, and Kenneth P. Miller. Berkeley: Berkeley Public Policy Press, Institute of Governmental Studies.

Misra, T. 2017. "Confronting the Myths of Segregation." October 12, www.citylab .com.

Mitchell, D. 1996. *The Lie of the Land: Migrant Workers and the California Landscape*. Minneapolis: University of Minnesota Press.

Mix, T. L. 2009. "The Greening of White Separatism: Use of Environmental Themes to Elaborate and Legitimize Extremist Discourse." *Nature and Culture* 4(2): 138–66.

Monger, W. I. 2008. "Commuter Tangles with Freight: California's Altamont Commuter Express Makes Plans to Combat Freight Interruptions." *Trains* 68(9).

Moore, S. A. W. 1989. *The Black Community in Richmond, California, 1910–1987.* Richmond: Richmond Public Library.

Moore, S. 2008. "As Poor Move to the Suburbs, Tensions Follow." *New York Times,* August 8.

Mouffe, C. 1998. "The Radical Centre." *Soundings* 9: 11–23.

———. 2005. *The Return of the Political, Volume 8.* New York: Verso.

Moulin, B. 2001. *La Ville et Ses Frontières: De La Ségrégation Sociale à l'Ethnicisation Des Rapports Sociaux.* Paris: Karthala.

Mumford, L., and G. Copeland. 1961. *The City in History: Its Origins, Its Transformations, and Its Prospects.* New York: Harcourt, Brace & World.

Municipal Research and Services Center of Washington. 1997. *Infill Development Strategies for Shaping Livable Neighborhoods,* Report no. 38 (June).

Murphy, A. K. 2007. "The Suburban Ghetto: The Legacy of Herbert Gans in Understanding the Experience of Poverty in Recently Impoverished American Suburbs." *City and Community* 6(1): 21–37.

———. 2010. "The Symbolic Dilemmas of Suburban Poverty: Challenges and Opportunities Posed by Variations in the Contours of Suburban Poverty." *Sociological Forum* 25(3).

Myers, D. 2007. *Immigrants and Boomers.* New York: Russell Sage.

Myers, J. S., and A. Dunning. 2011. "The Relationship between Megaregions and Megapolitans: Transportation Planning for the Two Scales." In *Transportation and Economic Development Challenges,* edited by K. Button and A. Reggiani, chapter 2. Cheltanham, UK: Edward Elgar.

Myhra, D. 1974. "Rexford Guy Tugwell: Initiator of America's Greenbelt New Towns, 1935 to 1936." *Journal of the American Planning Association* 40(3): 176–87.

Nalder, K. 2010. "The Paradox of Prop. 13: The Informed Public's Misunderstanding of California's Third Rail." *California Journal of Politics and Policy* 2(3).

Neary, J. P. 2001. "Of Hype and Hyperbolas: Introducing the New Economic Geography." *Journal of Economic Literature* 39(2): 536–61.

Nelson, K. 1986. "Labor Demand, Labor Supply and the Suburbanization of Low-Wage Office Work." In *Production, Work and Territory: The Geographical Anatomy of Industrial Capitalism,* edited by A. J. Scott and M. Storper, 149–69. New York: HarperCollins.

Nelson, A., and R. Lang. 2011. *Megapolitan America: A New Vision for Understanding America's Metropolitan Geography.* Chicago: American Planning Association.

Newburger, H. B., E. L. Birch, and S. M. Wachter, eds. 2011. *Neighborhood and Life Chances: How Place Matters in Modern America.* Philadelphia: University of Pennsylvania Press.

Newman, K. 2009. "Post-Industrial Widgets: Capital Flows and the Production of the Urban." *International Journal of Urban and Regional Research* 33(2): 314–31.

——— and E. K. Wyly. 2004. "Geographies of Mortgage Market Segmentation: The Case of Essex County, New Jersey." *Housing Studies* 19(1): 53–83.

———— and A. Schafran. 2013. "Assessing the Foreclosure Crisis from the Ground Up." *Housing Policy Debate* 23(1): 1–4.

Nicolaides, B. M., and A. Wiese. 2006. *The Suburb Reader.* New York: Routledge.

Norris, F. [1901] 1986. *The Octopus: A California Story.* New York: Viking Penguin.

Norris, M. 2006. "Brentwood Candidate Slams Antioch." *Brentwood Press,* October 13.

Office of Planning and Research, California. 1978. *An Urban Strategy for California.*

————. 2012. *California @ 50 Million: The Environmental Goals and Policy Report.* http://opr.ca.gov/docs/EGPR_backgrounder.pdf.

Omi, M., and H. Winant. 1994. *Racial Formation in the United States: From the 1960s to the 1990s.* London: Psychology Press.

Orfield, M. [1997] 2002. *American Metropolitics: The New Suburban Reality.* Washington, DC: Brookings Institution Press.

Orsi, R. J. 2005. *Sunset Limited: The Southern Pacific Railroad and the Development of the American West 1850–1930.* Berkeley: University of California Press

O'Toole, R. 2007. *The Best-Laid Plans: How Government Planning Harms Your Quality Of Life, Your Pocketbook, and Your Future.* Washington, DC: Cato Institute.

Palaniappan, M., D. Wu, and J. Kohleriter. 2003. *Clearing the Air: Reducing Diesel Pollution in West Oakland.* Oakland: Pacific Institute. www.pacinst.org/reports /diesel/clearing_the_air_final.pdf.

Pappademas, A. 2012. *Nate Dogg, b. 1969. New York Times Magazine,* December 12.

Painter, J. 1995. "Regulation Theory, Post-Fordism and Urban Politics." In *Theories of Urban Politics,* edited by D. Judge et al. London: Sage.

Parks, V., and D. Warren. 2009. "The Politics and Practice of Economic Justice: Community Benefits Agreements as Tactic of the New Accountable Development Movement." *Journal of Community Practice* 17(1–2): 88–106.

Pastor, M. 2001. "Looking for Regionalism in All the Wrong Places: Demography, Geography, and Community in Los Angeles County." *Urban Affairs Review* 36(6) (July): 747–82.

————. 2007. *Elections, Economics, and Coalitional Politics: Investigating California's Future(s).* Berkeley: Institute of Urban and Regional Development, University of California.

———— and D. Reed. 2005. *Understanding Equitable Infrastructure Investment for California.* Occasional Paper. San Francisco: Public Policy Institute of California.

————, J. Sadd, and R. Morello-Frosch. 2007. *Still Toxic after All These Years: Air Quality and Environmental Justice in the San Francisco Bay Area.* Santa Cruz: Center for Justice, Tolerance, and Community, University of California.

————, C. Benner, and M. Matsuoka. 2009. *This Could Be the Start of Something Big: Regional Equity Organizing and the Future of Metropolitan America.* Ithaca, NY: Cornell University Press.

Paul, B. 1999. "Proposition M and the Downtown Growth Battle." *The Urbanist,* July 1.

Peck, J. 2015. "Cities beyond Compare?" *Regional Studies* 49: 1–23.

——— and A. Tickell. 2002. "Neoliberalizing Space." *Antipode* 34(3): 380–404.

Pellow, D. N., and L. S. H. Park. 2002. *The Silicon Valley of Dreams: Environmental Injustice, Immigrant Workers, and the High-Tech Global Economy.* New York: NYU Press.

Pfeiffer, D. 2011. "Has Exurban Growth Enabled Greater Racial Equity in Neighborhood Quality? Evidence from the Los Angeles Region." *Journal of Urban Affairs* 34(4): 347–71.

———. 2012. "African Americans' Search for More for Less and Peace of Mind on the Exurban Frontier." *Urban Geography* 33(1): 64–90.

——— and E. T. Molina. 2013. "The Trajectory of REOs in Southern California Latino Neighborhoods: An Uneven Geography of Recovery." *Housing Policy Debate* 23(1): 81–109.

Phelps, N. A., A. M. Wood, and D. C. Valler. 2010. "A Postsuburban World? An Outline of a Research Agenda." *Environment and Planning A* 42(2): 366–83.

Pincetl, S. 1994. "The Regional Management of Growth in California: A History of Failure." *International Journal of Urban and Regional Research* 18(2): 256–74.

Pitti, S. J. 2003. *The Devil in Silicon Valley: Northern California, Race, and Mexican Americans.* Princeton, NJ: Princeton University Press.

Pope, C. 2004. "The Virus of Hate: The Sierra Club and the Immigration Debate." *Sierra Magazine.* http://vault.sierraclub.org/sierra/200405/ways.asp.

Presidio Trust. 2012. *Milestones: 2012 Year-End Report.*

Public Advocates, Inc., and Bay Area Legal Aid. 2007. *Policing Low-Income African-American Families in Antioch: Racial Disparities in "Community Action Team" Practices.* December.

Pulido, L. 2006. *Black, Brown, Yellow, and Left: Radical Activism in Los Angeles.* Berkeley: University of California Press.

Purcell, M. 2006. "Urban Democracy and the Local Trap." *Urban Studies* 43(11): 1921–41.

Pyatok, M. 2000. "Comment on Charles C. Bohl's New Urbanism and the City: Potential Applications and Implications for Distressed Inner-City Neighborhoods—The Politics of Design: The New Urbanists vs. the Grass Roots." *Housing Policy Debate* 11(4): 803–14.

Radford, G. 2000. "The Federal Government and Housing during the Great Depression." In *From Tenements to the Taylor Homes: In Search of an Urban Housing Policy in Twentieth-Century America.,* edited by John F. Bauman, Roger Biles, and Kristin M. Szylvian. University Park: Pennsylvania State University Press.

Radin, R. 2010. "Pittsburg Withdraws from Regional Transportation Agency." *Contra Costa Times,* July 6.

Ramsey-Musolf, D. 2016. "Evaluating California's Housing Element Law, Housing Equity, and Housing Production (1990–2007)." *Housing Policy Debate* 26(3): 488–516.

Rast, J. 2006. "Environmental Justice and the New Regionalism." *Journal of Planning Education and Research* 25(3): 249.

Rayle, L. 2015. "Investigating the Connection between Transit-Oriented Development and Displacement: Four Hypotheses." *Housing Policy Debate* 25(3): 531–48.

Reardon, S. F., S. A. Matthews, D. O'Sullivan, B. A. Lee, G. Firebaugh, C. R. Farrell, and K. Bischoff. 2008. "The Geographic Scale of Metropolitan Racial Segregation." *Demography* 45(3): 489–514.

Remapping Debate. 2011. *New Maps Show Segregation Alive and Well.* Accessed May 6, 2011, at www.remappingdebate.org/map-data-tool/new-maps-show-segregation-alive-and-well.

Rhomberg, C. 2004. *No There There: Race, Class, and Political Community in Oakland.* Berkeley: University of California Press.

Rifkin, J. 1995. *The End of Work: The Decline of the Global Labor Force and the Dawn of the Post-Market Era.* New York: Putnam.

Rittel, H. W. J., and M. M. Webber. 1973. "Dilemmas in a General Theory of Planning." *Policy Sciences* 4(2): 155–69.

Rivera, A., et al., and United for a Fair Economy. 2008. *Foreclosed: State of the Dream.* Boston: United for a Fair Economy.

Roberts, S. 2012. "Segregation Curtailed in U.S. Cities, Study Finds." *New York Times,* January 30.

Robinson, J. 2002. "Global and World Cities: A View from Off the Map." *International Journal of Urban and Regional Research* 26(3): 531–54.

———. 2006. *Ordinary Cities: Between Modernity and Development.* New York: Routledge.

Rodgers, C. N.d. "A Gift to San Anselmo from George Lucas." sananselmopark.org/our-history.

Rogers, P. 2002. "Hamann: San Jose's Growth Guru." *San Jose Mercury News,* February 28.

Rongerude, J., and M. Haddad. 2016. "Cores and Peripheries: Spatial Analysis of Housing Choice Voucher Distribution in the San Francisco Bay Area Region, 2000–2010." *Housing Policy Debate* 26(3): 417–36.

Rosoff, M. 2011. "We Don't Talk about Occupy Wall Street in the Valley Because We Don't Have Those Problems." *Business Insider.* Accessed December 28, 2011, at http://articles.businessinsider.com/2011-12-23/tech/30550152_1_bubble-unemployment-rate-silicon-valley.

Ross, C. L. 2009. *Megaregions: Planning for Global Competitiveness.* Washington, DC: Island Press.

Rothstein, R. 2014. *The Making of Ferguson: Public Policies at the Root of Its Troubles.* Washington, DC: Economic Policy Institute.

Roy, A. 2002. *City Requiem, Calcutta: Gender and the Politics of Poverty.* Minneapolis: University of Minnesota Press.

———. 2015. Urban Geography Lecture. American Association of Geographers Annual Meeting, Chicago, Illinois, April 21–25.

Rugh, J.S. 2014. "Double Jeopardy: Why Latinos Were Hit Hardest by the US Foreclosure Crisis." *Social Forces* 93(3): 1139–84.

—— and D.S. Massey. 2010. "Racial Segregation and the American Foreclosure Crisis." *American Sociological Review* 75(5): 629, 632, 634, 644–46.

—— and D. S. Massey. 2014. "Segregation in Post–Civil Rights America: Stalled Integration or End of the Segregated Century?" *Du Bois Review: Social Science Research on Race* 11(2): 205–32.

Rusk, D. 1993. *Cities without Suburbs.* Baltimore: Johns Hopkins University Press.

Ryan, B.D. 2012. *Design after Decline: How America Rebuilds Shrinking Cities.* Philadelphia: University of Pennsylvania Press.

Sampson, R.J. 2011. "Neighborhood Effects, Causal Mechanisms and the Social Structure of the City." In *Analytical Sociology and Social Mechanisms,* edited by P. Demeulenaere, 227–249. Cambridge and New York: Cambridge University Press.

Sandoval, J.O., and J.D. Landis. 2000. *Estimating the Housing Infill Capacity of the Bay Area.* Berkeley: University of California Press.

Sandoval, J.O., H.P. Johnson, and S.M. Tafoya. 2002. "Who's Your Neighbor? Residential Segregation and Diversity in California." *California Counts: Population Trends and Profiles* 4(1): 1–20.

San Francisco Chronicle. 2016. "Levi's Stadium Is a Model for Privately Financed Venues." February 4.

San Francisco Mayor's Task Force on African-American Out-Migration. 2009. *Report of the San Francisco Mayor's Task Force on African-American Out-Migration.* City of San Francisco.

Santacreu, O., E. Baldoni, and M.C. Albert. 2009. "Deciding to Move: Migration Projects in an Integrating Europe." In *Pioneers of European Integration: Citizenship and Mobility in the EU,* edited by E. Recchi and A. Favell, 52–71. Cheltanham, UK: Edward Elgar.

Sassen, S. 1990. "Economic Restructuring and the American City." *Annual Review of Sociology* 16: 465–90.

——. 2001. *The Global City: New York, London, Tokyo.* Princeton, NJ: Princeton University Press.

——. 2007. "Megaregions: Benefits beyond Sharing Trains and Parking Lots." In *The Economic Geography of Megaregions,* edited by K.S. Goldfeld, 59–83. Princeton, NJ: Policy Research Institute for the Region.

Saxenian, A.L. 1983. "The Urban Contradictions of Silicon Valley: Regional Growth and the Restructuring of the Semiconductor Industry." *International Journal of Urban and Regional Research* 7(2): 237–62.

——. 1994. *Regional Advantage: Culture and Competition in Silicon Valley and Route 128.* Cambridge, MA: Harvard University Press.

Schafran, A. 2008. *Catching the Green Wave: Developing an Industrial Land Use Strategy for Richmond's Green Economy.* Berkeley: Center for Community Innovation, University of California.

——. 2009a. "Outside Endopolis: Notes from Contra Costa County." *Critical Planning* 16: 10–33.

———. 2009b. *Discourses of the American Metropolis.* Unpublished Inside Field Statement. Berkeley: Department of City and Regional Planning, University of California.

———.2012a. "Origins of an Urban Crisis: The Restructuring of the San Francisco Bay Area." *International Journal of Urban and Regional Research* 37(2): 663–88.

———. 2012b. "The Cities of Carquinez." *The Urbanist,* June.

———. 2012c. "Entire Bay Area Must Take Ownership to Find Stadium Compromises." *Oakland Tribune,* April 5.

———. 2013. "Discourse and Dystopia, American Style: The Rise of 'Slumburbia' in a Time of Crisis." *City* 17(2): 130–48.

———.2014a. "Rethinking Mega-Regions: Sub-Regional Politics in a Fragmented Metropolis." *Regional Studies* 48(4): 587–602.

———.2014b. "Debating Urban Studies in 23 Steps." *City* 18(3): 321–30.

———. 2014c. "On the Road to Postsuburbia." *International Journal of Urban and Regional Research* 38(5): 1918–21.

———. 2015a. "Beyond Globalization: A Historical Urban Development Approach to Understanding Megaregions." In *Megaregions: Globalization's New Urban Form,* edited by J. Harrison and M. Hoyler, 75–96. Cheltanham, UK: Edward Elgar.

———. 2015b. "The Future of the Urban Academy." *City* 19(2–3): 303–5.

——— and J. Wegmann. 2012. "Restructuring, Race, and Real Estate: Changing Home Values and the New California Metropolis, 1989–2010." *Urban Geography* 33(5): 630–54.

——— and L. Feldstein. 2013. "Black, Brown, White and Green: Race, Land Use and Environmental Politics in a Changing Richmond." In *Social Justice in the Diverse Suburb: History, Politics, and Prospects,* edited by C. Neidt. Philadelphia: Temple University Press.

——— and Y. LeMoigne. 2016. "From the Suburbs to the Banlieue." In *From Dreamscapes to Nightmares? Suburban Imaginaries, Challenges and Prospects in the 21st Century,* edited by K. Anacker and P. Paginn. New York: Routledge.

———, C. MacDonald, E. Lopez-Morales, N. Akyelken, and M. Acuto. 2018. "Replacing the Services Sector and Three-Sector Theory: Urbanization and Control as Economic Sectors." *Regional Studies.*

———, M. N. Smith, and S. Hall. 2019. *The Spatial Contract* [working title]. Manchester: Manchester University Press.

Schlichtman, J. J., and J. Patch. 2014. "Gentrifier? Who, Me? Interrogating the Gentrifier in the Mirror." *International Journal of Urban and Regional Research* 38(4): 1491–508.

Schrag, P. 2004. *Paradise Lost: California's Experience, America's Future—Updated with a New Preface.* Berkeley: University of California Press.

Schwartz, J. 1997. "Prisoners of Proposition 13: Sales Taxes, Property Taxes, and the Fiscalization of Municipal Land Use Decisions." *Southern California Law Review* 71: 183–217.

Scott, A. J. 1980. *The Urban Land Nexus and the State.* London: Pion.

———— and M. Storper. 2015. "The Nature of Cities: The Scope and Limits of Urban Theory." *International Journal of Urban and Regional Research* 39(1): 1–15.

Scott, J. C. 1998. *Seeing like a State: How Certain Schemes to Improve the Human Condition Have Failed.* New Haven, CT: Yale University Press.

Scott, M. [1959] 1985. *The San Francisco Bay Area: A Metropolis in Perspective.* Berkeley: University of California Press.

Seidman, P. 2015. "Remaking the Suburbs: Is Marin the Next Stop in a Federal Government Crusade?" *Pacific Sun,* July 30.

Self, R. O. 2003. *American Babylon: Race and the Struggle for Postwar Oakland.* Princeton, NJ: Princeton University Press.

————. 2006. "Prelude to the Tax Revolt." In *The New Suburban History,* edited by Kevin M. Kruse and Thomas J. Sugrue. Chicago: University of Chicago Press.

Sexton, T. A., S. M. Sheffrin, and A. O'Sullivan. 1999. "Proposition 13: Unintended Effects and Feasible Reforms." *National Tax Journal* 52(1): 99–112.

Sheikh, N., 2008. "Community Benefits Agreements: Can Private Contracts Replace Public Responsibility?" *Cornell Journal of Law and Public Policy* 18(1): 223–42.

Shelley, K. 2002. *A History of California Initiatives.* Report prepared by the California Secretary of State's Office.

Sherbert, E. 2006. "Taylor Wins Brentwood Mayoral Race; Becnel, Richey Gain Council Seats." *Contra Costa Times,* November 8.

Silicon Valley Housing Trust. 2016. "List of Major Donors." Accessed August 23, 2016, at www.housingtrustsv.org/about-us/major-donors/.

Silicon Valley Institute for Regional Studies. 2015. *Income Inequality in the San Francisco Bay Area.* June. www.jointventure.org/images/stories/pdf/income-inequality-2015–06.pdf.

Slotkin, R. 1973. *Regeneration through Violence: The Mythology of the American Frontier, 1600–1860.* Norman: University of Oklahoma Press.

Smith, M. N. 2010. "Reliance." *Noûs* 44(1): 135–57.

Smith, N. 1996. *The New Urban Frontier: Gentrification and the Revanchist City.* New York: Routledge.

————. 2002. "New Globalism, New Urbanism: Gentrification as Global Urban Strategy." *Antipode* 34(3): 427–50.

Soja, E. W. 1989. *Postmodern Geographies: The Reassertion of Space in Critical Social Theory.* London: Verso.

————. 1992. "Inside Exopolis: Scenes from Orange County." In *Variations on a Theme Park: The New American City and the End of Public Space,* edited by Michael Sorkin, 94–122. New York: Hill and Wang.

————. 1996. "Los Angeles, 1965–1992: From Crisis-Generated Restructuring to Restructuring-Generated Crisis." In *The City: Los Angeles and Urban Theory at the End of the Twentieth Century,* edited by Allen J. Scott and Edward W. Soja, 426–62. Berkeley: University of California Press.

————. 2000. *Postmetropolis: Critical Studies of Cities and Regions.* New York: Wiley-Blackwell.

Solnit, R. 2002. *Hollow City: The Siege of San Francisco and the Crisis of American Urbanism.* London: Verso.

——. 2016. "Coming Apart." *Harpers,* November.

Soureli, K., and E. Youn. 2009. "Urban Restructuring and the Crisis: A Symposium with Neil Brenner, John Friedmann, Margit Mayer, Allen J. Scott, and Edward W. Soja." *Critical Planning* 16: 35–59.

Spectorsky, A. C. 1955. *The Exurbanites.* Philadelphia: J. B. Lippincott.

Spink Corporation. 1978. *Master Plan for Downtown and Waterfront Antioch, California.* November.

Spotswood, D. 2011. "County Supervisors Should Have Told HUD to 'Get Lost.'" *Marin Independent Journal,* October 16.

SPUR. 2010. "DIY Urbanism." *The Urbanist,* September.

Squires, G. D., ed. 2003. *Organizing Access to Capital: Advocacy and the Democratization of Financial Institutions.* Philadelphia: Temple University Press.

——. 2012. "Beyond the Mobility Versus Place Debate." *Journal of Urban Affairs* 34(1): 29–33.

—— and C. E. Kubrin. 2005. "Privileged Places: Race, Uneven Development and the Geography of Opportunity in Urban America." *Urban Studies* 42(1): 47.

Starr, K., and R. J. Orsi, eds. 2000. *Rooted in Barbarous Soil: People, Culture, and Community in Gold Rush California.* Berkeley and Los Angeles: University of California Press

Stehlin, J., 2015. "Cycles of Investment: Bicycle Infrastructure, Gentrification, and the Restructuring of the San Francisco Bay Area." *Environment and Planning A* 47(1): 121–37.

Steidtmann, N. 1985. "Citizen Lesher." *Bay Area Business Magazine* 4(3): 14–18.

Stein, S. M., and T. L. Harper. 2003. "Power, Trust, and Planning." *Journal of Planning Education and Research* 23(2): 125–39.

Steinberg, S. 2010. "The Myth of Concentrated Poverty." In *The Integration Debate: Competing Futures for American Cities,* edited by C. Hartman and G. D. Squires, 213–28. New York: Routledge.

Stern, A. M. 2005. "Eugenic Nation: Faults and Frontiers of Better Breeding in America." Berkeley: University of California Press.

Stevens, M. 2015. " Master-Planned Community at Risk of Losing All Water within Days." *Los Angeles Times,* June 18.

Storper, M. 2013. *Keys to the City: How Economics, Institutions, Social Interaction, and Politics Shape Development.* Princeton, NJ: Princeton University Press.

——. 2014. "Governing the Large Metropolis." *Territory, Politics, Governance* 2(2): 115–34.

——, T. Kemeny, N. Makarem, and T. Osman. 2015. *The Rise and Fall of Urban Economies: Lessons from San Francisco and Los Angeles.* Stanford, CA: Stanford University Press

Strasser, S. 2006. "Woolworth to Wal-Mart: Mass Merchandising and the Changing Culture of Consumption." In *Wal-Mart: The Face of Twenty-First-Century Capitalism,* edited by N. Lichtenstein. New York: New Press.

Sugrue, T. J. 1996. *The Origins of the Urban Crisis: Race and Inequality in Postwar Detroit*. Princeton, NJ: Princeton University Press.

Swain, C., and M. Tait. 2007. "The Crisis of Trust and Planning." *Planning Theory and Practice* 8(2): 229–47.

Sweeney, T. 1986. "Contra Costa Corridor: A Growing Problem?" *San Francisco Business,* September.

Szasz, A., and M. Meuser. 2000. "Unintended, Inexorable: The Production of Environmental Inequalities in Santa Clara County, California." *American Behavioral Scientist* 43(4): 602–32.

Tait, M. 2011. "Trust and the Public Interest in the Micropolitics of Planning Practice." *Journal of Planning Education and Research* 31(2): 157–71.

Talvitie, A. 2012. "The Problem of Trust in Planning." *Planning Theory* 11(3): 257–78.

Tarlock, A. D. 2014. "Zoned Not Planned." *Planning Theory* 13(1): 99–112.

Taylor, K. Y. 2016. *From# BlackLivesMatter to Black Liberation*. Chicago: Haymarket Books.

Taylor, L. 2011. "No Boundaries: Exurbia and the Study of Contemporary Urban Dispersion." *GeoJournal* 76(4): 323–39.

Teitz, M., and E. Barbour. 2007. "Megaregions in California: Challenges to Planning and Policy." Paper presented at the Healdsburg Research Seminar on Megaregions (April).

Teitz, M. B., and K. Chapple. 1998. "The Causes of Inner-City Poverty: Eight Hypotheses in Search of Reality." *Cityscape: A Journal of Policy Development and Research* 3(3).

Temple, J. 2008. "Brentwood: The Poster Child for Housing Bust." *San Francisco Chronicle,* May 11.

Thibert, J. 2016. *Governing Urban Regions through Collaboration: A View from North America*. New York: Routledge.

Toscano, P. 2012. "Obama Wins 8 of the Nation's 10 Wealthiest Counties." cnbc.com, November 7. www.cnbc.com/id/49726054.

Travis, W. R. 2007. *New Geographies of the American West*. Washington, DC: Island Press.

Trounstine, P. J., and T. Christensen. 1982. *Movers and Shakers*. New York: St. Martins Press.

Troutt, D. D. 2014. *The Price of Paradise: The Costs of Inequality and a Vision for a More Equitable America*. New York: NYU Press.

Tugwell, R. G. 1939. "The Fourth Power." *Planning and Civic Comment* 5(2) (April): 1–31.

Turner, F. 2006. *From Counterculture to Cyberculture: Stewart Brand, the Whole Earth Network, and the Rise of Digital Utopianism*. Chicago: University of Chicago Press.

Twomey, J. 2001. "Media Fuels Fear about Youth Crime; Perception: If Juvenile Crime Is at Its Lowest in Decades, Why Do So Many Americans Believe Otherwise?" *Baltimore Sun,* May 13.

United States Census Bureau. 2013. "Census Bureau Reports 265,000 Workers Commute into San Francisco County, Calif., Each Day." Release no. CB13-R.22 (March 5).

Vance, J. E. 1964. *Geography and Urban Evolution in the San Francisco Bay Area.* Berkeley: Institute of Governmental Studies, University of California.

Van Kempen, R., and B. Wissink. 2014. "Between Places and Flows: Towards a New Agenda for Neighbourhood Research in an Age of Mobility." *Geografiska Annaler: Series B, Human Geography* 96(2): 95–108.

Vorderbrueggen, L. 2010. "Brentwood Growth Measure Fight Heats Up." *Contra Costa Times,* May 30.

Wacquant, L. J. D. 1997. "Three Pernicious Premises in the Study of the American Ghetto." *International Journal of Urban and Regional Research* 21(2): 341–53.

Walker, R. A. 1981. "A Theory of Suburbanization: Capitalism and the Construction of Urban Space in the United States." In *Urbanization and Urban Planning in Capitalist Society,* edited by M. J. Dear and A. J. Scott, 383–430. New York: Methuen.

———. 1990. "The Playground of US Capitalism? The Political Economy of the San Francisco Bay Area in the 1980s." *Fire in the Hearth: The Radical Politics of Place in America,* edited by M. Davis et al., 3–82. London: Verso.

———. 1994. "Edgy Cities, Technoblurbs and Simulcrumbs: Depthless Utopias and Dystopias on the Sub-Urban Fringe." Paper presented at the University of California, Los Angeles. Institute for Social Science Research, Working Paper Series.

———. 1995. "Landscape and City Life: Four Ecologies of Residence in the San Francisco Bay Area." *Ecumene* 2(1): 33–64.

———. 1996. "Another Round of Globalization in San Francisco." *Urban Geography* 17: 60–94.

———. 2004a. *The Conquest of Bread: 150 Years of Agribusiness in California.* New York: New Press.

———. 2004b. "Industry Builds Out the City: The Suburbanization of Manufacturing in the San Francisco Bay Area, 1850–1940." In *Manufacturing Suburbs: Building Work and Home on the Metropolitan Fringe,* ed. Robert D. Lewis. Philadelphia: Temple University Press.

———. 2006. "The Boom and the Bombshell: The New Economy Bubble and the San Francisco Bay Area." In *The Changing Economic Geography of Globalization,* edited by Giovanna Vertova, 121–47. London: Routledge.

———. 2007. *The Country in the City: The Greening of the San Francisco Bay Area.* Seattle: University of Washington Press.

———. 2008. "San Francisco's Haymarket: A Redemptive Tale of Class Struggle." *ACME: An International E-Journal for Critical Geographies* 7(1): 45–58.

———. 2015. "Building a Better Theory of the Urban: A Response to 'Towards a New Epistemology of the urban?'" *City* 19(2–3): 183–91.

———. 2016. "Why Cities? A Response." *International Journal of Urban and Regional Research* 40(1): 164–80.

———— and Robert D. Lewis. 2001. "Beyond the Crabgrass Frontier: Industry and the Spread of North American Cities, 1850–1950." *Journal of Historical Geography* 27(1): 3–19.

————, M. Storper, and E. Gersh. 1979. "The Limits of Environmental Control: The Saga of Dow in the Delta." *Antipode* 11(2): 48–60.

Wallechinsky, D. 2010. "Chair of the Presidio Trust: Who Is Nancy Bechtle?" *Allgov.com,* November 22. www.allgov.com/news/appointments-and-resignations/chair-of-the-presidio-trust-who-is-nancy-bechtle?news=841786.

Walters, D. 1989. "The New California." *California History* 68(4): 224–29.

Warner, S.B. 1972. *The Urban Wilderness: A History of the American City.* New York: HarperCollins.

Webber, M.M. 1968. "The Post-City Age." *Daedalus* 97(4): 1091–110.

————. 1973. "Dilemmas in a General Theory of Planning." *Policy Sciences* 4(2): 155–69.

Wegener, T. 2001. *Toward a Typology of Regional Leadership Institutions: Examples from the San Francisco Bay Area.* Berkeley: Institute of Urban and Regional Development, University of California. http://escholarship.org/uc/item/7384x4s3.

Wegmann, J., A. Schafran, and D. Pfeiffer. 2017. "Breaking the Double Impasse: Securing and Supporting Diverse Housing Tenures in the United States." *Housing Policy Debate* 27(2): 193–216.

Weiher, G. 1991. *The Fractured Metropolis: Political Fragmentation and Metropolitan Segregation.* Albany: State University of New York Press.

Weir, M. 2004. "A Century of Debate about Regionalism and Metropolitan Government." University of California, Berkeley, Departments of Sociology and Political Science.

Weiss, M.A. 1987. *The Rise of the Community Builders.* New York: Columbia University Press.

Wellock, T.R. 1998. *Critical Masses: Opposition to Nuclear Power in California, 1958–1978.* Madison: University of Wisconsin Press.

Wenkert, R., J. Magney, A. Neel, and Survey Research Center. 1967. *Two Weeks of Racial Crisis in Richmond, California.* Berkeley: University of California, Survey Research Center.

Wheeler, S.M. 2001. "Infill Development in the San Francisco Bay Area: Current Obstacles and Responses." Paper presented at the Annual Conference of the Association of Collegiate Schools of Planning, Cleveland, Ohio, November.

————. 2002. "The New Regionalism: Key Characteristics of an Emerging Movement." *Journal of the American Planning Association* 68(3): 267–78.

————. 2009. "Regions, Megaregions, and Sustainability." *Regional Studies* 43(6): 863–76.

White, L. 2017. "Amid Housing Crunch, Bay Area Tenants Confront Landlords, Call for Rent Control." *San Jose Mercury News,* July 28.

White, R., P. N. Limerick, and J. R. Grossman. 1994. *The Frontier in American Culture: An Exhibition at the Newberry Library, August 26, 1994–January 7, 1995.* Berkeley: University of California Press.

Whyte, W., ed. 1958. *The Exploding Metropolis.* Berkeley: University of California Press.

Wiese, A. 2005. *Places of Their Own: African American Suburbanization in the Twentieth Century.* Chicago: University of Chicago Press.

Wildavsky, A. 1973. "If Planning Is Everything, Maybe It's Nothing." *Policy Sciences* 4(2): 127–53.

Wilson, W. J. 1987. *The Truly Disadvantaged: The Inner City, The Underclass, and Public Policy.* Chicago: University of Chicago Press.

Wolf-Powers, L. 2010. "Community Benefits Agreements and Local Government: A Review of Recent Evidence." *Journal of the American Planning Association* 76(2): 141–59.

Wollenberg, C. 1985. *Golden Gate Metropolis: Perspectives on Bay Area History.* Berkeley: Institute of Governmental Studies, University of California, Berkeley.

Wong, J. C. 2014. "Dropbox, Airbnb, and the Fight over San Francisco's Public Spaces." *New Yorker,* October 23. www.newyorker.com/tech/elements/dropbox-airbnb-fight-san-franciscos-public-spaces.

———. 2016. "Think Outside the Box: San Francisco's Horrible, No Good, Very Bad Housing." *The Guardian,* March 31.

Wood, M. 2016. "Oakland Struggles to Be the Anti-San Francisco." *Marketplace,* January 12.

Wood, R. C. 1961. *1400 Governments.* Cambridge, MA: Harvard University Press.

Wyatt, D. 1997. *Five Fires: Race, Catastrophe, and the Shaping of California.* London: Oxford University Press.

Wyly, E. K., M. Moos, E. Kabahizi, and D. Hammel. 2009. "Cartographies of Race and Class: Mapping the Class-Monopoly Rents of American Subprime Mortgage Capital." *International Journal of Urban and Regional Research* 33(2): 332–54.

Yglesias, M. 2012. "George Lucas, Facebook, and the Crisis of NIMBYism." *Slate,* May 23.

Zeiger, M. 2011. "The Interventionist's Toolkit." *Places: Design Observer,* January, 31. Accessed May 4, 2011, at http://places.designobserver.com/feature/the-interventionists-toolkit/24308/.

Zuk, M., A. H. Bierbaum, K. Chapple, K. Gorska, A. Loukaitou-Sideris, P. Ong, and T. Thomas. 2015. "Gentrification, Displacement and the Role of Public Investment: A Literature Review." Federal Reserve Bank of San Francisco, Community Development, Working Paper (August 24).

INDEX

community benefits agreements (CBAs), 147

"community benefits" movements: emergence of, 146; and gentrification dilemma, 144–49; Oak-to-Ninth agreement (2006), 146; search for, 146–49

Community Development Block Grant (CDBG), 183

commuters: out-of-county, 193; in San Joaquin County, 193–94

Concord Citizens for Responsible Growth, 107

Concord Naval Weapons Station, 279

Contra Costa Center, 91

Contra Costa County, 181, 198, 218; anti-growth backlash in, 102; Caldecott Tunnel, 90; construction of Interstate 680, 90–91; counties of, 89–93; development politics, 99; from edge cities to an axis of exclusion, 94–97; from failure to unholy alliance, 106–8; Fair Market Rents (FMR), 130; flats of West County, 91; forgotten government, 101–4; geographical area of, 90; grand bargain, 104–6; growth management plan, 107; median household income, 93*fig.;* open space preservation, 90; political circles, 90; residential units in, 98*fig.*, 102; socioeconomic divisions, 89; as 10th largest suburban county, 89; as 37th largest county, 89; Transportation Authority, 70, 105; transportation networks, 90; wealth generation, 90; *See also* East County

Contra Costa Development Association (CCDA), 102

Contra Costa Times, 102

Copeland, Brian, 31

corporate retail and amenities, 195–98

corruption, allegations of, 133

council of governments (COGs), 190, 216, 305

Council on Sustainable Development, 221

Covenants, Conditions and Restrictions (CC&R) violations, 74

crack cocaine, 32, 49

"creative class" havens, 52

criminal justice system, 251–52

critical habitat, 229

Crow, Jim, 49

Crown-Zellerbach, 58

Cutler, Kim-Mai, 171

decision-making, 260

Deer Valley, 67–68

deindustrialization, 134

DeLeon, Richard, 168–69

Delta-Mendota Canal, 234

Desmond, Matthew, 268

development: fees, 64, 103; political economy of, 260–61

devolution and retrenchment, program of, 104

Dewey, John, 115

Diablo County, 85

diesel pollution, 124

digital animation industry, 150

Dillon, Lindsey, 122

Discovery Bay project, 4

discrimination against nonwhites, 27

distant suburbs, 246

dividend, income, and rent (DIR) data, 101

dot-com boom, 129, 152, 163, 166

dot-com crash, 5, 8, 152, 166

Dougherty Valley, 85, 110–13, 121, 217, 220, 245, 257–59; battle over, 87, 114; and counties of Contra Costa County, 89–93; development controversy, 110; Dougherty Valley Dilemma, 113–16, 148, 151, 161, 164, 237; El Condado, 87–89; regional infill, 115; Specific Plan (1992), 111, 113; suburban life, 88; urban infill, 115

Dowall, David, 271

Dow Chemical, 105

drug trade, 49

Dumbarton Bridge, 159

Dust Bowl, 191

duty to protect, 268–70

Dyble, Louise, 178

East Bay Asian Local Development, 218

East Bay Municipal Utility District (EBMUD), 111, 214

East Bay Regional Park District, 103, 117

Panzer Division, 153, 156
Parsons Brinkerhoff Tudor Bechtel, 1
Pastor, Manuel, 253
Peirce, Charles, 115
Peninsula Open Space Trust, 157
People for Open Space, 103, 107, 218
people of color. *See* communities of color
Piedmont, 31*map*, 32, 33*tab.*, 202
Pittsburg, 4; *versus* Antioch city, 65–67; *versus* everyone else, 69–70; as New York on the Pacific, 65; racism issues, 69; regional transportation issues, 69
Plan Bay Area (2013): dream of a region, 229–33; economic prosperity strategy, 225–29; One Bay Area Grant (OBAG), 225
Pleasant Hill, 103
plebiscite, 242
pocket ghettos, 159
Point Reyes National Seashore, 179
Police Power and Particulate Matters, 128
political-business coalition, 206
political fragmentation, 15
pollution, from refineries and freeways, 124
Ponzi scheme, 64
pop sociology, 203
post-Civil Rights suburbs, 44
postindustrial garden, 49, 54–84; in Antioch city, 77; the bypass, 62–65; communities of color and, 56; in East County, 56, 84, 187; as employment centers, 58; house-rich and job-poor spaces of, 86; idea of, 55; lack of jobs, 57; small towns and big places, 65–70; structural instability of, 84
postwar: regionalism, 214–17; segregation, 38, 254; suburbanization, 19, 55, 81
poverty: in Alameda County, 144; of Latinx community, 160; rate among African Americans, 144; in Santa Clara County, 160; in South Bay, 159; suburbanization of, 36, 233
power plants, development of, 58
prices and paradoxes, notion of, 128–31
Priority Conservation Areas (PCAs), 225
Priority Development Areas (PDAs), 225
prison-building, 264

progressive communities, 167
Progressive Era, 88, 208, 214
property taxes, 61, 64, 132, 238
Public Policy Institute of California, 39, 301n3
public-sector jobs, 138
public sector organizations, 267
"push" and "pull" factors, of suburbanization process, 48

quality of life, 74, 75, 103, 109
quasi-public space, 32

racial coding, 251
racial discrimination, 35, 74, 159, 184, 217, 287n28
racial inequality, 160
racial injustice, 221
racial justice organization, 221
racial politics: BRAC and pace of redevelopment, 142–44; development mistakes, 138–42; and downtown redevelopment, 131–44; Emeryville's gain, 134–38; Oakland's loss, 132–34
racial profiling, 74–75
racial segregation, 38. 254, 42–44, 104
racist housing policies, 27
railway lines: San Ramon Branch Line of Southern Pacific, 109; Sonoma-Marin Area Rail Transit (SMART), 182
Ralston, Billy, 191
Reagan doctrine, 255
real estates, 89; of Bay Area, 171; boom in, 50; credit industry, 101; development of, 60; housing bubble, 77; industry location quotients, 100*tab.*; market, 39; political economy of, 101; prices for 5 zip codes, 129*fig.*; prices, rise of, 48; sales price per square foot, 79*fig.*
Redwood City, 41
refugee crisis, 123
regional governance, 218
Regional Housing Needs Assessment (RHNA), 223; performance by income categories by County, 226*tab.*; Plan Bay Area, 225–29; *versus* units permitted/built, by County, 224*tab.*
regionalization of diversity, 26